THE LEGAL PROTECTION
OF FOREIGN INVESTMENTS
AGAINST POLITICAL RISK

THE LEGAL PROTECTION
OF FOREIGN INVESTMENTS
AGAINST POLITICAL RISK

Japanese Business in the Asian Energy Sector

Thomas Nektarios Papanastasiou

qp

QUID PRO BOOKS

New Orleans, Louisiana

Published in 2015 by Quid Pro Books.

ISBN   978-1-61027-313-8 (pbk.)
ISBN   978-1-61027-319-0 (hbk.)
ISBN   978-1-61027-312-1 (ebk.)

QUID PRO BOOKS

Quid Pro, LLC
5860 Citrus Blvd., Suite D-101
New Orleans, Louisiana 70123 USA
www.quidprobooks.com

qp

Publisher's Cataloging-in-Publication

Papanastasiou, Thomas Nektarios.

The Legal Protection of Foreign Investments Against Political Risk: Japanese

Business in the Asian Energy Sector / Thomas Nektarios Papanastasiou.

p.   cm. — (Dissertation series)

Includes bibliographical references.

ISBN 978-1-61027-313-8 (paperback)

1. Investments, Foreign—Law and legislation. 2. Power resources—Asia—Finance. 3. Energy

industries—Law and legislation. I. Title. II. Series.

HD 9503 .U8 P15 2015   303'.03'71—dc22

2015543683

Cover photograph, "Power stations edge the sea at Rayong, Thailand," © by Sorapop Udomsri, used under license from Shutterstock.com. Author photo © Lucy Katefidi.

This book is also available in high-quality eBook editions from Quid Pro Books. It is presented as part of the *Dissertation Series*, which brings significant and useful original research to worldwide availability, for the benefit of scholars and professionals.

To My Mother and My Father

CONTENTS

LIST OF ABBREVIATIONS

ADB	Asian Development Bank
APEC	Asia-Pacific Economic Cooperation
B/C	Buyer's Credit
B/C I	Buyer's Credit Insurance
BIT	Bilateral Investment Treaty
BOO	Build-Own Operate basis
BOOT	Built-Own-Operate and Transfer
BOT	Built-Own-Transfer
BRICS	Brazil, Russia, India, China and South Africa
EBRD	European Bank for Reconstruction and Development
ECA	Export Credit Agency
EGAT	Thailand Public Electric Unity
EIB	European Investment Bank
EID	Export-Import Insurance Division
EPA	Economic Partnership Agreement
EPC	Engineering Procurement and Construction
EPRG	Extended Political Risk Guarantee
ERIA	Economic Research Institute for ASEAN and East Asia
EU	European Union
FDI	Foreign Direct Investment
FET	Fair and Equitable Treatment
FPS	Full Protection and Security
FTA	Free Trade Agreement
FTFs	Free Transfer of Funds
GATT	General Agreement on Tariffs and Trade
GGU	Government Guarantee Undertaking
HKIAC	Hong Kong International Arbitration Center

IBRD	International Bank for Reconstruction and Development
ICC	International Chamber of Commerce
ICSID	International Centre for the Settlement of Investment Disputes
IDA	International Development Agency
IFC	International Finance Cooperation
IIA	International Investment Agreement
IMF	International Monetary Fund
IPP	Independent Power Producer
JBIC	Japan Bank for International Cooperation
JFC	Japan Finance Corporation
JICA	Japan Investment and Cooperation Agency
KEPCO	Kansai Electric Power Co., Inc.
KLRCA	Kuala Lumpur Regional Centre for Arbitration
LCIA	London Court of International Arbitration
MDB	Multilateral Development Bank
METI	Ministry of Economy, Trade and Industry
MFN	Most Favoured Nation
MIGA	Multilateral Investment Guarantee Agency
MIT	Multilateral Investment Treaty
MNC	Multinational Corporation
MOFA	Ministry of Foreign Affair (Japan)
NAFTA	North American Free Trade Agreement
NEXI	Nippon Export Investment Insurance
NIEO	New International Economic Order
NT	National Treatment
ODA	Official Development Assistance
OECD	Organization for Economic Co-operation and Development
OII	Overseas Investment Insurance
OIL	Overseas Investment Loan
O&M	Operation and Maintenance
OPIC	Overseas Private Insurance Corporation
OUL	Overseas Untied Loan
OULI	Overseas United Loan Insurance
PCG	Political Credit Guarantee
PCIG	Permanent Court of International Justice

PCR	Partial Credit Risk
PIL	Public International Law
PPA	Power Purchase Agreement
PPIAF	Public-Private Infrastructure Advisory Facility
PPP	Public Private Partnership
PRG	Partial Risk Guarantee
PRI	Political Risk Insurance
PU	Performance Undertaking
RIETI	Research Institute of Economy, Trade and Industry (Japan)
RTA	Regional Trade Agreement
SIAC	Singapore International Arbitration Center
SOE	State Owned Enterprise
SPV	Special Purpose Vehicle
TEPCO	Tokyo Electric Power Co., Inc.
UN	United Nations
UNCITRAL	United Nations Commission on International Trade Law
UNCTAD	United Nations Commission on Trade and Development
WB	World Bank
WTO	World Trade Organization

PREFACE

This book examines the various ways in which political risks associated with foreign direct investment in public infrastructure (especially the energy sector) are managed, negotiated, and mitigated. The original version of this study was submitted as a doctoral dissertation in 2012 to the Graduate School of Asian Pacific Studies (GSAPS) of Waseda University, Tokyo, Japan, in partial fulfilment of the requirements of the Ph.D. degree with a focus on international investment law. Encouraged by the publisher to retain the original structure and approach as a dissertation and yet after making many necessary amendments and updates to the earlier version, the book's research is relevant and valid to date. Analysis of energy investment protection is specifically updated in the published edition of this study.

The study seeks to contribute to the literature on political risks mitigation, whose importance has been growing in recent years due to the global economic crisis and the increasing antagonisms among states and various private actors in the energy sector. Such contribution was recognized by the International Law Association (Hellenic Branch), by awarding the original work with the 2013 Argyrios Fatouros Prize as the best monograph by a young scholar in the field of International Economic Law (http://ilahellenic.gr/announcements/101-the-2013-fatouros-prize).

Political risk is defined in this book as the host government's unwarranted interference with the foreign investment, an interference which is political in nature and may cause damage to the investment's economic interests. Expropriation is the most traditional type of political risk but certainly is not the only form. The analysis focuses on two frameworks for dealing with political risks, namely 1) public international laws (PILs) such as international investment treaties and economic partnership agreements (EPAs), and 2) contractual arrangements, primarily in the form of political risk insurance (PRI)-policies and investor-state guarantees. For its specific empirical analysis, this study selects five Asian countries as host states of power investments and Japan as the home country, though of course the research and observations are intended to other countries and arrangements as well.

In connection with international investment treaties, this study examines both general and specific standards of treatment against political risks. As for political risk management through contracts, the study assesses the available legal means through PRI policy-tools provided by third-party actors such as Nippon Export and Investment Insurance (NEXI) and Multilateral Investment Guarantee Agency (MIGA), as well as investor-state contracts.

This work adopts both qualitative and quantitative methods for the two types of frameworks in order to engage the analysis of managing political risks. The qualitative method applied to international investment treaties involves an analysis of recent EPAs (2006 and after) entered into force between Japan and five countries (Indonesia, Malaysia, Philippines, Thailand and Vietnam) and an examination of the wording of eleven standards of treatment along with the legal interpretation of secondary sources. The qualitative approach to PRI mechanisms was conducted using primary information obtained from extensive interviews and meetings with NEXI and Japan Bank for International Cooperation (JBIC) executives, as well as information contained in their annual reports, organisation laws and secondary studies. Specifically as to power contracts, the analysis is based mainly on primary data contained in five real-world power projects implemented by Japanese companies in Asian countries. Turning to the quantitative methodology, an analysis of international investment treaties developed non-binary measures (a scoring card) to provide several snapshots of key legal elements for the protection of energy investments in each of the five Asian countries, based on investment and service trade chapters as well as on the treaties' appendices. In analysing the contracts in detail, the study undertook a non-numerical evaluation of critical elements examined in the power contracts, based on a five-scale index referring to the reservations or exceptions included in each case.

The study found that the suggested multi-tier legal framework can be effective in protecting against political risk, but such effectiveness depends on the wording of the legal components and on the nexuses among them. In particular, this analysis demonstrates that several factors – reservations in EPA clauses, lack of clarity in PRI tools and non-comprehensiveness in contractual guarantees – may weaken the protection against political risk. Finally, even if PRI (provided by NEXI) still plays the most dominant role in the protection of Japanese investments, the research asserts that the nexus of an institutionalised legal framework would be preferable in addressing future challenges of political risk mitigation.

This book is intended to contribute, in detail and with empirical support, to the literature on political risks of foreign investment in infrastructure, whose importance has grown in recent years as foreign investment in infrastructure such as the energy sector has rapidly increased. The previous studies on the subject, this book finds, have taken a rather one-sided or overly narrow approach by focusing on one aspect of political risk. Unlike these previous studies, this work adopts a holistic approach towards political risk management. In particular, by comparison to previous studies, the present research is different in applying this multi-angle assessment. It analyses a multi-tier legal framework by using different types of assessment techniques and by exploring the role of the following legal regimes: public international law consisting of international investment treaties such as BITs and EPAs; political risk insurance provided by export credit agencies (ECAs); and contractual guarantees included in investor-state contracts.

The book also contributes importantly in the adaptation of its scoring method in the analysis of the legal framework. The scoring techniques have been used in the discipline of international economics such as in studies measuring the impediments of host countries' FDI and EPA laws. However, this study takes a different approach from previous studies. Most importantly, it focuses on the relation of legal measures to the issue of political risk mitigation and not on broader investment liberalization or protection in general. Moreover, the study uses legal interpretative tools for the analysis of key legal elements, and of Japanese organizations' contracts, in a way that has not been used before as real cases. It develops non-binary measures (a scoring card) to provide several snapshots of the legal elements for the protection of power investments. Such elements are extracted from the investment and trade-in-services chapters in the EPAs as well as from the treaties' appendices. This approach is found to be very effective in making comparisons between different laws and treaties. It is hoped that the reader and future researchers will, in turn, have a better, more focused measure of the effectiveness of the political risk mitigation toolbox.

This project would not be complete without many important figures who have contributed to this study. It owes a lot to their support.

Professor Shujiro Urata has provided me with insightful advice and offered me the unique chance to challenge my ideas in an interdisciplinary forum consisting of international economics, law and business specialists.

Professor Yoshiaki Abe motivated me to do my research, and with his rich experience as a senior manager of the World Bank, guided me to the practice-area of public infrastructure projects and introduced me to crucial executives of multilateral and state agencies that were great sources of information for the development of this project.

Professor Junji Nakagawa of Tokyo University, functioning as my main advisor on issues of international investment law, was instrumental to my progress throughout my doctoral research. Thanks to his legal expertise, continuous feedback on my drafts and the long hours of discussion and consultation with him, I was able to clarify and strengthen my academic skills.

Apart from my Ph.D. committee, I am also deeply in debt to two pivotal and memorable figures: the late Emeritus Professor Hideo Nakamura of the Waseda University Faculty of Law, who brought me to Waseda University and supported my work in various ways over many years of study and research; and Emeritus Professor Kostas Beis of the Faculty of Law, Kapodistrian University of Athens, who introduced me to the basics of legal thinking and encouraged me to continue my studies in Japan.

I am also particularly grateful to the NEXI executives who were great sources of information for my project, especially to Mrs. Natsuko Harada (Vice President of Power & Mining Team) who kindly replied to my enquiries and devoted many hours in organising a series of meetings and interviews with several executives at NEXI, as well as to Mr. Haruyoshi Ueda (Senior Advisor of Structured & Trade Finance Insurance Department) who provided me with real-world contacts and contracts crucial for the completion of this study. Special acknowledgements are owed to the Ministry of Education, Culture, Sports, Science and Technology (Monbukagakusho) for the generous financial support that was offered to me for the largest part of my research in Japan.

Finally, there are not enough words to convey my gratitude to my colleagues and friends in Japan for their general support, and to my parents, to whom this book is dedicated, for their constant encouragement and patience.

THOMAS NEKTARIOS PAPANASTASIOU
Lecturer in Law
Law School of Neapolis University,
Paphos (Cyprus)
August, 2015

SUMMARY

Foreign investment is an important determinant for both countries and private businesses' economic welfare. Cooperation between host governments and foreign companies is a necessary requirement for the promotion and protection of foreign investments as well as for the success of any business project. However, the interests and the needs of host countries and foreign investors are diverging and sometimes contradictory, becoming the source of uncertainty. It is usually this uncertainty that triggers political risk such as expropriation of property, recall of licences, breach of contracts, discriminatory or unfair treatment, prohibition on capital repatriation, and even lack of physical or legal security against political violence and natural disasters.

How political risk can be legally managed and how one can assess the effectiveness of the legal responses to political risk is the central problem throughout this study, which deals with three areas of discussion: 1) the notion of political risk, 2) the legal framework for mitigation, and 3) the method of assessing the effectiveness of each legal mean. In particular, this study tests two assumptions sequentially: It asserts that political risk can be effectively managed through two legal tiers of protection: public international law (Part I: international investment treaties) and guarantees (Part II: provided by either insurance agencies or included in contractual agreements). In addition, it argues that there is a nexus among different tiers of the legal framework which has a complementary result on the mitigation of political risk. When this study refers to the effectiveness of the legal protection, it means how strong and comprehensive the legal responses to political risk can be.

In particular, the power sector is by nature more prone to political risk than any other industry due to its politically strategic and socially sensitive character. The present study is unique with respect to its empirical research and its legal assessment. It selects five Asian countries (Indonesia, Malaysia, Philippines, Thailand and Vietnam) as the host states of power investments because of the size and the number of private power-projects placed in their territories. It also selects Japan as the home country of the investors' residence-state because of the high Japanese participation into the power-projects of the above Asian economies, as well as due to the recent signing of Economic Partnership Agreements (EPAs) between Japan and the five respective countries.

In Chapter 2, the three main areas of discussion are explored. *First*, the present volume describes the categories of risks that exist when investing in the infrastructure sectors. It distinguishes commercial from political risks as those that usually exist when doing business. This study, after examining definitions given by previous studies, broadly conceives the notion of political risk as the host government's unwarranted interference with the foreign investment, an interference which should be political in nature and should cause damage to the investment's economic interests. Thus, the classification of political risk cannot be comprehensive unless the reason behind the state's unwarranted behaviour is investigated (relationship among damage, breach and the reason that triggered the breach is required).

Second, this study focuses on identifying the legal framework that is available to foreign investors in order to manage political risks. There are only a handful of studies that have undertaken a holistic approach towards different measures of political risk management, though based on general assumptions with limited empirical observations. In comparison to the previous studies, the present study is an empirical study of law. It is unique in the analysis of a multi-tier legal framework by using different types of assessment techniques and by exploring the role of the following legal regimes: public international law (PIL) consisting of international investment treaties such as EPAs, political risk insurance (PRI) provided by export credit agencies (ECAs) and contractual guarantees included in investor-state contracts such as power project-financing forms.

Third, this study is also unique in its method of assessing the effectiveness of the examined legal regimes. It follows a combined analytical method comprised of qualitative assessment and scoring evaluation. The qualitative assessment is based on the analysis of the comprehensiveness of legal countermeasures to political risks, examining the breadth and clarity of wording, the inclusiveness of content with regards to the existence or lack of a reference to particular elements, and the number of exceptions made in the relevant clauses or policies. With regards to the scoring method, the evaluation follows scoring-techniques that have been used in the discipline of international economics. However, the present study is different from previous studies in many aspects. This study uses legal interpretative tools for the analysis of the key legal elements. It develops non-binary measures (a scoring card) to provide several snapshots of the legal elements for the protection of power investments. Such elements are extracted from the investment and trade-in-services chapters as well as from the treaties' appendices (Part I). In Part II, this book undertakes a non-numerical evaluation of critical elements analysed in the power contracts, based on a five-scale index referring to the reservations or exceptions included in each case's contractual clauses. The scoring results are better for those treaties or contracts that contain fewer restrictions conceiving them as a symptom of a low possibility of political risk occurrence, thus higher level of protection.

Chapters 3, 4 and 5 (Part I) examines the international standards of treatment and their relation to political risk mitigation. In particular, Chapter 3 examines the standards of treatment responsible for the protection against expropriation and the risk of non-compensation for the damages suffered by foreign investors. These two risks are the most traditional type of political risks. This study analyses what constitutes direct and indirect expropriation, lawful and illegal expropriation, and examines what international arbitration tribunals require in order to accept a claim of expropriation and to award compensation. Most importantly, this chapter examines the conditions that make a taking non-compensable focusing on the distinction between general regulatory takings that are permissible and those that are not permissible (regulatory or creeping expropriation), requiring compensation to the affected investor. However, such a distinction is not an easy exercise especially in relation to the nature of taxation measures issued by the host country. According to the scoring results, it is found that some of the Japan's Treaties exclude the application of some substantive principles from taxation measures, resulting to more uncertainty. Such treaties are conceived as being less effective in the protection against expropriation, resulting to lower scores. However, in relation to compensation standards, most of the treaties receive high scores due to the clear reference to full compensation rights according to Hull's formula.

Chapter 4 assesses the role of general standards of treatment, namely national treatment (NT), most favoured nation (MFN), fair and equitable treatment (FET) and full protection and security (FPS) in the protection of Japanese power-investments against political risk. It argues that clauses containing general standards have not received appropriate attention as a tool for protecting foreign investments. NT and MFN protect against the risk of discrimination requiring the same treatment as that domestic or third-countries' investors receive. FET and FPS protect against any arbitrary or unfair host government's behaviour, as well as against the risk of civil disturbance, violence and strife. Especially in relation to power investments, the general standards of treatment have significant value due to the dominance of state owned enterprises within the electricity sector of most countries. However, assessing the effectiveness of general standards in the examined Japan's Treaties, it is found that almost all of them obtain exclusions and limitations. In relation to NT and MFN standards, low scores are given for those treaties that exclude general provisions (e.g. subsidies and other incentives) and even lower scores are given when general standards are excluded from applying to investments that are specifically related to power sector. The protection-capacity of FET and FPS standards is substantively limited (resulting to lower scores of effectiveness) when treaties include an additional note which prescribes the minimum standard of treatment to be afforded to Japanese investments.

Apart from these general standards, Chapter 5 assesses the role of specific standards of treatment in mitigating political risk, such as the free transfer of funds (FTFs) clause, the protection from strife clause and the umbrella clause. It also examines the treaties' deterrence through the provision of investor-state arbitration and subrogation clauses. These standards address the protection of investments against specific dangers: prohibition on capital repatriation, no remedy for damages due to civil disturbance or violence, breach of contracts, difficulty in enforcing legal orders or absence of an impartial judicial forum and the non-recognition of the home-country's substitution rights. The host states are allowed to limit these standards' application. However, any restriction on these standards shall be legitimate (permitted under specific conditions) and follow concrete legal principles such as non-discriminatory treatment that shall be compelled. According to the study assessment, it is found that only few treaties refer explicitly to the above principles, when legitimate restrictions occur, and some of them impose excess (non-legitimate) restrictions, resulting to a lower score on the effectiveness of their protection-degree. As for the umbrella clause, almost all treaties receive the lowest score due to the absence of such clause in their investment-chapters. Finally, with respect to the investor-state arbitration clause, all Japan's Treaties include such clause, though with several exceptions and different wordings. In relation to the wording-differences, this study categorises arbitration-clauses according to the Broches-index, assessing the degree of host-state's consent to direct arbitration right.

Chapters 6 and 7 (Part II) examine the PRI policies and contractual guarantees focusing on their relation to political risk mitigation. Chapter 6 assesses the available legal means in PRI policy-tools provided by Japanese state-agencies, such as the Nippon Export Insurance Agency (NEXI) and the Japan Bank for International Cooperation (JBIC) and by multilateral actors, such as WB agencies, mainly the Multilateral Investment Guarantee Agency (MIGA). In theory, PRI agencies are known as the *prominent victims* because of their involvement in deterring the harmful behaviour of host governments and in indemnifying the investors for the damage suffered. According to this chapter's analysis, it is found that NEXI has played a crucial role not only in protecting Japanese power-investments against several political risks, but also in promoting the economic and industrial interests of Japanese enterprises against other countries' competitors. However, this chapter highlights that there are some implications in NEXI's insurance-tools and MIGA's guarantees, which are related to the ascertainment of investors' claims. It is found that signing a PRI contract does not constitute an automatic elimination of all possible cases of political risk. Some risks are not covered by PRI tools and others are not clearly addressed. In particular, there are technicalities such as a list of insured events that shall occur and a number of unclear check-points required by ECAs in order to decide whether an insurance-claim is valid or not. The vagueness of such technicalities results to limitations in addressing some political risks, especially expropriation or infringement of rights and the change in laws risk.

In addition, along with the PRI measures, Chapter 7 analyses the role of specific guarantees included in investor-state contracts. It selects the arbitration, stabilization, waiver of sovereign immunity and *force majeure* clauses as the most essential in mitigating political risk. Today, there is a need for signing contracts that on the one hand, do not impose heavy contingent liabilities and on the other hand, offer a good design in managing political risk. Assessing the design of the four mentioned guarantees, this chapter evaluates the contracts based on the inclusion of specific legal elements in each clause, as well as on the comprehensiveness of their wording. It is found that some contracts contain a best-design clause of political risk management, thus unsatisfactory design exists in several others. In particular, almost all contracts provide an arbitration clause without choice-of-law other than the domestic law; only two contracts obtain a sovereignty clause guarantying that they irrevocably waive the host state's immunity over jurisdiction of a foreign award, the enforcement and the attachment of its assets. Moreover, only one contract provides a separate clause on the stability-of-laws guarantee, while others contain no any form of stabilisation clause. In addition, even if all contracts provide a force-majeure clause, their risk-transfer design between private and public, parties varies significantly, resulting to several uncertainties.

Finally, Chapter 8 examines the effectiveness of the three legal-regimes when they function in pairs or combined in one body. Four potential combinations are made: [*PIL* + *PRI*], [*PIL* + *Contracts*], [*PRI* + *Contracts*] and [*PIL* + *PRI* + *Contracts*]. This chapter compares such combinations of legal regimes by looking into two types of interactions. First, it analyses the interface (overlapping) of political risk that can be mutually covered. Second, when no overlapping exists, it examines whether there is a nexus, meaning a complementary result of mechanisms that uniquely exist in each legal regime. It is found that there is an overlapping of several types of political risk that can be covered under each combination of legal regimes. The most important finding is that the legal mechanisms that exist only in one regime can also complement the others' regimes framework. Therefore, they can enhance the degree of legal protection against political risk when bound together. In particular, synthesising the core argument of such complementary roles, PIL regime is unique for its preventive nature of measures (*ex-ante protection*) and for its broader coverage of political risk due to the inclusion of general standards of treatment. PRI is unique for offering measures of deterrence (*ex-post protection*) that can address on-time specific types of political risk better than any other regime (e.g. natural events-*force majeure*). Finally, investor-state contracts are unique for their specific-preventive nature (*tailor-made protection*) offering an independent structure of risk-transfer design, according to the needs and priorities of the parties. However, such nexus constitutes an ideal situation occurring in nominal terms, and it does not take into consideration the variations that exist under each regime. In reality, as assessed by this study, due to several limitations or weaknesses in each legal regime, the actual nexus is more limited than the nominal case described above.

In conclusion, this study offers three contributions to the legal literature on investment protection: the determination of political risk under new areas of law (e.g. PIL); the structure of a comprehensive framework composed of multi-legal regimes analysed separately and in a nexus manner; and the assessment of the framework's effectiveness by using qualitative and scoring methodology. Chapter 9 summarises the strengths and the weaknesses in each of Japan's treaties, in the NEXI and the MIGA insurance policies, and in each of the five investor-state contracts that have been analysed throughout the book. This study finds that the multi-tier legal framework can be effective in protecting against political risk, but such effectiveness depends on the wording of the legal components and on the nexuses among them. In particular, this analysis demonstrates that several factors – limitations in EPA clauses, lack of clarity in PRI tools and non-comprehensiveness in contractual guarantees – may weaken the protection against political risk.

Finally, even if PRI (provided by NEXI) still plays the most dominant role in the protection of Japanese investments, this book proposes that the nexus of an institutionalised legal framework would be the most preferable in addressing future challenges of political risk mitigation. This leads to the conclusion that Japan needs to expand the number of EPA treaties with other nations, to take a more balanced-approach between informal (negotiations) and formal legal institutions (litigious-means), and to implement its own EPA Model Law, as is the case for other capital-exporting countries. As for Japanese businesses themselves, they would be well advised to depoliticize their disputes with host-states through the direct-right to investor-state arbitration, reducing their dependence on Japan's politics.

THE LEGAL PROTECTION
OF FOREIGN INVESTMENTS
AGAINST POLITICAL RISK

1

INTRODUCTION

1.1. About the subject study: Managing political risk in power-sector investment

1.1.1. Background

Foreign investment is an important determinant for both countries and private businesses' economic welfare. The power sector (electricity) has been globally one of the most attractive infrastructure sectors for private participation and foreign direct investment (FDI).[1] Telecommunications and energy (including electricity) have attracted the majority of private investments. These two sectors experienced the first deregulation and market reforms that led to privatisation and liberalisation, and experienced them more than any other infrastructure sector.[2] Since the 1990s, inward FDI for some ASEAN countries' power sectors has increased significantly, with Japanese investors playing a dominant role.[3]

Even if foreign investment in the power sector is desired by both governments and investors, the specific interests and needs of host countries and foreign investors (including their home country) are diverging and sometimes contradictory, affecting the profitability of projects and the behaviour of foreign businesses.[4] On one hand, foreign investors seek *stability* and *protection* of their economic interests from unwarranted governmental intervention. On the other hand, host countries seek political interference for the sake of their own political and public interests, regulatory autonomy, and protection of their sovereignty.

---

[1] UNCTAD, *World Investment Report 2008: Transnational Corporations and the Infrastructure Challenge* (United Nations, New York and Geneva, 2008) p. 101.

[2] J.P. Doh and R. Ramamutri, 'Reassessing Risk in Developing Country Infrastructure', *Long Range Planning* 36:4 (2003) p. 339.

[3] The World Bank-PPIAF database contains updated information about foreign investments by sector and provides details about private sponsors' nationalities. See http://www.ppiaf.org/ppiaf.

[4] Some of the most controversial cases occur when privatisation of SOEs are followed by lay-offs, as in the LAC region; also, with regards to the power sector, issues such as responsibility for environmental protection measures, increases in tariff of electricity sold per unit and state policy of subsidies (especially after enterprises become private), discrimination in competition-policy, free access to the network, discrimination of the regulatory authorities in favour of foreign enterprises, etc. For example, see: I.N. Kessides, *Reforming Infrastructure: Privatization, Regulation, and Competition* (World Bank, Washington, DC, and Oxford University Press, New York, 2004) p. 1. See also: F. Sader, 'Attracting Foreign Direct Investment into Infrastructure: Why Is It So Difficult?', Occasional Paper no. 12, *Foreign Investment Advisory Service-IFC* (World Bank, Washington, DC, 2000) pp. 21-29, 39-40. However, this study focuses on the legal aspect of host state's governance of foreign investments in the power sector in relation to political risk.

The real challenge is to keep a balance between these different needs and objectives. When a balance cannot be sustained by the involved parties, it is then that potential political risks occur.

Figure 1   The Challenge of Balancing[5]

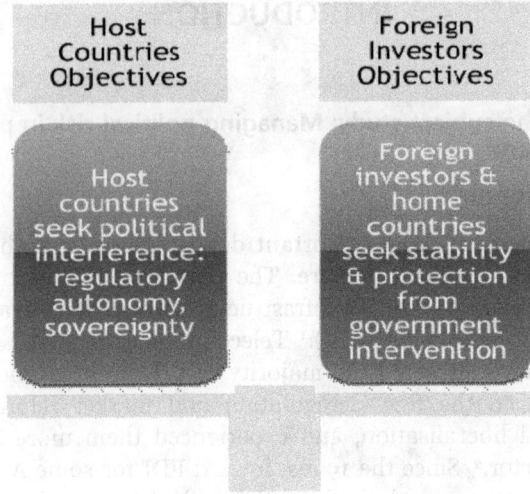

Host Countries Objectives	Foreign Investors Objectives
Host countries seek political interference: regulatory autonomy, sovereignty	Foreign investors & home countries seek stability & protection from government intervention

Discussion over this challenge will be explored throughout this study with a focus on the foreign investors' perspective. Moreover, the purpose of this study is to analyse the multi-tier legal framework of foreign investment protection against political risk by emphasising the peculiarities of the power sector. In particular, the present study asserts that political risk can be effectively managed and mitigated through two crucial legal regimes: *public international law* consisting of several international treaty standards, and *contractual guarantees* contained in either political risk insurance (PRI) policies or investor-state contracts. In addition, it is argued that a nexus between different legal regimes can be established with a complementary result in the management of political risk.

The most important issues that are dealt with within this study are related to three areas of discussion: the notion of political risk, the legal framework in managing political risk and the method in assessing the degree of protection (i.e. the effectiveness) of multi-tier legal regimes. Thus first, it should be explained why power-sector investment is selected, why five Asia countries are examined as host states of power investments and why this study focuses on Japan as home country of power investments.

1.1.2.   Energy sector as case study

Aside from addressing the protection of foreign investment against political risk, this study asserts that there is an intense need to manage political risk in infrastructure and especially in the power sector. This section explains why political risks are more likely to occur in the infrastructure sector than any other

---

[5] Figure compiled by the author.

industry. It argues that infrastructure by its nature requires a high level of government involvement and co-operation with the private sector, and, as a result, whenever intervention causes problems for investors or their co-operation fails, the possibility of political risks materialising significantly increases. In particular, the high possibility of political risk occurrence can be explained due to several peculiarities that are related to the nature of infrastructure industries and the complexity of private sector participation in power investments.

The opening of infrastructure sectors to foreign investment has happened much more slowly than in other industries.[6] The opening up has started very recently, in the early 1990s, compared with other industries like the manufacturing sector that started from World War II.[7] Although there is a variation in the degree of openness, most developed or transitioning countries have now, for the most part, introduced foreign entities into their infrastructure industries. However, infrastructure is still characterised as the most restrictive sector among all other sectors.[8]

Private investment in public infrastructure sectors differs from investments in any other industry or service sector for two primary reasons. Firstly, the infrastructure sector is characterised as a socially and politically "sensitive" industry.[9] Issues such as the price of electricity, accessibility and quality of services are always at the core of public interest and politics. Any increase in prices or deterioration of services would be immediately noticed by local communities and social unrest could result. The operation and provision of public infrastructure services can become an even more "delicate" situation when foreign investors are involved, raising nationalistic concerns among the local societies.[10]

Secondly, infrastructure is regarded as a "strategic" industry.[11] It plays an indispensable role in the economic growth and economic development of countries. The strategic function of infrastructure also seems to be related to national security and public interest concerns,[12] something that is highly significant when determining whether an expropriation is legitimate or not.[13] The energy industry could be considered to be one of the most strategic infrastructure sectors for most countries. There are limitations and restrictions found in the FDI policies and laws related to infrastructure sectors, included not only in

---

[6] UNCTAD, *World Investment Report 2008*, pp. 152-153.

[7] *Ibid.*

[8] S.S. Golub, 'Measures of Restrictions on Inward Foreign Direct Investment for OECD Countries', *OECD Economic Studies* no. 36 (OECD, Paris, 2003) pp. 87 and 100.

[9] The social dimension of infrastructure is stronger in sectors like water and electricity provisions; UNCTAD, *World Investment Report 2008*, pp. 161-162.

[10] J. Gomez-Ibanez, 'Private Infrastructure in Developing Countries: Lessons from Recent Experience' (paper presented to the Commission on Growth and Development at the Workshop 'Global Trends and Challenges', New Haven, 28-29 September 2007); see also: I.N. Kessides, *Reforming Infrastructure*.

[11] UNCTAD, *World Investment Report 2008*, p. 155.

[12] *Ibid.*

[13] As explained in this volume, one of the requirements for an expropriation to be considered legal is when it fulfils a "public purpose".

developing and emerging economies (e.g. China[14] and the Russian Federation[15]), but also in developed countries such as the United States.[16]

In parallel with the above characteristics, another important issue related to infrastructure is private participation. The private sector is increasingly needed for improvement, maintenance and expansion of infrastructure services. Most countries, both developed and developing, either need private capital to bypass public finance constraints or look for private managerial skills in order to improve efficiency and modernise their infrastructure services. In many cases, multinational corporations (MNCs) have proved successful at providing efficient and affordable services to both developed and emerging economies.[17]

Moreover, the role of the state as the main actor in providing infrastructure services has changed and, to a great extent, governments' activities have been replaced by private sector. Often, market mechanisms have successfully provided solutions to problematic public infrastructure services that were previously, traditionally and solely, operated by the state.[18]

One of the most popular structures of private participation in the power-infrastructure sector is the *project finance*. In relation to power plants in specific, or infrastructure in general, there are usually a variety of parties that are directly or indirectly involved with a particular investment project.

Some of the main parties are the sponsors of the project – usually construction companies (contractors), financiers (such as big investment banks-lenders), suppliers of machinery and natural resources important for the project, operating-companies (operators), and many other subcontractors.[19] Usually, the abovementioned companies are private companies and each of them is responsible for undertaking a certain risk that is connected to the nature of their contribution to the project. For instance, the banks will bear the financial risks, the contractors the construction risk, the suppliers the supply risk. This follows the basic principle of project finance that "risks should be allocated to the party that is best able to control the risk or influence its outcome".[20] Nevertheless, in power project financing, risks are eventually allocated according to the will of the parties in the contractual agreement. In developing countries the state party

---

[14] According to Chinese foreign investment policy, power generation and electricity distribution are considered to be critical to the national economy. UNCTAD, *World Investment Report 2008*, p. 155.

[15] The Russian Federation defines all natural monopolies as strategic sectors, *ibid*.

[16] The US Foreign Investment and National Security Act of 2007 requires "investigation of any transaction by a company controlled by foreign government, especially when it concerns critical infrastructure..."; *ibid*.

[17] ADB, *Developing Best Practices for Promoting Private Sector Investment in Infrastructure* (Asian Development Bank, Manila, 2000).

[18] See also: Doh and Ramamurti, 'Reassessing Risk', pp. 337-353: Multiple roles of government in infrastructure as: sponsor/investor, consumer/customer, rule-maker/regulator and mediator/moderator.

[19] S. Babbar and J. Schuster, 'Power Project Finance: Experience in Developing Countries', *RMC Discussion Paper Series* no. 119 (World Bank, Washington, DC, 1998) pp. 23-32.

[20] S.L. Hoffman, *The Law and Business of International Project Finance* (3rd edn, Cambridge University Press, New York, 2008) p. 28.

[Government or State Owned Enterprise (SOE) purchaser] usually assumes more risks, including some types of risks that they are not in the position to control. In more developed countries where the investment climate is less uncertain, host governments assume less risk.[21]

The empirical evidence for this has been supported strongly by the "neo-liberal" and globalisation movements advocating for more liberalisation and privatisation of economic activities that are controlled by governments, such as infrastructure industries.[22]

However, it is not always clear whether the market's "invisible hand"[23] or the host state's own strategy is the only factor responsible for private participation in infrastructure.[24] There have been many instances when exogenous factors pushed states to open up their infrastructure industries. Since the 1980s and especially in 1990s, international organisations of great influence – such as the Breton Woods sister organisations, the International Monetary Fund (IMF) and the World Bank (WB) – have included in their lending policies to developing countries loan conditionality related to the privatisation of infrastructure industries and liberalisation.[25]

As for the power sector, there are different degrees of openness depending on the geographic region and on the industry's constituent segments. According to UNCTAD (World Investment Report-2008), the Asian region retains more

---

[21] Babbar and Schuster, 'Power Project Finance', p. 20.

[22] Classical economic theory has influenced and, to some extent, shaped international economic law, supported by the "North", the capital exporting countries. It has emphasised the free movement of capital and the protection of investments through better standards of treatment and neutral arbitration tribunals for the resolution of investment disputes; M. Sornarajah, *The International Law on Foreign Investment*, 2nd edn (Cambridge University Press, Cambridge, 2004) pp. 51-57, 293-294.

[23] It has been asserted that infrastructure financing should be guided by the capital market's invisible hand. See: A. Chen, 'A New Perspective on Infrastructure Financing in Asia', *Pacific-Basin Finance Journal* 10:3 (2002) pp. 227-242.

[24] It is argued that there is a need to redefine the role of the State rather than see its full withdrawal from infrastructure sectors. Countries should adopt simpler reform models and gradual implementation of reform, through steps such as restructuring, competition and regulation. See: T. Jamasb, 'Between the State and the Market. Electricity Sector Reform in Developing Countries', *Utilities Policy Journal* 14:1 (2006) pp.14-30. In addition it should be stated that different State policies are adopted towards liberalisation. For example, China is following a gradual "step-by-step" liberalisation, compared to India that is following a quicker process. See: Doh and Ramamurti, 'Reassessing Risk', pp. 337-353.

[25] It was first in this WD report that the WB articulated their policy for more privatisation and liberalisation in order to tackle the mismanagement and inefficiencies of SOEs and also to reduce the government debts created from some infrastructure operations. Even though the World Bank still continues asserting the role of private sector in infrastructure, it currently does not explicitly impose privatisation conditionality as it did previously, especially after failures in water concessions in Latin American countries and the renegotiation of Independent Power Producer (IPP) during and after the Asian financial crisis of 1997. Although there has been to date some attention paid to new policies, such as Public Private Partnerships (PPP) and public sector capacity building (corporate governance methods), privatisation is still the mainstream of the WB's policy orientation. WB, *World Development Report, 1994. Infrastructure for Development* (World Bank, Washington, DC, 1994); see also: Gomez-Ibanez, 'Private Infrastructure' and UNCTAD, *World Investment Report 2008*, p. 153.

restrictions than the Latin America and Caribbean ones.[26] In general, Asian countries are still more reluctant to open and deregulate their electricity sectors than countries of other regions such as Eastern Europe, Central Asia or Latin America. However, the power generation segment of the electricity sector is more attractive to foreign investors than the transmission and distribution segments[27] (figure below).

Figure 2   Cumulative Investment in Electricity Projects with Private Participation by Region and Subsector, 1984-2003[28]

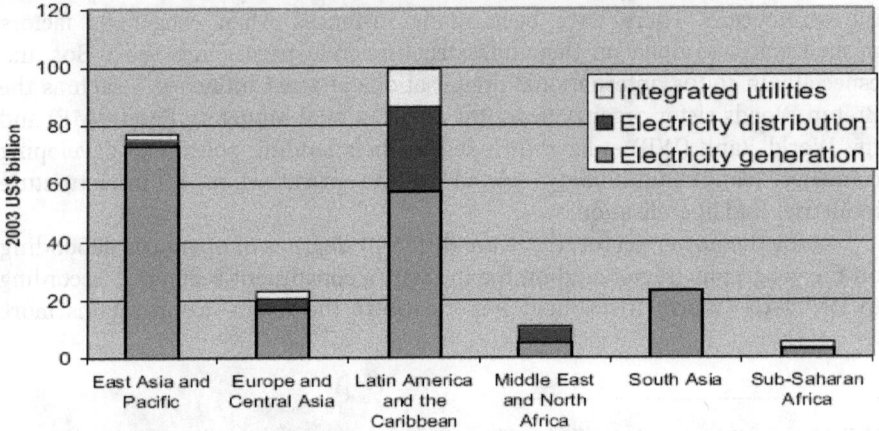

One of the main reasons for this is that the construction and operation of power plants (greenfield projects) are usually the BOT type of contracts between the private sector and the government (ministries or its SOEs), according to which the private companies are required to build, maintain and (sometimes) operate the plants and the government is obliged to pay for the services provided. On the contrary, operation of the electricity networks (throughout the country or a large geographic area) and the provision of distribution services to the end-users (final consumers) requires the awareness and understanding of many factors that are related to metering of the electricity consumed, collection of the bills, enforcement procedures in case of non-payment, social policy towards poor or other social groups, subsidies and many other issues that do not occur in the up-stream services of generation segment; therefore, even aside from govern-ments' behaviours, in terms of both political and commercial risks, operating

---

[26] UNCTAD, *World Investment Report 2008*, p. 153; see also: A. Estache and A. Coicoechea, 'How Widespread Were Infrastructure Reforms During the 1990s?', World Bank Research Working Paper no. 3595 (World Bank, Washington, DC, 2005).

[27] In 2008, UNCTAD made a survey in World Association of Investment Promotion Agencies (WAIPAC). Almost half of the respondents said they are actively promoting foreign investment in electricity generation (in Asia almost all) but very few do the same for the transmission or distribution segments; UNCTAD, *World Investment Report 2008*, p. 157.

[28] M.A. Covindassamy, D. Oda and Y. Zhang, 'Analysis of Power Projects with Private Par-ticipation Under Stress', no. 311/05 Joint UNDP/WB (ESMAP) Report (World Bank, Washing-ton, DC, 2005) figure 2.8, p. 17.

services in the distribution segment of electricity industry makes business more complicated and investment projects riskier.[29]

In addition, this book prefers using the power sector as its case study in order to better identify and test the specific reservations or restrictions that host countries retain in the annexes of their respective Economic Partnership Agreements (EPAs). In relation to the EPA assessment exercise, the power sector is selected mainly because of two reasons: Firstly, all examined EPAs comment on the power sector and incorporate some degree of restrictions or reservations, and therefore, for consistency, this study is able to compare them. On the contrary, other industries (e.g. manufacturing, transportation etc.) are not always specifically referred to in the respective EPAs. Moreover, the power sector is a relatively equally important industry for every country. Other more commercial sectors such as the manufacturing or mining sectors differ from country to country according to the specific circumstances and market characteristics that occur in each country's business environment. Secondly, it is not feasible for the purpose of a qualitative legal assessment to analyse the whole spectrum of sectors and sub-sectors that are reserved in each EPA. For example, in some EPAs, such as the Japan-Indonesia EPA, Annex 4 of Chapter Five (Part II) of the respective Treaty, there are about one hundred (100) economic activities that do not conform with regards to NT provision and most of them include some different kind of exceptions. Therefore, the selection of a specific industry such as the power sector which is referred to in both investment and trade in services chapters, is justified, among others, for practical reasons as well.

1.1.3. Five Asian countries as host states

With regards to the reason for selecting the five particular Asian countries – Indonesia, Malaysia, Philippines, Thailand and Vietnam – this study has conducted research on some important country-selection criteria such as: the size and number of private power projects implemented in several Asian countries including all segments of the electricity industry, the type of private participation as well as the origin of the projects' sponsors in each power project. This information was extracted from the World Bank's Public-Private Infrastructure Advisory Facility (PPIAF) database and the findings are the results of the author's calculations (see the table on the following page).

The five selected countries have shown the largest concentration of private power investments in terms of both the amount of investment commitment and the number of power projects. The Philippines is the country with the largest number of investment commitment and number of power projects, while Vietnam shows a substantially lower concentration of private investments in the power sector, thus it is among the countries with a current trend of attracting large amounts of FDI in its power sector. Another characteristic that is matched

---

[29] In East Asian countries, private investments are concentrated in greenfield generation projects compared to Latin American region where concession and divestitures of electricity distribution companies take a much greater part of private investments. However, openness to private investors is more possible for the generating segment because of the easiness in unbundling the segment and in creating conditions for competition. See UNCTAD, *World Investment Report 2008*, p. 155.

Table 1   Country Selection Criteria[30]

Countries/ Selection criteria	Indonesia	Malaysia	Philippines	Thailand	Vietnam
PSP-1st Year	1992	1992	1990	1993	1996
Projects/$ Million	12245.10	12950.20	17909.91	10893.50	1783.08
No of Projects	34	42	84	63	18
Projects/Generation	34	34	65	63	18
Projects/Distribution Transmission	0	8	19	0	0
Greenfield/$ Million	12245.1	10345.2	11841.7	9349	1238
Concession-Divestiture /$ Million	0	2605	6068.2	1544.5	544.9
No Projects- 1st sponsor=Non-Asian	16	0	34	17	4
No Projects - 1st Sponsor=Asian	16	42	66	52	16

with the findings of several infrastructure studies is that the generation segment and the greenfield projects monopolise the attraction of power investments as well as the participation of Asian sponsors is higher than investors of non-Asian origin and relatively high compared to the evidence in other regions of the world, e.g. Latin America and Africa.

1.1.4. Japan as home country

Finally, as for the selection of Japan by this study as the home country of international power investments' residence place, there are three reasons. The first has to do with the result of an investigation made by this research about the nationality of the largest sponsors participating in power-investment projects in the territory of the five Asian countries. It is observed that Japanese investors (trading, manufacturing or power companies) held either the first or the second position among foreign investors in terms of the amount of investment-commitment or in terms of being recorded as the first or second sponsor in joint-ventures with sponsors of other countries, in the period from 1990 to 2008. The biggest competitors with Japanese companies are investors from the Organisa-tion for Economic C-operation and Development (OECD) countries such as the USA, UK, Australia, Germany and France, as well as from economies in transi-tion (China). An additional important element for the selection of Japan as home country is the fact that Japan has recently signed and entered into force EPA treaties with all of the five selected Asian countries. Thus, other capital exporting

---

[30] Source: Table compiled by the author (based on the author's own calculations of private investments in each country/year; data extracted from the WB-PPIAF: Private Participation in Infrastructure (PPI) Database, 2009).

countries do not obtain international investment agreements (IIAs) for example USA or they have only obtained them with some of the host countries. In addition, other home countries have only signed Bilateral Investment Treaties (BITs), which differs from the EPA type of treaty (see Table 2 below).

Table 2   Foreign Sponsors in Power Sector & IIAs[31]

Coun-tries	Indo-nesia	IIA	Malay-sia	IIA	Thai-land	IIA	Philip-pines	IIA	Viet-nam	IIA
USA	No 1	n/a	n/a	n/a	No 4	n/a	No 2	n/a	n/a	n/a
Japan	No 2	EPA	No 2	EPA	No 1	EPA	No 1	EPA	No 1	BIT+ EPA
UK	No 4	BIT	No 1	DIT	No 3	BII	No 3	BIT	No 4	BIT*
Australia	No 3	BIT	No 3	BIT	n/a	n/a	n/a	n/a	n/a	n/a
Ger-many	No 6	BIT	n/a	BIT	n/a	BIT	No 4	BIT	n/a	BIT
France	n/a	BIT	n/a	BIT	No 2*	n/a	n/a	BIT	No 2	BIT
H.K. (China)	n/a	n/a	n/a	n/a	No 3	BIT	n/a	n/a	n/a	n/a

The second reason for choosing Japan is the fact that Nippon Export Investment Insurance Agency (NEXI) is one of the most active export credit agencies in the area of PRI business. However, compared with the large amount of research that has analysed bilateral or international agencies such as Overseas Private Insurance Corporation (OPIC-USA), Multilateral Investment Guarantee Agency (MIGA) of WB or European Export Credit Agencies (ECAs), studies on NEXI have not thoroughly examined its policies. In this regard, this study is unique in analysing comprehensively and in-depth the specific policy-tools of NEXI by conducting meetings and interviews with NEXI executives and using primary and secondary information about its function and organisation. Moreover, this study has also benefited by receiving from NEXI five real-world case studies of power contracts with Japanese participation in Asian projects and in relation to the subject-matter of this book, the legal framework in managing political risk.

Third, as can be observed in Table 3 (on the following page), comparing Japan with some of the main capital-exporting countries, Japan lags behind in terms of the number of IIAs signed until recently. Such a low number of IIAs signed by Japan causes implications in the legal management of political risk weakening Japanese investors' position. Moreover, this study attempts to analyse the particular added-value of recent Japanese EPA treaties in the mitigation of political risk and the legal empowerment of Japanese investments.

---

[31] Table compiled by the author (based on the author's calculation; data extracted from the WB-PPIAF database (1998-2008), UNCTAD and Japan's MOFA database).

Table 3   Number of IIAs Signed by Selected Countries[32]

Countries	The number of IIAs
Germany	135
China	119
Switzerland	114
UK	103
Egypt	100
Italy	100
France	98
Netherlands	91
Republic of Korea	86
Belgium	84
USA	46
Canada	25
Japan	12

1.2.   Risks in general

In general, there are two main categories of risk: the commercial and the political risk. The risks which are covered by the private sector are commercial risks. Although private companies play the most significant role in assuming the various commercial risks, there are some other risks that private investors must also assume, while still being incapable of controlling: the political risks.[33] Before determining the notion of political risk, it is necessary to understand what kinds of risks exist when investing in the infrastructure sector, especially with regards to the commercial risks.

There is not any universally accepted definition of what political risk is. The majority of studies on political risk agree that the distinction between commercial and non-commercial risks is blurred mainly because the difficulty in determining political risk. Moreover, an attempt to list all potential reasons that can trigger a political risk is a difficult exercise. Investing in infrastructure sectors changes significantly according to the evolving form of contractual agreements between investors and state enterprises, thus it is not easy to create an exhaustive list of political risks.

The main concern of investors when they invest abroad is the uncertainty related to the behaviour of the host state. The reason for this uncertainty is the possibility that the host government will interfere in the foreign investors' business (the unpredictable behaviour of the host government). Regardless of industry-specific characteristics, foreign investors always need to consider how

---

[32] As of June 2007 except for Japan's case (September 2011). Table compiled by the author (information taken from UNCTAD website and NEXI).

[33] Sometimes political risks are also referred as regulatory risks, especially in a domestic context.

they can protect their investment against any change of the host state's policies (actions or inactions), a change that may damage or negatively influence the profit of their business. This concern or fear towards any potential host government's change of behaviour is exactly what political risk is all about.

Therefore, the main difference between commercial and political risk is that the former can be controlled and calculated by the private investor but the latter is outside of the business's control and depends solely on the government's behaviour. The private sector cannot predict the government's behaviour and therefore political risks are considered to be non-calculated risks. Moreover, the private sector cannot take the control of the reasons that trigger political risk therefore political risks are neither predictable[34] nor controllable risks.

1.3.   Focus of the study

This study does not simply delineate the political risks and determine the legal factors that increase their likelihood when foreign investors invest in the power sector of host countries. More than that, it focuses on identifying the legal framework that is available to foreign investors in order to manage political risks – and to mitigate them. Therefore, to resolve in legal terms the management of political risk for foreign investments is the priority of this study. Next, this study focuses on an equally critical task: assessing the effectiveness of the legal framework in protecting power sector investments against political risks.

The legal framework used in this study for the management of political risk is composed of two important tiers of protection:

- Public international law, and
- Contractual guarantees (contained in political risk insurance and investor-state contracts).

With regard to public international law, this study investigates the protection provided by a crucial source of international law – contemporary treaty-based international investment law combined, when necessary, with other sources such as customary international law.[35] In particular, the study aims to explore the protection provided by Japan's EPA and BIT treaties through standards of treatment such as: expropriation and compensation treatment, general standards and specific standards of treatment. With regard to the second tier of managing political risk, the contractual guarantees consist of two separate components: the political risk insurance (PRI) tools provided by bilateral agencies such as NEXI or multilateral organisations such as the World Bank Group (mainly MIGA) and the specific guarantees that are included in investor-state contracts.

---

[34] M. Stephens, 'A Perspective on Political Risk Insurance', in T.H. Moran (ed.), *Managing International Political Risk* (Blackwell Publishers Ltd., Oxford, 1998) p. 154.

[35] This study also takes into account subsidiary sources of international law such as: "general principles" (e.g. *unjust enrichment* and that of *equity* principle, which have been used to support claims for the payment of full compensation upon the expropriation of foreign property, or the *sanctity of contracts*), "judicial decisions" (e.g. arbitral of *ad hoc* or *institutional tribunals*), and "international practices" (e.g. commercial practices and usages – BOT practices or model law related to infrastructure-projects – that have shaped the *lex mercatoria*).

In addition, this research focuses on an assessment exercise of each of the legal framework's components mentioned above. It attempts to assess the effectiveness of these components in reducing the possibility of political risk occurrence by using qualitative and scoring assessment-methods.

1.4.   Questions

After analysing the multi-tier legal regime of foreign investment protection, and determining the concept of political risk, this study tests two assumptions sequentially:

First, the existence of concrete standards of treatment included in international investment treaties, insurance mechanisms provided by PRI programs and specific guarantees contained in investor-state power contracts have a positive impact on (or increase) the effectiveness of the legal protections against political risk.

Second, there is a nexus among different tiers of the legal framework which has a complementary result on the protection of foreign investments against political risk.

When this study refers to the *effectiveness* of the legal protection, it means *how strong and comprehensive can the legal responses to political risk be*. However, there are several questions that should first be examined. To begin with: what is the connection between each tier's legal framework and the protection from political risk? In other words, do standards of treatment included in EPAs and BITs or insurance tools provided by ECAs or contractual clauses negotiated in power contracts respond to the particular task of political risk mitigation? If each of the above multi-tier legal frameworks responds positively, then we need to address how effective this legal response is. In a more tangible way, what are the objective criteria for strong and comprehensive responses in each of the tiers of legal protection? Or, in contrast, what are the factors that increase the likelihood of political risk?

This study attempts to show that, however challenging the arrangements for the implementation of power investments have been, the impact of the legal frameworks is crucial. Nevertheless, to speak about the assessment of this legal impact would be a unique exercise. Therefore, a question central to this study is: How can we assess the effectiveness of the multi-tier legal framework in terms of political risk management? In particular, what specific methodological tools (qualitative and scoring) are appropriate for such an assessment exercise?

Building on the result of this assessment, this study will furthermore address the gaps in or disadvantages of each tier of the legal framework for protecting from political risk and will attempt to respond to the questions: can any interrelation be established between two tiers of protection and how this could happen? Which particular political risks could be covered by a multi-tier legal framework and which risks could not?

These questions are addressed in the following chapters as well as within this chapter by explaining the methodological tools that are adopted by this study. Thus, it is necessary first to explore the problems in managing political risk and the ways of mitigating them as identified by previous studies, and then to compare them with the particular framework that is adopted herein.

1.5.   Methodology

As explained previously in this chapter, this study aims to examine how specific legal tools can manage and mitigate political risks in international power investments and to evaluate the effectiveness of these tools, meaning to find out how strong and comprehensive the legal responses (measures) to political risk can be. In order to achieve this purpose, this study follows a method combined of qualitative assessment and scoring evaluation.

First, the legal framework used in this study for the management of political risk is composed of two important tiers of protection: public international law (Part I), and contractual guarantees (Part II). Additionally, an analysis of the combination of these two tiers is also included (nexus). The methodology used for each tier of protection is not similar with regards to the scoring evaluation method. However, the qualitative analysis is focused on the same issues, namely: the comprehensiveness of the legal countermeasures to political risk (breadth and clarity of wording), the inclusiveness of content (existence of or lack of reference to particular elements) and the number of exceptions made in the relevant clauses or policies.

In brief, Part I consists of three categories (legal measures) of analysis: expropriation and compensation standards, general standards and specific standards of treatment. Part II consists of two legal measures of analysis: PRI tools and guarantees included in investor-state power contracts.

The methodology adopted for Part I is a combined qualitative and evaluation approach. The qualitative aspect consists of review and analysis of sources such as Japan's EPA treaties and BIT as well as studies of international foreign investment law and international investment tribunals' awards (jurisprudence). There are five bilateral EPAs (Japan with Indonesia, Malaysia, Philippines, Thailand and Vietnam) that have recently been concluded (the period from 2006 to 2009) and one BIT between Japan and Vietnam (December 2004). All the EPAs' and BIT's relevant legal documents and annexes are publicly available on Japan's Ministry of Foreign Affairs (MOFA) and the United Nations Commission on Trade and Development (UNCTAD) web pages. The evaluation approach consists of a scoring methodology which is a modification of the assessment methods used by previous economic studies. The results of the scoring along with the findings are presented in the appendix: "Scoring-Card of Japan's EPAs".

Table 4   Japan's IIAs with ASEAN-5 Countries

ASEAN-5	Type of IIA	Entry into force
Indonesia	EPA	Jul. 1, 2008
Malaysia	EPA	Jul.13, 2006
Philippine	EPA	Nov.11, 2008
Thailand	EPA	Nov. 1, 2007
Vietnam 1	EPA	Oct. 1, 2009
Vietnam 2	BIT	Dec.19, 2004

The methodology in Part II is mainly based on a qualitative approach (for both PRI tools and investor-state contracts) and, partly, on a non-numerical evaluation method (guarantees in investor-state contracts). The qualitative approach to PRI tools consists of a review and analysis of primary information obtained from interviews and meetings with NEXI in the period between March and August of 2010 and two meetings with Japan Bank for International Cooperation (JBIC) executives (in November 2009 and April 2010), as well as secondary sources such as policies contained in the above organisations' annual reports and organisation laws, and studies on PRI. The qualitative approach to investor-state contracts consists of a review and analysis of the primary data contained in five real-world power contracts implemented in different Asian countries with the participation of Japanese investors. These data (contracts) were provided to the author by NEXI. This methodological approach also includes secondary sources, studies on contractual guarantees. In addition, this study undertakes a non-numerical evaluation assessment of the analysed clauses that are included in each contract by adopting a tailor-made method for this part of the research.

1.6.   Study roadmap

This study consists of nine chapters and is divided into two parts. The current chapter is the introduction dealing with issues such as the background of this study, explaining why the power sector, the five Asian countries and Japan were selected as the subject matter, and it provides the hypotheses and the main research-questions. In Chapter 2, the three main areas of discussion are explored. The chapter analyses the political risk concept, the legal framework of managing political risk and the methodology of the risk-assessment that is undertaken by this study. In addition, this chapter reviews previous studies that are related to the above areas of discussion and signifies this study's unique approach.

In Part I, Chapter 3 analyses how the particular function of expropriation and compensation treatments that are provided in investment treaties function as political risk mitigation tools with regard to overseas investment in the power sector. In particular, this chapter explains the difference between direct and indirect expropriation, emphasises the many manifestations existing in the latter and investigates the various tests adopted by international investment tribunals in relation to the character of the host government's regulatory or administrative measures. It analyses the criteria of the expropriation's legality and the various characteristics of compensation; it examines the treatment provided by the specific clauses included in each IIA, and assesses their comprehensiveness by scoring them.

Similarly, Chapters 4 and 5 deal with the function of general and specific standards of treatment and their role in managing political risk. This study investigates the scope and application of four general standards of treatment: NT and MFN as relative standards, and FET and FPS as absolute standards. Chapter 4 assesses the treaties based general standards' degree of protection of Japanese investments against political risk. Chapter 5 investigates the scope and application of each specific standard of treatment provided by the reviewed treaties and in particular: free transfer of funds, protection from strife, the umbrella clause, as well as the dispute resolution clause and subrogation ability. It also assesses their comprehensiveness in mitigating political risk through a scoring methodology.

Part II consists of Chapters 6 and 7. These chapters specify the affirmative or active mechanisms of investment protection against political risk through the use of PRI and specific contractual guarantees respectively. Chapter 6 analyses the role and function of NEXI as an insurance provider of Japanese overseas investment in the power sector, and identifies several policy-tools' effectiveness in mitigating political risk by exploring the conditions under which NEXI accepts the validity of the insured-investors' claims. In addition to the evaluation of NEXI, this chapter also analyses its co-operation with JBIC and it compares the function of the two Japanese agencies with specific guarantees provided by the World Bank's agencies, mainly MIGA as well as IBRD, IDA and IFC. Part II is completed with Chapter 7, which undertakes an analysis of the role of sovereign guarantees provided to specific power projects that were insured by NEXI and then it investigates five real-world contract cases. In particular, it examines the comprehensiveness of four clauses that are important to the mitigation of political risk – the arbitration, waiver of sovereign immunity, stabilisation and *force majeure* clauses. This chapter also assesses the degree of managing political risk by using a non-numerical evaluation method for each contract's clause separately.

Finally, Chapter 8 addresses the interfaces and complementary role of the multi-tier legal framework, investigating whether there is a nexus created by different mechanisms of risk management. The overall findings and conclusions of this book, as well as some policy implications and notes for future research, are presented in Chapter 9.

2

POLITICAL RISK, THE LEGAL MEANS OF PROTECTION, AND THE ASSESSMENT OF THEIR EFFECTIVENESS

2.1.   The notion of political risk

As was mentioned in Chapter 1, risks in general are categorised into political and commercial risks. Risk-categorisation is related to either some general criteria, such as the nature and function of groups of risks or to specific criteria, depending on how the parties (public and private) in a contractual agreement assume and allocate certain risks. Before examining the criteria that determine the notion of political risk, it is helpful to introduce what a commercial risk is all about.

2.1.1.   Commercial risks

Commercial risk is the risk that usually exists when doing business. According to Hoffman, commercial risks are changes in economic and business conditions such as cost demand, competition, or project management and more specific risks related to credit, construction, operation and other contractual undertakings of a project.[36] These are the types of risks that every investor needs to assume when he implements a project, whether in his home country or overseas. On the one hand, commercial risks are related to the microeconomics of a particular investment (endogenous risk) and, on the other hand, to the way the market generally functions (exogenous risk). Thus, there is also a broader category of risks that are related to the economic and fiscal environment of host countries. In relation to power projects, most usual types of endogenous commercial risk are related to the construction of the project such as a failure to complete the power plant on time, as technically specified and within the agreed budget, the failure or delay of the suppliers to provide the necessary equipment or fuel to the project company, or the default of the counterparty in making the payments for the delivery of the agreed services.[37] In relation to the project completion risk and the technical performance risk, the investor (project-company) usually outsources the construction of the project to independent contractors and operators through specialised agreements – the engineering procurement and construction (EPC) and the operation and maintenance (O&M) contracts. In complicated power project financing, contractors, operators, suppliers and even lenders of the project participate along with the sponsors (main investors) as shareholders in a joint venture company which is a special purpose

---

[36] Hoffman classifies commercial risks into nine categories. Hoffman, *Law and Business*, pp. 58-68.

[37] Babbar and Schuster, 'Power Project Finance', p. 20.

vehicle (SPV) responsible for the undertaking of all phases of the project.

Exogenous commercial risks are related to the market of the particular industry. With regard to power sector, the most well known risk is the increase of the fuel price that is needed for the operation of the power plant. For example, the majority of power plants still operate today by using conventional types of fossil fuel energy such as oil, coal and gas. The price fluctuation of these primary energy resources is an exogenous commercial risk that affects the income projection of the investment's project company. Another commercial risk is related to the competition that an investor may face in a certain economy, though in the power sector of most countries (especially developing countries) there is a public monopoly with vertically integrated power systems run by an SOE who is the sole purchaser of the electricity produced.[38]

Another category of risks which may or may not be counted among the commercial risks to a project is related to the macroeconomic situation of the host state where the investment project is located. For example, the inflation risk, the sovereign default risk, the foreign exchange risk and the high cost of borrowing from the domestic market are some general economic risks that an investor needs to study carefully before investing in a particular country. These risks are not similar to the previous types of commercial risks as private parties (investors) are not able to control them, thus investors are able to use tools offered by financial market (e.g. swaps-derivative market).[39] Some types of commercial risks that are often assumed by host states are the foreign exchange risk, the public utility's payment performance to the private counterparty, the SOE's default, the fuel supply risk when the host government or an SOE is the sole supplier of fuel to the project company. These risks are commercial in nature, but when the host government guarantees them, as analysed later, they become political in function under one important condition: they are materialised due to political reasons.

Moreover, this study asserts that there should be a demarcation line between normal commercial risks (such as the above) assumed by the state, and risks that the state is unable to assume. Macroeconomic risks are included in the core notion of business risk inherent in every investment project that investors should unavoidably assume when they decide to invest overseas. Investors always have the freedom to proceed with an investment plan or to stay out of the market. When investors decide to invest in a highly uncertain environment they do that after they obtain and thoroughly examine the country's risk environment[40] and demand very high rates for the assumption of the macroeconomic risks.[41] The

---

[38] Kessides, *Reforming Infrastructure*, pp. 2 and 141-157.

[39] In practice, host states with uncertain economic environments usually offer to assume some of such types of commercial risks in order to attract investments into their infrastructure industries.

[40] Large multinational corporations keep an in-house department that makes assessments on country risk. There are also well known global private companies focusing on the assessment of countries' credit risk and others providing various analyses of sovereign risk issues.

[41] However, there is always a psychological factor of "irrationality" in the way investors decide to conduct business which should also be included in the notion of commercial risk. See: C.A.

degree of success and profitability of a business should always be a purely commercial matter calculated by the investor.

2.1.2. The source of political risk in the power sector: the obsolescing bargain

Nevertheless, the threat of political risk occurrence is more eminent in infrastructure (including the power sector) compared to other business-activities. Foreign investors would like to secure their investments against any potential political risk by increasing or maintaining their leverage over the supporting role of the host state.[42] However, Raymond Vernon was among the first scholars[43] to notice that the foreign investors' bargaining power in host countries "would obsolesce or diminish over time, especially in industries such as infrastructure which is characterized by high fixed costs and the inability to transfer capital investment to the home country or another host country". He states that, "on the one hand, governments are under constant pressure to raise their demands on the foreign investor. On the other hand, investors are increasingly committed to a project by the sinking of commitments and by the sweet smell of success".[44] There is empirical evidence in the extracting industries – such as oil and copper – that host governments over the years have managed to elevate their share of the profits substantially.[45]

The power sector especially belongs among the capital intensive industries that require large amount of capital to be invested in specific assets. The construction of power plants and electricity networks, purchase or lease of real estate such as land and buildings, import of expensive machinery including power generators and other electrical machines are some of the important assets of the electricity industry. The investment commitment in assets like the above is what economists call the "asset specificity" problem.[46]

After an investment project is implemented, it is then quite difficult or impossible for investors to divert their investment to another project or transfer their invested capital to another country. Their engagement with the specific investment project and dependence on those specific assets usually lasts for several years. This incapacity of investors to *move out* from the power industry of the host country weakens their bargaining position towards the host government in case of disagreement, conflict or unwarranted interference. Keeping the

---

Hill, 'How Investors React to Political Risk', *Duke Journal of Comparative and International Law* 8:2 (1997) pp. 289-290 and 307.

[42] An argument that emphasises foreign investors' influence on host countries derives from their promise to bring jobs, capital, technology, and in general to contribute to the economic growth and development of host states.

[43] See: R. Vernon, *Sovereignty at Bay: The Multinational Spread of U.S. Enterprises* (Basic Books, New York and London, 1971); and also some later studies such as: L.T. Wells and E.S. Gleason, 'Is Foreign Infrastructure Investment Still Risky?', *Harvard Business Review* (September/October 1995) pp. 44–53; Doh and Ramamurti, 'Reassessing Risk', pp. 337-353.

[44] Vernon, *Sovereignty at Bay*, p. 53.

[45] *Ibid.*

[46] Williamson is one of the more recent scholars that stressed the issue of asset specificity as closely related to that of opportunism. O.E. Williamson, *The Economic Institutions of Capitalism* (Free Press, New York, 1985).

government's commitments *alive* in long term power projects is not an easy task. Good co-operation with the host state and its agencies throughout the implementation and operation period of the project is indispensable.

On the host state side, governments are willing to attract private investments in infrastructure for various important reasons.[47] In order to succeed in attracting foreign investors, host states are most of the time ready to promise them favourable treatment and to guarantee protection against any future unjustified interference or unpredictable regulatory action. However, even if host governments give such assurances to foreign investors, it cannot be absolutely guaranteed that their promises will be kept until the completion of the project. As described by Vernon, "the returns to the foreign company no longer seem appropriate to the risk bared before implementation of projects, and the government feels justified in demanding more out of the project".[48] It is true that, before a foreign investor decides to proceed with the implementation of an investment project, host governments are likely to unilaterally waive some part of their sovereign rights in relation to their infrastructure regulatory authority in favour of the foreign investors' interests. However, the assurances given to foreign investors by host governments are nothing more than one-sided and one-time promises for future behaviour. Thus, it is argued that "unilaterally enacted, however, such measures could easily be unilaterally revoked".[49] After investments are implemented, the host government finds itself in a superior bargaining position compared to the foreign investor's situation. From the time the foreign investor proceeds with his investment plan, he is dependent on the host government's promises and guarantees.

In conclusion, the asset specificity problem appears when foreign investors have already committed to invest in a certain country and to a specific project. In the pre-investment period, host countries are competing with each other to attract investments by promising foreign investors the friendliest treatment. During this period, foreign investors compete against each other as well. They tend to promise the best business solution for the benefit of the host country. However, in the post-entry period, foreign investors have already taken on legal obligations and have committed large amounts of capital and time to one specific project and country. At this point, it is the investors who need to carefully maintain friendly and smooth co-operation with the host government and its state agencies. Foreign investors make their calculations based on the good will of host governments and their agencies that they will keep, in the long term, their promises and obligations.

---

[47] Some of them are the constraint on public finance, lack of technology and managerial skills, or even a decision to deregulate and privatise the industry.

[48] Vernon, *Sovereignty at Bay*, p. 48.

[49] A. Ziegler and L.P. Gratton, 'Investment Insurance', in P.T. Muchlinski,, F. Ortino, and C.H. Schreuer (eds.), *The Oxford Handbook of International Investment Law* (Oxford University Press, Oxford, 2009) p. 528.

2.1.3. Previous studies on political risk

This section describes, in particular, some of the previous researchers' efforts in defining what political risk is and explains the all-embracing approach of this book on political risk. It is argued that listing analytically all possible political risks in a contract depends on the specific party's interests.[50] Nevertheless, the problem in determining political risk derives from two factors. Firstly, there is a different approach to political risk among different disciplines, namely economics and political economy compared to law. Secondly, political risk is quite heterogeneous.

In international and development economics, there is a different approach to political risk than in law. Political risk is determined in a broader way, including all those factors that make future expectations unpredictable.[51] Some economic studies focus on political risks, such as the expropriation of private property as restrictions to FDI, "as a reason why capital does not flow from rich to poor countries",[52] or "as an impediment to foreign investment in developing countries".[53] In addition, political economy studies focus on the reasons of political risk occurrence, indicating, for example, "the lower weight of foreign investors in the political process that eventually decides on the redistribution of income and wealth in the host country" or whether the immediate gain of host country's expropriation or default can outweigh the "long-run cost" of losing a "good reputation" or the "reluctance of foreign investors to provide further capital".[54] Political risk can be any "political discontinuities" that result in losses.[55]

On the contrary, law studies focus on political risk neither as FDI determinants nor as political shifts in the redistribution of income and power. Law focuses more on the legal protection of foreign investment against political risk. This legal framework of investment protection can be determined according to a set of legal sources such as domestic laws and regulations about foreign investment, legal principles about the protection of private property, international law,

---

[50] Stephens, 'Perspective', pp. 161-162: For example, in an insurance contract by Export Credit Agencies, ECAs would prefer the political risks that are covered to be listed in the contract so any other risks (that are not listed) would be considered to be commercial risks and therefore the ECAs would not be responsible to bear them (the exclusive approach). On the contrary, commercial banks would like to specify that those kinds of risks that are not covered by the insurance contract should be regarded as commercial risks, so that any other unspecified risk would be considered to be political in nature, and therefore the responsibility of covering them would fall to the ECAs (inclusive approach).

[51] P. Harms, *International Investment, Political Risk, and Growth* (Kluwer Academic Publishers, Boston/Dordrecht/London, 2000) p. 72.

[52] N.G. Mankiw, D. Romer and D.N. Weil, 'A Contribution to the Empirics of Economic Growth', *Quarterly Journal of Economics* 107:2 (1992) pp. 407-437.

[53] R.E. Lucas Jr., 'Why Doesn't Capital Flow from Rich to Poor Countries?', *American Economic Review* 80:2 (1990) pp. 93-96.

[54] For a detailed reference to the New Political Economy literature-survey, see: Harms, *International Investment*, pp. 103-111.

[55] D.R. Lessard, 'Country Risk and the Structure of International Financial Intermediation', in D.K. Das (ed.), *International Finance – Contemporary Issues* (Routledge, London, 1993) pp. 451-470.

international treaties on foreign investment and contractual agreements that legally bind the parties.[56]

However, one problem in determining political risk is also observed within legal studies. Some of the reasons may be connected to the difference of states' legal systems or to the absence of an explicit coverage of the political risk notion under international law. The term "political risk" is mainly found in studies related to project finance and much less frequently in those focused on the international law of foreign investments.[57] Nevertheless, the main problem is that political risks are quite "heterogeneous" in nature.[58] There are many different events that can constitute a form of political risk and as complicated new market structures are added, there is also an increase in new types of political risk which investors, countries, and courts need to interpret and acknowledge. For example, in the infrastructure industry, there are "on-going sources of threat".[59] Most of these are related to the liberalisation trend and the reform process that developing countries are undertaking. Especially with regards to investments in the power sector, the structure of contracts which differ according to the parties' specific needs and the interaction of a multiple number of actors make the understanding of the allocation of risks a quite delicate exercise. Moreover, the involved role of PRI agencies in covering some new categories of risk such as the devaluation risk or the sub-sovereign risk which "do not readily fall under the established political risk categories"[60] create some more confusion in defining political risk.

Nevertheless, the lack of a universally accepted definition of political risk does not mean that there are no demarcation lines that can distinguish political risk from any other type of risk. A comprehensive definition of political risks is given by Professor Louis Wells, specifying them as "those risks that are principally the result of forces external to the industry and which involve some sort of government action or, occasionally inaction".[61] In another effort to determine political risk, a distinction is made when the relationship in a contractual agreement is between a private party and a foreign government or a state owned enterprise as usually occurs within foreign investments in infrastructure sectors.

---

[56] T.H. Moran, 'Political and Regulatory Risk in Infrastructure Investment in Developing Countries: Introduction and Overview', *The Centre for Energy, Petroleum and Mineral Law and Policy Journal* (CEPMLP) vol. 5:6 (1999).

[57] Several such studies are referenced in M. Inadomi, *Independent Power Projects in Developing Countries: Legal Investment Protection and Consequences for Development* (Kluwer Law International, Oxford, 2009) p. 133 n. 46.

[58] Hill, 'How Investors React', p. 288.

[59] Moran, 'Political and Regulatory Risk', p. 7.

[60] T. Matsukawa and O. Habeck, 'Review of Risk Mitigation Instruments for Infrastructure Financing and Recent Trends and Developments', *Trends and Policy Options Paper*, no. 4, PPIAF (World Bank, Washington, DC, 2007) p. 6.

[61] L.T. Wells, 'God and Fair Competition: Does the Foreign Direct Investor Face Still Other Risks in Emerging Markets?', in T.H. Moran (ed.), *Managing International Political Risk* (Blackwell Publishers Inc., Oxford, 1998) p. 15: Wells adds that any other risk that threatens investors such as risks of using new technology, or risks of better marketing policies by competitors and even risks triggered by natural disasters should be considered to be commercial risks or acts of God.

In this case, it is argued that the "source of the risk, the sovereign, is not extraneous to the business or contractual relation".[62]

The determining factor or reason for the occurrence of political risk is considered to be the involvement of the government and its agencies in the implementation of an investment project. The more the government's involvement in an investment project is needed, the more sensitive to political risk the project becomes. In the case of infrastructure industries, such as building and operating energy, transportation, or telecommunication networks, it is obvious that the participation of the government is a prerequisite and therefore these sectors are politically sensitive.[63] An effort to give an as inclusive as possible definition of political risks determines them as "risks associated with business or investment in a country which would not be present in another country with a more stable and developed business and economic climate and regulatory regime".[64]

In particular, with regard to foreign investments, political risk is "the risk faced by an investor that a host country will confiscate all or a portion of the investor's property rights located in the host country".[65] Expropriation or nationalisation of private enterprises by host states has been the most recognised risk under international law and along with the threat of war and civil disturbances they have been long focused on.[66] However, this definition of political risk is considered to be exclusive rather than inclusive, concentrating on only one of the dangers that investors face in a foreign country.

Moran, in an attempt to be inclusive, offers a large list of potential political risks that infrastructure investors are exposed to. He divides the political risks into a list of three overlapping categories: the "traditional political risk", the "regulatory risks" and the "parastatal performance risks".[67] The last category,

---

[62] When the public entities do not comply with their contractual obligations, invoking "the use of some specific state power, de jure or de facto", then this is a peculiar instance of cases covered under the term "quasi-commercial" risk; G. Sacerdoti, 'The Source and Evolution of International Legal Protection for Infrastructure Investments Confronting Political and Regulatory Risks', *The Centre for Energy, Petroleum and Mineral Law and Policy Journal* (CEPMLP) 5:7 (1999) p. 5.
Another study takes a broader approach to defining political risk, stating that "political risk can be broadly defined as the risk that the laws of a country will change to the investor's detriment after it has invested capital in the country, reducing the value of its investment. Put simply, it is the risk of government intervention". P. Comeaux and S.N. Kinsella, *Protecting Foreign Investment under International Law. Legal Aspects of Political Risk* (Oceana Publications Inc., New York, 1997) p. 1.

[63] UNCTAD, *World Investment Report 2008*, pp. 161-162.

[64] Hill, 'How Investors React', p. 294: This definition comes from the idea that even if the right to private property is recognised and protected today by all states, developing countries, due to lack of modernised legal systems, are unable to protect these rights and therefore the possibility of political risk increases.

[65] Comeaux and Kinsella, *Protecting Foreign Investment*, p. xxv.

[66] Wells, 'God and Fair Competition', p. 15.

[67] In the first category, the included risks are related to political violence, currency convertibility and transferability, expropriation, creeping expropriation and breach of investment agreement. The second category, regulatory risks, consists of all those risks that, in general, arise from the "application and enforcement of regulatory rules, both at the economy-wide and the industry-or project-specific level". Moran, 'Political and Regulatory Risk', p. 4. This type of risk is more about the large scope of a government's regulatory intervention into the domestic marketplace

parastatal performance risks, consists of risks that could be also termed as quasi-commercial risks, invoking the risk that the public utilities or the host government itself will not comply with specific performance obligations toward the foreign investors such as the duty to purchase the output (electricity) under the Power Purchase Agreement (PPA) or to supply the needed fuel for the project's power plant under the supply agreement. This category of risks can also provoke uncertainty about whether a quasi-commercial risk can be considered to be a political risk or what the criteria in accepting the political nature of such risks should be.[68]

Whatever the categorisation of political risk is, scholars that research political risk-related issues acknowledge that some of the most important risks, such as indirect expropriation, breach of contract and regulatory risks, overlap significantly. Moreover, there is a grey area where the ability to distinguish political risk from commercial risk is quite an ambiguous exercise.[69] Most of the investments in infrastructure sectors are mega-projects with complicated legal structures such as project-financing techniques consisting of large number of agreements and contracts, and a sophisticated business organisation. The legal peculiarity and the complexity that are often observed under such structures make the identification and listing of events related to political risk an unmanageable task. Therefore, an exhaustive list of political risks may not be inclusive enough as they are undergoing great changes and new kinds of political risk may occur.

2.1.4. Study approach to political risk

This study recognises that certain conditions should be met in order to classify a risk as political. First of all, the mere involvement of the public sector in a private infrastructure project means neither that it will result in a political risk occurrence nor that any potential infringement of contractual rights will be political in nature.

In an effort to make a more specific determination of political risk, this study considers it to be: the host government's *unwarranted interference*[70] with the foreign investment which should be *political in nature* and should *adversely affect* the investment's operation or *damage* its economic interests.[71] Unwar-

---

attempting to correct market failures or to protect the general public's health or prosperity. This is a category in which it is not easy to exclusively list all the potential cases of political risks and moreover, there is a blurred distinction between what a legitimate legislative measure is and what constitutes a political risk. *Ibid.*

[68] Other studies have categorised these risks differently. For example, Rubins and Kinsella divide risks into seven categories in an attempt to be more descriptive: outright expropriation including confiscation and nationalisation, regulatory interference (including indirect and creeping expropriation), currency risk, civil unrest, breach of state contracts, corruption and trade restrictions; N. Rubins and N.S. Kinsella, *International Investment, Political Risk and Dispute Resolution: A Practitioner's Guide* (Oceana Publications, New York, 2005) pp. 5-6. Hoffman makes an even larger list of risks according to cross-border risks covered in project finance: Hoffman, *Law and Business*, pp. 40-57.

[69] Stephens, 'Perspective', p. 148.

[70] The concept of interference could be defined broadly, including laws or regulations but also including any action or inaction by the government.

[71] This definition is the result of combining ideas and concepts related to political risk contributed to the literature by previous authors.

ranted interference occurs when host government or its state enterprises act discriminatorily or against the promises and guarantees that were provided to foreign investors at the time of the decision to invest in the territory of the host state.[72] Moreover, the above described behaviour of the host state needs to cause a loss to the investors' business. Lastly, the reason behind the host sate's interference with foreign investor's property cannot be any reason but only "political and speculative".[73] Thus, any commercial or business-oriented matter that is behind the state enterprises' behaviour does not constitute a political risk even if there is damage to investor's property or interests.

However, the above mentioned criteria cannot always guarantee the effective protection of foreign investments against political risk. It is not always easy to realise what constitutes an unwarranted behaviour. For example, in order to decide the discrimination basis of a host government's act, identification of an appropriate comparator is needed. Moreover, whether there is a guarantee or promise by the host state towards the foreign investor depends not only on the content and scope of the particular agreement but also on whether this agree-ment is legally binding or not. It is an even more difficult case to clarify whether the damage to a foreign investment is caused by host government's actions or by any other non-political reason. In complicated power investments, it is likely that the damages suffered by a change in the investment conditions of a project would be partially attributable to both political and commercial reasons.[74]

Another uncertainty arises when the state acts simultaneously in its sovereign capacity as a regulator and in its commercial function as a *businessman*. This often occurs in services related to infrastructure. Especially in relation to power contracts, when the host government provides assurances (promises) or guaran-tees to foreign investors covering the state enterprises' non-performance risk, even if these risks are commercial in nature (e.g. electricity price under a PPA, currency exchange-rate, minimum level of revenue guaranteed, supply of oil for the power plant), a breach of any of these obligations (guaranteed by the govern-ment) can be considered to be a political risk.[75]

However, it cannot be asserted that any breach of a contract by a government or its entities constitutes a political risk. There should be a relationship between the breach and the reason that triggered the breach. For example, if the reason behind a contractual breach is commercial in nature, then the risk should not be

---

[72] In particular, according to this study, unwarranted behaviour may occur when government acts discriminatorily or arbitrarily, when it breaks its assurances or guarantees toward investors, or even when it is opposed to the principle of the good faith and the legitimate expectations of investors about what the State has promised to offer.

[73] Inadomi points out that a definition of political risk should "capture the essence that is the host government's ill will, opportunism and a purpose of appropriation which is the cause behind the government actions leading to reduced profits"; Inadomi, *Independent Power Projects*, p. 134.

[74] That would be more obvious during regional or global financial crises affecting the state enterprises' performance obligation. It is difficult to ascertain what makes host governments liable and when the investors should be held responsible for assuming certain external risks.

[75] It is also asserted that even a macroeconomic risk could become political risk "as long as a government entity breaches a contractual relationship"; Inadomi, *Independent Power Projects*, p. 134.

characterised as political risk. Therefore, the classification of political risk cannot be comprehensive if the reason for the public counterparty's default or breach in an investor-state contract is not investigated.[76] An exception to this rule is the case of natural disasters which, despite the fact that they are not considered to be political risks (according to international project finance literature), are covered by ECAs as if they were political risks (as part of political risk insurance schemes).[77]

In conclusion, what the private sector cannot deal with is the unpredictable behaviour of the government. It is not about what government offers but about how it keeps its promises (obsolescing bargains). The assurances given to foreign investors by host governments are nothing more than one-sided and at-one-time promises for future behaviour.[78] Because of the inherent political discontinuities which are especially prevalent in developing countries, foreign investors should be interested not only in the concrete content of laws and contracts but also in general guarantees that increase the possibility of a risk being political and thereby keeping the host government bound to their obligations.[79] These issues among others are related to a central question in this study: what is the legal framework under which political risks are managed and foreign investments are protected?

2.2. The legal means of protection against political risk

2.2.1. The role of international investment treaties

The issue of foreign investment protection is at the heart of international investment law. Even if promotion of investment is the desired result for both states and private actors, there is not the same significance placed on the issue of investment protection. Promotional policies are based on states' intentions and choices.[80]

However, the issue of foreign investment protection is different than that of promotion and attraction. Protection of foreign investment is not a choice but a necessity. It derives from the possibility of a conflict occurred due to the divergence between the private interests of foreign investors and public measures of

---

[76] For example, if there is a default of the public utility in paying the project company, this risk will be considered to be political if government had guaranteed the payment obligation of the utility. Thus, if the same default occurred because of "lack of funds due to mismanagement", then the risk is a commercial one"; see Hoffman, *Law and Business*, p. 57.

[77] For example NEXI covers losses due to force majeure insuring investments against a broad list of natural events which include in the political risk category; NEXI, *NEXI Business Guide*, 'Overseas Investment Insurance' section (Nippon Export Insurance Agency, 2009) p. 12.

[78] Ziegler and Gratton, 'Investment Insurance', p. 528.

[79] Fatouros was among the first scholars who used the terms guarantees, promises (or assurances) interchangeably in a sense to do or not to do certain things (referring to government obligations). A.A. Fatouros, *Government Guarantees to Foreign Investors* (Columbia University Press, New York and London, 1962) p. 190.

[80] At an initial stage, before any agreement is completed, there is no specific obligation for states to take measures for promotion or attraction of foreign investments. It depends on each state to decide how and when should it attract (if it is the host state) or promote (if it is the home country) foreign investment.

host countries.[81] This potential conflict can lead to a great danger of private sector interests being harmed by the host state's behaviour. And it is this danger that materialises political risks. But, before it is explained how international law and particularly investment treaties help foreign investors mitigate political risks, it is better to answer why protection of private interests (foreign investments) should be regulated by international law.

First, it is important to note that foreign investors bring capital and undertake business projects in the territory of the host state which is a different country than their home country. It is obvious that such process of foreign investment has an international character because it involves at least two sovereign countries. Moreover, both home state and host state have an obvious right in claiming a strong interest in regulating the flow and completion of investments from one country to another.[82] Whereas there is a recognised interest of the home country and its investors, after foreign investment is incorporated in the territory of the host state, it still needs to be regulated according to the laws and the legal system of the host state. Foreign investments shall also be under the host state's jurisdiction, being regulated in a similar way to domestic investments. But saying that, the question of why international law is needed for the regulation of foreign investments still remains unanswered.

The necessity of international law in regulating foreign investment could be explained by the different levels of development among countries.[83] Home countries are usually well-developed economies and states with organised institutions, rule of law, and political and social stability. On the contrary, most of the host countries are still in their developing process, with closed markets or economies in transition with trade barriers and political disturbances including corruption, rule of man, lack of governance, social conflicts, and wars, to mention some of the main problems. Even if the host states include in their domestic investment codes important guarantees and generous privileges for foreign investors (guarantees and privileges that are not offered by developed states), there is still one critical problem. They cannot satisfy the need of foreign investments for protection against the unpredictable and unwarranted interference of their governments.[84] In other words, because of the above mentioned problems of developing countries, foreign investors feel insecure about mitigating potential political risks on their own. They need a more institutionalised forum that can guarantee them security of their investments.

---

[81] The threat of the obsolescing bargain is what usually happens. Theodore Moran states that "the vulnerability of firms with large fixed investments (i.e. power companies) to find the terms of their operating agreements changed or renegotiated, once their operations are in place". T.H. Moran, 'The Changing Nature of Political Risk', in T.H. Moran (ed.), *Managing International Political Risk* (Blackwell Publishers Inc., Malden, 1998) pp. 9-10.

[82] UNCTAD, *World Investment Report 2008*, pp. 3-7.

[83] R. Pritchard, 'The Contemporary Challenges of Economic Development' in Robert Pritchard (ed.), *Economic Development, Foreign Investment and the Law: Issues of Private Sector Involvement, Foreign Investment and the Rule of Law in a New Era* (Kluwer Law International, International Bar Association, London, 1996) pp. 3-5.

[84] T. Ginsburg, 'International Substitutes for Domestic Institutions: Bilateral Investment Treaties and Governance', *International Review of Law and Economics* 25:1 (2005) p. 107; see also Fatouros, *Government Guarantees*, p. 121.

It is the international investment agreements that have been found by both host and home states to be the appropriate forum to secure foreign investments against governmental interference and eventually to mitigate political risk.[85] In particular, EPAs provide a specific framework for foreign investment protection. On the one hand, they guarantee that foreign investments receive an internationally appropriate standard of treatment by the host state. On the other hand, in the event of violation of these standards by the host state, they provide a neutral and objective dispute resolution mechanism which can force a host state to respect the agreed standards of treatment and compensate investors for any damage incurred.[86]

The most significant contribution of international investment treaties is their private standing. The private standing of bilateral investment treaties is something of an "anomaly" in international law.[87] According to Alan Sykes, "private actors have the right to bring an action against a government alleged to have violated the treaty and further require a government adjudged to have breached its obligations to pay money damages to the aggrieved investor".[88] The private standing of international investment treaties is a legitimate way to waive countries' sovereignty in favour of the foreign investments' protection. In other words, even if these treaties are negotiated and signed between sovereign states, their provisions are directly addressed to the private actors (foreign investors originating from the home country in the treaty). These treaties offer specific treatment in favour of foreign investments and they provide measures that limit the host state's regulatory sovereignty in several ways. This function of private standing in international treaties is one of the most important representations of enhancing the bargaining capacity of foreign investors which is promoted through the use of international law.

2.2.2. The role of political risk insurance (PRI)

One of the greatest challenges for infrastructure investors is finding reliable mechanisms that can ensure the credibility of host government's commitments.[89] In complicated power investment projects where many uncertainties occur and the credibility of promises by state agencies is doubted, foreign investors and lenders require the involvement of third-party actors who will cover them against any potential occurrence of political risk. These third-party actors, being the ultimate level of protection for private sector, become the so-called "prominent

---

[85] UNCTAD, *Bilateral Investment Treaties in the Mid-1990s* (United Nations, New York and Geneva, 1998).

[86] By using international tools such as EPAs, the international law can protect foreign investments in two ways. First, the standards of treatment that are guaranteed by host state are internationally bound to the home country and its investors. Second, foreign investors have the ability to satisfy their claims against a potential host state's unwarranted behaviour through an effective state-to-investor dispute resolution forum; Sacerdoti, 'Bilateral Treaties', p. 253.

[87] A. Sykes, 'International Law', in M. Polinsky and S. Shavel (eds.), *Handbook of Law and Economics*, vol. 1 (Elsevier, Amsterdam, 2007) p. 811.

[88] *Ibid.*

[89] Moran, 'Political and Regulatory Risk', p. 9.

victims",[90] deterring the dynamics of the obsolescing bargain. Such actors are international financial institutions like the World Bank Group's independent organisations (e.g. MIGA) and bilateral ECAs like NEXI or credit enhancement agencies like (JBIC). This study argues that the involvement of bilateral and multilateral agencies in the contractual agreement of power investment projects can both mitigate risks and strengthen the bargaining position of investors towards the host state.[91] Host governments are less likely to repudiate or neglect their contractual obligations or their promises that are derived from IIAs when international organisations and important countries are involved. Any damage to the involved international organisations' or home countries' interests in an investment project could politically and economically harm the host state that caused this damage.

2.2.3. Contractual guarantees and power project-financing

Foreign direct investments are not always implemented through legally binding contractual agreements with the host state. However, infrastructure investments and especially power projects almost always involve some type of contract with the host government directly or indirectly through its agencies or SOEs.[92] These contracts or sets of legally binding documents are usually called state contracts (or investor-state contracts) because of the particular dual nature of the host state's role.[93] The argument that state contracts serve to internationalise the agreement between the investor and the host state resulting in the international liability of the state and the unlawful character of the state's act in case there is a violation of these contracts is still not entirely accepted by legal theory.[94] Nevertheless, whether the internationalisation theory has a real effect or not, in infrastructure business practice, it is undoubted that investor-state investment agreements have a valuable application in the mitigation of political risk with a variety of results, depending on the provision of specific types of guarantees by the host government or its agencies.

In infrastructure practice there is a certain type of investment contract that

---

[90] A term first used by Robert Shanks in Theodore Moran's 1998 book: R.B. Shanks, 'Lessons in the Management of Political Risk: Infrastructure Projects (A Legal Perspective)' in T.H. Moran (ed.), *Managing International Political Risk* (Blackwell Publishers Ltd., Oxford, 1998) pp. 85-108.

[91] The role of multilateral and bilateral agencies are analysed in Part II: 'Political Risk Insurance and Investor-State Agreements'.

[92] Sacerdori points out: "Because of the problem of sunk costs, and the historical negative experience especially in developing countries, investors are typically unwilling to make investments in infrastructure without adequate, frequently complex, contractual protection". G. Sacerdoti, 'The Source and Evolution of International Legal Protection for Infrastructure Investments Confronting Political and Regulatory Risks', *The Centre for Energy, Petroleum and Mineral Law and Policy Journal* (CEPMLP), vol. 5-7 (1999), section A, p. 2.

[93] On the one hand, host state acts as the counterparty of the agreement with the foreign investor; and on the other hand, it has some authoritative power being the regulator of the investment (a dominant position).

[94] Sornarajah asserts that there is little support that "such agreements are akin to treaties and their violation is unlawful": Sornarajah, *The International Law*, pp. 402, and see also pp. 417-429.

comes in the form of a concession agreement or public private partnership (PPP) and it varies according to the specific arrangement adopted in each case. The most common form is the build-own-operate and transfer (BOOT) contract[95] or, in its simplest form, the build-own-transfer (BOT) contract.[96] Power projects are usually structured based on a project financing technique (most often on a limited-recourse basis), whether the flow of project's revenue comes from the end-users (retail customers) or from the public utility (the host government) (a take-or-pay arrangement). Most of the political risk consists in the danger that the host government will interfere with the operation of the power project during the life of the project, resulting in a reduction of the pre-determined calculation of the project's revenue. It is this danger that foreign investors need to be aware of at the time of entering into a BOT or any similar agreement with host states and look into specific ways of reducing that risk.

In general, there is a variety of legal documents that are used for power projects (infrastructure investments) and each one of them legally binds the parties to concrete project agreements.[97] For example, a concession is used for the granting of a specific licence or exclusive right by the host government to a foreign investor in order to implement the BOT agreement,[98] a PPA or take-or-pay contract is used to guarantee to the private sponsors that a certain amount of electricity will be purchased and at an agreed tariff, and a performance agreement is frequently provided by the host government in order to guarantee the public utility's performance obligations toward the private investor throughout the project's operational life.[99]

Thus, when it comes to complicated power project financing, the most important legal document in relation to political risk mitigation is the implementation agreement (sometimes called a stability or support agreement).[100] An implementation agreement is particularly important in cases of foreign investments in developing countries where the possibility of political risk materialisa-

---

[95] Under the BOOT structure, in the case of a power-plant project, the foreign investor or the special purpose corporation (consortium of sponsors) signs a contractual agreement with the host government or its power utility which is a SOE to construct the power plant (build), to own and operate the facility (investment) for an agreed period of time (usually twenty to twenty-five years), and eventually to transfer the ownership of the asset to the public electric utility; Sacerdoti, 'The Source and Evolution', p. 3; see also: Rubins and Kinsella, *International Investment*, pp. 34-36.

[96] P. Bernardini, 'Development Agreements with Host Governments' in Robert Pritchard (ed.), *Economic Development, Foreign Investment and the Law: Issues of Private Sector Development, Foreign Investment and the Role of Law in a New Era* (Kluwer Law International, International Bar Association, London, 1996) p. 168; see also: F. Sader, 'Attracting Foreign Direct Investment into Infrastructure: Why Is It So Difficult?', Occasional Paper no. 12, *Foreign Investment Advisory Service-IFC*, World Bank, Washington, DC, 2000, pp. 12-14.

[97] In many infrastructure projects, a letter of intent or a memorandum of understanding which are signed prior to the formal contractual agreement is also included. Even though they are non-binding written statements they include description of specific obligations that the parties should undertake after the signing of the formal contract: Hoffman, *Law and Business*, p. 144.

[98] The term *concession* can be used interchangeably with other terms such as *license, service contract* and *development agreement*: see *ibid.*, p. 145.

[99] Rubins and Kinsella, *International Investment*, pp. 36-37.

[100] Hoffman, *Law and Business*, p. 147.

tion is higher. The implementation agreement usually consists of all the above set of contracts but its main function is to address some of the uncertainties that are related to the host government's responsibilities, such as sovereign guarantees, and with assurances that mitigate specific political risks.[101]

2.3. The legal framework of managing political risk and the assessment of its effectiveness

2.3.1. Political risk management (previous studies and present approach)

2.3.1.1. Methods of mitigating political risk

Firstly, when referring to the "management" of political risk, it means the methods of mitigating political risk. In general, the issue of risk mitigation is interconnected with the issue of looking into ways of how to secure financing. When it comes to foreign infrastructure investments such as construction and operation of power plants in a host country, securing financing is always a difficult or sometimes impossible mission, particularly in relation to the invest-ment climate of developing countries.[102]

Foreign investors, financiers and governments would not achieve the imple-mentation of infrastructure mega-projects if there were not the various home countries' and international institutions' measures for tackling political risk. Some of the most important types of interventions by home countries and international organisations that have been developed in order to complement investments in the public infrastructure sector are mainly related to official development assistance (ODA) for infrastructure projects,[103] capacity-building measures[104] and promotion of regional infrastructure projects with an emphasis in the energy sector.[105] Thus the strong political back-up by the involved govern-

---

[101] This will be explained analytically in Chapter 7 of this book, where real-world implementa-tion agreements are analysed.

[102] UNCTAD, *World Investment Report 2008*, p. 169.

[103] As far as the ODA is concerned, multilateral development banks such as the WB, EBRD for Europe and ADB for Asia and donor states which are capital-exporting countries, such as the US, Japan, European countries and recently emerging economies e.g. China, have played a significant role in securing financing by making more funds available, as well as attracting more FDI into the infrastructure industry of developing countries. About the synergies between ODA and foreign investments in electricity and other infrastructure industries: UNCTAD, 'Foreign Direct Investment and Financing for Development: Trends and Selected Issues', doc. TD/B/COM.2/80 (United Nations, New York & Geneva, 2008).

[104] Another area of foreign investment facilitation is related to capacity building measures or technical assistance programs. In order to successfully attract foreign investments in infrastruc-ture sectors such as electricity, a strong legal and regulatory environment is required for the successful preparation of complex projects such as PPPs or power project financing based on limited recourse sources. In order for infrastructure projects to become bankable for foreign promoters, several multilateral and bilateral institutions have allocated large amounts of funds to providing technical assistance to central and local governments, as well as to their regulatory authorities and public utilities, relating the assistance programs to the improvement of the business environment in infrastructure industries. UNCTAD, *World Investment Report 2008*, p. 175.

[105] In addition, regional integration trends around the globe, such as in the ASEAN community in South-East Asia, has encouraged the development of cross-border infrastructure especially in

ments is a *sine qua non* for the involvement of transnational companies which need a high degree of protection against the multi-level occurrence of political risks.

Nevertheless, the effectiveness of the above interventions has not been always clear.[106] Moreover, in relation to political risk mitigation, the above interventions have not been specialised enough to facilitate foreign investor's involvement with public infrastructure sectors unless host governments offer excessive sovereign guarantees or generous subsidies that most of the time impose big financial burden and large contingent liabilities on the host governments.[107]

Mitigating all kind of political risks in sectors such as infrastructure network-industries is a complicated matter that should be addressed through different tools. According to a traditional approach of studies on political risk and business practices, the focus has been on *affirmative* or *active* methods that investors can take to reduce their exposure to political risk. In particular, several studies have analysed examples of methods that require an affirmative action by investors, such as arrangements with ECAs for the provision of political risk insurance,[108] agreements with IFIs for the provision of full or partial risk guarantees (RRGs)[109] as well as the signing of investor-state contracts with host states which in infrastructure sectors they are usually project finance contracts or PPPs.[110]

However, apart from these affirmative measures, the present volume asserts that there are also passive or non-controllable methods of mitigating risk, such as the understanding and acknowledgment of the protection offered by general and specific standards of treatment that are included in international investment

---

sectors such as the energy industry with the development of power generation mega-projects and interconnection of the regional grid system (e.g. construction of the *Nam Theun II Hydropower Project* in Laos supplying electricity to Laos and to Thailand); B. Thomson, 'Laos and Thailand: Exploring Cross-Border Hydropower Projects', *Allen & Overy*, note written on 17/5/2010, as retrieved on 20/6/2011.

[106] It has been questioned with regards to the host countries' improvement of their capacities and the time that is needed for such an effort, with regards to the optimal use of the private and public sectors' cooperation for the benefit of the local population (especially the low-income customers), and with regards to the final result in successfully reforming the electricity sector of host countries; A. Estache, 'Argentina's 1990s Utilities Privatization: A Cure or a Disease?', Mimeo (World Bank, Washington, DC, 2002).

[107] A. Estache and M. Fay, 'Current debates on Infrastructure Policy', *Policy Research Working Paper*, no. 4410 (World Bank, Washington, DC, 2007); see also: Babbar, 'Power Project Finance'.

[108] L. William, 'Political and Other Risk Insurance: OPIC, MIGA, EXIMBANK and Other Providers', *Pace International Law Review* 5:1 (1993) pp. 59-113.

[109] M.D. Rowat, 'Multilateral Approaches to Improving the Investment Climate of Developing Countries: The Cases of ICSID and MIGA', *Harvard International Law Journal* 33:1 (1992) pp. 103-144; Matsukawa and Habeck, 'Review of Risk Mitigation Instruments'; J. Delmon, 'Mobilizing Private Finance with IBRD/IDA Guarantees to Bridge the Infrastructure Funding Gap', Finance, Economics and Urban Development Department/Sustainable Development Network (World Bank, Washington, DC, 2007).

[110] T. Irwin, M. Klein, G.E. Perry and M. Thobani (eds.), 'Dealing with Public Risks in Private Infrastructure', *World Bank Latin American and Caribbean Studies* (World Bank, Washington, DC, 1997); F. Sader, 'Attracting Foreign Direct Investment into Infrastructure: Why Is It So Difficult?', Occasional Paper no. 12, *Foreign Investment Advisory Service-IFC* (World Bank, Washington, DC, 2000) pp. 22-24.

treaties. There is a substantial difference between affirmative and passive function measures.

According to the function of passive methods, protection against political risk can be achieved without the requirement of any action or measure by foreign investors whose investments are at risk. On the contrary, according to the function of affirmative measures, investors need to take several actions.[111] In the function of passive methods, foreign investors are benefited by legal instruments that mitigate political risk and protect their investments without any direct action required by them.[112] It is about a pre-set legal framework of foreign investment protection. That is achieved through the protective framework established by legal mechanisms such as the general and specific standards of treatment included in investment treaties.[113]

2.3.1.2. Holistic approach in managing political risk

There are many studies that have researched the mitigation of political risks by focusing on the various methods separately, but there are very few that adopt an integrated analysis of political risk and only a handful of studies that undertake a holistic approach focusing on both active and passive measures of political risk mitigation. In reviewing them, this study has adopted several points related to the structure of the study as well as to the legal framework in managing political risk. Nevertheless, there are some substantial differences as well as secondary variations between the present volume and previous research.

Beginning with the oldest study that is relevant to this book (1994), Paul Comeaux and Stephan Kinsella advocated a multi-tier legal framework for reducing political risk by invoking international treaty law (BITs), contractual protection through stabilisation and arbitration clauses and the PRI policies available in MIGA and OPIC as well as in private investment insurance.[114] Later, their 1994 article became a monograph[115] with expanded coverage, and it was

---

[111] For example, in the case of PRI agreements, investors need to negotiate with the related ECA and convince it about their desired coverage for their investment's political risk. If the ECA agrees to insure the investment, then in return for the ECA's coverage, investors are obliged to pay a premium. Similarly, in the case of a direct contract agreement with the host state, foreign investors need to negotiate about risk allocation among the contract parties, structure the most appropriate contractual agreement and undertake several responsibilities in exchange of guarantees given by the host government.

[112] However, indirectly, private sector, and especially export oriented industries and trading companies, are very active in lobbying and influencing their home country's political institutions to proceed with the signing of investment treaties and free trade agreements with the countries wherein their export and investment interests lay.

[113] This book argues that the awareness and understanding of these mechanisms by all the involved parties in an investment project can enhance an effective protection against political risk.

[114] In the article, the authors introduced the concept of protection against political risk through both general and specific standards of treatment based on the US-Russia BIT, as well as through concession contracts and PRI policies. See: P. Comeaux and N.S. Kinsella, 'Reducing Political Risk in Developing Countries: Bilateral Investment Treaties, Stabilization Clauses, and MIGA & OPIC Investment Insurance', *New York Law School Journal of International and Comparative Law* 15:1 (1994) pp. 1-48.

[115] Comeaux and Kinsella, *Protecting Foreign Investment*.

finally updated by a new study in 2005, this time by Noah Rubins and Stephan Kinsella.[116] The latest study addresses similar issues including three parts: 1) the pre-investment management of political risk,[117] 2) the international legal framework for protecting investments against political risk,[118] and 3) the last part of this study is devoted to dispute resolution in general, addressing issues related to political risk mitigation.

Another set of studies that have influenced the present study's adoption of an integrated analysis of political risk are two articles published in the *The Centre for Energy, Petroleum and Mineral Law and Policy Journal* (CEPMLP) in 1999. In contrast to other studies that do not address political risk problems in a particular industry, both of these articles are related to the protection of infrastructure sectors against political risk.[119] In the first one,[120] author Theodore Moran – one of the key scholars who have initiated and empowered the legal debate related to political risk and foreign investment protection – identifies the sources of political risk and examines three levels of reducing or mitigating political risks: the use of "self-help" measures which consist of domestic laws and regulatory reforms by host states that they undertake in order to reduce risks in their jurisdictions, the use of international treaties (BITs) focusing on the role of general and specific standards of treatment and international arbitration and finally, the use of insurance and guarantees offered by third parties such as ECAs and the World Bank Group's agencies.[121] Similarly to Moran's paper, the second article's[122] author, Georgio Sacerdoti, argues for the importance of addressing political risk in infrastructure sectors. Sacerdoti also examines the various types of risks affecting international infrastructure investment, distinguishing them from commercial risks, and provides a list of various kinds of political risk.[123]

---

[116] In the new book there is an expansion in the analysis of the role of international arbitration: Rubins and Kinsella, *International Investment,* pp. 261-365.

[117] It consists of listing all categories of political risk, referring to basic transaction structures (such as investor-state contracts and main clauses that affect political risk), as well as investment insurance consisting of the description of insurance policies (mainly through an analysis of OPIC and MIGA). There is also reference to other national insurance programs such as NEXI, thus there is a limited analysis on them.

[118] It includes both general and specific standards of treatment (contained in BITs) analysing their roles in reducing political risk.

[119] Thus, there is in general discussion about infrastructure sectors and not a specific reference to the power industry.

[120] This paper was used in the International Conference 'Promoting Infrastructure Investment in Developing Countries by Reducing Political and Regulatory Risk' held in Rome on 8-10 September 1999 and sponsored by the World Bank and the Government of Italy; Moran, 'Political and Regulatory Risk'.

[121] This article particularly analyses the role of MIGA guarantees as well as IFC policy and IBRD, PRG and PCG tools. In its final part, the article gives attention to future developments in relation to project finance techniques instead of using sovereign guarantees that impose heavy contingent liabilities on host states; *ibid.*

[122] Sacerdoti, 'Source and Evolution'.

[123] After giving the general framework of multilateral and bilateral investment treaties, he examines the role of BITs in connection to the pre-establishment investment stage, the role of general and specific standards of treatment in the post-establishment stage and the settlement

2.3.1.3. Study approach

In comparison to the previous studies reviewed above, this study is different in respect of two primary facts as well as in relation to some secondary aspects. Firstly, the present study is an empirical study of the legal protection of power investments against political risk. By "empirical", it means that on the one side, it investigates the wording of specific clauses that are included in five of Japan's EPAs and one BIT and it compares their differences. On the other side, it focuses on a particular industry, the power sector, making some practicable findings by analysing elements that particularly affect Japanese investments in the power sector of the host countries. The empirical character of this study changes the analytical approach compared to the previous studies as it focuses not only on the general framework of investment protection but also on the micro-level elements that affect the management of several political risks with regards to power investments. One result of the different analytical approach of this study is that it contains specific observations of the treatment available to the power industry that is included not only in the wording of the analysed clauses but also in annexes that are attached to the end of the respective EPA treaties. In these annexes, there are interesting findings related to specific reservations or restrictions that are taken by the host countries treating Japanese power investments in a different way in each case.

The difference in approaching the legal framework of foreign investment protection is also apparent when the subject matter is EPA treaties compared to BITs. The previous research focused on BITs which, until very recently, were the most common type of international investment agreement.[124] However, this study asserts that the management of political risk under the framework of EPA treaties differs from that under BITs being larger in scope and in their details. Since the end of the 1990s and especially during the last decade, a new type of economic agreement has arisen. Free Trade Agreements (FTAs), or EPAs in the case of Japan, are modern bilateral (or regional) tools that promote free trade between countries, in a way similar to the General Agreement on Tariffs and Trade (GATT) model.[125] However, what makes FTAs useful and unique tools is their regulatory framework. Even if the primary reason for using FTAs has been the liberalisation of trade, their greatest contribution has been their inclusion (in the majority of the cases) of a section devoted to the promotion and protection of investments from one party (country) to the other, and vice versa. Moreover, even if the FTAs' methods of regulating foreign investments is similar to the

---

of disputes between investors and the host states or between contracting parties. However, Sacerdoti does not include PRI policies in his legal framework related to the management of political risk in infrastructure investments because the focus of his article is limited to the international treaty-law (mainly BIT) protection.

[124] BITs have gained momentum mainly because of the failure to create a multilateral investment agreement. They offered an alternative, more flexible path, being ad hoc agreements created on a bilateral level between an export-capital (home country) and an import-capital country (host state).

[125] FTAs are the response of the international community to the limitations faced by multilateral trade arrangements (under the WTO). They represent increasing *bilateralisation* between states that wish to open their markets to an even greater extent than the level provided by GATT.

methods of BITs, the content of the FTAs' regulations are much larger in scope and greater in their details compared to the regulatory framework of BITs.

In particular, as far as investment is concerned, there is a substantial difference in the scope of the FTA provisions compared with those of BITs. The majority of FTAs (such as those analysed by this paper – Japanese EPAs with five ASEAN countries) include two separate chapters: one on trade in services and one on investments. This division of chapters is important because FTAs succeed in regulating investments with a greater perspective. FTAs include the investment in services through the commercial presence mode [mode no. 3 of the World Trade Organisation (WTO)–GATS].[126] By including a trade in services chapter in FTAs, disputes about investment definitions can be substantially reduced (though still not eliminated).[127] There is no fixed concept of host state and home state in FTA treaties. Both parties are considered to be potential capital exporting and capital importing states. Both parties can be host states and home states according to the origin of each individual investment project. FTAs also differ in their details. They include concrete protection of foreign investments in two different stages: there are measures addressed to investment in the pre-establishment phase, and separate provisions for the post-establishment phase, which is considered to be the main phase of investment protection. However, this book analyses provisions that are included in the post-establishment phase only.[128]

Another difference that is related to the empirical character of analysis is that this study does not investigate the legal protection provided by domestic laws in each of the host countries' jurisdictions. Moran, as referenced above, argues for the use of "self-help" measures, municipal laws and regulations, in the protection against political risk.[129] Thus, among other problems, the main constraint on the use of domestic laws is the general and fragmented nature of municipal legal systems.[130] For the purpose of an empirical analysis, it is necessary to examine a large set of specific municipal laws in each jurisdiction separately, including not

---

[126] This is a substantial difference from the BITs; this volume, as analysed in the methodology section below, examines the legal framework of managing political risk under both chapters, on investment and on trade in services for each EPA.

[127] A. Kaushal, 'Revisiting History: How the Past Matters for the Present Backlash against the Foreign Investment Regime', *Harvard International Law Journal* 50:2 (2009) p. 491.

[128] The main reason is that the pre-establishment phase contains provisions about market access, restrictions on acquisition of real estate, restrictions on foreign ownership and performance requirements in general which are related mainly to the promotion and liberalisation of FDI. On the contrary, this study, as previously explained, does not focus on FDI promotion policies but instead focuses on the legal protection of foreign investments against political risk. Moreover, post-establishment provisions deal with barriers to investment that are not related to the notion of political risk according to this research. Such provisions are the percentage of foreign-shareholding permitted by the host-country or the maximum number of foreign managers allowed in the Board of Directors, issues related to visa of foreign employees etc.

[129] However, his study, similar to the other reviewed studies, does not include any empirical test on any particular group of countries. His aim is to advocate for the role of a multi-tier legal framework in managing political risk by including self-help measures that are available to host countries to reduce risk in their own jurisdictions.

[130] This is highlighted also in Moran's article: Moran, 'Political and Regulatory Risk', pp. 1-2.

only FDI laws, which are usually the main legal instrument in treating foreign investments, but also several decrees or specific legislative acts that are usually issued *ad hoc* per project-case.[131] For this reason, under the scope and structure of this study, domestic laws cannot be tested.[132]

The second important difference between this volume and the previous research with regards to the legal framework of foreign investment is in its assessment of the effectiveness of the legal framework. As a first step, this study provides an in depth analysis of potential factors that increase or decrease the possibility of political risk materialisation. This is implemented through particular examination of the wording in treaties' clauses and annexes, PRI tools in NEXI's and World Bank's mechanisms and through guarantees that are contained in investor-state power contracts. Nevertheless, the most significant contribution of this research is the assessment of the findings mainly in investment treaties and investor-state contracts by qualitative and scoring methods. The present study aims to create a comprehensive guide which can show the degree of protection against political risk. Especially with regards to investment treaty protection, it develops a score card which measures the effectiveness of the various standards of treatment in each treaty.

In addition to the empirical character of this study and the assessment exercise, this research is also unique in the following ways: it examines for the first time the legal protection of recently entered-into-force Japanese EPAs [133] combined with a review of the latest international jurisprudence, it explores for the first time the functionality of NEXI in-depth with the help of primary data (interviews) and secondary data, [134] and it offers case-studies from power contracts between foreign investors and host countries adding real-world examples that are applicable to this study's framework. Finally, this book differs from previous research in that it pays attention to the interface among different tiers of legal framework, looking at whether there is a complementary result (nexus) on the protection of foreign investments against political risk.

2.3.2. Assessment exercises on foreign investment regimes

When it comes to the crucial issue of assessing the effectiveness of the legal framework of foreign investment protection, this study follows techniques that have been used in the discipline of international economics. Firstly, there are two groups of previous research that have initiated assessment exercises related to FDI regimes. One group of studies undertook research on measuring the

---

[131] That is often observed in power investments which, due to the complexity of the projects and because of the participation of a large number of sponsors and lenders, specific legislative or administrative actions are taken in order to justify the commitment and engagement of the host government to the project requirements.

[132] However, an analysis based on empirical tests of specific host countries' laws would be an independent future research.

[133] The reviewed Japan's EPAs entered into force in the period from 13 July 2006 (Japan-Malaysia EPA) to 1 October 2009 (Japan-Vietnam EPA); Source: Japan's Ministry of Foreign Affairs.

[134] Rubins and Kinsella's work refers to NEXI, but not to the extent of the present study; see: Rubins and Kinsella, *International Investment*, p. 91.

impediments of various countries' FDI laws and FTAs for the openness of the investment regime (investment promotion) and the other group assessed the economic impact of provisions existent in regional and bilateral trade agreements (promotion and protection of foreign investments).

In the oldest study within the first group of research assessing the restrictiveness of domestic FDI laws, Golub examined the restrictions on FDI for OECD countries in the period 1998-2000 by assessing rules on foreign equity, screening and approval procedures, as well as restrictions on boards of directors, movement of people, and input and operations.[135] He used a scoring system to calculate the overall restrictiveness indicators for each industry and country based on FDI regulations in each of the above areas. The total score ranged between zero (0) and one (1), also using a weighting scheme.[136] In a similar way, a PECC study evaluated the FDI regimes of Asia-Pacific Economic Cooperation (APEC) economies by investigating wider areas of FDI regulations such as most favoured nation (MFN) treatment, profit repatriation, work permits, performance requirements, dispute settlement, investment incentives and capital exports.[137] Based on the above studies, an expanded approach was taken in more recent research undertaken by the Economic Research Institute for ASEAN (ERIA)[138] and the Research Institute of Economy, Trade and Industry (RIETI).[139] For example, in the first study, Shujiro Urata and Mitsuyo Ando scored the restrictiveness of FDI rules of all ten ASEAN countries by measuring the six areas similar to Golub's study: market access, national treatment, screening and approval procedures, composition of board of directors and management, movement of investors and performance requirements. In the RIETI study, the same assessment methodology was used[140] but with an important difference: it was adopted in order to measure the degree of restrictions of selected FTAs instead of host countries' FDI laws.[141] However, the main weakness of the above

---

[135] S.S. Golub, 'Measures of Restrictions on Inward Foreign Direct Investment for OECD Countries', *OECD Economic Studies*, no. 36 (OECD, Paris, 2003).

[136] In his assessment exercise, zero was given to FDI laws that had no restrictions on inward investment flow providing the best regime for FDI openness, and a unit was given to those regulations that were restrictive to inward FDI, imposing several constraints and exceptions.

[137] PECC, 'An Assessment of Impediments to Foreign Direct Investment in APEC Member Economies' (Pacific Economic Cooperation Council, Tokyo, 2002).

[138] S. Urata and M. Ando, 'Investment Climate Study on ASEAN Member Countries' in J. Corbett and S. Umezaki (eds.), *ERIA Report No 1, 2008: Deepening East Asian Economic Integration* (ERIA Institute, Jakarta, 2009) pp. 125-195.

[139] S. Urata and J. Sasuya, 'Analysis of the Restrictions on Foreign Direct Investment in Free Trade Agreements' in C. Findlay and S. Urata (eds.), *Free Trade Agreements in The Asia Pacific*, World Scientific Studies in International Economics vol. 11 (World Scientific Publishing Co., Singapore, 2010) pp. 81-130.

[140] In another study of the RIETI's publication, an attempt to score expropriation, transfer of payments and investor-state dispute was also included but to a limited extent. See: R. Ochiai, P. Dee and C. Findlay, 'Services in Free Trade Agreements' in C. Findlay and S. Urata (eds.), *Free Trade Agreements in the Asia Pacific*, World Scientific Studies in International Economics, vol. 11 (World Scientific Publishing Co., Singapore, 2010) pp. 56-57.

[141] In March 2007, RIETI organised a policy symposium entitled 'Assessing Quality and Impacts of Major Free Trade Agreements' which initiated the assessment exercise on FTAs.

studies is that they measured elements that are limited to FDI promotion and liberalisation, without covering the issue of FDI protection. Notwithstanding their important contribution to the way FDI restrictions affect investment openness, regulations about the market access, the national treatment (NT) and MFN treatment in the pre-establishment phase or restrictions on the investors' movement and the composition of board of directors are not as important as (or at least no more important than) the regulations related to the post-establishment phase and, in particular, the crucial issue of various reservations with regards to the treatment of investments under international investment treaties (or investment chapters of FTAs).

The second group of assessment research undertakes a different exercise than the first group based on provisions existed in FTAs. This group's significance is their attempt to measure non-trade provisions that are related to both promotion and protection of foreign investments. An early study by Adams *et al.*[142] made an index of liberalisations to measure the breadth and depth of RTAs by including a category for investment rules. When these rules prohibit any restriction on investment, they are treated with the highest score (1.00).[143] A similar assessment exercise is undertaken in another study by te Velde and Bezemer.[144] This study also uses an index focusing on investment and scores the various findings in a similar way. In particular the authors categorise the findings in RTAs according to the degree of inclusiveness related to investment provisions and make a scale from -1 to 3.[145] However, the assessment criteria that are used by both studies in relation to the prohibition of restrictions on investment or the inclusion of investment provisions are general and abstract without addressing particular threats to the protection of foreign investment. These criteria are focused only on whether there is a reference by the reviewed treaties to restrictions on FDI flow or to the provision of assurances for investors without specifying the findings and, more importantly, without analysing in depth the essence of each restriction or provision accordingly. For example, if there is a clause providing NT or MFN treatment, it will be scored fully without taking into account interpretative variations in the wording or reservations included in annexes when comparing different treaties.

---

[142] R. Adams, P. Dee, and G. McGuire, 'The Trade and Investment Effects of Preferential Trading Arrangements – Old and New Evidence', Australian Productivity Commission Staff Working Paper (Canberra, 2003).

[143] In the case of a prohibition of restrictions only on NT, a 0.75 score is given, and if there is a mere provision for initiatives to reduce restrictions and facilitate investment, then a lower score (0.25) is given. If no any provisions of the above are found, then the lowest score to be given is zero (0). Their scoring results were used in a gravity model showing that non-trade provisions significantly impact investment flows.

[144] D.W. te Velde and D. Bezemer, 'Regional Integration and Foreign Direct Investment in Developing Countries', 2004 (http://www.odi.org.uk/iedg/Projects/ec_prep2.pdf), cited in M. Lesher and S. Miroudot, 'Analysis of the Economic Impact of Investment Provisions in Regional Trade Agreements', *OECD Trade Policy Working Papers* no.36 (OECD, Trade Directorate, Paris, 2006).

[145] For example, 0 is given if there are no provisions at all, -1 if there are restrictive provisions, 1 if there are some investment provisions in the region, 2 with more advanced regulations and 3 if there are complete provisions. This study also finds a correlation between a country's membership in a specific RTA and extra-regional inward FDI flows.

A more recent and comprehensive study that expanded the assessment method of the above research is an OECD paper by Lesher and Miroudot.[146] This research examines investment provisions in relation to both goods and services contained in 24 RTAs as of November 2005, based on six categories.[147] The strength of the OECD study is the broad coverage of investment provisions compared with the previous research.[148] However, due to similar reasons as mentioned above about the previous studies, this research has also several weaknesses. As is acknowledged by the authors, "the purpose of this analysis is not to provide a full analysis of the provisions, but rather to lay the foundation for the study of the impact of these provisions on trade and FDI flows".[149] The weakest point is that it treats the provisions of investment-related standards such as NT, expropriation or fair and equitable treatment (FET) without analysing the specific wording and their connotation depending on the particular case. Moreover, the assessment exercise of investment regulation and protection elements is built upon a binary approach based on a yes or no methodology. That leads to a scoring result which cannot represent the full spectrum of restrictions and legal variations that are included in different types of treaty clauses. Nevertheless, it should be recognised that all of the above exercises are part of an economic quantitative assessment which does not aim to qualitative measure of the value of each provision. They rather focus on creating an index that can be utilised for ranking exercises of various investment-related clauses that are included in different types of trade and investment agreements. This is a central difference with the present study's assessment methodology as detailed in the following section.

Before analysing the present methodology, it is also important to discuss the assessment exercise in relation to the effectiveness of the contractual guarantees included in insurance and investor-state contracts. There is not any relevant study that has undertaken an assessment based on specific guarantees that are included in contractual clauses or insurance policies. The only assessment exercise is related to project performance as it is defined by the evaluation groups in international financial institutions such as the World Bank (WB), the Asian Development Bank (ADB), the European Investment Bank (EIB) and others, in line with the work of OECD-DAC Working Party on Aid Evaluation and based on criteria of project's relevance, efficacy, efficiency, and sustainability.[150] This book does not examine any of the above criteria in relation to power projects because

---

[146] Lesher and Miroudot, 'Analysis of the Economic Impact'.

[147] Access to markets and non-discrimination in the pre-establishment phase, non-discrimination in the post-establishment phase, the same provisions for investment in services, provisions for investment protection such as expropriation, FET, free transfer of funds among others, dispute settlement including state-state and investor-state dispute mechanisms and finally investment promotion and cooperation mechanisms.

[148] Apart from including provisions for investment not only in relation to market access but also to the post-establishment phase, it also provides assessments of the provisions included in the trade in services chapters via mode 3 of the WTO, commercial presence.

[149] *Ibid.*, p. 10.

[150] See, for example: EIB, 'Evaluation of PPP Projects Financed by the EIB', Evaluation Report, Operations Evaluation Department (European Investment Bank, Luxembourg, 2005).

they have no direct connection with the issue of protection against political risk. However, the general approach of assessment exercises by international organisations, based on non-numerical project-ratings such as *good, satisfactory, unsatisfactory,* and *poor,* is similarly adopted for the needs of this study's assessment.

2.4. Methodology

2.4.1. Qualitative assessment

Starting with the qualitative approach to Parts I and II, this study categorises the various tools provided by the multi-tier legal framework into two mechanisms: the *non-controllable* or *passive* mechanisms,[151] consisting of standards of treatment in international treaties (Part I), and the *active* or *affirmative* tools which are controllable,[152] such as PRI and contractual guarantees (Part II). For the passive tools, this study analyses specific determinants included in the wording of the examined treaties' clauses and annexes. In particular, it identifies those criteria that increase or decrease the possibility of political risk occurrence (i.e. the effectiveness of protection).

As mentioned above, passive tools are the standards of treatment that are contained in BITs and EPAs (or FTAs) treaties. In general, the notion of treatment is broad. It means any kind of legislative, administrative or judicial measure, or any kind of action or inaction by the host state or its agencies affecting the real or legal situation (or just the behaviour) of foreign investors and their investments. The implementation of a law, the issuance, denial or cancellation of a licence, a judicial decision, an administrative fine, a measure of expropriation, the denial of transfer of funds outside the country, a giving of a subsidy are only some of the measures that are included in the concept of foreign investment treatment. In any case, the measures, actions or inactions shall really affect the condition of foreign investments (positively or negatively). The issuance of a law, which has never been implemented or, being inactive, is not considered to be a measure that affects foreign investments, thus is not treated.

In the past, both states and investors were exclusively concerned about the risk of expropriation. While expropriation remains a fundamental element of international investment agreements, there are also some other equally significant elements included in the body of most investment agreements. A variety of element-clauses has been recently utilised in claims by international investment law arbitrations.[153] A variety of standards of treatment would be contained in one article or in many articles.[154]

There are two main categories of treatment included in the majority of international investment agreements and owed by states to foreign investors and their

---

[151] When foreign investors do not need to take any particular action in relation to the structuring of these measures.

[152] Investors need to take the initiative (actions) in negotiating and structuring the various contracts.

[153] Fair and equitable treatment is one of the most used elements in investors' claims and arbitration decisions (mainly by ICSID and UNCITRAL tribunals).

[154] Sornarajah, *International Law,* p. 233.

investments: the general and the specific standards of treatment. The former consist of the host state's guarantees against non-specific risks that may occur in relation to the pre-establishment or post-establishment of the foreign investments in the territory of the host country. In particular, host states promise that foreign investors and their investment will be treated fairly, with no discrimination or arbitrary behaviour and according to international law, international principles and customs. The general standards of treatment guarantee the foreign investment's protection in general, without specifying any particular source of violation. This book examines provisions (wordings) that exist in NT, MFN treatment, FET and full protection and security (FPS) treatment. On the contrary, the latter category of treatment provides guarantees against specific risks which may occur only after the establishment of the foreign investments in the territory of the host state and throughout the period of the investment operation. The study examines provisions (wordings) that exist in expropriation and compensation standards of treatment, free transfer of funds (FTFs) treatment, protections from strife, umbrella clause and two additional clauses related to international dispute resolution and subrogation which, as explained below, play the role of deterrence.

The study further asserts that the general and the specific standards of treatment consist of a dual application function. Protection of foreign investments against political risk can be achieved through both prevention and deterrence. On the one hand, both general and specific standards clauses prevent a host state from violating its obligations in relation to the promised treatment of foreign investments. The preventive application of these standards of treatment consists of a legally binding obligation. The host state, by signing an investment treaty and by promising general and specific treatment towards the investments of the home country, undertakes a direct international obligation towards the other party of the treaty (the home country) and consequently towards its investors.

On the other hand, in the event the host state violates these standards, the treaty comprises in most occasions a neutral dispute resolution forum that home states or even their investors can utilise.[155] If a host state neglects or violates its international obligations derived from the standards of treatment clauses, the *state responsibility* can be established according to international law before the agreed juridical or arbitration forum. International investment arbitration offers states and investors an effective and impartial way to protect their interests and satisfy their claims by providing remedies such as adequate compensation or in rare cases, restitution. The possibility of a host state being condemned by one of the agreed arbitration tribunals or accused of maltreatment of foreign investments in its territory increases the deterrent function of the standards of treatment. Therefore, the combined effect of promised standards of treatment and the treaty's dispute resolution mechanisms establishes the "rescue" or deterrence application of these measures.

In the case of active measures taken under PRI and under investor-state contracts, this book focuses on the factors that increase or decrease the deterrence of

---

[155] This depends on the provision of the arbitration clause: State-to-State or State-to-Investor arbitration forum.

insurance instruments in relation to the protection of investments insured against political risk (i.e. the effectiveness of instruments' deterrence) or the preventive function of contractual guarantees in relation to a host government's assurances towards investors (i.e. the comprehensiveness of contractual clauses).

In particular, for the PRI framework, the present study examines the political risk coverage offered by NEXI and JBIC in relation to foreign investments in the power sector by analysing specific policies in four insurance instruments: overseas investment insurance (OII), overseas untied loan insurance (OULI), buyer's credit insurance (B/C Insurance) in the case of NEXI, and the extended political risk guarantee (EPRG) provided by JBIC. Apart from identifying which types of political risk are covered by each instrument, the qualitative methodology focuses on the comprehensiveness of NEXI's specific requirements based on the following criteria. Firstly, it investigates the insured events that NEXI requires with regards to its liability to insure the claim of the investor for losses suffered due to certain political risks. Such events required by NEXI are an inability to continue business operations, bankruptcy of the investor's subsidiary, suspension of banking transactions and suspension of business operations for three months or longer. Secondly, the analysis deepens the investigation on the claim ascertainment. This study analyses what list of check-points for claim ascertainment are required by NEXI in order to verify whether the insured's claim for insurance is valid or not. As analysed in this volume, the check-points for claim validity differ depending on the insured risk. With regards to power project finance, the ascertainment exercise becomes more difficult due to the complexity of the projects. The comprehensiveness of the check-points is a crucial determinant of political risk deterrence because if they are not verified by NEXI, then the insured's claim is declared to be invalid. In addition to these criteria, this study also examines some broader factors such as the eligibility criteria set by NEXI (and JBIC) in relation to the insured product, the direct and indirect beneficiary as well as the contents of NEXI and JBIC policies in relation to the maximum repayment term for the projects' insurance, the maximum amount that can cover claims for losses due to political risk and the premium rates according to country-risk and type of product. Finally, this study compares the findings of the above analytical method with those found by examining the deterrence of guarantees provided by the World Bank Group's agencies such as MIGA, International Bank for Reconstruction and Development (IBRD), International Development Agency (IDA) and International Finance Cooperation (IFC). In particular, this study examines the political risk coverage offered by WB (mainly MIGA) in relation to foreign investments by analysing specific policies included in MIGA policies (guarantees covering four types of political risk: expropriation, currency inconvertibility and transfer risk, breach of contract and war and civil disturbance), as well as partial risk guarantees (PRGs) provided by IBRD/IDA (and IFC loans). The analysis is conducted in a similar way as that of NEXI, and it compares the two sets of findings. This comparison facilitates our understanding of the differences between the two systems and focuses on the evaluation of each agency's effectiveness towards the protection of Japanese investments against political risk.

Finally, in the case of active measures taken under investor-state power contracts, this book analyses first the strength and weaknesses of various forms of sovereign guarantees that were utilised in power projects insured by NEXI. It then investigates the implementation agreements of five power projects (the case studies) and tests the degree of protection against political risk by examining the comprehensiveness of four contractual clauses that are considered to be the most relevant in mitigating political risk: international arbitration, waiver of sovereign immunity, stabilisation and *force majeure* clauses. The comprehensiveness of each clause is dependent on specific criteria related to the mechanism of risk-allocation between the host government and the foreign investor. When this allocation is favourable to the investor side (provision of specific guarantees against political risk), then the exposure of the project is considered to be low and therefore, the possibility of political risk occurrence is held to be low too. The qualitative methodology consists of an examination of the content and the wording of each clause.

In particular, for the arbitration clause, this study pays attention to several criteria, such as: the recognition of an international tribunal (institutional or *ad hoc*) that sits outside the host country, the existence of a governing law other than domestic law, and the choice of international arbitration procedures such as UNCITRAL. In the case of the waiver of sovereign immunity clause, it is important whether the clause incorporates three types of immunity-waivers: a) from suits in other jurisdictions, b) from recognition of the awards, c) from enforcement procedures (*attachment of assets*). The inclusion of the last type can significantly decrease the exposure of the power project to political risk of the government's non-compliance with an award or decision. Finally, some variation in the wording of the waiver clauses is also crucial for the effective allocation of political risk. For example, the inclusion of the two words "irrevocably" and "unconditionally" in the waiver clause plays a determining role. In the case of the stabilisation clause, the effectiveness of political risk mitigation varies according to the degree of stabilisation. Some of the most important variations of stabilisation degree are: a) "freezing", b) "consistency", c) "balancing", and d) "allocates the burden" forms. A combination of the above forms can occur according to the specific wording in each clause. As for the last clause, *force majeure*, the analysis is focused on the design of the allocation of risk related to *force majeure* events between the investors and the host government. This study treats as best *transfer-design*, when the private party is excused from its obligations due to a *force majeure* event occurrence but the state party is still liable for its payment obligation. The contracts that contain such designs are conceived as the best in terms of their effectiveness towards political risk mitigation. However, there is a variation of transfer-design that depends on the events covered as well as on other requirements towards the parties of the contract. For these reasons, specific wording-analysis is conducted.

2.4.2. Scoring evaluation (numerical and non-numerical assessment)

The assessment of the effectiveness of the multi-tier legal framework in terms of political risk management is a central issue for this study. Apart from the qualitative analysis, there are also some scoring tools used mainly in Part I (dealing with public international law).

This study assesses the treaty-based international standards of treatment in five EPAs and one BIT using information obtained from the legal documents of the relevant treaties. The methodology used for the analysis is described in detail in Part I for each standard of treatment along with the discussion of the findings. However, this section aims to provide an overall picture of this assessment-study's characteristics.

In particular, an extensive index and score-card of the five ASEAN countries' performances is created for the Part I assessment, based on concrete legal elements related to political-risk mitigation.[156] This study uses the chapters on "trade in services" and on "investment" of each EPA and abstracts those provisions that are relevant to protection of Japanese investments in the respective host states (*content analysis*). The Japan-Vietnam EPA has only a "trade in services" chapter because a Japan-Vietnam BIT was previously concluded including all the relevant investment protection clauses.

All elements are used as proxies for creating a positive or negative (according to their variation) environment for foreign investment protection against political risk. When a host country promises favourable treatment (fewer restrictions) to foreign investments through its bilateral EPA, this is conceived of as a "symptom" of the low possibility of political risk occurrence, thus higher level of protection and greater degree of effectiveness.

With regards to the assessment exercise, a scoring-method is used in order to measure the degree of "reservations" or "restrictions" found after the qualitative analysis of the clauses referred to above in the qualitative approach section. It is acknowledged by this study that this way of conducting a scoring experiment does not reveal the actual degree of political risk occurring in each country. It is only a method of facilitating the quantitative observation of restrictions and reservations that are referred to in the body-text of each respective EPAS. The maximum score for each element is a unit -1- which indicates the highest level of protection against potential political risk (the best treatment) that foreign investment may receive. The minimum score for each element is zero -0- which indicates the lowest level of protection against potential political risk (the worst treatment or no provision) that foreign investment may receive according to bilateral investment agreements. However, this study does not keep only a binary approach to scoring-methodology but it furthermore introduces several other scoring variations (0.50, 0.75, 0.80, 0.90) in order to measure the diversification in the wording existent in each clause and the differences from treaty to treaty.

In the case of the expropriation standard, in contrast with previous studies, this study measures more types of variations than the mere inclusion of legitimate expropriation (public purpose, non-discrimination, due process of law, compensation). It evaluates several criteria of indirect expropriation such as exceptions related to taxation measures or restrictions over the submission of investors' claims before international fora. In the case of the compensation standard, this assessment exercise differs from previous ones in measuring the provision of important elements such as the requirements of prompt, adequate

---

[156] For details see the present book's appendix, "Scoring-Card of Japan's EPAs".

and effective compensation (Hull formula), as well as whether the compensation is freely transferable and convertible or whether there are restrictions on that.

Similarly, in the case of the general standards of treatment, the present research does not only score the provision of a clause referring to NT or MFN treatment; it also evaluates the various reservations or exceptions that are usually included in the annexes of the respective treaties with regards to Japanese investments in the power sector of the host countries. Most of the variations are found in the trade in services chapters related to commercial presence. When a treaty contains general reservations which apply to all sectors and not specifically to power investments (e.g. different treatment of subsidisation policy between local and foreign companies) the score given is higher compared to reservations that introduce concrete exceptions related to the power sector (e.g. different treatment in the provision of electricity services between domestic and foreign operators). In the case of FET and FPS standards of treatment, the criteria of assessment are related to the wording of the clauses. When the wording of a respective treaty recognises FET/FPS standards as the *minimum standards of treatment*, then this study treats such wording with a lower score compared to the clauses that do not contain such wording. This study asserts that there is a crucial difference in the effectiveness of the above clauses analysing the scope of its standard depending on the wording.

Finally, with regards to specific standards of treatment, there are also important variations that affect the degree of political risk occurrence. Provisions of FTFs are included in both chapters of trade in services and investment. The FTFs standard appears with the greatest number of variation and receives various scores accordingly. One of the reasons for these variations is the different provisions for the case of balance of trade payments. There are different criteria in the restrictions to FTFs that are permitted by each treaty such as omission of the non-discriminatory requirement to provide treatment to FSFs that is "no less favourable than that accorded to the transfer originating from investments made by investors of any third State" or to domestic investments. A similar assessment exercise is conducted for the standard of protection from strife. If there is no provision of NT and MFN in the wording of each clause then a lower score is given. Low scoring is also given when there are restrictions to the non-freely convertible or non-transferability of the compensation payments required under the protection from strife clause. In the case of the umbrella clause, its absence from some treaties is more evident than with other standards. When an umbrella clause is not provided by a treaty, then the minimum score -o- is given. However, there are also cases according to which there is a provision of an umbrella clause but with limitations. Such a limitation is observed in the following type of wording: The promised treatment shall be kept by the host state but "in accordance with its (host state) laws and regulations"; this case is treated with a score lower than a unit because the inclusion of such a wording creates uncertainty in investors about the sustainability of the host state's assurances. Finally, the final indicator is the applicability of an impartial dispute resolution comparable to an international adjudication and the inclusion of a subrogation clause. This study adopts several criteria that are important elements for the effectiveness of the dispute resolution forum. It gives the lowest score when the respective treaty does not include a state-investor arbitration process. In addition, a low score is given when there is a requirement to exhaust local remedies before activating the international arbitration procedure. There are also several exceptions in the wording of the dispute resolution clauses such as the exclusion of NT disputes from international arbitration or the requirement for prior consultation before the claim is made in an international arbitration process. Such exceptions are treated with different scores.

In the case of the assessment exercise related to the specific guarantees that are provided by the investor-state contracts (Part II), this study undertakes a non-numerical assessment method. It evaluates the provisions found under the four clauses (arbitration, waiver of sovereign immunity, stabilisation, and *force majeure*) according to the criteria determined in the qualitative analysis mentioned above. Then, it creates a five-scale evaluation index similar to those used by multilateral development banks for the evaluation of their appraisal reposts. However, the purpose of this study is to assess the comprehensiveness of the above clauses that are related only to political risk mitigation and not to the overall quality of a project or contract. In particular, it evaluates as "best" those clauses whose *almost all* of their critical elements contain positive (+) provisions. "Good" are those clauses whose *most* elements are positive (+), "satisfactory" are those clauses whose *many* elements are positive (+), "unsatisfactory" are those whose *many* elements are negative (-), and "poor" are those whose *most* elements are negative (-). The assessment-technique is that the more positive (+) elements found, the lower possibility of political risk occurs and the higher degree of contract-effectiveness is achieved.

Table 5   Non-Numerical Assessment of Contractual Guarantees[157]

Evaluation method	Critical elements	Positive (+)	Negative(-)
Best	Almost all	+++++	
Good	Most	+++	
Satisfactory	Many	++	
Unsatisfactory	Many		- -
Poor	Most		- - - -

The main reason for adopting such a non-numerical evaluation is that it is difficult to measure the degree of restrictions or the *strictness* of various wordings that are included in each clause. For example, in the case of the arbitration clause, it is not feasible for a scoring exercise to assess whether the existence of a governing law other than the domestic law should be considered as a better treatment for investments receiving better score than the provision of international arbitration procedures or the reverse. Or in the case of the stabilisa-

---

[157] Table compiled by the author.

tion clause, there is no specific rule regarding whether to treat the "consistency" form as a better or worse treatment than the "balancing" form. Therefore, it is a more reliable technique to conduct the assessment exercise based on a non-numerical method by giving an aggregate result for the evaluation according to the quantity of positive (+) or negative (-) elements that are found in each contractual clause.

In conclusion, the assessment methodology of this volume differs substantially from other studies. Previous assessment research has been monopolised by empirical studies of the international economics discipline that assess the impact of certain provisions to trade and investment liberalisation, focusing on numerical ranking without any qualitative interpretation of the law. On the contrary, the present research is an empirical study of international law, assessing the effectiveness of provisions with a focus on protection against political risk, and not on the impact on promotion or liberalisation of FDI. Moreover, this book provides qualitative criteria of different wordings and other variations existent in each clause. Accordingly, the typology used in the scoring evaluation builds upon a multi-level scoring system based on a detailed matrix of investment provisions which allows for a more accurate assessment of each provision. On the contrary, previous studies have taken a binary approach to elements that are related to investment protection. Finally, even if there are many studies in international law that have focused on the analysis of treaty-based provisions related to the protection of foreign investment, an attempt to evaluate these provisions quantitatively has been neglected. This study's methodology is unique in attempting to do that by combining legal analysis and scoring assessment techniques.

PART I
THE INTERNATIONAL LAW STANDARDS OF
TREATMENT AND THE JAPANESE EPAs

3

THE RISK OF EXPROPRIATION AND
THE COMPENSATION STANDARD[158]

3.1.   Introduction

It is well stated by both theory and jurisprudential practice that expropriation
and the risk of non-compensation for the damages suffered by foreign investors
is one of the most traditional and broadly occurring political risks. It appears in
traditional forms such as the direct expropriation or confiscation of the investor's
real and personal property by the host government, or the nationalization of
certain industries (e.g. power plants or energy distribution networks), but also in
more complicated and indirect ways such as the imposition of obligations and
taxes by the host government to such an extent that the investment becomes
practically infeasible, or the recall of a license by the host country's agency that is
important for the business operation of the investment (e.g. license for the
production or sale of electricity), which have been characterized as either
creeping or *regulatory* expropriation.

The danger of expropriation or nationalization constitutes one of the greatest
political risks that threatens foreign investments after their establishment in the
territory of the host country. According to Paul Comeaux and Stephan Kinsella,
political risk is defined as "the risk faced by an investor that a host country will
confiscate all or portion of the investor's property rights located in the host
country"[159] and expropriation as "the taking by a host state of property owned by
an investor and located in the host state, ostensibly for a public purpose".[160] It is
obvious that according to these definitions, political risk and expropriation mean
almost the same thing. Both definitions refer to a classic situation according to
which political risk and expropriation exist when the host state instead of
protecting the investment or the economic rights of foreign investors, it seize
them. However, under the influence of the recent international jurisprudence
and the latest academic theories, on the one hand, the notion of political risk has
expanded into a new concept that does not solely mean an illegal governmental
taking of property. In addition to the expropriation risk, international law
recognizes a diverse number of factors that can also provoke the materialization
of political risk. On the other hand, it is also evident that the expropriation
concept has evolved into a more complicated element than the classic definition

---

[158] This chapter is partially based on a previous study conducted by the author: T.N. Papanastasiou, 'Protecting Foreign Investments against Expropriation: A Comparative Study of Japan's
EPAs', *International Journal of Public Law and Policy* 1:2, (2011) pp. 171-201.

[159] Comeaux and Kinsella, *Protecting Foreign Investment*, p. 1.

[160] *Ibid.*, p. 3.

of a property-seizure, requiring the development by the legal theory and the application by international tribunals of various doctrines.

Finally, with regards to compensation for expropriation, it is obvious that for investors who have been damaged by a host state's expropriation, after proving the host state's liability for an expropriation, their highest priority and interest would be to examine how to obtain compensation for their grievances. In particular, securing an appropriate level of compensation is the best tool of political risk mitigation that foreign investors can ever obtain. Any kind of remedies but especially monetary compensation is the ultimate level of invest-ment protection against any kind of investment treaty's breach but especially against the risk of expropriation.

3.2. The expropriation risk

3.2.1. Expropriation or nationalization clause

As an initial matter, to understand political risk and expropriation, it is im-portant to clarify the meaning of *property* and *property rights*. According to common law, property consists of *tangibles* and *intangibles* such as rights under contracts. The terminology used by civil law is different referring to property as *things* divided into *immovables* and movables. However, whatever is followed in each instance of terminology for property, both common law and civil law accept that property rights are related to *ownership* comprising three specific elements: the exclusive rights to use, to enjoy and to dispose of property within the limits of the law. Explaining the above three functions of ownership, for example in the case of a power-plant investment, property rights consist of: ownership of the land, the power-plant on the land including the inventory and all equipment (movables or not), the right to operate the plant, the right to produce electricity and sell it to the wholesale or retail market (depending on the license taken by the host state), the right to receive usable currency and to export the currency and so on. All these elements that are referred to as the ownership right deter-mine the essence of the property rights that need to be protected by the host state.

Another issue that needs clarification is the term nationalization that is often used interchangeably with expropriation. Even if nationalization is often treated as expropriation, it is a different notion. In the past, the most used term was nationalization. It appeared after the de-colonialisation period when poor and underdeveloped states gained their independence and tried to take the control of important natural resources that were under foreign ownership.

The main difference is that nationalization is a general and impersonal form of expropriation which governments use in order to implement social and economic reforms in a particular sector of the economy. Expropriation is a more personal action which states take in order to possess individual foreign investors' assets and rights. Nationalization usually happens in natural resource industries such as the energy sector (oil, gas, minerals exploitation plants). Electricity sector is also likely to be nationalized especially when host states manifest the im-portance of electricity for the economic development and nation's wealth. Finally, in addition to expropriation and nationalization, there is another similar term that is also broadly used: confiscation. The main difference between expropria-tion, nationalization and confiscation is that the latter is used to "refer to seizure of property by a state without compensation, usually to punish the owner for who he is or for what he has done".[161] However, even if the above three notions have some differences, in reality, distinguishing the various measures taken by a host government does not have any practical importance. In contrast, the most important element is the consequences of each measure. In international investment law the terms *expropriation* and *nationalization* are used to date without discretion as they both indicate the same phenomenon in two manners: first, the deprivation of the property or the investment rights of the foreign investor because of the host state's taking for its own benefit (direct expropriation), and second, the partial or full denial of the foreign investor's right to use or dispose its investment (indirect expropriation).

Expropriation or nationalization are the legal terms that are likely to apply in most cases and, as will be analysed below, the crucial element is whether or not the action of expropriation is legal. Moreover, expropriation or nationalization is not a thing of the past. There are a growing number of recent re-nationalizations in the area of infrastructure that has brought the expropriation article back into the limelight. Most of these cases appear in Latin America countries but also in Eastern Europe and Russia Federation. The most recent cases exist in Venezuela where President Hugo Chavez has advanced a series of foreign industries' nationalizations in multiple sectors starting from the oil and minerals extracting industry and continuing to various manufacturing sectors.[162]

In general, states provide guarantees through their domestic law (Constitution or special laws such as Foreign Investment Law) about the protection of private property. However, it is acknowledged by international law that host states obtain the sovereign right to expropriate or confiscate private property inside its territory, "subject to exceptions".[163] Thus, there are some general principles and requirements in respect to the rule of law and the protection of property right that prevent states' from expropriating private property. Apart from the guarantees of domestic law for the protection of private property, general international law and international investment treaties determine the protection of aliens' property and rights. Therefore, two of the most important issues for international tribunals and jurists are to define what constitutes an expropriation and to determine when expropriation is legal or not.

3.2.2. Direct expropriation

When a host state takes measures to seize the property or the property rights of foreign investments, usually involving a transfer of ownership rights to the state or to a third person, these measures constitute what is known as direct expropriation. Direct expropriation in a sense of an outright taking of private property by the state has been a major public international law issue throughout

---

[161] *Ibid.*, p. 7.

[162] A recent example is the nationalisation of FertiNitro, a US-Italian JV company producing fertilisers which President Chavez accused of price speculation damaging the agricultural sector in Venezuela. See: http://www.npk-world.com/site/flash/flashDetail.asp?flash_id=752053 (retrieved on 10/12/2010).

[163] Sornarajah, *International Law*, p. 239.

the 20th century.[164] In recent times, the most well-known cases of direct expropriation consist of the 1979 Iranian nationalization of banks and insurance companies that were brought before the Iran-US Claims Tribunal.[165] Since then, cases of direct expropriation seemed to be gradually disappearing until a new wave of nationalizations in Latin America and East Europe. In general, there are two categories of direct expropriation: the *de iure* and the *de facto* expropriation.

3.2.2.1. De iure expropriation

When the taking of the private property and the transfer of the ownership rights from the foreign investor to the host state is implemented through domestic laws or administrative decrees, then the expropriation is called *de iure* or expropriation by law. This is the most usual type of foreign investors' property-taking by host states. The taking results to either foreign investor losing the ownership of an immovable thing such as land, real estate or a factory, acquired with capital imported to the host state for the purpose of an investment or losing the stocks of an enterprise that was the investment vehicle inside the host country's territory. When the ownership of the above property or property rights are transferred to the host country's government or agencies through a measure imposed by domestic laws, then the expropriation is considered as blatant or property taking.

3.2.2.2. De facto expropriation

This type of expropriation consists of actions that result in the absolute and permanent taking of foreign investors' property without any due legal process. It exists when host governments declare hostile actions of expropriation without maintaining any official formality and proceed to the taking by using force, e.g. using the army to take over the control of an energy plant or factory and expelling the foreign owners without recognizing their ownership rights over the seized property. According to international investment law, de facto expropriation is an arbitrary action of the host government and, therefore, it is always considered to be illegal. Moreover, de facto expropriation is also contrary to human rights-law, especially the economic dimension of human rights. Projects that are joint ventures between state companies and foreign investors or partly owned and controlled by states, such as oil projects, mining projects and power projects, are characterized as high profile expropriation risk projects.[166] The de facto expropriation may be perceived as a case of indirect expropriation too.[167] However, this study categorizes de facto expropriation under direct expropriation.

---

[164] A. Reinisch, 'Expropriation', in P.T. Muchlinski, F. Ortino and C.H. Schreuer (eds.), *The Oxford Handbook of International Investment Law* (Oxford University Press, Oxford, 2008) p. 407.

[165] *Ibid.*

[166] Comeaux and Kinsella, *Protecting Foreign Investment*, p. 6.

[167] C. Yannaca-Small, '"Indirect Expropriation" and the "Right to Regulate" in International Investment Law', OECD Working Paper on International Investment no. 2004/4, (OECD Financial and Enterprise Affairs Directorate, Paris, 2004) p. 4.

3.2.3. Indirect or creeping expropriation

3.2.3.1. In general

To date the majority of disputes before the international investment tribunals are related to the issue of foreign investment regulation and to what is called indirect expropriation. Indirect expropriation is also known as creeping expropriation and as measures tantamount or equivalent to expropriation. There are different expressions used by the investment treaties in the relevant clauses. For example, the Japan-Philippines EPA article 95.1 states that:

> "Neither Party shall expropriate or nationalize investments in its Area of investors of the other Party or take any measure *equivalent to*[168] expropriation or nationalization (hereinafter referred to in this Chapter as 'expropriation')."[169]

Another expression similar to the above is used in the Japan-Indonesia EPA. Article 65.1 of the respective Treaty states the following:

> "Neither Party shall expropriate or nationalize investments in its Area of investors of the other Party or take any measure *tantamount to*[170] expropriation or nationalization (hereinafter referred to in this Chapter as 'expropriation')."[171]

Indirect expropriation consists of a host state's measures that do not result in the direct taking of investor's property but which gradually or abruptly deprive the investor of the use and benefit of its assets. In other words, indirect expropriation is a more complicate process than the direct taking, because it is hidden and its results cannot be immediately felt. Most importantly, the majority of the indirect expropriation cases do not affect the nominal ownership of the investor but deprive investors of the effective ownership of their property rights. Other than that, international investment law treats creeping expropriation in a similar way as it does with direct cases of expropriation.

Some of the most common cases of indirect expropriation and potential threats of political risk are the increases in taxes, harsh regulations that affect the operation of the investment, and restriction or denial of exports. The most important case of indirect expropriation exists when host states revoke the license or the permit necessary for operation or establishment of a foreign investment and prevent investors from continuing their business activities. It is obvious that in infrastructure investments, a license or governmental permit is always required along with concession or other public contracts signed between the private investor and the host state. Any revocation of license or change in the rights given to foreign investors by public contracts could constitute indirect expropriation. In all of the above cases, the expropriation act is not about the taking of property or the transfer of ownership from the foreign investors to the

---

[168] Italics added by the author for emphasis.

[169] Japan-Philippines EPA, article 95.1.

[170] Emphasis added by author.

[171] Japan-Indonesia EPA, article 65.1.

host state, actions that occur in the case of direct expropriation. In indirect expropriation, the foreign investor retains the ownership but without the substantial rights to use and dispose its investments.

Moreover, because of the host state's unreasonable interference with the investor's use or control of its property rights, foreign investments are substantially damaged or cannot make any profits. In this case, there is no need to clarify concretely the asset that has been expropriated. The subject matter of indirect expropriation can be generally any asset or property right, including the foreign investment as a whole. However, there may be some implications in calculating the compensation ought to the foreign investor. The issue of compensation becomes more complicated when the indirect expropriation consists of measures taken by the host government in order to regulate several business operations.

3.2.3.2. Regulatory expropriation

The most sophisticated type of indirect expropriation is the so called regulatory expropriation or regulatory taking. The problem of indirect expropriation arises, when general or specific government actions that are applicable to regulatory measures, affect the value of property. The issue of regulatory taking needs to be determined according to whether a measure is attributable to the sovereign right of the states to legislate or to the foreign investors' right to protect their property. To balance between these two rights, it is an important and difficult process that international tribunals need to undertake. On the one hand, it is a generally established principle that host state's interference with property through regulatory measures is part of states' sovereignty right. On the other hand, in case there is a deprivation of foreign investment's value because of a governmental regulatory interference, the affected foreign investors require compensation for their damage. The problem, that international tribunals need to address, is whether the political risk of indirect expropriation is materialized or not, and to determine if the host state owes to the affected foreign investor compensation.

A number of international tribunals' decisions attempt to articulate a comprehensive framework of what constitutes indirect expropriation. According to international jurisprudence, a regulatory measure may constitute an indirect expropriation even if the state's interference with the private property does not benefit the host state. For example, in the International Centre for the Settlement of Investment Disputes (ICSID) case *Metalclad Corporation v. Mexico*, it is stated that:

> "[E]xpropriation includes not only open, deliberate and acknowledged takings of property, such as outright seizure or formal or obligatory transfer of title in favour of the host State, but also covert or incidental interference with the use of property which has the effect of depriving the owner, in whole or in significant part, of the use or reasonably-to-be-expected economic benefit of property even if not necessarily to the obvious benefit of the host State".[172]

---

[172] ICSID Case No.ARB (AF)/97/1, Award of 30 August 2000, para. 103.

3.2.4. Determining legality and manifestation of the indirect expropriation

3.2.4.1. In general

In this section, it is necessary to clarify the context of two important issues that influence the protection of foreign investments against expropriation. The first is related to the difference between legal and illegal expropriation and its importance. The second consists of the distinction between regulatory takings that are permissible and those that become expropriatory (indirect expropriation) requiring compensation to the affected investor. On many an occasions, the above cases create some confusion about the level of protection provided by international law to foreign investments in regards to compensation and materialization of the expropriation risk.

3.2.4.2. Criteria of the expropriation's legality

In the case of direct expropriation (except for de facto expropriation)[173] or indirect expropriation, the customary international law does not rule out takings of foreign investments provided certain conditions are met. In order for a taking to be "lawful",[174] there are four criteria that are required. In the World Bank's Guidelines on the Treatment of Foreign Direct Investment, it is stated that an expropriation shall be for a public purpose, in accordance with applicable legal process (due-process), without a discriminatory manner on the basis of nationality and with compensation.[175] The above four criteria determine whether an expropriation is legal or not. All of the reviewed by this study, Japanese investment agreements contain these four criteria. For example, the Japan-Thailand EPA, article 102.1 affirms that:

> "Neither Party shall expropriate or nationalize investments in its Area of investors of the other Party ... except: (a) for a public purpose; (b) on a non-discriminatory basis; (c) in accordance with due process of law; and (d) upon payment of prompt, adequate and effective compensation".[176]

An expropriation cannot be viewed as legal unless these four criteria prevail altogether.

However, the Japan-Indonesia EPA contains one additional element that the other EPAs do not affirm. Article 65.1(c) of the respective Japan-Indonesia EPA requires that lawful expropriation shall be in accordance with not only "due process of law" but also with "Article 61" of the Agreement. According to this article, the host state shall accord to foreign investments *general treatment* sustaining FET and FPS. It could be argued that this additional requirement

---

[173] *De facto* expropriation is, as analyzed above, by definition (*eo ipso*) illegal.

[174] Sornarajah, *International Law*, p. 395.

[175] I. Shihata, *Legal Treatment of Foreign Investment: The World Bank Guidelines* (World Bank, Washington, DC, 1993). See also: C. Yannaca-Small, 'Indirect Expropriation', p. 3. And Sornarajah adds one more characteristic of "illegal" expropriation, when the taking is done in violation of a treaty; Sornarajah, *International Law*, p. 395.

[176] Japan-Thailand EPA, article 102.1.

added in para. (c) of article 65.1 is a clarification of what due process of law means. This study in fact asserts that it is something more than a mere clarification: it is an expansion of the "due process" notion imposed by the Japan-Indonesia EPA. It requires the host state to be compatible not only with the classic concept of "due-process of law" but also with the much broader meaning of FET and FPS, as modern jurisprudence has construed.

According to the above widely accepted international law principles, a state is allowed to expropriate a foreign investment only if the purpose of its action satisfies the public interest. The requirement of public purpose receives more practical use in terms of the regulatory expropriation when host state's measures refer to public utility purpose but, in reality, they hide political or ideological reasons.[177] The host government shall justify the motive of the taken measures according to the principles of good faith, proportionality and fair treatment. Moreover, all measures applied need to adopt the established legal procedures according to the domestic law (due process) which at least shall not violate the minimum international standards.[178]

Similarly, when a taking or a measure is discriminatory, targeting only the nationals or the foreign investments of one country, the expropriation is considered as illegal. "The principle against racial discrimination is an *ius cogens* principle of international law".[179] Host states usually justify their expropriatory actions by referring to the public purpose of their measures. However, the public purpose alone cannot justify the expropriation, if the proposed measure is addressed against the investors of one only country and does not include domestic investors or nationals of third countries. In this case, even if the public-purpose nature of the proposed measure is justified, thus the taking is discriminatory, the measure should be considered as illegal expropriation.

Finally, according to international law, it is required that an appropriate compensation shall be given to the damaged foreign investor by the host state in order an expropriation to be lawful. The requirement for compensation is considered as the most important issue for foreign investors who would like to secure their economic interests in case of damage or property taking. Moreover, examining the compensation standard from the political risk aspect and in connection with the international treaty-law, compensation is considered by investors as the most genuine and tangible tool of risk mitigation.

However, it is not clear whether the compensation works as a condition for the legality of an expropriation or as just the consequence of the expropriation. In practice, it is observed that arbitral tribunals consider compensation more as the result of a taking and less as a requirement of the legality.[180] It seems that

---

[177] Sornarajah, *International Law*, p. 397.

[178] For example, domestic legal procedures shall provide fair treatment to foreign investments. See: P. Glavinis, *Diethnes Oikonomiko Dikaio: Genikes Arhes, Diethnes Emporio, Xenes Ependiseis* [*International Economic Law: General Principles, International Trade, Foreign Investments*] (Sakkoulas Publications, Athens, 2009) p. 642.

[179] Sornarajah, *International Law*, p. 398.

[180] Glavinis, *International Economic Law*, p. 647. See also the case *Former King of Greece and others v. Greece* of the European Court of Human Rights–Award of 23.11.2000, para. 90. The

whether an expropriation is characterized as lawful or illegal, this characterization does not affect the obligation of the host state to compensate. In summary, if a host state's expropriatory measure complies fully with the requirements of public purpose, non-discrimination and due process, it will not be declared as illegal, provided that as a result of this measure, adequate compensation will be given to the damaged foreign investment.

The tendency of approaching the compensation element more as a result and less as a requirement, for the legality of an expropriation, is not of an insignificant value. The study asserts that it can affect the full scope of the foreign investment protection. On the one hand, in terms of protection against political risk, the recognition of the legality of an expropriation may play a decisive role. As is analysed in Part II, according to some investment contracts and ECAs insurance policies, it is likely that the deprivation of the insured foreign investor, whose damage is caused by a lawful (according to the domestic law) expropriation, may not be adequately covered by them.[181] In addition, it is argued that even when the right to compensation is recognized by the international tribunals, their calculation method of compensation between a lawful and an unlawful expropriation might differ. In the case of a lawful expropriation, it is argued that compensation might not cover the full scope of the investor's claim. For example, compensation shall not cover the loss of future profits claim which could be fully accepted in the case of illegal expropriations.[182] On the contrary, other jurists argue that there should be no distinction between lawful and unlawful takings in regards to compensation payable for a governmental expropriatory act.[183] Regardless of the different views in academia, it is argued here that investment tribunals have not really followed the academic dialogue making no distinctions in the compensation payable for a lawful or unlawful expropriation.[184]

On the other hand, the majority of the expropriation disputes brought before the international tribunals are based on claims related only to the compensation element. This could be explained because of two main reasons: First, the

---

Court stated that "the lack of compensation does not make the taking of the applicant's property eo ipso wrongful".

[181] It is difficult for ECAs to accept a claim for additional or partly compensation. Furthermore, Cameron asserts that: "Even the presence of a stabilization clause in the energy investment contract will not be sufficient to prevent a lawful expropriation by the host state (although it will almost certainly increase the claimant's chances of obtaining a higher level of compensation)"; P.D. Cameron, *International Energy Investment Law: The Pursuit of Stability* (Oxford University Press, Oxford, 2010) p. 220.

[182] D.W. Bowett, 'State Contracts with Aliens: Contemporary Developments on Compensation for Termination or Breach', *British Year Book of International Law* 59:1 (1988) p. 63. And see Brownlie, who asserts that there should be a distinction between lawful and unlawful expropriation: I. Brownlie, *Principles of Public International Law* 6th edn. (Oxford University Press, Oxford, 2003) pp. 509-514; Brownlie also refers to the EHCR Judgment of 21 February 1986, EHCR no 98, para. 54: "Article 1 does not, however, guarantee a right to full compensation in all circumstances. Legitimate objectives of "public interest", such as pursued in measures of economic reform on measures designed to achieve greater social justice, may call for less than reimbursement of the full market value", *ibid.*, p. 538.

[183] J. Crawford, *The International Law Commission's Articles on State Responsibility: Introduction, Text and Commentaries* (Cambridge University Press, Cambridge, 2002) p. 226.

[184] C. QC. McLachlan, L. Shore and M. Weiniger, *International Investment Arbitration: Substantive Principles* (Oxford University Press, New York, 2008) p. 332.

international arbitration tribunals are likely neither to doubt the host state's arguments based on the public purpose and due process of their applied measures nor to make it easy to bring cases of investors of third countries that have not been treated equally by the host state. The essence of public interest or rule of law is located in the core of the states' sovereignty which arbitration tribunals find difficult to challenge. In addition, an international tribunal would avoid addressing an argument on the basis of racial discrimination between the claimant (foreign investor) and a third country's investor who has not been included in the host state's measure. Second, in most of the expropriation cases, host states argue that compensation is not required because they do not construe the nature of the measure as an expropriation. Therefore, other than examining the legality-criteria of the expropriation and the requirement for compensation, prior to that, it is more important to realize whether there has been an expropriation, and to clarify the conditions specifying governmental measures as a taking or just as a non-compensable regulation.

3.3. The international law standard for compensation

3.3.1. General

The international law standard for compensation has been, practically, the most compelling issue from the foreign investor's point of view. Investors whose property and economic rights have been damaged have a key interest in first looking into how to prove that the host state is liable for an expropriation and ultimately into how to obtain compensation for their grievances. With regards to the international law framework of investment protection against political risk, it can be argued that remedies in general and compensation in particular have the closest relation to what, in political risk insurance, are called instruments of risk mitigation, such as the various types of guarantees offered. In the case of the risk of expropriation that foreign investors need to assume and mitigate, the standard of compensation has a dual function. It not only guarantees investors reimbursement in case of damages suffered but also works as a disincentive for the state. The disincentive originates, on the one hand, in the threat of a sanction imposed for the alleged action (breach of an international treaty's rule) and, on the other hand, in the removal of the enrichment motive by the state (returning the illegal profit through the compensation mechanism unjust enrichment).[185]

3.3.2. Compensation as reparation

Compensation for an expropriation is not the only remedy that is available for the investor's protection. Following the debate in customary international law, a state found liable to an international wrong is obliged to make reparation by way of restitution and if this is not possible, to pay monetary compensation for the alleged damage. In particular, the seminal decision of the Permanent Court of International Justice (PCIJ) in its 1928 judgement in the Chorzow Factory Case made a crucial separation between the notion of compensation and that of

---

[185] T.W. Walde and B. Sabahi, 'Compensation, Damages, and Valuation', in P.T. Muchlinski, F. Ortino and C.H. Schreuer (eds.), *The Oxford Handbook of International Investment Law* (Oxford University Press, Oxford, 2008) p. 1053.

restitution in kind (restitution *in integrum*).[186] The Court argued about the priority of restitution, regarding it as a first rank remedy by stating that "[r]estitution in kind, or, if this is not possible, payment of a sum corresponding to the value which restitution in kind would bear".[187]

Since the Chorzow Factory judgement, international jurisprudence has nearly never applied the restitution remedy. Among the very few exceptions, the Texaco/Calasiatic case is the most important case in which a tribunal indemnified the foreign investor by ordering the host state to undo the nationalisation of the oil industry and restore the status quo ante.[188] The decision of the Tribunal to order a specific performance (restitution) towards a sovereign state received criticism from the majority of legal scholars from Third World countries, politicising the issue of reparation.[189]

Since then, the majority of investment arbitration tribunals have considered restitution to be an impractical remedy mainly because states are unwilling to undo actions that were based on political decisions or constitutional constraints and because after expropriation occurs, in most of the cases it is impossible to return to the pre-expropriation situation.[190] In addition, the most important reason against the use of restitution as a remedy is the element of interference with the state's sovereignty. Governments shall obtain a degree of autonomy and discretion in deciding which measure is appropriate to indemnify investors. Being enforced by an arbitration tribunal to follow a particular course of conduct would be an intrusive action into the state's regulatory authority. On the contrary, choosing monetary compensation as an alternative type of remedy can satisfy the government's sovereign right to regulate and the protection of private property can be better sustained.

Thus, there are scholars who continue to argue about the necessity to reconsider the practicality of restitution. Walde and Sabahi argue that the exclusion of restitution as an alternative remedy "may no longer be appropriate to the new disciplines in investment treaties".[191] They support the necessity of restitution as a remedy by referring to the WTO dispute settlement (it does not use financial compensation), to European Union (EU) practice (ordering EU member states to take measures), to public law and international human rights practice and finally to the difficulty of compelling compensation for breach of other treaty standards such as denial of justice, fair and equitable or national treatment.[192] Even though the discussion on the applicability of both types of reparation (compensation and restitution) may have a significant effect on investment protection, the large majority of investment arbitration tribunals avoid compelling states to restitution.

---

[186] The *Chorzow Factory* Case, *Germany v. Poland* (Merits), PCIJ Collection of Judgments, Series A, no. 17, Award of 13.09.1928, p. 47.

[187] *Ibid.*

[188] *Texaco/Calasiatic v. Libyan Arab Republic*, ILM 17 (1978), p. 3.

[189] About the criticism from scholars see Glavinis, *International Economic Law*, p. 650.

[190] Walde and Sabahi, 'Compensation', pp. 1058-1059.

[191] *Ibid.*, p. 1060.

[192] *Ibid.*, pp. 1060-1062.

As a result, compensation is regarded by this study as the main or only available international law instrument of political risk management.

3.3.3. Characteristics of compensation and its appropriateness

To date, it is not only recognised by the large majority of jurists that monetary compensation is the established type of reparation for breach of the expropriation standard but also it is generally agreed that an investor's claim to payment of compensation (in some amount) following an expropriation is an undisputed right.[193] However, there has always been a debate over the character and the appropriate standard of compensation in different paradigms of expropriation.

According to the Chorzow Factory case, when an illegal expropriation occurs, compensation is considered to be a sanction on a host state's behaviour and it must have similar consequences to restitution.

> "Reparation must, as far as possible, wipe out all the consequences of the illegal act and re-establish the situation which would, in all probability, have existed if that act had not been committed. Restitution in kind, or, if this is not possible, payment of a sum corresponding to the value which restitution in kind would bear; the award, if need be, of damages for loss sustained which would not be covered by restitution in kind or payment in place of it – such are the principles which should serve to determine the amount of compensation due for an act contrary to international law".[194]

Since the Chorzow Factory's influential judgement, scholars have been arguing over the issue of whether awarding compensation is a punitive or compensatory measure. The determination of the character of compensation itself would not have been of any practical meaning if it were not connected to a more crucial issue, the amount of compensation owed by the alleged host state. Moreover, the effort to determine the standard of compensation for expropriation became more complicated after the politicisation of this matter. On the one hand, capital exporting states (in the past developed countries in the West)[195] have always insisted that there is a general international law rule of full compensation for expropriation determined by Hull's formula.[196] And on the other hand, capital importing countries (in the past Communist countries and then-developing countries in general) have maintained the New International Economic Order

---

[193] Brownlie argues that "the right to compensation on whatever basis is recognized in principle". Brownlie, *Principles*, p. 519.

[194] The *Chorzow Factory* Case, *Germany v. Poland* (Merits), PCIJ Collection of Judgments, Series A, no. 17, Award of 13.09.1928, p. 47.

[195] Today it is also non-Western countries that belong to the category of capital-exporting countries such as the East Asian countries, i.e. Japan, Korea, Singapore, China, or countries in transition such as Brazil and Chile in Latin America.

[196] The Hull Formula is referred to Cordell Hull who was Secretary of State during the Mexican expropriations of 1938. See: Sornarajah, *International Law*, p. 38; see also: McLachlan, Shore and Weiniger, *International Investment Arbitration*, p. 316.

(NIEO) position that compensation problem should be exclusively resolved under national law, a principle based on Calvo's doctrine.[197]

Both of the positions denote their principles with the term *appropriate compensation*. The Hull formula of full compensation is expressed in specifications such as "prompt, adequate, and effective", "market" or "genuine value".[198] Compensation is prompt when is paid without delay either at the time of the taking or it has been determined to be paid with interest from the time of the taking. It is adequate when equivalent to the fair market value of the expropriated property, when the expropriation occurred or at the time that was publicly announced. Adequate is the term used to express the principle that investor should be indemnified in whole, in other words for the full value of the damage occurred or property taken. And, effective means that compensation will be paid in a freely convertible and transferable currency. Even if the majority of scholars agree with the argument that the standard of "full compensation" is the appropriate one in case of unlawful expropriation,[199] the proponents of the Hull formula insist on their argument that the "full compensation" standard is a general requirement based on customary international law that should apply to all cases of expropriation, accepting only some "exceptional circumstances" that may justify the provision of less than full compensation.[200]

Thus, it is today observed in both theory and jurisprudence that there is still a divergence of arguments about the standards for compensation that should apply. In particular, there is a logical assumption that different cases of expropriation such as "racially discriminatory" takings or acts with "clear lack of a public purpose" should be treated with a different standard of compensation than lawful expropriations.[201] Even if there is a level of conformity over the issue of "full compensation" standard for unlawful takings, there are issues such as the compensation for nationalisation that are "acknowledged to be one of the most controversial areas of international law" and therefore, as Professor Sornarajah argues, it is not possible to accept that there is a custom of "full compensation" in international law practice.[202]

However, even if there is not yet consensus on the notion of appropriate

---

[197] Carlos Calvo, a distinguished Argentinean diplomat and jurist. See: Sornarajah, *International Law*, p. 38; see also: McLachlan, Shore and Weiniger, *International Investment Arbitration*, p. 316.

[198] Walde and Sabahi, 'Compensation', p. 1068.

[199] Opponents of the principle of the Hull formula argue that in circumstances other than unlawful expropriation (e.g. lawful expropriation), and in cases such as regulatory or creeping expropriation, international law requires the payment of "appropriate" (non-full) compensation. See, for example: Sornarajah, *International Law*; C.F. Amerasinghe, 'Issues of Compensation for the Taking of Alien Property in the Light of Recent Cases and Practice', *International and Comparative Law Quarterly* 41:1 (1992) pp. 22-23; see also: Bowett, 'State Contracts with Aliens', p. 59.

[200] Brownlie, *Principals*, p. 508; Rubins and Kinsella, *International Investment*, pp. 157, 179; Glavinis, *International Economic Law*, p. 653.

[201] Sornarajah, *International Law*, pp. 438-439.

[202] *Ibid.*, pp. 436, 441-442. See also: McLachlan, Shore and Weiniger, *International Investment Arbitration*, pp. 316-319; R. Dolzer, 'New Foundations of the Law of Expropriation of Alien Property', *American Journal of International Law* 75 (1981) p. 553.

compensation, it should be indicated that the current standard of compensation for expropriation "in light of the language" of international investment treaties is inclusive of the principle of full compensation referring either to the Hull formula (adequate, prompt, effective) or using the terms "market/genuine value" and "adequate".[203] With regards to the importance of the compensation standard for political risk management, foreign investors have found bilateral investment treaties to be the appropriate tool to eliminate the uncertainties raised from the controversy over the issue of the compensation's appropriateness.

The majority of BITs and investment chapters of FTAs, making most of the time clear that their aim is not only protection but also promotion of foreign investments between states, specify the Hull formula as the appropriate standard of compensation. Thus, even if it has become common practice for bilateral investment agreements to adopt the full compensation standard, this cannot mean that "BITs could convert that norm into a principle of international law".[204] BITs are instruments of agreement that are used only between the particular signatory states without imposing any binding obligation on other states.[205] A bilateral agreement between states over the full compensation standard cannot be construed as an acceptance of this standard as a general rule of law, but rather it is a tool of capital-importing states to attract investments by offering the highest level of protection against the political risk of expropriation. This method of bilaterally securing foreign investments with the highest standard of compensation treatment has a practical application with regards to political risk. It does not only guarantee foreign investments the full compensation standard but it also separates investments, with only those that are in conformity with the particular treaty's requirements qualifying for protection, leaving aside all those that "do not have approval" by the host state.[206] Therefore, investors need to take into consideration that not all investments are protected with the full compensation standard and that the language of the respective treaty matters.

In addition, foreign investors need to be aware that the calculation of compensation does not follow a uniform practice, but rather it depends on the circumstances of each particular case. For example, there are suggestions that cases of indirect expropriation such as regulatory takings should not always result in the same (full) compensation standard as direct expropriation does.[207] The issue of lost profits can also be a difficult case for tribunals to assess. For example, there have been cases where tribunals have not awarded full compensation for lost profits of expropriated companies in order to avoid awarding a large sum to a wealthy foreign investor against a poor state. This tendency is perceived

---

[203] Walde and Sabahi, 'Compensation', p. 1069.

[204] Sornarajah, *International Law*, pp. 440-441.

[205] The controversy over the compensation standard is one of the reasons that states as yet have not achieved any multilateral investment agreement.

[206] *Ibid.*, p. 245.

[207] It is often the case that in indirect expropriation the investor retains some part of his property compared with formal expropriation, and it is important to take into account the legitimacy of a state's action regarding "intention, good faith, legitimate purposes pursued, proportionality of measure and purpose"; Walde and Sabahi, 'Compensation', p. 1080.

as courts treating the compensation standard as a "punitive rather than compensatory" measure.[208]

Furthermore, there can be a meaningful distinction between a legal and illegal nationalisation. It is argued that only in the case of unlawful nationalisation can present and future profits be included in the compensation standard.[209] The role of specific contractual guarantees provided to an investor also plays an important role. Guarantees of host states (especially those against nationalisation), the existence of a stabilisation clause, or when an investor is invited by the government to implement a specific project (as happens in most power plant investments) could justify the full compensation standard even when a legal nationalisation occurs. It is argued that the above circumstances create a significant degree of "legitimate expectations" for investors, so that arbitration tribunals tend to treat them as exceptional cases requiring full compensation against the government's fraudulent conduct.[210] These implications, as well as the controversial methods that are used for determining the precise amount of compensation (especially whether to measure future profits or intangibles such as goodwill),[211] makes the management of political risk (expropriation) an even more dubious process.

3.4. Indirect expropriation or non-compensable regulation?

3.4.1. In general

The problem becomes complicated when it is difficult to distinguish between regulatory takings that are permissible and those that become expropriatory. It could be a substantial involvement in a state's sovereign right to regulate if, whenever it introduces general regulatory measures for a public purpose, such as environmental, health or taxation measures that affect both domestic and foreign investment, it is obliged to pay compensation to affected foreign investors. Therefore, not all state measures that affect foreign investments are expropriation.[212] As a result, if there is no expropriation, there is no occurrence of political risk either.

To detect a measure of indirect or creeping expropriation is a difficult task. In most of the direct expropriation cases, there is usually an act of nationalisation, confiscation or outright seizure of property by the host state and the damage to the foreign investor interests can be realised clearly and immediately. On the contrary, in the case of indirect expropriation, there is a series of measures that indirectly and over time deprive the foreign investor of property rights or its fundamental economic interests. In indirect or creeping expropriation, it is difficult to determine the nature of the state's measures, the degree of damage to

---

[208] McLachlan, Shore and Weiniger, *International Investment Arbitration*, p. 319.

[209] Sornarajah, *International Law*, p. 482.

[210] *Ibid.*, p. 483.

[211] Tribunals use a variety of different economic methods such as calculating the liquidation value, the replacement value, the book value or assessing the value using the Discounted Cash Flow (DCF) principles. See: McLachlan, Shore and Weiniger, *International Investment Arbitration*, pp. 319-333.

[212] Sornarajah, *International Law*, pp. 85-86.

the investment and, most importantly, it is a complicated process to diagnose the causal relation between governmental interference and investor's deprivation.

The acknowledgement of non-compensable takings has been recognised by several authorities.[213] The most important are the European Convention on Human Rights and the Harvard Draft Convention on International Responsibility of States for Injuries to Aliens. The European Convention in article 1 of Protocol 1 implicitly says that the obligation to compensate does not apply when the state's laws or measures are enforced "in accordance with the general interest or to secure the payment of taxes or other contributions or penalties".[214] The European Court of Human Rights based on the above article has consistently maintained the argument of non-compensable takings.[215] Additionally, the Harvard Draft Convention makes a more explicit and clear statement saying that an uncompensated taking shall not be wrongful if it results from several measures such as "the execution of tax laws; a general change in the value of currency; the maintenance of public order, health or morality; or the normal operation of the laws of the State".[216]

However, except for the limited examples of the authorities mentioned above, the majority of bilateral (BITs) and multilateral investment treaties (MITs) acknowledge indirect expropriation without addressing non-compensable regulation.[217] Thus, it is important to mention that in the most recent FTAs signed by the United States, there are exclusive criteria determining what constitutes indirect expropriation and what the right to regulate.[218] In the case of Japan's recent EPAs concluded with Indonesia, Malaysia, Philippines, Thailand and Vietnam, there is no exclusive reference to non-compensable regulation or to what specific factors or situations constitute an indirect expropriation. However, in two of Japan's investment agreements (Japan-Philippines EPA and Japan-Vietnam BIT), there are some general and security-related exceptions that address indirect expropriation implicitly by invoking cases that constitute the right of the State to regulate.[219] Thus, even if host states are recognised as having the right to regulate under certain conditions with no restriction by the respective investment agreements, it is not clear whether tribunals will permit the non-

---

[213] Cameron, *International Energy Investment Law*, p. 221 n. 145. See also, for a more extensive list of international legal texts: Yannaca-Small, 'Indirect Expropriation', pp. 7-9.

[214] The European Convention on Human Rights, Article 1 of Protocol 1; Entry into force: 1954.

[215] Yannaca-Small, 'Indirect Expropriation', p. 7 n. 16.

[216] The Harvard Draft Convention on International Responsibility of States for Injuries to Aliens, 1961, Article 10.5.

[217] Most of the developed countries' BITs, and important multilateral treaties or legal texts, such as the Energy Charter Treaty, the NAFTA, the 1992 WB Guidelines do not include any reference to non-compensated regulatory measures; See Yannaca-Small, 'Indirect Expropriation', pp. 6-7.

[218] Some examples can be found in the US-FTAs that are concluded with Australia, Chile, Central America, Morocco, and Singapore, as well as in Canada's updated model of Foreign Investment Promotion and Protection Agreement (FIPA). For further information see Yannaca-Small, 'Indirect Expropriation', p. 21.

[219] The right to regulate addresses cases such as the protection of life, health, public order, environment and security interests etc. Article 99 of Japan-Philippines EPA and article 15 of Japan-Vietnam BIT.

compensable character of the taken measures. This issue remains blurred as there is no consistency to the international jurisprudence.

Even if states tend to clarify the conditions of indirect expropriation through their international investment agreements, the difficulty of distinguishing between legitimate state measures and expropriation remains unchanged. Moreover, "the line between the concept of indirect expropriation and governmental regulatory measures not requiring compensation has not been clearly articulated and depends on the specific facts and circumstances of the case".[220] One of the most difficult cases is when a country issues taxation measures that result to a substantial interference with the property of foreign investments. It is difficult to determine when a taxation measure constitutes a non-compensable regulation and when is expropriation. According to the findings of the study, even if all Japanese investment agreements acknowledge that expropriation shall also apply to taxation measures, there are some exemptions that exclude taxation measures from the application of general principles and increase the uncertainty of indirect expropriation. The most important question is when can a measure affect the foreign investment property without having to provide compensation and what criteria should determine that?

The case-by-case investigation of international tribunals about the nature of regulatory measures further blurs the concept of indirect expropriation and the inconsistent approach to define it, thus scholars have identified a number of "tests or doctrines of expropriation" in their analyses of arbitral awards.[221] The most important criteria that arbitral tribunals have applied in determining expropriation are the degree of governmental interference with the investment (the sole effect test), the character of the governmental measures (the purpose test) and the degree of expectation of the investor (the legitimate expectations test).[222]

3.4.2. The degree of governmental interference (the sole effect test)

In order to determine a regulatory measure as an indirect expropriation and therefore compensable, one of the most important criteria, according to several tribunals' awards, is the deprivation of foreign investor's property. More specifically, according to international jurisprudence, the deprivation of property has to be substantial.[223] Substantial deprivation consists of either a property taking or when "the owner[224] is not able to use, enjoy or dispose of the property".[225] If the state's interference with property does not affect the ownership

---

[220] Yannaca-Small, 'Indirect Expropriation', p. 3.

[221] Cameron, *International Energy Investment Law*, p. 222.

[222] Cameron has also introduced the proportionality test; see: *ibid.*, p. 228. However, other scholars either do not analyse it separately or they include it in the three criteria mentioned above. E.g., McLachlan, Shore and Weiniger, *International Investment Arbitration*, p. 301.

[223] ICSID Case *Pope & Talbot Inc. v. Canada*, Interim Award of 26 June 2000, para. 96-105. See also: ICSID Case *LG&E v. Argentine Republic*, Decision on Liability 3 October 2006, para. 190; ICSID Case *Azurix Corp. v. Argentine Republic*, Award of 14 July 2006, para. 322.

[224] In the case of foreign investments, the owner is the foreign investor.

[225] ICSID Case *Pope & Talbot Inc. v. Canada*, Interim Award of 26 June 2000, para. 102.

rights of the investor or it just reduces the profit of the investment,[226] then such an interference cannot be substantial and therefore it is not an expropriation. Even if there is an interference with ownership rights, this effect according to the *Tecmed* Tribunal needs to be lasting with a certain degree of permanence:

> "[I]t is understood that the measures adopted by a State, whether regulatory or not, are an indirect de facto expropriation if they are irreversible and permanent".[227]

However, according to *S.D. Myers v. Canada*, while it is agreed that the effect has to cause "a lasting removal", under some circumstances an indirect expropriation could exist even when the effect is not permanent:

> "Expropriations tend to involve the deprivation of ownership rights; regulations a lesser interference".[228]

And the Tribunal continues, stating:

> "[A]n expropriation usually amounts to a lasting removal of the ability of an owner to make use of its economic rights although it may be that, in some contexts and circumstances, it would be appropriate to view a deprivation as amounting to an expropriation, even if it were partial or temporary".[229]

Thus, even with this exceptional recognition of the temporal effect of the governmental interference as a criterion of indirect expropriation, the *S.D. Myers* Tribunal did not accept the position of the claimant that the Canadian Government's decision to impose restrictions in the export of waste products constituted an indirect expropriation.[230]

Therefore, the right to compensation requires substantial deprivation of the investor's property which depends on the duration and the severity of the economic impact caused by the governmental interference (degree of interference). The degree of interference has been an important factor that has been employed by the majority of international tribunals to judge whether a regulatory measure constitutes an indirect expropriation and whether it is compensable. However, arbitral awards have not been consistent in the application of the "degree of interference test", mainly because of the given conditions of each case and the combination of more than one doctrine or test.

Moreover, it is more controversial whether the economic impact of the degree of interference with the investment should be considered as the only criterion for assessing a government's liability for expropriation. According to the sole effect test or doctrine, it is argued that:

---

[226] ICSID Case *Methanex Corporation v. USA*, Award of 9 August 2005.

[227] ICSID Case *Tecmed SA v. United Mexican States*, Award of 29 May 2003, para. 116.

[228] ICSID Case *S.D. Myers v. Canada*, Partial Award of 13 November 2000, para. 282.

[229] ICSID Case *S.D. Myers v. Canada*, Partial Award of 13 November 2000, para. 283.

[230] Yannaca-Small, 'Indirect Expropriation', p. 14.

"If a regulatory measure or a series of measures has a sufficiently restrictive effect on the owner's rights to use, enjoy the benefits of or dispose of its property, it will constitute expropriation ... the state's intent is therefore irrelevant in a strict application of this test".[231]

In the *Metalclad v. Mexico* case, the Tribunal adopted the sole effect doctrine and found a violation of the North American Free Trade Agreement's (NAFTA) expropriation clause[232]. It concluded that the deprivation of Metalclad's ability to use its property was a sufficient harm to constitute expropriation and it was not necessary to "decide or consider the motivation, nor the intent of the adoption of the Ecological Degree".[233]

However, in contrast to Cameron's argument that "the sole effect doctrine is the dominant one",[234] it is argued that even if other criteria (like the motivation of the state) are less important than the economic impact of the measure, they can contribute to the tribunal's judgement as to whether there has been an expropriation or not.[235] Moreover, according to other scholars,[236] even if the degree of governmental interference is recognised as the one of the main criteria in order to distinguish an indirect expropriation from a regulatory measure, it is argued that it is not exclusive, and it seems that most of the cases in international jurisprudence have been based on a more balanced approach, accepting the combination of multiple factors.

It is also the position of this study that no matter how important the severity of the economic impact caused by governmental interference is, the sole effect test contains within it innate disadvantages which, as a result, might decrease the level of protection against the political risk of indirect expropriation.

First, the sole effect test may limit the capacity of host states to defend themselves against investors' claims for compensation even when the damage is caused by general regulatory measures. If tribunals adopt the *stricto sensu* approach in regards to the sole effect doctrine, then any other factor such as the public purpose and the character of the state's measure or the specific conditions under which the measure was taken (e.g. a state of emergency) will not be applicable. Such an approach would also lead to an unfair situation against domestic investments. Sornarajah states that:

"[T]he foreign investor entered the state voluntarily, knowing the risk of such regulatory laws being applied against him, and that he

---

[231] Cameron, *International Energy Investment Law*, p. 223.

[232] NAFTA article 1110.

[233] ICSID Case *Metalclad Corporation v. United Mexican States*, Award of 30 August 2000.

[234] Cameron, *International Energy Investment Law*, p. 222.

[235] McLachlan, Shore and Weiniger, *International Investment Arbitration*, p. 301.

[236] Sornarajah, *International Law*, p. 375. See also: Yannaca-Small, 'Indirect Expropriation', p. 15.

should bear the risk of such adverse changes as any citizen of the state would".[237]

Therefore, if general regulatory measures that affect similarly domestic and foreign investors are compensable only in regards to foreign and not to domestic investors, it would be an unfair treatment for the affected domestic investments whose damage is not covered by any compensation.

Moreover, it is also difficult for a claimant-foreign investor to win a case based on the sole effect doctrine. As is analysed above, when the state's measure merely reduces the profit of the investment without depriving the investor of ownership rights or when the effect of the measure is not lasting (a temporary deprivation), then such an interference cannot be substantial and therefore it may not be an expropriation. As Cameron states: "[A] claim will be much harder to maintain when most of the value of the investment remains".[238] It is evident that the application of the sole effect test cannot effectively mitigate the political risk of governmental interference with foreign investments. The requirement of substantial deprivation of property makes foreign investors not that confident in protecting their property against indirect expropriation, especially when they invest in sectors such as infrastructure, which is heavily regulated and controlled by state agencies.

3.4.3. The character of the governmental measures (the purpose test)

The majority of international tribunals undertake a balanced approach to what constitutes expropriation, accepting a combination of multiple criteria. In establishing their judgement over expropriation, the examination of the character of the governmental measures plays an important role in distinguishing indirect expropriation from regulations.

Although governments usually claim that regulatory activity cannot constitute expropriation, international tribunals have firmly stated that regulatory actions are not per se outside the scope of expropriation.[239] However, there are some criteria that are related to the character of the measures which tribunals have used in order to exclude regulatory measures from expropriation.

One important characteristic of the governmental measures is their purpose. Examining whether the respective measures aim to promote general public welfare and social purpose is an important factor. The purpose of these measures is related to the hard-core functioning of states. It is the sovereign right of states to protect essential issues such as public health, environment and life or to comply with human rights and promote safety and national security. When states take measures that aim to satisfy such primary rights as those referred to above, they are allowed to impose restrictions on foreign investments (and individuals in general) without having the obligation to compensate unless the restrictions are discriminatory.

---

[237] Sornarajah, *International Law*, p. 376.

[238] Cameron, *International Energy Investment Law*, p. 223.

[239] E.g., *Pope & Talbot Inc. v. Canada*, Interim Award of 26 June 2000, states: "Regulations can indeed be exercised in a way that would constitute creeping expropriation".

The international jurisprudence has been influenced by the approach of the European Court of Human Rights which has recognised the right of states to deprive or control the use of private property establishing measures for the public interest, unless the state's judgement is "exercised in a manifestly unreasonable way". The rationale behind this approach is a legitimate goal of states: to satisfy society's stability, transparency and the rule of law.[240] In recent international investment arbitration, *S.D. Myers v. Canada* is a well-known case that applied the purpose test by accepting Canada's prohibition of the S.D. Myers company's export of waste products. The Tribunal rejected Myers' claim that the ban amounted to an expropriation of his investment because, after examining the real interests involved on behalf of the Canadian Government's intention, its measures were found to be legitimate environmental measures.[241]

The purpose of the state's measures is related to another characteristic: the context of governmental measures or the police powers of state. The notion of police powers includes all measures that constitute state's regulatory power and therefore, according to international law their "normal exercise merit no compensation, irrespective of the scale of the effect upon the investment".[242] According to the American Law Institute's Restatement of US Foreign Relations Law, it is stated with regards to indirect expropriations that:

> "[A] state is not responsible for loss of property or for other economic disadvantage resulting from bona fide general taxation, regulation, forfeiture for crime, or other action of the kind that is commonly accepted as within police powers of the states, if it is not discriminatory...."[243]

Similarly, the Tribunal in the *Tecmed v. Mexico* case stated:

> "The principle that the State's exercise of its sovereign power within the framework of its police power may cause economic damage to those subject to its powers as administrator without entitling them to any compensation whatsoever is indisputable".[244]

In the application of the purpose test (intention and police powers), arbitration tribunals take into consideration the characteristics of the state's measures and reject compensation claims unless the taken measures are discriminatory. Discrimination occurs when for example, a taxation measure applies only to alien enterprises and not to locally-owned. However, even in this case, it is not

---

[240] Yannaca-Small, 'Indirect Expropriation', p. 17.

[241] ICSID Case *S.D. Myers v. Canada*, Partial Award of 13 November 2000, paras. 281 and 285.

[242] Cameron, *International Energy Investment Law*, p. 227.

[243] 'Restatement of the Law Third, the Foreign Relations of the United States', American Law Institute, vol. 1, 1987, Section 712, Comment g, cited in Yannaca-Small, 'Indirect Expropriation', p. 8. Similar expressions were used in *Too v. Greater Modesto Insurance Associates* of Iran-US Claims Tribunal, Award December 29, 1989, cited in Yannaca-Small, 'Indirect Expropriation', p. 19.

[244] ICSID case no. ARB (AF)/00/2, *Tecmed S.A. v. United Mexican States*, Award of 29 May 2003, cited in Yannaca-Small,'Indirect Expropriation', p. 19.

always clear if a discriminatory regulation intends to achieve expropriation. The monopolistic nature of most infrastructure sectors or their strategic role for the economic development of states could excuse under certain circumstances a legitimate taking of discriminatory measures against specific investments. In general, if a state falsely purports the public purpose of a respective measure in order to avoid its obligations derived from investment treaties and international law or to merely expropriate property of a particular foreign investor, then this measure is declared unlawful expropriation and it should be compensable.

Considering that it is difficult to practically examine the intention of the state, international tribunals have adopted an alternative way of assessment which is related to the proportionality of the taken measure. According to some scholars, the proportionality exercise is approached as an additional test.[245] Thus, this study treats proportionality not as a separate test but as a tool in weighting the purpose test by tribunals.[246] Whether the measures taken by the state kept a balance between the general interest of the community and the private interests or unjustifiably deprived the alleged foreign investment and whether the measures benefited the public welfare or not, are some of the specific exercises that tribunals may use in order to investigate the character and the aim of the taken measures. Therefore, according to the *Tecmed* case, "a reasonable relationship of proportionality between the charge or weight imposed to the foreign investor and the aim sought to be realized by any expropriatory measure"[247] was an important element for the Tribunal in order to exercise the balanced approach test by combining the effect and the purpose of the state's taken measure.

However, such a purpose test that reflects on the intention of the state, the *bona fides*, the proportionality or any other element relevant to the characteristics of governmental regulation is not an easy task for the investors to prove. Tribunals are not likely to doubt a government's assessment about measures in the public interest. National authorities know better what is good for their societies than any international tribunal. Moreover, even if the effect test of the governmental measures plays the most important role in tribunals' judgement over the expropriatory character of a taken measure, governmental intentions or the context of measures cannot be ignored by tribunals in assessing whether there has been an indirect expropriation or merely a non-compensable regulation.[248] Thus, it is not always clear whether tribunals will adopt a balanced approach to their assessment of a particular case or follow the sole effect test

---

[245] E.g., Cameron, *International Energy Investment Law*, pp. 228-229. Similarly, Reinisch, besides referring to proportionality, also adds a test on legality, transparency and consistency: Reinisch, 'Expropriation', pp. 447-450.

[246] In support of the study's position, it is important to mention that in the most recent EPA signed between Japan and India (16 February 2011), there is an additional annex (no. 10) which explains all potential methods (tests) of determining a measure as expropriation but without referring to the proportionality test. Retrieved in May 2011 from the Japan's Ministry of Foreign Affairs (MOFA) website: <www.mofa.go.jp/policy/economy/fta/index.html>.

[247] ICSID Case *Tecmed SA v. United Mexican States*, Award of 29 May 2003, para. 122.

[248] "It may be that the effect on the investment weights more heavily in the balance than the motivation of the State, but the motivation can nonetheless assist in assessing whether there has been an indirect expropriation". McLachlan, Shore and Weiniger, *International Investment Arbitration*, pp. 301-302.

looking solely at "the objective impact of measures ... not the subjective intention behind those measures".[249]

The inconsistency of tribunals' approaches towards the purpose test adds some more uncertainty over the assessment of the governmental measures and the state's intention. How to prove the subjective intention behind host state's behaviour is a quite difficult and ambiguous task. Moreover, with regards to the innate public character of infrastructure sectors, international tribunals are less likely to doubt the public purpose of the taken measures, adding some more uncertainty in the protection of investment against regulatory takings, thus increasing the possibility of political risk occurrence.

3.4.4. The degree of expectation of the investor (the legitimate expectations test)

Finally, another criterion that has also been used by tribunals in combination with the previously analysed tests is the foreign investor's legitimate expectation test. In order for tribunals to determine whether an indirect expropriation has occurred, they investigate to what degree governmental measures affect the investor's legitimate and reasonable expectations. The investor's legitimate expectation exercise is applied in a similar way to the sole effect test. The latter is related to the degree of governmental interference with the investment. In contrast, the legitimate expectation test is about the level of governmental interference with the investor. The legitimate expectation is, similarly to the sole effect test, "a question of degree".[250]

It is argued that the notion of adopting the investor's legitimate expectations for the protection of foreign investments is associated with the general principles of international law (as well as domestic law) such as the FET standard.[251] However, it is not always clear how to weigh up the investment-backed expectations and furthermore, how to assess the degree of governmental interference with them. There are important issues such as the "focus on the legal situation in the host country at the time of the investment" and to what extent "the investor accepted (it) when investing", the chronological factor concerning whether the "objective conditions and social priorities may have changed" since the time of investment implementation, and other factors that need to be addressed *eo ipso* in order to settle "precisely where the line is crossed such that we can no longer speak of an effective protection of the individual's right to hold and enjoy property".[252]

According to the international jurisprudence, in the *Metalclad* case, the Tribunal accepted the investor's claim that the municipality's denial of the local construction permit constituted an indirect expropriation. The Tribunal took this decision because it weighed up "these measures taken together with the rep-

---

[249] *Ebrahimi (Shahin Shaine) v Islamic Republic of Iran* (1994), 30 Iran-USCTR 170, p. 190, cited in McLachlan, Shore and Weiniger, *International Investment Arbitration*, p. 302.

[250] Cameron, *International Energy Investment Law*, p. 226.

[251] D. Dolzer, 'Indirect Expropriations: New Developments?', *New York University Environmental Law Journal* 11:1 (2002) pp. 78-79.

[252] *Ibid.*, p. 79.

resentations of the Mexican federal government, on which Metalclad relied".[253] Similarly, in the *Tecmed v. Mexico* case, the Tribunal investigated whether the Mexican government's measures were "reasonable with respect to their goals, the deprivation of economic rights and the legitimate expectations of who suffered such deprivation"[254] and it therefore accepted the foreign investor's claim for indirect expropriation, acknowledging that the investor "had legitimate reasons to believe that the operation of the Landfill would extend over the long term".[255] In a more recent case, the *Methanex* Tribunal referred to the role of specific commitments offered by the State to the investor and recognising that:

> "[A]s a matter of general international law, a non-discriminatory regulation for a public purpose, which is enacted in accordance with due process and, which affects, inter alios, a foreign investor or investment is not deemed expropriatory and compensable unless specific commitments had been given by the regulating government to the then putative foreign investor contemplating investment that the government would refrain from such regulation".[256]

The degree of expectation of the investor could gain some additional utility for the protection of infrastructure investments. For example, most power investments are implemented after some special permits and contractual agreements such as the signing of concession-contracts with the host state directly or its governmental agencies has been completed, providing concrete guarantees and assurances to foreign investors. Despite the importance that reasonable and legitimate expectation could have in the protection of infrastructure investments, there are only a few cases where international tribunals have applied the legitimate expectation test in combination with some other tests in determining a governmental measure as an indirect expropriation provoked by the host state. On the contrary, the legitimate expectation element has been utilised and applied by tribunals in a broader and more efficient manner under the FET standard.

3.4.5. Test of expropriation determined by the EPA-Treaty

Tribunals are free to select the appropriate doctrine in order to determine the nature of the taken measures and decide whether they constitute indirect expropriation or non-compensable regulation. However, it is also observed that in some investment treaties between countries, specific provisions are included that clarify which tests should be applied by tribunals in case of dispute on matters related to indirect expropriation.

A very recent example of investment chapters included in international treaty is the EPA between Japan and the Republic of India which was signed on 16

---

[253] *Metalclad Corporation v. United Mexican States*, para. 107.

[254] ICSID case no. ARB (AF)/00/2, *Tecmed SA v. United Mexican States*, Award of 29 May 2003.

[255] *Ibid.*, para. 149.

[256] UNCITRAL case, *Methanex Corporation v. United States of America*, Award of 5 August 2005.

February 2011.[257] According to Annex 10 that refers to the investment chapter of the Treaty (expropriation clause), it clarifies the possibility the application of four "factors" (tests) by tribunals in order to determine the nature of a taken governmental measure. In addition, the Treaty excludes the sole effect doctrine and adopts the more established test of balance approach. In order to determine what constitutes expropriation, the tribunal shall take into consideration factors such as the impact of governmental interference with investment, stating that:

> "The economic impact of the government action, although the fact that such action has an adverse effect on the economic value of an investment, standing alone, does not establish that an indirect expropriation has occurred."

Thus, in the case of Japan's previous EPAs (which are the subject of this study's research), there is no such clause included in an annex as is the case in the Japan-India EPA. In general, the absence of any reference to specific tests does not affect the tribunal's decision in choosing freely the appropriate method of how to determine indirect expropriation. However, it could be argued that the existence of annex similar to the one in Japan's EPA with India could reduce to some extent the now-inconsistent approach of tribunals in investigating the nature of indirect expropriation measures which are the most important source of uncertainty and political risk occurrence.

3.5.   Assessment of standard of expropriation/compensation-scoring

The results of the assessment are shown in the table below:

Table 6   Result of Assessment: Expropriation and Compensation Standard of Treatment[258]

ASEAN-5	Indonesia	Malaysia	Philippines	Thailand	Viet-nam
Expropri-ation	0.75	1.00	0.50	0.75	0.75
Compen-sation	1.00	1.00	1.00	0.75	1.00

The inclusion of concrete provisions and clarity in the wording of the bilateral investment agreements in relation to the expropriation and compensation standard is of great significance. In order to assess the degree of bilateral treaties' effectiveness in managing political risk, this study analyses the provisions related to the expropriation and compensation standard and attempts to measure them, adopting the following methodology.

---

[257] Retrieved in May 2011 from the Japan's Ministry of Foreign Affairs (MOFA) website: <www.mofa.go.jp/policy/economy/fta/index.html>.

[258] Table compiled by the author.

3.5.1. Methodology–Expropriation

The maximum score for the protection against expropriation standard is a unit -1- which indicates the highest level of protection against the political risk of governmental interference with the foreign investment's property though expropriation. This score is given when treaty clauses grant to foreign investments a comprehensive framework of protection against any kind of expropriation (direct or indirect) making clear reference to the imposition of host states using taxation measures for expropriatory purposes (creeping or regulatory expropriation).

Given the fact that all treaties include a general provision of declaring protection against illegal expropriation, a minimum score -0- would be given to those treaties that omit one of the four requirements that are needed in order for a host state to undertake the measure of legitimate expropriation: public purpose, non-discrimination, due process of law, compensation.

The most frequent restrictions that treaties impose in their expropriation clauses are related to the complicated issue of when a taxation measure constitutes expropriation. If investment treaties set looser conditions for the legitimacy of taxation measures in relation to expropriatory takings, then the risk of indirect expropriation through taxation measures becomes higher and therefore they receive a lower average score of 0.75. One additional restriction also occurs when investors cannot direct their claims about the expropriatory character of a taxation measure before a court, unless they first consult an established 'sub-committee' who will decide on whether an investor can submit its taxation dispute to an international tribunal.

Finally, when treaties include an additional note, with regards to when a taxation measure becomes expropriatory, according to which taxation measures can be exempted from the general rule of the four requirements mentioned above, then this exemption is treated as a strict divergence from what is needed for an expropriation to be lawful. This last reservation, combined with other restrictions related to taxation measures, is considered to be the lowest level of protection against indirect expropriation (through expropriatory taxation) and therefore it is scored at 0.50.

**Table 7   Standard of Protection against Expropriation /
Scoring Methodology[259]**

If the 4 principles (public purpose, non-discriminatory, due process of law, compensation) are *not* indicated in the expropriation clause	0.00
Exemption of taxation measures from the above principles	0.50
Other exemptions regarding taxation measures	0.75
Full protection against direct and indirect expropriation	1.00

---

[259] Table compiled by the author.

3.5.2. The findings–Expropriation[260]

First of all, it should be mentioned that the expropriation clause is applied in a more fixed manner than what is the case in other general and specific standards of treatment included in investment chapters of international treaties. It is more about a provision of a general declaration stating each party's consent in respecting the investments in its area of the other party from an expropriation or any measure equivalent to that (indirect expropriation). Such a declaration is addressed to all investment-activities related to any sector or industry. Therefore, as far as the sector-level is concerned, there is not any difference or reservation as is the case for FET, NT or other provisions. However, as far as the wording is concerned, there are some differences that, according to the findings below, could result in a different degree of protection against expropriation and to a varying level of political risk uncertainty. When the wording of each treaty introduces exemptions from the general declaration of expropriation-clauses, the study assigns them different scores. If the effects of these exemptions are uncertain or undermine the protection of investment against expropriation, then the study perceives that the possibility of political risk is higher, and therefore a lower score is given.

Examining the average scores for Japan's investment agreements with the five ASEAN countries, the study found that the Japan-Malaysia EPA has no restrictions on the provision of protections to Japanese investments in Malaysia against expropriation and therefore it receives the highest score (1.00). The rest of the treaties receive lower average scores mainly because of their restrictions with respect to when a taxation measure constitutes expropriation. The study takes into consideration in its assessment exercise any restriction related to taxation. It is quite a frequent phenomenon for countries to indirectly expropriate foreign investments by using taxation measures. Japan's treaties with Indonesia, Thailand and Vietnam receive average scores of 0.75 and the Japan-Philippines EPA receives the lowest score, 0.50. Japan-Philippines EPA has a combination of more restrictions with regards to when a taxation measure can constitute expropriation and to when an investor can submit its taxation-dispute to an international tribunal.

In particular, as analysed by the study, there is not any test of expropriation determined by the five reviewed Japanese investment treaties as is the case for the latest Japanese EPA with India. Thus, the study does not give any score related to the test of expropriation as this depends not on the respective investment treaties but, on an *ad hoc* basis, on the selection of the doctrine (sole effect or balanced approach) that international tribunals would pursue in a potential adjudication.

One difference which is considered as having positive result on the level of protection against expropriation is introduced in the Japan-Indonesia EPA. There is an additional element required by this Treaty in order for an expropriatory measure taken by the host state to be allowed. Article 65.1 (c) of the respective treaty requires that the host state's measures shall be compatible not only with the classic concept of "due-process of law" but also with FET and FPS

---

[260] For review of the findings, see the appendix: "Scoring-Card of Japan's EPAs".

standards. This study argues that this additional requirement of FET and FPS standards, included among other requirements into the "expropriation clause" of the respective Treaty, could maximise the degree of investment protection against government claiming that a taking has been an eligible (lawful) measure. It is easier for an investor to claim and prove that a governmental measure has interfered with his property and violated his legitimate expectations than confronting the state's procedures and arguing against their legitimacy. However, this study compares only restrictions found in the reviewed treaties and assesses only differences that have negative effect to the degree of protection against expropriation.

A difference that may reduce the level of protection against expropriation is introduced by the Japan-Philippines EPA and the Japan-Vietnam BIT. Article 99 of the Japan-Philippines EPA permits the Parties to take any measure without being obliged to comply with the expropriation clause (art. 95) in case there is a necessity to adopt measures for the protection of health, life, environment, to maintain morals and public order, to protect essential security interests or finally to comply with their obligations under the UN Charter for the maintenance of international peace and security (art. 99.1 [a], [b], [c], and [d]). A similar provision is found in the Japan-Vietnam BIT (art. 15). It should be noted that despite these exceptions, the referred-to clauses do not recognise explicitly the right of state to take non-compensable measures as can be observed in other investment agreements (e.g. the most recent US-FTAs). It is argued that it is the tribunals' decision to judge whether a measure that falls under the cases referenced above should be compensable or not and therefore, the study does not take into account this element for the scoring-assessment. However, taking into consideration that other treaties such as Japan-Malaysia EPA, Japan-Indonesia EPA and Japan-Thailand EPA do not contain any similar clauses, it is argued that tribunals could be less likely to accept a compensation claim by investors under the Japan-Philippines EPA or the Japan-Vietnam BIT.

The most important difference among the five investment agreements found by the study is related to taxation measures. All treaties recognise that a taxation measure taken by governments can also constitute an (indirect) expropriation unless the taken measure complies with all of the following four requirements: public purpose, non-discriminatory, due process of law and compensation.

Accordingly, article 104.1 of the Japan-Philippines EPA acknowledges that article 95 of the Treaty (expropriation) shall also apply to taxation measures unless the four principles occur. Similarly, the rest of the EPA treaties recognise taxation measures as potential expropriation. However, the Japan-Philippines EPA provides an additional note under article 104 (taxation measures as expropriation) that introduces an exemption from the general rule of the four principles which are necessary for an expropriation to be lawful. According to the note for article 104.1, from the four principles, only the "non-discriminatory" element is required in order that a taxation measure be lawful. This means that in the case of taxation measures taken by the host state (e.g. Philippines), the respective government can argue about the non-compensable character and prove the legitimacy of such measures even when they lack a public purpose or when they do not comply with the due process of law.

Investors conceive of taxation measures as a serious source of political risk, especially in relation to the infrastructure sectors where the state's interest and governmental interference is likely to be significant. If investment treaties set looser conditions for the legitimacy of taxation measures and in relation to expropriatory takings, then the risk of indirect expropriation through taxation measures becomes higher. For this reason, the study treats such an exemption of the "expropriation clause" concerning taxation measures with a lower score (0.50) than it treats the relevant clauses of the other treaties (e.g. Japan-Malaysia EPA) in which there is no such exemption and therefore receive a perfect score.

Except for the Japan-Philippines EPA, similar exemptions are not found in any other investment agreement reviewed by this study. The Japan-Vietnam BIT in its "Agreed Minutes" which is attached to the main body of the BIT agreement, records the understanding of the Parties in relation to taxation measures, stating that "the imposition of taxes does not generally constitute expropriation". It continues by referring to some examples, such as "a claim of excessive burden that is imposed by a taxation measure cannot be indicative of an expropriation". The purpose of this statement, even though it is not found in the rest of the Japan's investment agreements, is not believed to be the introduction of one more restriction on what can constitute an expropriation. It is only the recognition of a general principle of international law: a state's sovereign right to regulate its economic and fiscal policies by imposing taxation measures. However, the Japan-Vietnam BIT, the Japan-Thailand EPA and the Japan-Indonesia EPA introduce, along with the Japan-Philippines EPA, another restriction which is related to the establishment of a special sub-committee and results in a lower score, as analysed below.

Article 106 of the Japan-Philippines EPA establishes a "sub-committee on investment" which among others is responsible for discussing any matter related to taxation measures as expropriation (art. 106.2 [c]). The provisions of this article imply that investors cannot direct their claims about the expropriatory character of a taxation measure before a court, unless they first consult the respective "committee" of article 106. Furthermore, it is not clear what will be the procedure in case the sub-committee does not agree with the arguments of the investor or it determines that the taken taxation measures are not expropriation. Similar provisions are included in the Japan-Vietnam BIT (art. 20). This study asserts that this procedural uncertainty makes the protection of investments against creeping expropriation (taxation) more blurred. Moreover, looking at the wording of the Japan-Indonesia EPA, article 73.3 and 73.4, the study finds that the investor loses the right to submit its investment dispute to an international tribunal in case the committee determines that the taken measure is not expropriation. For example, article 73.3 of the Japan-Indonesia EPA explicitly states that no investor may invoke the expropriation claim as the basis of an investment dispute if the committee of article 73.4 has determined that the taxation measure is not an expropriation. For this reason, the expropriation clauses the Japan-Indonesia EPA, the Japan-Thailand EPA and the Japan-Vietnam BIT receive a lower score (0.75).

In the case of the Japan-Malaysia EPA, there is no such restriction requiring the establishment of a sub-committee for taxation measures. More specifically, article 81.5 recognises that taxation measures can constitute expropriation under the requirements of the four principles, and in article 85.1 (Settlement of Investment Disputes), it is confirmed with a special note that any settlement related to investment disputes "shall apply in respect of taxation measures". Therefore, investors are not required to submit their claims for expropriatory taxation to any sub-committee but they can directly apply their dispute to the Treaty's recognised international tribunal. The study believes that this facility increases substantially the confidence of investors in protecting their economic interests against indirect expropriation (taxation measures).

3.5.3. Methodology–Compensation

The maximum score for the compensation standard is a unit -1- which indicates the highest level of protection against political risk of expropriation through the provision of full compensation (best treatment) that foreign investments can receive according to each treaty's wording by making clear reference to the full compensation standard. In particular, clear reference to the full compensation standard is considered to exist when the key words prompt, adequate and effective compensation or fair market value (the Hull formula) is adopted by the relevant treaty's clause. The minimum score is zero -0-, which indicates the lowest level of protection against a potential political risk of expropriation and it occurs when no compensation treatment for expropriation is provided by the respective treaty (worst treatment/no provision). Score 0.50 indicates a case when compensation payments are not freely transferable, effectively realisable and convertible, elements that are required in order compensation to be effective, and 0.75 when the wording of a particular treaty provides for appropriate – prompt – compensation by referring to the requirement of payment without delay but without clear reference to an appropriate interest payment. An important issue that arises here is in relation to the date from which interest should be payable, taking into account the length of time from the time of expropriation until the time of payment that is required. (See table below).

Table 8   Standard of Compensation/Scoring Methodology[261]

If no compensation treatment then	0.00
If compensation – payment not effective (freely transferable and convertible)	0.50
If compensation – payment not prompt (without determining the date from which interest should be payable)	0.75
Prompt adequate and effective compensation (Hull formula)	1.00

---

[261] Table compiled by the author.

3.5.4. The findings–Compensation[262]

In analysing the five bilateral investment agreements between Japan and Indonesia, Malaysia, Philippines, Thailand and Vietnam, very few differences were found among them in relation to the issue of the compensation standard.

More specifically, all of them include (as was expected) the full compensation standard by adopting the wording of the Hull formula. All of the four EPAs (in their respective investment chapters – the Japan-Vietnam EPA does not include an investment chapter) and the Japan-Vietnam BIT refer to the Hull formula by stating that expropriation or its equivalent is not allowed except "upon payment of prompt, adequate and effective compensation". The full compensation standard (adequate compensation) is completed by a concrete statement included in all the Treaties that "such compensation shall be equivalent to the fair market value of the expropriated investments (a) at the time when the expropriation was publicly announced or (b) when the expropriation occurred, whichever is the earlier". The Japan-Malaysia EPA adds in article 81.2 (a) that the fair market value can be determined even "immediately before the expropriation was publicly announced", however this addition does not influence the overall assessment of this clause as all treaties acknowledge that "the fair market value shall not reflect any change in market value occurring because the expropriation had become publicly known earlier".

Similarly, with regards to the requirement of effective compensation, all treaties provide that compensation shall be "effectively realisable, freely transferable and freely convertible at the market exchange rate prevailing on the date of the expropriation into the currency of the country of the investors concerned and freely usable currencies". In addition, all the treaties repeat their guarantee of freely transferable compensation in their relevant articles concerning "transfer of payments".

However, the previous uniform expression of the adequate and effective compensation is not found in the last requirement of the Hull formula, the requirement of a prompt compensation and particularly in relation to appropriate interest. Actually, four of the investment treaties comply fully with the prompt compensation standard by stating that "compensation shall be paid without delay and shall carry an appropriate interest, taking into account the length of time from the time of expropriation until the time of payment". However, the Japan-Thailand EPA is the only one that does not conform to the above expression. In relation to the date of interest payable, article 102.3 of the Japan-Thailand EPA states that compensation "shall carry an appropriate interest, in accordance with the laws and regulations of the Party making the expropriation". It is obvious that in the case of an expropriation by the Thai Government, Japanese investments are not guaranteed that compensation payment will carry an appropriate interest dated from the time of the expropriation (as is the case for the rest of the Treaties), but the amount of the interest will be determined by the Thai Government's discretion according to its municipal laws and regulations. This study assesses the Japan-Thailand provision's interest-determination as restrictive to the notion of prompt compensation,

---

[262] For further review of the findings, see the appendix: "Scoring-Card of Japan's EPAs".

construing it as an element that causes more uncertainty about the method of calculating the amount of compensation including interest. Therefore, any kind of uncertainty about the issue of prompt compensation is also conceived of as a higher degree of political risk. For these reasons, the Japan-Thailand EPA is scored less (0.75) compared with the other treaties, which receives the maximum score (1.00).

3.6. The alternative protection against expropriation provided by the FET standard[263]

It is highly unlikely that foreign investments will be implemented unless states also determine, along with general standards, specific standards of treatment and provide certain guarantees. Thus, the book compares the content of two clauses (expropriation-clause and FET standard) and highlights the complementary function of the evolved FET-standard in protecting foreign investments against the risk of expropriation.

Due to the difficulty in construing the concept of indirect or tantamount expropriation, especially in relation to regulatory takings that are not compensable, international tribunals have shown "reluctance to support claims based on the expropriation provisions that are found in the texts of BITs, as well as MITs".[264] Tribunals justify their difficulty in distinguishing between valid regulations and expropriatory activities by indicating, among others, that there are different criteria that "each of them alone would be insufficient (to constitute expropriation),[265] although their combination could amount to expropriation".[266] Therefore, determining whether a taken measure constitutes expropriation or not, is a process "often difficult to predict".[267] This difficulty increases the uncertainty of expropriation risk, and thus the possibility of political risk occurrence. Cameron indicates that, because of the tribunals' difficulty in determining indirect expropriation, there are recently very few awards that have found a government responsible for expropriation.[268] However, the most interesting finding is that in most of the cases when tribunals rejected the expropriation claim, they found that "host states had violated other treaty provisions, especially the FET standard".[269]

In contrast to the tribunals' reluctance to support expropriation claims, there is a large number of arbitral awards that have relied upon the FET standard in their decisions. In relation to FET doctrine, it is important to analyse the evolu-

---

[263] The FET standard is analysed in Chapter 4: 'General Standards of Treatment'.

[264] Cameron, *International Energy Investment Law*, p. 184.

[265] Parentheses added by the author.

[266] McLachlan, Shore and Weiniger, *International Investment Arbitration*, p. 298.

[267] *Ibid.*

[268] Cameron further states that "of seven awards that examined claims based on expropriations in 2007, only two decided in favour of the investor and five rejected such claims altogether." Cameron, *International Energy Investment Law*, p. 223. See also notes 154 and 155, *ibid.*, for more information about the list of the specific awards.

[269] *Ibid.*, p. 223.

tion of its role in providing a complementary (and sometimes more sufficient) protection of foreign investments against expropriation.

The use of the FET general standard for the protection of foreign investments against a specific political risk such as expropriation not only complements but also expands the scope of protection. Even when the criteria that are required by international law for constituting an expropriatory measure as lawful expropriation exist (due process, non-discriminatory action, public purpose and adequate compensation), the taken measure may still be considered illegal in the event of a violation of the FET standard. A claim of violation of the FET standard can be supported more easily than can an expropriation-claim do. It is often the case, especially for the attraction of foreign investments in infrastructure sectors, that host governments or their agencies offer concrete promises and specific guarantees to foreign investors about the stability of the regulatory environment and the government's support in implementing and undertaking a particular investment project. This assurance provided by states creates reasonable and legitimate expectations to foreign investors. Any later-taken measure that infringes the host state's promises, cancels the investors' expectations and affects their economic interests could be enough reason for tribunals to decide on the illegality of such a measure, and thus to accept a claim for protection and compensation by the investors.[270]

In the case of the FET standard, in order to decide on a violation of legitimate expectations, the claimant-investor needs to specify what the state's guarantees were, how the taken governmental measure infringes these guarantees and to prove the level of damage caused by that measure. In contrast, in order to decide on an expropriation breach, the interacting factors, especially in the case of indirect expropriation, create a more complicated situation. Tribunals need to identify the existence of multiple criteria and apply various tests in order to examine issues such as the degree of damage, the public purpose of the taken measure, the intention of the government, the due process and the non-discrimination of the government's behaviour, the proportionality of the taken measure, the appropriateness of the compensation and many others. Each of these factors alone or in combination, as explained above, can play a decisive role in determining whether a measure constitutes an expropriation or a non-compensable taking. However, international tribunals are not likely to keep a consistent approach in determining expropriation factors and as a result, it is ambiguous and difficult to predict to what extent they can provide an effective protection against creeping or regulatory expropriations.

In particular, a detailed investigation of an indirect expropriation by an arbitration tribunal would cause some problems of a political dimension. For example, if an arbitration tribunal rejects the position of a state on the necessity and the public purpose of the alleged measures, it is likely the tribunal's decision would be accused of intervening in issues of sovereignty with the respective country.

---

[270] Thus, it is stated that the FET standard "will not be understood to amount to a stabilization clause but will leave some measure of governmental space for regulation". R. Dolzer, 'Fair and Equitable Treatment: A Key Standard in Investment Treaties', *International Lawyer* 39:1 (2005) p. 105.

In addition, tribunals face a constraint in evaluating the degree of a host state's interference with a foreign investment. As explained before, there are two important criteria determining the degree of the taken measure's interference. First, the economic impact of the measure, meaning that tribunal needs to examine whether there is an effective change of control or ownership of the foreign investment and second, the duration of the measure. However, concerning complicated economic activities such as infrastructure-related investments, it is possible that various regulatory measures do not result in an effective change of the foreign investor's control but yet other serious economic impacts could be identified causing economic damages to the foreign investment at a later stage. In energy sectors, one of the most *common* risks is the revocation of concessions or licenses by the host state for an assumed failure of the investor to comply with some regulatory requirements imposed by the government. Even when revocation does not occur, the investor may face serious economic problems when, for example, state authorities veto necessary tariff increases in the operation of infrastructure networks such as the distribution and transmission of electricity.[271] Thus, in these cases, it is difficult for a foreign investor to protect its interests based solely on the expropriation provision provided by a treaty.

For example, in the ICSID case *Telenor v. Hungary*, the host state introduced a new administrative measure forcing all mobile operators (foreign companies in the majority), including Telenor (a Norwegian operator), to subsidise the services provided by fixed-line operators (SOEs in their majority). This measure interfered with the investment of the foreign investors causing large damages (Telenor sought damages of up to $152 million). However, the ICSID Tribunal rejected Telenor's claim of indirect expropriation judging that the measures at issue (taken by the Hungarian Government) were found to fall short of a substantial economic deprivation of the investment that is required to constitute expropriation (no change of control or ownership was found).[272] The Tribunal accepted the argument of the respondent-state that if "any form of interference with the investor's property or diminution of its value constitutes expropriation [it] would be out of line with expropriation jurisprudence".[273] On the contrary, Telenor could protect its investment under the provision of the FET standard if the Hungary/Norway BIT would permit arbitration in regards to FET claims, though as this treaty permits arbitration only for expropriation claims, the Tribunal rejected the FET claim having no jurisdiction.[274]

Similarly, in other ICSID cases, tribunals have denied allegations of interference with investments by regulatory agencies or administrative authorities stating that "such interference did not rise to the level of an international treaty violation, and ICSID's function was not to serve as an administrative review body

---

[271] Cameron, *International Energy Investment Law*, p. 199.

[272] ICSID Case No. ARB/04/15 *Telenor Mobile Communications A.S. v. Republic of Hungary*, Award of 13 September 2006.

[273] UNCTAD, *World Investment Report*, Box V.8, p. 166.

[274] *Ibid.*

in the absence of such violation".[275] There are cases such as *LG&E v. Argentina*, where tribunals have accepted the host state's claim of a "state of necessity" exempting it from the obligation to compensate for damages to the investors' property that were provoked by adjustments of tariffs.[276] In the *Nykomb v. Latvia* case, the state changed its previous promise to purchase electricity at a "double tariff" and finally gave an offer at only 75 per cent of the average tariff. The investor claimed that this regulatory change constituted a regulatory taking tantamount to indirect expropriation. Thus, the tribunals rejected the claim stating that "there was no possession taking ... no interference with the stake-holders' rights or with the management's control over and running of the enterprise – apart from ordinary regulatory provisions laid down in the production license, the off-take agreement."[277]

Tribunals have continued the tendency of rejecting investors' claims of indirect expropriation, especially in sectors related to the energy industry, mainly because of the effect test requiring that the taken measures entail a substantive degree of possession or control over the enterprises. Contrary to the indirect expropriation test, tribunals have started accepting claims based upon the breach of FET standards, as in the *BG Group v. Argentina* case. In this case, the tribunal rejected the indirect expropriation claim comparable to the other cases because of the non-permanent impact of the disputed measure upon the investor's property and the "non-deprivation of the BG's control over the investment or management of its day-to-day operations". However, the tribunal acknowledged the difficulties faced by the investors in making claims of indirect expropriation and, therefore, it accepted the investor's claim of violation of its legitimate expectations based on the FET standard.[278]

3.7. Chapter's conclusion

Several factors have decreased the confidence of investors in protecting their investments against political risks by basing their claims only on violation of

---

[275] *EnCana Corporation* v. *The Republic of Ecuador*: The Tribunal rejected jurisdiction over claims arousing out of tax regulations except only an expropriation claim. UNCITRAL, LCIA No UN3481, IIC 91 (2006), Award of 3 February 2006, cited in Cameron, *International Energy Investment Law*, p. 205.

[276] *LG&E Energy Corporation and Others v. Argentina*, Discussion on Liability, ICSID Case No ARB/02/1, IIC 152 at 126, cited in Cameron, *International Energy Investment Law*, p. 205.

[277] *Nycomb Synergetics Technology Holding AB v. Latvia*, SCC Case No 118/2001, IIC 182 (2003), Award of 16 December 2003, cited in T.W. Walde and K. Hober, 'The First Energy Charter Treaty Arbitral Award', *Journal of International Arbitration* 22 (2005) pp. 83-104. Similarly, in *PSEG* v. *Turkey*, ICSID case No ARB/02/5, IIC 198 (2007), award of 19 January 2007 (dispute over the development of a power sector), the Tribunal accepted that only extreme forms of interference can constitute indirect expropriation requiring "deprivation of the investor in the control of the investment" as well as deprivation in the "management of day-to-day operations of the company, interfering in the administration, impeding the distribution of dividends, interfering in the appointment of officials and managements, or depriving the company of its property or control in total or in part": PSEG case, para. 278, cited in Cameron, *International Energy Investment Law*, p. 229.

[278] *BG Group plc v. Argentine Republic*, UNCITRAL Arbitration, IIC 321 (2007), Final Award of 24 December 2007. See also other cases according to which tribunals fount state-liability based on FET such as: *Occidental v. Ecuador, Saluca v. Czech Republic*, and *Azurix v. Argentine Republic*, cited in Cameron, *International Energy Investment Law*, p. 229.

expropriation clauses. International jurisprudence has recently changed its previous support for investors with regards to expropriation claims and there has been an increasing series of awards based on both bilateral and multilateral investment agreements that follow a stricter approach on what determines indirect expropriation.

First of all, the shift of states' practice from direct expropriation to the more sophisticated creeping expropriation has blurred the distinction between expropriation and non-compensable regulatory measures. In the face of divergent interpretations of the concept of indirect expropriation, different tribunals have examined each case *ad hoc*, and on many occasions they have rendered inconsistent decisions. To some extent, the difference in tribunals' judgements is rooted in the existence of different investment treaties that tribunals need to apply in each case and in the various factual circumstances of each case. However, the most significant difficulty in keeping the output of awards consistent is the different jurisprudential approaches to the application of various expropriation tests, or to the different combinations of these tests (balanced approach). Issues such as how to define the permanent and substantial deprivation of property, or how to evaluate the exercise of a state's police powers and identify the intention of government or, finally, how to diagnose governmental interference with investors' legitimate and reasonable expectations are complicated processes that result in a lot of uncertainty on the investor's side. It is obvious that in order to decide on the substantial level of a government's interference with the investment or with the investor's expectations, and in order to accept the government's non-legitimate purpose or the unlawful nature of its measures, the legal burden of proving these arguments should be carried by the party whose legal position will be ameliorated, and this party is the claimant-investor.

It is evident from the various arbitral awards discussed in this section that the global adjudication system is evolving with regards to expropriation and FET principles and therefore what constitutes a compensable expropriatory measure is still an unclear issue in international investment law. However, it can also be observed that in recent international jurisprudence, claimants have achieved a more efficient protection of their investments against alleged regulatory measures under the provision of FET standards, while tribunals have found it difficult to apply the various indirect expropriation tests in order to determine specific facts and state measures.

Moreover, given the wording of each treaty's expropriation clause, there are also differences that may change the degree of political risk relating to expropriation. As was found by the study's assessment, there are differences in the treatment of taxation measures and in particular the conditions required for taxation measures to be lawful. Judging taxation measures as a serious source of political risk, especially in relation to infrastructure sectors, it has influenced the final scoring exercise. Most of the reviewed investment Treaties set looser conditions for the legitimacy of taxation measures in relation to expropriatory takings resulting in a higher risk of indirect expropriation, thus a stricter score (e.g. Japan-Philippines EPA).

In relation to the compensation standard for the expropriation of foreign property, the international law provisions of compensation are regarded as instruments of political risk management with similar function to mechanisms used in political risk insurance (compensation as guarantee). Moreover, this study takes into consideration international investment jurisprudence on the matter of monetary compensation being the main or only instrument of reparation available to international law. However, determining the amount of compensation payable to the investor has been one of the most controversial debates between the two conflicting norms relating to the "full compensation" standard. The controversy founded in the theory about what constitutes an appropriate standard of compensation has been solved in practice by the selected language of the majority of the international investment treaties which include the Hull formula. This study has confirmed this practice by reviewing and analysing the wording of the relevant Japanese Treaties.

All of the reviewed Treaties follow quite a uniform approach, providing the maximum level of investment protection by adopting the full compensation standard of the Hull formula. However, examining each of the requirements separately (adequate, effective, prompt), the study assessed that the vagueness in the determination of the date from which to calculate interest payable (found in the Japan-Thailand wording) is an element that creates uncertainty about the requirement of prompt compensation and, therefore, can result in a higher degree of political risk.

Finally, the study acknowledges that even when the Treaties' language is conclusive about the full compensation standard, investors should be aware that, in practice, there are implications for international investment tribunals, judging each expropriation case separately, in determining the precise amount of compensation or contractual arrangements existing parallel to the treaty that may make the management of political risk (expropriation) an even more dubious process.

4

GENERAL STANDARDS OF TREATMENT

4.1. Introduction

As stated previously, the expropriation clause is not the only investment treaty protection that will engage the international responsibility of host states if breached. Host states guarantee the provision of general standards of treatment in international investment agreements. These standards are common features of international investment treaties such as BITs and investment chapters of FTAs (or EPAs in the case of Japan).[279] In addition, the majority of capital importing countries tends to introduce new national investment codes that include similar promises of foreign investment treatment.

There are four general standards of treatment the role of which this study analyses: national treatment (NT), most favoured nation treatment (MFN) and the most significant, full and equitable treatment (FET) and full protection and security (FPS). The first two address issues of protection from discrimination and the last two (FET and FPS), a more inclusive protection from any discriminatory and arbitrary host government's behaviour or a reasonable level of police power with due diligence in case of acts of violence and strife, being also summarised as a minimum standard of treatment.[280] In the case of national treatment and MFN treatment, the introduced standards involve a comparative test, whereas in the FET and FPS cases, there is an absolute test.[281]

In a comparative test, there are some relative standards embodied in national treatment and MFN principles which define the required treatment by reference to the treatment accorded to other investment.[282] When a foreign investor claims a violation of the non-discrimination principle of national treatment and MFN, he is required to identify a comparator (national in the case of NT or another foreigner in the case of MFN principle) and to indicate that he has received less favourable treatment from the host state. If a comparator is successfully indicated then the burden falls upon the host state to prove that there has not been any

---

[279] A previous study conducted by the author examines the role of Japan's EPAs in mitigating political risk; T.N. Papanastasiou, 'The Role of Economic Partnership Agreements in Protecting Foreign Investments against Political Risk: An Analysis of Japan's EPAs', *Journal of the Graduate School of Asia-Pacific Studies* 21:2 (2011) pp. 95-124.

[280] T.J. Grierson, J. Weiller and I.A. Laird, 'Standards of Treatment', in P.T. Muchlinski, F. Ortino and C.H. Schreuer (eds.), *The Oxford Handbook of International Investment Law* (Oxford University Press, Oxford, 2008) pp. 261-262.

[281] *Ibid.*, p. 262.

[282] UNCTAD, *Bilateral Investment Treaties in the Mid-1990s* (United Nations, New York and Geneva, 1998). See also: Fatouros, *Government Guarantees to Foreign Investors*, pp. 135-141, 214-215.

different treatment or justify (a more difficult case) the validity of its behaviour based on reasonable and non-discriminatory decisions.[283]

In an absolute test, when a foreign investor claims a violation of fair and equitable treatment or a failure of full protection and security, he is not required to identify a comparator as the FET/FPS standards are absolute.[284] He only needs to demonstrate that the treatment received by host state was below the standard required by the concrete international investment treaty (between his home country and the host state).

When the host state adopts a measure (treatment) that affects a foreign investment, it is examined whether this measure is or is not in accordance with the content of the two standards (relative and absolute) guaranteed by the Treaty's general standards clauses. In other words, the general standards mentioned above serve as guidelines for foreign investors in identifying the scope and the extent of the protection promised to them. This study particularly focuses on the protection of general standards of treatment against political risk within the infrastructure industry and more specifically electricity. According to the UNCTAD Investor-State Disputes Database, electricity is involved in most of the infrastructure related investment disputes during the last decade.[285]

However, this study does not address the issue of standards of treatment in the pre-establishment phase of foreign investments. Even if the issue of granting standards of treatment (i.e. NT or MFN treatment) at the entry stage is regarded as important right, it is considered as an issue irrelevant to the focus here: the protection against political risk. The pre-entry rights of establishment are substantially different than the post-establishment rights of investments. Investment treaties that contain pre-entry rights aim at liberalization.[286] On the contrary, the post-establishment standards of treatment aim at host country's regulatory stability and foreign investment protection. For example, when an investment treaty grants NT or MFN treatment at the stage of entry, it is regarded as an important requirement of opening the host country's economy to investments of the home country. National treatment at the stage of entry entitles foreign investors to a right of entry and establishment in the host state. This right result to foreign investors being able to invest in those sectors of host country that domestic investors are allowed to invest. Accordingly, MFN treatment at the stage of entry, it contributes to the liberalization process. It entitles investors of the home state the right to enter and establish into those sectors of host country that foreign investors of third countries are allowed to do.

Therefore, standards of treatment at the entry stage constitute of a promise for liberalization, assuring an "open economy" towards investors of home country. However, these rights do not provide any additional guarantees for the protection of foreign investments after their establishment and during their operation. As explained before, because of the "asset specificity problem" foreign

---

[283] Grierson, Weiller and Laird, 'Standards of Treatment', p. 259.

[284] *Ibid.*, p. 262.

[285] UNCTAD, <www.unctad.org/iia>. Retrieved in February 2011.

[286] Sornarajah, *International Law*, p. 234.

investors are in their weakest bargaining position towards host government's discrimination or arbitrary behaviour during the post establishment period. During that period political risks are likely to materialize. This study attempts to analyse the role of post-establishment general standards of treatment in protecting foreign investments against political risk.

4.2. The standard of national treatment (NT)

4.2.1. In general

NT signifies the host state's guarantees for non-discriminatory treatment to the investors (or the service suppliers in the case of electricity services) of other countries (investors of the home country). It connotes that their investments (or services) will receive treatment no less favourable than the treatment host state accords to investments in its territory of its own nationals and companies.

For example, the Japan-Indonesia EPA reads in article 59.1 of the investment chapter or article 79 of the trade in services chapter that: "Each Party shall accord to investors of the other Party and to their investments treatment no less favourable than that it accords in like circumstances to its own investors and to their investments with respect to investment activities". Additionally, the other EPAs of Japan with Malaysia, Thailand, Philippines and the BIT with Vietnam contain similar expressions, though they specify various kinds of investment activities: "with respect to the establishment, acquisition, expansion, management, operation, maintenance, use, possession, liquidation, sale, or other disposition of investments-referred as investment activities". There is additionally a clarification clause, found in all Japan's EPAs, with regards to any case of inconsistency between MFN treatment in chapters on services and in chapters on investment. For example, article 57.2 of the Japan-Indonesia EPA states that "in the event of any inconsistency between the Investment Chapter and the Trade in Services Chapter and with respect to matters covered by MFN article, the latter Chapter shall prevail to the extent of inconsistency".

However, there is an important difference with regards to the national treatment included in the EPA treaties that Japan negotiated with the five ASEAN member-countries. In the Japan-Indonesia EPA (article 59.2) and the Japan-Malaysia EPA (article 75.3) there is a general restriction:

> "Notwithstanding paragraph 1, each Party may prescribe *special formalities*[287] in connection with investment activities of investors of the other Party in its area, provided that such formalities do not materially impair the protection afforded by the former Party to investors of the other Party and to their investments pursuant to this Chapter".

It is argued that these special formalities introduce some form of limitation to the standard of national treatment and they consist of an exemption that other treaties do not require (cf. Japan's EPAs with the Philippines, Thailand and Vietnam).

---

[287] Italics added by the author for emphasis.

4.2.2. Scope

Discrimination occurs in different forms, variously based on race, religion, political ideology or affiliation, disability, and many other reasons. With regards to the treatment of foreign investment, nationality is the most important criterion of discrimination.[288] It is argued that discriminatory treatment on the basis of nationality is not always illegal under general international law.[289] However, when an international investment treaty (or an investment chapter of a FTA or an EPA), contains a national treatment clause, then the provisions of this clause are guaranteed and every differential treatment on the basis of nationality shall be confirmed as illegal. This obligation to treat all aliens as equal or to treat them as favourably as nationals established by treaty is confirmed in the *Genin v. Estonia* Tribunal's decision.[290] The Tribunal notes:

> "[I]nternational law generally requires that a state should refrain from discrimination treatment of aliens and alien property. Customary international law does not, however, require that a state treat all aliens (and alien property) equally, or that it treats as favourably as nationals. Indeed, even unjustifiable differentiation may not be actionable. In the present case, of course, any such discriminatory treatment would not be permitted by Article II (1) of the BIT, which requires treatment of foreign investment on a basis no less favourable than treatment of nationals".[291]

The promise of non-discrimination by the host state does not imply that domestic law needs to change in order to provide to foreign investments more favourable treatment than that provided to its national investors. The purpose of the NT is not to offer more benefits or better protection to foreign investments compared to local investments. Even if it is not against the meaning of NT when the host state treats foreign investments better than local investments, it is not what NT is supposed to stipulate. NT imposes on the host state only a negative obligation: to avoid treating foreign investments less favourably than investments made by its own nationals and companies. In the case of the power sector, NT plays more crucial role in the protection of foreign investments than any other industry. In most of the countries, the power sector is usually serviced exclusively by State Owned Enterprises (SOEs).[292] Therefore the negative obliga-

---

[288] However, this does not mean that the issue of discrimination is necessarily restricted to nationality. See: C.H. Schreuer, 'Protection against Arbitrary or Discriminatory Measures', in C.A. Rogers and R.P. Alford (eds.), *The Future of Investment Arbitration*, Institute for Transnational Arbitration—The Center for American and International Law (Oxford University Press, New York, 2009) p. 193.

[289] *Ibid.*

[290] *Genin, Eastern Credit Ltd. Inc. and AS Baltoil v. Republic of Estonia*, Award, 25 June 2001, cited in Schreuer, *ibid.*

[291] *Genin, Eastern Credit Ltd. Inc. and AS Baltoil v. Republic of Estonia*, Award, 25 June 2001, cited in *ibid.*

[292] In both developing and developed countries a large part of investments and business in the infrastructure sector, including power sector, are usually implemented by SOEs. See, for example: R. Bacon and J. Besant-Jones, 'Global Electric Power Reform, Privatisation and Liberalisation of the Electric Power Industry in Developing Countries', *Energy and Mining*

tion of NT is important for the protection of foreign investments in the power sector as it can also result in the mitigation of political risk. Moreover, the violation of national treatment has emerged as an important claim in recent investment treaty arbitration decisions, though only under the NAFTA treaty, where there are a significant number of awards that address what "treatment no less favourable" means.[293]

4.2.3. Application

This study asserts that the provision of NT plays two important roles related to political risk mitigation:

1) On the one hand, national treatment enhances the host country's rule of law and increases the predictability of the government's behaviour. In developing countries, institutions are not strong enough to support order and justice. Moreover, corrupt governments or oligarchic regimes are unpredictable and arbitrary, especially towards foreign investments.[294] Providing NT, the host state is obliged by an internationally binding tool (e.g. an EPA treaty) to protect foreign investments against arbitrary and discriminatory discretion. In a sense, NT improves the host state's rule of law by improving the predictability of host government's actions.

The specification of the standard of NT for "no less favourable treatment" calls attention to any treatment provided by municipal laws, regulations, procedures or any host state's administrative measures that may affect the investments covered by the Treaty between the host and the home country. Therefore, in the case of the electricity legal framework, if foreign investors are aware of the host country's specific laws, regulations and treatment towards domestic energy investments with regards to construction and operation of power plants (investment) and electricity supply (trade in services), then the NT clause can guarantee a certain standard of treatment similar to that made already available to domestic investments. In this case, with the provision of NT investors of the home country are able to know in advance the exact treatment owed to them by the host state, improving their ability to predict the regulatory environment. Similarly, if foreign investors are not aware of the domestic laws' full context, then the national treatment standard loses a great part of its significance in predicting the applicability of domestic laws.

This function of NT clause minimizes the risk of uncertainty with regards to the host country's regulations and reduces the political risk of the host government's unpredictable behaviour towards foreign investments. Foreign investors need only to be acquainted with the host country's laws and its treatment of domestic investments. By clarifying and defining the treatment that the host state provides to its nationals, foreign investors can feel more confident that they will receive the same or similar treatment and they will not be discriminated against

---

Sector Board Discussion Paper: No. 2 (World Bank, Washington, DC, June 2002); see also: Estache and Fay, 'Current Debates on Infrastructure Policy', *Policy Research Working Paper*, no. 4410 (World Bank, Washington, DC, 2007).

[293] Some important cases between the US and Canada: see ref. 72 in Sornarajah, *International Law*, p. 234; see also: Grierson, Weiller and Laird, 'Standards of Treatment', pp. 290-296.

[294] Glavinis, *International Economic Law*, p. 614.

compared to their domestic competitors. If NT is responsible for the creation of a more confident and stable regulatory environment, then political risk mitigation is also attributable to the NT's provision to foreign investments. For example, if a privilege such as a state's subsidy is reserved for an SOE (in the infrastructure-power sector domestic investors are usually SOEs), it could contradict national treatment of an international investment treaty if it is not given to a foreign investment of the home country who conducts investments in the same infra-structure industry (unless it is exempted in advance by one of the Treaty's Parties).

However, it is a prerequisite that all relevant laws or any administrative rulings of the host state to be promptly published or made publicly available by the time a foreign investor needs to know the content of the host country's regulations related to the NT. This is an important obligation that requires the host state make fully transparent its regulatory environment (affirmative obligation). The obligation for transparency is complementary to the NT and it shall be always referred in the body of the investment Treaty.

2) On the other hand, NT determines the limits of the host state's discretionary decisions and the scope of foreign investments' protection against discrimination. NT limits the discriminatory behaviour of host state. This is the most important function of NT especially in respect to political risk mitigation. NT is not meant to guarantee the anti-trust practices among similar businesses in the territory of a host state. Competition issues are regulated by NT in the case of trade law under GATT agreement of WTO.[295] However, the violation of NT on trade issues does not have the severe effects of discriminatory or arbitrary treatment on foreign investments in sectors such as the infrastructure industry. In the case of trade, when the products of a foreign company are maltreated, the foreign company can take measures on its own to reduce the damage. For example, it can stop its export delivery to the host country and divert its products to some other, friendlier markets. In the case of investment, it is much more difficult for a foreign investor to take any measure to reduce its damage. Especially in the case of large capital-intensive establishments in the territory of the host state, such as infrastructure projects (e.g. construction of power plants), foreign investments are totally exposed to the host state's behaviour.[296]

Therefore, the significance of NT is the host state's legally binding promise, taken under international law (EPA treaty), that can guarantee the protection of foreign investments by offering security of law and predictability of the government's behaviour. Additionally, it is the host state's guarantee that helps foreign investors to mitigate political risk when they undertake large infrastructure investment projects in the territory of the host country. However, by promising to foreign investments equal treatment with the one given to local investors according to the domestic law, it does not mean that the local standards are adequate. This is something that foreign investors need to investigate carefully by hiring local lawyers and consulting local businesses and international agencies in order to acquire a complete understanding of the standards provided by the host

---

[295] *Ibid.*

[296] Ginsburg, 'International Substitutes', p. 107.

country's law. It is also for this reason that host countries make efforts to modernise or update their investment codes according to international standards that foreign investors are familiar with.[297]

4.3. The standard of most favoured nation treatment (MFN)

4.3.1. In general

First of all, the direct beneficiary of MFN clause is the home country because the created obligation is inter-state, between the granting and the beneficiary state.[298] "The granting state cannot be discriminatory against the beneficiary state in favour of a third state".[299] The consent or not of the third state does not matter. The relation of the MFN granting state and the third country is used only as a reference to the extent of favourable treatment that the beneficiary state can claim.

However, the practical meaning of MFN treatment is that the host state guarantees to the investors of the home country (foreign investors) that their investments will receive treatment no less favourable than the treatment it accords in similar situations to investments in its territory of investors of any third country. For example, if a host state gives to a foreign investment of a third country license to produce and sell electricity or financial incentives to operate its business or any kind of privileges that it does not normally provide to other power investments, then the host country is obliged to provide to the investments of the home country, with whom it signed the international investment treaty, the same treatment for the implementation and operation of similar power projects.

4.3.2. Scope

The MFN treatment for investment and for services is included in separate clauses, in the investment chapter and in the trade in services chapter according-ly. For example, the Japan-Malaysia EPA,[300] in article 76 (investment chapter) under the title "most-favoured-nation treatment", states that: "Each country shall accord to investors of the other Country and to their investments treatment no less favourable than that it accords in like circumstances to investors of a third State and to their investments, with respect to investment activities".[301] This wording on most favoured treatment is followed in a similar way in all of Japan's EPAs. There is additionally a clarification-clause, found in all of Japan's EPAs, in

---

[297] Indonesia has already updated its domestic investment code (2008) and Malaysia is also doing the same (2010).

[298] R.M. Islam, 'The Most Favoured Nation Clause', in K.C.D.M. Wilde (ed.), *International Transactions: Trade and Investment, Law and Finance* (The Law Book Company Ltd., Sydney, 1993) p. 215.

[299] *Ibid.*

[300] The Japan-Malaysia EPA entered into force in 13 July 2006.

[301] Accordingly, article 101 (trade in services chapter) of the Japan-Malaysia EPA states under the title "most-favoured-nation treatment" that: "Each country shall accord to services and service suppliers of the other Country treatment no less favourable than that it accords to like services and service suppliers of any third State".

regards to any case of inconsistency between MFN treatment in chapter on services and in chapter on investment. For example, article 73.2 of the Japan-Malaysia EPA states that "in the event of any inconsistency between the Investment Chapter and the Trade in Services Chapter and with respect to maters covered by MFN article, the later Chapter shall prevail to the extent of inconsistency".

The significance of the MFN treatment included in an international treaty (e.g. an EPA) is the guarantee of the host country to the investors of the home country (contracting countries to the EPA) that they will receive at minimum the same standard of treatment and the same level of protection as the treatment foreign investors from third countries receive in the territory of the host country. Considering that most of the countries have created particular economic relations and specific co-operation among each other because of political, geographical, economic or even historic reasons,[302] the use of the MFN standard has a practical meaning. When countries create specific economic partnerships, it is obvious that favourable treatment is reserved for the investors of the partner countries. Whenever an MFN clause is included in a new investment treaty between two countries, the investors of these countries will "receive the best treatment that each of the contracting countries has granted to the investments or investors of any other country".[303] Otherwise, in the absence of any special undertaking between the granting country and a third country, the MFN clause would lack any practical use or real substance.[304]

4.3.3. Application

With regards to the infrastructure industry, the MFN standard plays an important role in determining the level of protection foreign investments receive. An important issue related to infrastructure is the private participation. Private sector is increasingly needed for improvement, maintenance and expansion of the infrastructure services. Throughout the power investment practices, governments and foreign investors enter into specific contracts for the supply of energy. For example, the construction and operation of power plants (greenfield projects) are usually implemented through BOT type of contracts or concessions between the private sector and the Government (Ministry or its SOEs). According to these contracts, private companies are required to build maintain and (sometimes) operate the plants and government is obliged to pay for the services provided. Power sector investments are different than those of other sectors (e.g. manufacturing) because one of the above types of contracts is required.

However, the question raised is whether the specific provisions of these con-

---

[302] For example, European states have special economic partnerships with ex-colonies. Former Soviet Union countries have strong co-operation especially on issues of trade and investment and they keep privileges of the past. Japan makes a special effort to promote the economic development of South-East Asian countries because of its proximity to them and of the high Japanese-MNCs interests.

[303] An argument used by UNCTAD paper for the significance of MFN clause included in BIT. UNCTAD, *Bilateral Investment Treaties 1995-2006: Trends in Investment Rulemaking* (United Nations, Geneva, 2007) p. 38. See also: Glavinis, *International Economic Law*, p. 617.

[304] Glavinis, *International Economic Law*, p. 617.

tracts are included in the host state's obligation to provide MFN treatment when an EPA treaty enters into force. According to the internationalization of contracts theory, it is argued that the content of the investment contracts is covered by the provisions of the investment treaties and therefore, the State is also responsible in the case of less favourable treatment towards the power investments of the home-country's investors.

It is also argued that the MFN clause used by bilateral investment treaties is very important for the international economic system because it facilitates the "multilateralisation" of international investment law.[305] However, in the case of customs unions, common markets or economic communities of a group of countries, the MFN standard does not apply to the investments of a third country which has signed an investment treaty with one of the above countries. For example, if a state belongs to a regional organisation like ASEAN and gives some privileges to other member countries, these privileges should be excluded from the MFN clause that this state has granted to a third country (beneficiary). This is an exclusion from the general application of the MFN clause.[306] Even if there is no requirement for the States to explicitly recognise the above exclusion from the MFN connotation, the Japan-Malaysia EPA includes a statement in the Annex no. 4 of the Treaty that "MFN may also not be accorded to foreign investors with respect to preferential treatment granted under any ASEAN agreement".[307]

Another important issue concerning the MFN function is whether the dispute resolution mechanisms that are provided by a bilateral investment treaty should be extended through the MFN clause to a third country (that is benefited by the MFN treatment). It is argued that the MFN effect should also apply to the investment arbitration mechanisms.[308] However, it seems that the opposite argument is the most appropriate. Glavinis argues that a dispute over the violation of a MFN treatment between countries that are parties to an investment treaty needs to be solved by using the resolution mechanisms of their treaty and not any other's treaty mechanisms. A different solution would "multilateralise" the resolution mechanisms of bilateral investment agreements "from the window".[309]

Finally, similarly to the significance of the NT, the host state's promise of MFN treatment is a legally binding obligation to the foreign investors of the home country. The MFN standard of treatment protects investors of the home

---

[305] A.F. Rodriquez, 'The Most-Favored-Nation Clause in International Investment Agreements – A Tool for Treaty Shopping?', *Journal of International Arbitration* 25:1 (2008) p. 89.

[306] This exclusion also applies in the case of GATT/WTO when a contracting country reserves favourable treatment for the product of a third country with which it has a common market, e.g. the European Union. Glavinis, *International Economic Law*, p. 618. However, the exclusion of several privileges from the MFN application has to be stated by the granting country in the investment treaty. Sornarajah, *International Law*, p. 236.

[307] Japan-Malaysia EPA, Annex no. 4, Schedule of Malaysia, note no. 5.

[308] M. Valenti, 'The Most Favored Nation Clause in BITs as a Basis for Jurisdiction in Foreign Investor-Host State Arbitration', *Arbitration International* 24:3 (2008) p. 447; and E. Gaillard, 'Establishing Jurisdiction through a Most-Favored-Nation Clause', *New York Law Journal* 233:105 (2005) p. 3.

[309] The only legitimate way to multilateralise them could be through a multilateral treaty, like the attempt made by the OECD for the signing of the MAI Treaty for dispute resolution mechanisms in 1998; Glavinis, *International Economic Law*, p. 619.

country against the potential political risk of the host government's discrimination and unfair treatment. By identifying the host government's treatment towards investors from third countries, the home country's investors have a better understanding of the host government's behaviour. The MFN standards of treatment make the host government's behaviour more predictable and foreign investors more confident of the host country's rule of law.[310]

4.4. The standard of fair and equitable treatment (FET)

4.4.1. In general

The FET standard is a principle that derives from international customary law and is related to the treatment of aliens. According to international law, there is a general obligation for every state to refrain from violating the basic rights of aliens. Protection of aliens includes also protection of their economic rights, their property and their investments.

In the failed attempt of the MAI Treaty, it was stated that "each Contracting Party shall accord to investments in its territory of investors of another Contracting Party fair and equitable treatment" and that "in no case shall a Contracting Party accord treatment less favourable than that required by international law". The meaning of FET is that an international minimum standard of treatment is introduced. In case the standard of treatment given to domestic investors is less than the standards required by the international customary law, then the host state is obliged to provide at least a minimum of fair treatment to foreign investments.[311]

The obligation for a minimum standard of treatment is important in order to avoid any confusion that the NT standard may create. Even if the host state treats foreign investments not less favourable than local investments (NT), in case the local standards are lower than the international standards, the host state is still obliged to a minimum of fair treatment. In other words, FET introduces an absolute standard of fair treatment which is not determined by reference to any other level of treatment. On the contrary, the NT and the MFN standards are relative standards because they refer to the treatment accorded to local and third country's investors accordingly.

4.4.2. Scope

In Japan's EPA treaties, there is a different wording of the FET standard. In Japan's EPA with Indonesia, Malaysia and in its BIT with Vietnam, the FET clause comes under the title "general treatment" and states: "Each Party shall

---

[310] However, it is not very clear whether investors can acquire all the necessary information about the treatment that the host government reserves for specific investment projects. For example, the infrastructure project agreements between the host government and private contractors are, most of the time, secret. Private companies usually demand from all partners to keep contracts and all relevant agreements confidential because they are considered business secrets. It is, for example, difficult to know what kind of incentives or privileges are offered to private investors in a specific power plant project. There are many details about different parts of the agreement i.e. the PPA contract, the project finance arrangement, facilitation of the construction, O&M, etc. It is not clear how the MFN standards can be fully applied in the above cases.

[311] Sornarajah, *International Law*, p. 337.

accord to investments of investors of the other Party fair and equitable treatment and full protection and security".[312] Thus, in Japan's EPA with Thailand and Philippines, the relevant to the FET clauses come under the title "minimum standard of treatment" and state: "Each Party shall accord to investments of investors of the other Party treatment in accordance with international law, including *fair and equitable treatment*[313] and full protection and security".[314] In the EPAs with Thailand and Philippines, there is an additional "explanation note" that is not included in the other EPAs.[315] These differences are substantial and play an important role in the protection of foreign investments.

The obligation of host countries to provide the FET standard is often stated as part of their obligation to protect inward FDI.[316] Even if "minimum standard of treatment" and "general treatment" refer to the FET standard, they are not the same. The latter may include the former, but it goes further.[317] Under the title of FET, contracting parties are free to determine its connotation according to their intention, which may differ treaty by treaty. The core of the FET is the protection of the expectations of investors, and it may justify claims against host country measures which violate the expectations of investors. It is stated that: "Among the most discussed standards of protection that investment treaties provide are 'fair and equitable treatment' and 'full protection and security.' These concepts and their relation to the minimum standard of treatment of aliens under customary international law have inspired significant debate. This discussion has mainly centred on whether these standards provide only as much protection as foreign investors receive in their capacity as aliens under the customary international law minimum standard of protection of aliens, or whether they offer a higher level of protection."[318]

Both "minimum standard of treatment" and "general treatment" may overlap significantly with respect to issues such as arbitrary treatment, discrimination and unreasonableness.[319] However, as explained above, some of the Japan's Treaties (EPAs with Indonesia, Malaysia and BIT with Vietnam) describe FET as a standard which entails obligations at least as great as those imposed by general international law and on the contrary, some others (Japan's EPAs with Thailand and Philippines) regard FET as one general rule of international law which cannot impose obligations greater than those imposed by general international law.

---

[312] E.g., Japan-Indonesia EPA, article 61/Japan-Malaysia EPA, article 77/ Japan-Vietnam BIT, article 9.1

[313] Italics added by the author for emphasis.

[314] E.g., Japan-Thailand EPA, article 95 and Japan-Philippines EPA, article 91.

[315] This note's significance is analysed in the findings section of the present chapter.

[316] UNCTAD, *Bilateral Investment Treaties 1995–2006*; see also: UNCTAD, *Bilateral Investment Treaties in the Mid-1990s*.

[317] Fatouros, *Government Guarantees*, p. 215; see also: C. Yannaca-Small, 'Fair and Equitable Treatment Standard in International Investment Law', OECD Working Paper on International Investment no. 2004/3, (OECD Financial and Enterprise Affairs Directorate, Paris, 2004) p. 40.

[318] C.F. Dugan, D. Wallace Jr. and R.D. Noah, *Investor-State Arbitration* (Oxford University Press, Oxford, 2008) p. 491.

[319] Grierson, Weiller and Laird, 'Standards of Treatment', pp. 261-262.

As a typical exposition of the minimum standard, the seminal *Neer* decision cited that the host government's treatment of aliens would violate international law only if the treatment amounted "to an outrage, to bad faith, to wilful neglect of duty, or to an insufficiency of governmental action so far short of international standards that every reasonable and impartial man would recognize its insufficiency."[320] According to the *Neer* case, violation of the minimum standard could be established only if "bad faith" and intention of the host government to damage foreign investments were proven.

The international minimum standard was addressed in the first half of the 20th century, as it applies to the "physical security" (personal property) of an alien. However, the modern treaties' purpose is to protect foreign investments. Moreover, as Sornarajah explains,[321] the content of the minimum standard, when it comes to investment protection, will always be problematic and it is up to the tribunal to decide, each time, its content. There are only three potential cases according to which violation of the international minimum can prompt "state responsibility". They are related to compensation for expropriation, responsibility for destruction or violence by non-state actors and denial of justice.[322] Thus, the first two cases overlap with the "expropriation" and the "full protection and security" standards accordingly. Therefore, the minimum standard is relevant and limited to the denial of justice.

Since the *Neer* case, the minimum standard has evolved to become the fair and equitable standard gaining independent elements, beyond the principles of customary international law, such as the protection of investors' "legitimate expectations". Thus, the meaning of fair treatment is not always concrete. Recent arbitration practice[323] has tended to interpret it in a broad manner and under an autonomous interpretation.[324] Violation of the fair treatment principle is included in the notion of denial of justice and can also appear in the forms of absence of due process, discrimination, lack of transparency, absence of good faith, violation of legitimate expectations,[325] and even as lack of proportionality.[326] As is explained below (regarding the *TecMed* case), the expanded concept of FET standard does not require proving the host state's "bad faith" which was one of the requirements in the *Neer* case in order to accept the violation of the minimum standard. The violation of the FET standard can be objectively established.

---

[320] See *L.F.H. Neer and Pauline E. Neer v. Mexico* [U.S.-Mexico Claims Commission] (Opinion rendered on 15 October 1926).

[321] Sornarajah, *International Law*, pp. 328-332.

[322] *Ibid.*, p. 330.

[323] For reference about the arbitration tribunal's decisions on FET notion, see *ibid.*, pp. 332-342.

[324] "The scope of the undertaking of fair and equitable treatment under the Agreement ... resulting in an autonomous interpretation, taking into account the text of the Article (FET) of the Agreement or from international law and the good faith principle, on the basis of which the scope of the obligation assumed under the Agreement and the actions related to compliance therewith are to be assessed". ICSID, *TecMed v. Mexico*, decision of 29.05.2003, para. 155.

[325] Sornarajah, *International Law*, p. 340.

[326] Proportionality as part of the FET notion has been argued in the ICSID, *MTD Equity Sdn. Bhd. and MTD Chile S.A. v. Republic of Chile*, decision of 25.5.2004, para. 109.

The notions of denial of justice and legitimate expectation are especially considered as sub-categories or extension of fair treatment. Denial of justice is
strictly defined as unfair justice by the State's judicial organs. However, in
ICSID's jurisprudence,[327] a broader concept is also accepted. Denial of justice
can also apply when a judicial decision violates the investor's rights. In this case,
it is argued[328] that the host state is responsible even when its judiciary issues a
decision that is against the principles of international law in relation to foreign
investment protection. Regarding the second sub-category of fair treatment, the
"investor's legitimate expectations", it is stated in the ICSID case, *TecMed v.
Mexico*,[329] that "the foreign investor expects the host State to act in a consistent
matter, free from ambiguity and totally transparently in its relations with the
foreign investor ... without arbitrarily revoking any pre-existing decisions or
permits issued by the State that were relied upon by the investor to assume its
commitments as well as to plan and launch its commercial and business activities". It has become obvious that, after the *TecMed* decision, the protection of
foreign investors can take greater horizons and new dimensions dependent in
each case on the arbitration tribunal's interpretation of host state's behaviour.

However, it is important to state that if an EPA provides the FET clause under the title "minimum standard of treatment" (e.g. the Japan-Philippines and
the Japan-Thailand EPA) instead of "general standard of treatment", foreign
investments cannot be benefited by the broader framework of protection as
established by the *TecMed* case and the tribunals will follow a narrower approach
to the protection of foreign investments.

4.4.3. Application

Several investment disputes are related to the infrastructure sector and particularly to the energy industry.[330] In most of these known investment disputes,
violation of the FET clause has been used to a great extent and applied in the
protection of foreign investments.[331] According to ICSID's award in *Parkerings-
Compagniet AS v. Lithuania* (para. 331), the notion of the investors' legitimate
expectations have been determined using specific criteria: "The expectation is
legitimate if the investor received an explicit promise or guarantee from the host-
State, or if implicitly, the host-State made assurances or representation that the
investor took into account in making the investment. Finally, in the situation
where the host-State made no assurances or representation, the circumstances
surrounding the conclusion of the agreement are decisive to determine if the
expectation of the investor was legitimate. In order to determine the legitimate

---

[327] ICSID, *Robert Azinian, Kenneth Davitian & Ellen Baca v. Mexico*, Award of 1.11.2009, paras.
97-99.

[328] *Ibid.* See also ICSID, *Saipem SpA v. Bangladesh*, Award of 21.03.2007, paras. 132 and 137.

[329] ICSID, *TecMed v. Mexico*, Decision of 29.05.2003, para. 154.

[330] Number of known infrastructure-related investment disputes, 1996-2007. UNCTAD, *World
Investment Report 2008*, p. 164.

[331] The large majority of arbitral decisions have addressed three clauses: the fair and equitable
treatment, the expropriation and the "umbrella" clauses. *Ibid.*, p. 166.

expectation of an investor, it is also necessary to analyse the conduct of the State at the time of the investment".[332]

The scope of the FET standard remains unclear as tribunal arbitration is continuously evolving. Thus, if future arbitration follows the reasoning in the *Parkerings-Compagniet* dispute, the FET clause is likely to continue offering to investors an even greater potential for protection against a host state's actions. Any related explicit promise or even implicit assurance by the host state could become a binding obligation through the fair treatment clause that is included in an international investment agreement. This study asserts that the notion of legitimate expectations reflects the *lato sensu* definition of political risk. The risk of "government's unpredicted behaviour towards foreign investments" can be reflected in the notion of explicit or implicit guarantees given by host states.

In relation to the infrastructure sectors, the expanded scope of FET through the concept of the protection of legitimate expectations increases the degree of investment protection against the unwarranted behaviour of the host state. The upgraded FET clause benefits investments in the infrastructure more than in any other sector. As mentioned before, infrastructure is regarded as a "strategic" industry.[333] It plays an indispensable role for the economic growth and economic development of countries. The strategic function of infrastructure seems to be related to the national security and public interest concerns,[334] something that is of high significance for the determination of an expropriation as legitimate or not.[335] Especially, in regards to the energy industry it could be considered as one of the most strategic infrastructure sectors in most countries. However, the strategic role of the infrastructure sectors has been often manipulated by governments in order to interfere into foreign investments claiming their sovereign right to protect their interests. In many cases, foreign investors successfully protected their investments by utilizing the legitimate expectation claim.

However, determining whether the FET standard has been infringed or not is not an easy process. It does not only depend on the nature of government's behaviour, but the investors' actions and overall business conduct is also relevant.[336] For example, it would be a more balanced approach to investigate whether the investor carries out the assessment of the project feasibility with due diligence or whether the investor is negligent in conducting business but then blames the commercial loss on government action.

With regards to political risks, the FET standard (under its expansionist evo-

---

[332] ICSID, *Parkerings-Compagniet AS v. Republic of Lithuania* Award of 11.09.2007. See also: UNCITRAL Award, para. 1 in *International Thunderbird Gaming Corp. v. United Mexican States.*

[333] UNCTAD, *World Investment Report 2008*, p. 155.

[334] *Ibid.*

[335] As is explained in a later section, one of the requirements for an expropriation to be considered as legal is when there is a reason of "public purpose".

[336] P.T. Muchlinski, 'Caveat Investor? The Relevance of the Conduct of the Investor under the Fair and Equitable Treatment Standard', *International and Comparative Law Quarterly* 55:3 (2006) p. 527.

lution) could possibly become the "magic wand" for foreign investors to protect their interests when a host state's behaviour is decisive for their expectations but finally fails to fulfil them. Expectations of investors towards the government's behaviour depend on the level of predictability. However, the government's behaviour can never become fully predictable, especially in relation to the infrastructure services because of the nature of risks being out of the investors' control (uncontrollable risk = unpredictable risk = political risk). Therefore, the purpose of the FET general standard is to provide to foreign investors an additional tool in order to mitigate unpredictable (political) risks that are hidden in complicated-by-nature frameworks such as those required in power projects.

FET standards could easily be applied by using only objective requirements in order to determine whether there has been a violation of a host state's obligations or not.[337] In other words, whether a host state is in "bad faith" or not is not required for the establishment of the violation of its obligation towards a foreign investment. It is stated:[338]

> "The commitment of fair and equitable treatment included in the Article of the Agreement is an expression and part of the *bona fide* principle recognized in international law, although bad faith from the State is not required for its violation: To the modern eye, what is unfair or inequitable need not equate with the outrageous or the egregious. In particular, a State may treat foreign investment unfairly and inequitably without necessarily acting in bad faith".

Finally, according to ICSID's award in *Duke v. Republic of Ecuador* (para. 381), "contractual breaches do not amount, in themselves, to arbitrary conduct", indicating that violation of the FET standards go "beyond a normal contract dispute". In other words, there is a difference between a state's treatment and a contract party's behaviour. FET standards include something more than just a breach of contract. It is more about the overall government's behaviour acting as a State. If the host State does not honour its obligations from its promises, foreign investors have extra protection provided by international law through the FET clause of an investment treaty.

4.5.   The standard of full protection and security (FPS)

4.5.1.   In general

The full protection and security (FPS) standard is the second element of the non-contingent standard that is found commonly in all modern investment treaties (the first is the FET element). It is a guarantee that the host state will provide a degree of protection and security to investors and investments of the home country. This guarantee has a significant utility in the protection of foreign investments against the political risk of civil disturbance, disorder or violence. The threat of violence or any civil strife as well as the absence of host state's

---

[337] According to ICSID's jurisprudence and theory, the subjective obligation of host states is not a requirement for the application of fair treatment, ICSID, *Duke Energy Electroquil Partners & Electroquil S.A. (Duke) v. Republic of Ecuador*, 18.08.2008, paras. 380-383.

[338] ICSID, *TecMed v. Mexico*, Award of 29.05.2003, para. 153.

protection that investors may face in a politically volatile or hostile environment is a political risk that can cause damage to foreign property or substantive economic loss.

The FPS standard is usually combined with the FET standard (most of the time under the same clause in the treaty). However, in the beginning, it appeared separately in bilateral treaties of friendship, commerce and navigation, relating to the physical protection of aliens or their property and based on claims of state responsibility and diplomatic protection.[339] The main reason for the inclusion of FPS in the early bilateral treaties FCN was to face the "fear of xenophobic violence and the inadequacy of local police forces in some capital-importing countries, including the defeated power after World War I".[340] The reasoning for the necessity of the FPS standard in the 19th and early 20th centuries is still valid. Especially after the domino effect of recent uprisings in several Arab countries in early 2011,[341] the FPS standard's necessity regains momentum.

This section analyses the nature of the international law standard of FPS and assesses the degree of protection provided by the reviewed Japanese treaties.

4.5.2. Characteristics

The inclusion of the FPS standard plays an important role in the mitigation of the political risk of civil disturbance. It is not clear if there is any international treaty standard where the host state can be held liable for damage caused to a foreign investment by third parties such as rioters, rebels or looters.[342] The provision of FPS in an investment treaty consists of an explicit guarantee to safeguard the foreign investment's property and the foreign investor's security. However, it cannot be considered to be an absolute guarantee. First of all, as for any other standard of treatment that is provided for by an international treaty, the FPS standard applies only to those investments or investors that are covered by the specific treaty. Moreover, determining what constitutes security is an issue that need clarification and cannot be solved by using the vague language of most investment treaties. As professor Salacuse highlights, it is necessary to define the host state's obligation under investment treaties by answering three important issues: against whom the state must protect investments, against what actions and with what measures.[343]

In theory, there is a controversy about the scope of protection provided by FPS, whether it covers only the traditional concept of physical security or an extended meaning of security such as legal security as well. On the one hand, some scholars assert that the FPS standard is based on the customary international law which consists of the host state's duty to protect aliens' physical security and of the state's responsibility "arising from the failure to fulfil that

---

[339] McLachlan, Shore and Weiniger, *International Investment Arbitration*, p. 247.

[340] Rubins and Kinsella, *International Investment*, p. 218.

[341] The popular rebellions in Tunisia, Libya, Egypt, and Bahrain (as well as efforts at political changes in Syria) referred to in the western media as the "Arab Spring".

[342] Rubins and Kinsella, *International Investment*, p.19.

[343] J.W. Salacuse, *The Law of Investment Treaties* (Oxford University Press, Oxford, 2010) p. 208.

duty either wilfully or negligently".[344] Moreover, it is stated that such treatment of FPS that is owed "cannot be higher under investment treaty"[345] and therefore the host state is not liable for damage that is caused to the foreign investor's interest by "violence that could be reasonable anticipated".[346] In other words, it is about the failure of the host state to protect foreign investments from physical damage caused by "either miscreant State officials, or by the actions of others where the State has failed to exercise due diligence".[347] As will be analysed below, the FPS standard is, according to international jurisprudence, the exercise of police power by the host state.

On the other hand, it is argued that the scope of the FPS standard has been expanded by the later evolvement in arbitration tribunals' jurisprudence on this matter, becoming a "strict or absolute" standard and adopting the view that "arbitrators will consider that standard to be a guarantee against negligent State omissions of a more general sort than mere police inaction".[348] No matter what the theoretical approach, it is agreed by all commentators that the wording of each investment treaty and the tribunals' view on the nature of FPS will eventually determine the scope of foreign investment protection under the FPS standard. Therefore, in order to define the nature of the FPS standard, it is necessary to examine the treaties' language and to analyse the jurisprudential interpretation given on this matter.

4.5.3. Application

As mentioned above, the FPS standard is included in all modern investment treaties. Thus, there is variation in the precise formulation of the standard and the diversity of treaty text in the area of FPS is being increased. There is a simple variation in the wording used by several treaties, such as "full protection" or "most constant protection", which is not believed to make a significant difference in the level of protection owed by host governments.[349] However, there are some other variations in the language that are considered to be worthy of attention in relation to the degree of investment protection. Regardless of the level of variation, this study contemplates the precise wording of the clause which is important for the assessment of the degree of protection against political risk.

Reviewing the investment chapters of Japan's EPAs, most of them introduce a simple and uniform language combining FPS with the FET standard. For example, Japan-Indonesia EPA (Chapter 5: Investment) article 61 under the title "General Treatment" provides that: "Each Party shall accord to investments of

---

[344] Sornarajah, *International Law*, p. 342.

[345] *Ibid.*

[346] *American Machine Tools v. Zaire* (1997) and *Wena Hotels v. Republic of Egypt* (2002), both cited in *ibid.*, p. 237.

[347] McLachlan, Shore and Weiniger, *International Investment Arbitration*, p. 247. See also: Salacuse, *Law of Investment Treaties*, p. 210 ("A host state satisfies its due diligence obligation when it takes all the reasonable measures of protection that a well-administered government would take in a similar situation"), and *ibid.*, note 19, about the meaning of due diligence.

[348] Rubins and Kinsella, *International Investment*, p. 224.

[349] *Ibid.*, p. 219.

investors of the other Party fair and equitable treatment and full protection and security".[350] The Japan-Vietnam BIT (article 9.1) uses the expression "full and constant protection and security". Moreover, in Japan's EPAs with the Philippines and Thailand there is a more complicated variation in the language of FPS treatment. For example, article 95 of the Japan-Thailand treaty, under the title "Minimum Standard of Treatment", affirms that: "Each Party shall accord to investments of investors of the other Party treatment in accordance with international law, including fair and equitable treatment and *full protection and security*";[351] and the clause is followed by an additional note that is not included to the rest of the treaties, in a similar way to the FET section, as is analysed in that section of this book.[352]

Considering the above differences in the formulation of the FPS wording, it is important to examine briefly the international arbitration tribunals' interpretation of FPS. As is mentioned above, there is no uniform approach followed by different tribunals on this matter. In one of the first cases, the *Asian Agricultural Products Ltd* v. *Sri Lanka* (the *AAPL* case)[353] the Tribunal rejected the claim of the investor that FPS goes beyond the minimum standard of customary international law and that it establishes an unconditional obligation of protection on the host country (strict or absolute liability). Thus, the Tribunal found the Sri Lankan government responsible for its inaction and omission and for violating "its due diligence obligation which requires undertaking all possible measures that could be reasonably expected to prevent the eventual occurrence of killings and property destructions".[354] According to this seminal decision relating to the FPS standard, the Tribunal also clarified that the protection owed should be according to the international standards and not in respect to the domestic standards when such protection *en droit* is inadequate. Furthermore, the obligation of the host state to take certain measures shall be based on "an objective standard of vigilance in assessing the required degree of protection" regardless of what its intention was. The host state's liability should be an objective and not subjective fact.[355] Similarly, later cases repeated the *AAPL* reasoning,[356] but with the addition of an important requirement on the investor-claimant side: If the claimant fails to carry the burden of proving the government's inadequate response and the connection of this response to the damage suffered, then this will result in a denial of the government's liability.[357] The difficulty in providing

---

[350] Similarly, article 77 of Japan-Malaysia EPA.

[351] Italics added by the author for emphasis.

[352] Article 91 of the Japan-Philippines EPA states the same expression and includes the same note as the Japan-Thailand note (but under the title 'General Treatment' as the other EPAs).

[353] ICSID case No ARB/87/3, Final Award of 27 June 1990.

[354] *Ibid.*

[355] *Ibid.*

[356] Such as the ICSID Tribunals in *American Manufacturing and Trading Inc (AMT)* v. *Zaire* and *Wena Hotels Ltd v. Arab Republic of Egypt*.

[357] *Wena Hotels Ltd v. Arab Republic of Egypt*, ICSID Case, No ARB/98/4, Award on Merits of 8 December 2000. See: Salacuse, *Law of Investment Treaties*, p. 212.

sufficient evidence to establish a causal link between the investment's damage and the host state's behaviour has been the main reason in rejecting investors' claims in several arbitration cases.[358]

However, the most complicated issue in international jurisprudence has been the scope of FPS protection. In the *CME* case it was asserted for the first time that FPS protection included not only physical injury, as it had been traditionally interpreted until that time, but also the legal rights of foreign investors.[359] The controversy increased when in another case with the same parties and the same set of facts as in *CME*, the Tribunal made a different decision adopting the traditional approach on the scope of FPS.[360] Since these two influential judgements, there have been a few cases that have adopted the *CME* approach, accepting the expansion of the FPS standard to the protection against legal injury[361] with some important clarifications. For example, in relation to the scope of protection under the FPS standard, the Tribunal in the *Azurix* case made a clear interpretation of the treaty's wording stating that if there is an omission of the words "full" or "fully", then it is limited to the level of police protection (physical injury) only, rejecting the argument about expansion of the FPS-protection to legal rights. However, this approach was not adopted uniformly. For example, it was rejected by a later Tribunal which asserted that the difference in the wording between "full protection" and just "protection" does not affect the level of protection owed by the host state.[362] Finally, in the *Saluca* case, the Tribunal repeated the argument of the earlier cases as *Lauder* did, adopting the traditional interpretation of the FPS notion and by stating that the FPS standard is not meant to cover anything else but only "to protect more specifically the physical integrity of an investment against interference by the use of force".[363]

Looking into the divergent interpretations of the FPS standard, there is not any clear position on whether tribunals should adopt the limited scope of FPS, being part of the international minimum standard, or the expansive approach, being "an independent and self-contained treaty standard without the reference to the limitations of customary international approach".[364] It is obvious that the divergence in the jurisprudence's view on the degree of FPS protection against government's interference constitutes one more reason for investors' increasing uncertainty towards political risk. No matter what the tribunals' approach is, it is agreed that the treaty-standard of FPS guarantees the investor's property from damage caused by either host state's organs or by others acting within the host

---

[358] Such as *Tecmed SA v. United Mexican States*, ICSID Case No ARB (AF)/00/2, Award of 29 May 2003.

[359] *CME Czech Republic BV v. Czech Republic* Case, Partial Award of 13 September 2001.

[360] *Lauder v. Czech Republic* Case, Award of 3 September 2001.

[361] For example, *Azurix v. Argentine Republic*, ICSID Case No ARB/01/12 of 23 June 2006.

[362] *Parkerings-Compagniet AS v. Republic of Lithuania*, ICSID Case No ARB/05/08, Award of 14 August 2007.

[363] *Saluca Investments BV (The Netherlands) v. Czech Republic*, UNCITRAL Partial Award of 17 March 2006, para. 291.

[364] Salacuse, *Law of Investment Treaties*, p. 216.

state's jurisdiction.[365] Whether a strict liability obligation on a host state can be established, expanding the coverage of FPS from cases of physical damage to legal injury depends on the specific treaty-wording of the FPS standard, which is an important factor for the overall assessment of the treaty's degree of protection against political risk, as analysed below.

4.6. Assessment of general standards of treatment–scoring

The results of the assessment are shown in Table 9.

Table 9   Result of Assessment: General Standards of Treatment[366]

ASEAN-5	National Treatment	Most Favoured Treatment	Fair & Equitable Treatment	Full Protection & Security
Indonesia	0.50	0.50	1.00	1.00
Malaysia	0.50	0.50	1.00	1.00
Philippines	0.75	1.00	0.75	0.75
Thailand	0.75	0.50	0.75	0.75
Vietnam	0.75	0.50	1.00	1.00

4.6.1. Methodology: NT and MFN

The maximum score for both NT and MFN standards is a unit -1- which indicates the highest level of protection of an investment's property against the political risk of discriminatory governmental interference. This study analyses the wording used for NT and MFN in the respective clauses that are included under the Investment Chapters and the Trade in Services Chapters of Japan's EPA Treaties. NT and MFN standards appear under separate articles in both Investment and Trade in Services Chapters for each reviewed treaty.

As far as the NT and MFN standard is concerned, the maximum score of 1.00 is given only to those treaties that do not contain any reservation or exception relating to the NT/MFN standard, either in general (for all sectors) or, specifically, restrictions only related to power investments. When a treaty only contains some general reservations that do not impose strict rules (e.g. reservations in the subsidisation policy) and are applied to all sectors without exemption, they are scored at 0.75. On the contrary, when there are stricter reservations which are not only general but also specific to the power industry, introducing many exceptions from the NT/MFN standards, and which are usually included in annexes at the end of the treaties, then these treaties are assessed at a lower score: 0.50. Additionally, in the case of the MFN standard, strict reservations are considered those rules that exempt the MFN provision with regards to investments of third countries that had entered the host country before the treaty

---

[365] C. Schreuer, 'Full Protection and Security', *Journal of International Dispute Settlement* (2010) pp. 16-17; see also: McLachlan, Shore and Weiniger, *International Investment Arbitration*, p. 262.

[366] Table compiled by the author.

entered into force or those rules that allow the host country to take unilateral measures that limit the MFN standard in various aspects.

Finally, it should be mentioned that it is quite unusual in the conventional international law to find a treaty with no NT/MFN-provisions at all, according to which a zero-score (0.00) would be assigned. A detail of the NT and MFN standard's scoring-methodology is provided in the tables below:

Table 10   Standard of National Treatment/Scoring Methodology[367]

No any provision of National Treatment	0.00
Strict & specific reservation on National Treatment	0.50
General exceptions to National Treatment	0.75
National Treatment with no limitation	1.00

Table 11   Standard of Most Favoured Nation/Scoring Methodology[368]

No any provision of Most Favoured Nation	0.00
Strict & specific reservation on MFN treatment	0.50
General exceptions to MFN treatment	0.75
Most Favoured Nation with no limitation	1.00

4.6.2.   Methodology: FET and FPS

The maximum score for both FET and FPS standards is a unit -1- which indicates the highest level of protection of an investment's property against the political risk of governmental interference. This study analyses the wording used for FET and FPS in their respective clauses that are included under the Investment Chapters of Japan's EPA Treaties. Both of these standards are combined under the same clause in all reviewed treaties.

As far as the FET standard is concerned, the maximum score 1.00 is given when the language of the treaty provides the general expression of the FET standard which contains the evolved scope of FET including the crucial protection of investors' legitimate expectations. In connection to FPS standard, the maximum score 1.00 is given when the language of the treaty provides the general expression of FPS standard without limiting tribunals' ability to interpret the standard as independent, protecting investments from both physical and legal damage occurred by the government's interference through the use of force or failure of duty.

However, when the FET and FPS standards appear under the title "Minimum Standard of Treatment" or provide the expression treatment in accordance with international law including a specific note (as analysed in the findings-section),

---

[367] Table compiled by the author.

[368] Table compiled by the author.

then this is considered to be a restriction imposed by the language of the treaty following the reference to the limitations of the customary international approach and therefore such clauses are treated with score 0.75.

Finally, it should be mentioned that it is quite unusual in the conventional international law to find a Treaty with no FET/FPS-provisions at all, according to which a zero-score (0.00) would be given. A detail of the FET and FPS standard's scoring-methodology is provided in the tables below:

Table 12 Standard of Fair & Equitable Treatment/Scoring Methodology[369]

No FET provision	0.00
FET as minimum standard of treatment	0.75
FET as evolved treaty-standard	1.00

Table 13 Standard of Full Protection and Security/Scoring Methodology[370]

No FPS provision	0.00
FPS as minimum standard of treatment	0.75
FPS as evolved treaty-standard	1.00

4.6.3. The findings[371]

Examining each standard and the specific wording, not all of the countries receive the highest score (1.00) in regards to the provision of FET and FPS standards. In the case of the Japan-Philippines EPA (art. 91) and Japan-Thailand EPA (art. 95), there is an additional provision which is not construed by the rest of the EPA treaties.

This additional provision is named an "explanation note" and indicates that: "This article prescribes the international law minimum standard of treatment of aliens as the minimum standard of treatment to be afforded to investments of the other Party." The concept of FET/FPS "does not require treatment in addition to or beyond that which is required by the customary international law minimum standard of treatment of aliens".[372] "A determination that there has been a breach of another provision of this Agreement, or of a separate international agreement, does not *ipso facto* establish that there has been a breach of this Article".[373]

---

[369] Table compiled by the author.

[370] Table compiled by the author.

[371] For a more detailed review of findings, see appendix: "Scoring-Card of Japan's EPAs".

[372] Article 91 (investment chapter) of Japan-Philippines EPA (entry into force: 11 November 2008).

[373] *Ibid.* See also, to the same effect: Article 95 (investment chapter) of Japan-Thailand EPA (entry into force: 1 November 2007).

This additional note has a particular importance because it limits the scope of both FET and FPS standards substantially. It can be interpreted as protection only as much as investors receive in their capacity as aliens under the customary international law minimum standard of protection of aliens. On the contrary, in the case of the Japan's EPAs with Indonesia, Malaysia and the BIT with Vietnam there is no such additional explanatory note. In these EPAs, the FET and FPS standards come under the title of "general treatment". In relation to the FET standard, it is interpreted according to international jurisprudence as investments receiving the extended scope of FET protection including the crucial protection of investors' legitimate expectations. Therefore, the Japan-Philippines and the Japan-Thailand EPAs, excluding the important function of the legitimate expectations from their FET clause, they are assessed as more restrictive and therefore scored less (0.75 each). On the contrary, in the case of Indonesia, Malaysia, and Vietnam, there is no restriction derived by any explanatory note and therefore they receive the highest score (1.00). Accordingly, in the case of the FPS standard, Japan's EPAs with Indonesia, Malaysia and the BIT with Vietnam receive the highest score 1.00 following the same assessment method as in the case of FET standard (*mutatis mutandis*). On the contrary, Japan's EPAs with the Philippines and Thailand adopt restrictions by limiting their scope to the obligation of host states to protect foreign investments from physical damage only. Therefore, such language is considered to be a concrete imposition on tribunals to interpretation of the FPS standard in an expansive approach for the interest of foreign investments.

With regards to NT, all countries except Indonesia and Malaysia receive the same score (0.75). First of all, the reason that no country receives full score is that all of them impose some reservations or exceptions to the NT standard that apply in general to all sectors including the power investments. These reservations are referred in either the EPA-clauses or in annexes. One exception common in all EPAs is that subsidies provided by the Party or its SOEs including grants, government supported loans, guarantees, insurance, and some other incentives that are limited to nationals of the country do not apply in the treaty. In the case of the Japan-Indonesia EPA and the Japan-Malaysia EPA, there are both some general restrictions on the NT standard that address to all sectors (not exclusively to the power sector) and some specific restrictions to the power sector which are responsible for their lower scores compared to the other EPAs (0.50). For example, article 79 (services chapter) and annex 8 of the Japan-Indonesia EPA Treaty, there is an exemption from NT concerning the income tax of non-resident taxpayers if their income derives from an Indonesian source (interest, royalties, dividends, fees from services performed in Indonesia). Additionally, article 64.1 adds more reservations and exceptions to NT on certain activities related to electricity sectors described in Annex 4 such as EPC-construction services, power plant, transmission and distribution of electric power, M&O of electric power instruments, nuclear power plant. Last but not least, there is a general restriction in both of the above EPAs, affecting all foreign investments. They introduce through an "additional note" the possibility to prescribe special formalities in connection with investment activities of investors of the other

Party in their areas, reducing the protective function of the NT standard and increasing the unpredictability of the host state's behaviour.

Finally, with regards to MFN treatment, it is only the Philippines that receive a perfect score (1.00). The Philippines do not retain any reservation or exception about MFN treatment towards Japanese investments in the power sector (art. 76 of the Japan-Philippines EPA). On the contrary, there is a variation of reservations and exceptions for the rest of the countries that score much lower (0.50). Thailand (art. 79) applies MFN only to services that have been conducted after the agreement enters into force and not to previous investments. In other words, if a Japanese power company enters into an investment contract with the Thai Government, it will not be able to receive the more favourable treatment that one foreign company receives if the later conducted its investment before the entry into force of the respective Japan-Thailand EPA. In the case of Vietnam, there is a provision in article (2.2 and 5.3 of the Japan-Vietnam BIT) indicating that exceptional measures might be taken in the future after notifying the other Party (Japan), something that creates ambiguity. Finally, Indonesia and Malaysia also adopt similarly strict measures indicating that MFN treatment may not be accorded in certain issues related to the provision of loans, grants, incentives and other subsidies. Considering that government's credit and guarantees are usually addressed to the infrastructure providers, the above exception influences substantially the foreign investments in the power sector. The Japan-Indonesia EPA (art. 64.1) imposes several restrictions on certain economic activities that are included in Annex 4 of the Treaty in relation to EPC-construction services, power plant, transmission and distribution of electric power, M&O of electric power instrument and nuclear power plant. Finally, the Japan-Malaysia EPA may not accord MFN treatment in the case of privatisation or divestment of assets owned by the Government (annex 4 of the EPA Treaty). Considering that infrastructure industries such as the power sector consist of the core of privatisation policies, the above reservation could lead to discrimination of foreign investors based on their nationality. According to Annex 7 of the Japan-Malaysia EPA (Part II-trade in services), a MFN restriction may be posed in all sectors through any kind of measure and by all modes of supply.

4.7. Chapter's conclusion

This chapter has discussed the four general standards of treatment that are provided by EPAs: the national treatment, the most favoured nation treatment, the fair and equitable treatment, and the full protection and security. The study used as a basis legal-research techniques, analysing the international investment law through the six Japan's investment treaties (five EPAs and one BIT) as well as the related jurisprudence. It mainly focused on the wording (terminology) of the relevant clauses. It emphasised that the real nature of political risk is the unpredictable behaviour of host governments towards foreign investors' interests. In addition to that, it focused on the function and significance of the general standards. This paper addressed the general standards of a treatment's potential in mitigating "non-calculated" risks by emphasising aspects such as awareness of the standards, transparency of regulations, discriminatory and arbitrary discretion, predictability of government's behaviour, investors' legitimate expectations and the protection from physical injury or legal damage by the use of violence.

It is recognised that concluding EPA itself reduces the possibility of political risk occurrence. Thus, this study analyses that EPA to EPA is different even when concluded by the same home country (Japan) and that each EPA offers different levels of protection. In particular, this study asserts that infrastructure sectors such as electricity are more restricted to foreign investments than other industries. Furthermore, comparing the five EPAs, it is found that the power sector is reserved to a different extent with regards to NT, MFN, FET and FPS standards. General standards of treatment do not provide the entire solution to an investor seeking to reduce political risks. However, when a host country promises general principles of favourable treatment to foreign investments through its bilateral EPA, this is conceived as a "symptom" of low possibility of political risk occurrence, thus an additional tool of protection. Finally, the study by using its assessment method (scoring exercise) indicated in a quantitative way that the level of protection against political risk, under a given treaty, depends on its precise wording and the interrelationship of different standards of investment treatment.

5

SPECIFIC STANDARDS OF TREATMENT

5.1.   Introduction

The significance of general standards of treatment is that they can guarantee or assure the protection of foreign investments against discriminatory, unpredictable, unwarranted or arbitrary host state's behaviour. As explained before, the general standards of treatment serve as an important framework including general guidelines and basic concepts of foreign investments protection against potential threats that derive from government's various kind of intervention. However, these guidelines, general in nature, they do not specify the concrete danger or risk against which foreign investments seek protection. Throughout history and empirical evidence of issues related to the protection of aliens and their economic rights, there are specific risks that have seriously threatened foreign investors' interests.

Some of the most known and well observed specific risks consist of dangers of governmental interference with the foreign investor's property rights, and thus they are considered as political risks. Some representative examples are the forced renegotiation or repudiation by the host government of the contract with a foreign investor, the full or partial restriction of the capital repatriation or limitations on the free transfer of funds from the host state, the loss of assets or economic damage due to security threats caused by political conflicts, wars, social unrest, internal and external political instability and the government's breach of foreign investors' contractual rights especially when these rights should be respected under international law, the difficulty in enforcing the legal orders and the absence of an impartial judicial forum. All of the above mentioned dangers are specific risks that foreign investors cannot calculate as they do in the case of commercial risks when they decide to implement a business project in the territory of another country. They are unpredictable risks related directly or indirectly to host government's actions, inactions or its behaviour and therefore, they are considered as political risks.

Apart from the general standards of treatment, host states are also required to provide some specified guarantees to foreign investments that shall be clearly referred to particular clauses in their international investment agreements. These specific guarantees are based in generally recognized principles of international law, such as the rule of law, the fair and non-discriminatory treatment, and the need of transparency and legitimacy of state's actions which are clustered by the general standards of treatment. However, when it comes to particular cases of risks and to the rights and obligations of the treaty-parties, specificity, clarity and accuracy in contractual language are *sine qua non* elements. Especially in terms of mitigating specific political risks, foreign investors seek security and full awareness of host State's obligations. It is highly unlikely for foreign investments to be implemented unless states determine, along to the general standards, specific also standards of treatment such as the free transfer of funds (FTFs), the protection from strife and the umbrella clause, and provide certain guarantees in relation to investor-state international arbitration forum and subrogation capacity. These specific standards and provisions are examined in this chapter by analysing their content and comparing them through six Japanese Treaties' specific clauses (five EPAs and one BIT).

5.2.   The standard of free transfer of funds (FTFs)

5.2.1.   In general

The main goal of every investor is to make profits and, particularly for foreign investors, to be able to remit those profits to their home country or elsewhere. In case a host state directly or indirectly intervenes in the foreign investors' right to repatriate their profits, then the political risk of non-transfer of funds materialises. The protection of the free transfer of funds is an objective of international investment treaties and this section analyses the main characteristics of this objective as well as assessing the degree of protection provided by each of Japan's investment treaties.

5.2.2.   Characteristics

The risk of prohibition of the transfer of funds is as important as the risk of expropriation. Though the foreign investor does not face any danger of losing its ownership rights over the property, by not being able to repatriate the capital after a potential liquidation of its investment, a substantial economic loss could be incurred (similar to the results of creeping expropriation).[374] If an investor cannot allocate freely or promptly its capital from one country to another, following the business opportunities that occur, there is a deprivation of basic economic rights. The economic loss is even more evident when the repatriation problem is connected to the convertibility of the local currency into hard currencies. For this reason, most of the treaties (such as Japan's EPAs) add a provision for the right to transfer funds in a freely usable currency and at the market rate in order to avoid the exchange rate adopted by the central bank of the host state. For example, article 83.2 of the Japan-Malaysia EPA recognises: "Each Country shall allow transfers to be made in a freely usable currency at the market rate of exchange prevailing on the date of the transfer".

However, despite the above provision, it is obvious that, especially in countries with a high inflation risk, when the local currency is devaluated, it is not only about the convertibility problem but mainly about losing large amounts of money after converting local currency to hard currencies. In particular, looking into the infrastructure industries and power project financing practices, the majority of the investments are funded through foreign debt or equity participation. Thus the financing must be repaid out of the project's profits that are made, most of the time, in local currency but should be converted into the agreed hard

---

[374] Glavinis, *International Economic Law*, pp. 656-658.

currency in order to satisfy the project's creditors (financiers) and promoters (shareholders).

5.2.3. Application

The inclusion of the free transfer of funds standard is a common practice for most (if not all) international investment treaties.[375] However, there are some differences in the wording of the FTFs clauses that may affect the degree of the investment's protection.

First of all, there may be a difference in the scope of the payments that are included in the treaty's standard of capital repatriation. There are treaties that follow an "exhaustive" and others an "illustrative" approach in relation to the scope of the fund's repatriation guarantee.[376] The exhaustive approach is considered to be more strictly relating to political risk because it provides a guarantee of capital repatriation only to a list of payments that are contained under the treaty's provision. The issue of funds related to a particular investment can be so broad that an exhaustive list of payments is likely to exclude potential cases and result in a limitation in the degree of protection. Most often, the wording of such an exhaustive approach explicitly states that the contracting parties shall guarantee "the following payments related to investments",[377] and a list of payment categories follows. On the contrary, the illustrative approach uses more flexible language, not restricting the number of payments that can fall under the article's protection by referring to some of them indicatively. It usually comes under the expression that each contracting party shall guarantee "payments relating to investments and in particular of..."[378] followed by a list of examples. All of the reviewed Japanese investment treaties (EPA investment chapters and a BIT with Vietnam) follow the illustrative approach by repeating a similar (to the above: in particular of) wording: "such transfers shall include those of...". For example, the article 83 of the Japan-Malaysia EPA states that: "Each Country shall allow all transfers to be made into and out of that Country freely and without delay in any freely usable currency. Such transfers shall include..." and a list of payments is provided such as different kinds of profits and dividends, capital from the sale or liquidation of the investment, loan payments, remuneration of the investment's personnel, the monetary compensation for an expropriation, or any other payment arising out of a dispute settlement.

However, even if a particular treaty follows the broader approach of illustrating a list of payments, the transfer of funds must be related to an investment covered by the respective treaty in order for the foreign investor to claim the protection of the treaty's guarantee. In other words, "the investor must demonstrate that there is a link or connection between the investment and the funds

---

[375] There are also a large number of national investment codes that contain a repatriation of funds guarantee. This is evident mostly in developing countries which are capital-importing countries and they often provide unilateral guarantees as to the free transfer of funds in order to make their territory more attractive to foreign investments and a business-friendly place.

[376] Rubins and Kinsella, *International Investment*, pp. 242-243.

[377] For example, see article 5 of the Egypt-Kazakhstan BIT (1993), cited in *ibid.*, p. 243.

[378] For example, see article 6 of the Finland-Kazakhstan BIT (1992), cited in *ibid.*

sought to be transferred".[379] Similarly, in the *Continental Casualty v. Argentina* case, the tribunal rejected the claim of the foreign investor for a breach of host state's obligation under the repatriation guarantee because funds held by the claimant in his bank-account did not fall within the "transfers related to an investment" under the respective BIT and highlighted that "not every cross-border movement of funds by an investor would be protected under the transfer provisions of a BIT".[380]

Moreover, even if treaties tend to contain "absolute statements" about the protective scope of the transfer of funds standard, as professor Sornarajah indicates, the provision of such statements is "unrealistic as problems will arise when a contracting party has exchange shortfalls necessitating currency controls".[381] It is a practical problem that an absolute obligation for free transfer of funds cannot be established. That is especially evident during times of financial crisis when, due to extreme balance of payment constraints, the host government may invoke the state of necessity principle and be excluded from the obligation for free repatriation until the situation becomes stable again as in normal times.[382] In other words, it is argued that even if modern investment treaties (such as the Japanese EPAs-investment chapters) contain no explicit exception to the free repatriation of funds, in the case of restricted access to foreign exchange or a balance of payments problem,[383] the investors need to be aware that in time of crises an absolute right of repatriation cannot be feasible. That was the case during the Asian financial crisis in 1997 when some Asian states such as Malaysia imposed currency controls, despite the opposition of the IMF, in order to deal with the serious situation at that time.[384] Accordingly, during the today's global financial crisis, the possibility of states imposing restrictions on the free transfer of funds increases, thus investors need to assume the political risk in alternative ways.[385]

The argument of no absolute right of repatriation could be also based on what treaties provide for the trade in services. The trade in services is an important

---

[379] A. Kolo, 'Transfer of Funds: The Interaction Between the IMF Articles of Agreement and Modern Investment Treaties: A Comparative Law Perspective', in S.W. Schill (ed.), *International Investment Law and Comparative Public Law* (Oxford University Press, New York, 2010) p. 358.

[380] For more detailed review of the international investment jurisprudence on this matter, see Kolo, 'Transfer of Funds', p. 358 n. 51.

[381] Sornarajah, *International Law*, p. 238.

[382] *Ibid.*, p. 239; similarly, Kolo argues that "notwithstanding the absence of such an explicit stipulation on balance-of-payment or national security exceptions in an investment treaty, nonetheless, when faced with such situations, the host state may still be able to restrict capital transfers under the doctrine of necessity in general international law as codified in Article 25 of the International Law Commission's (ILC) Articles on State responsibility"; Kolo, 'Transfer of Funds', pp. 357-358.

[383] In contrast to the wording of the latest agreements, investment treaties that were signed before 2000 contain exceptions to the free repatriation of funds in case of serious balance of payments problem. See: Rubins and Kinsella, *International Investment*, p. 243 n. 253.

[384] Later, the IMF accepted that such measures by the Malaysian government were a "possible solution"; Sornarajah, *International Law*, p. 310.

[385] Some of these ways are analysed in Part II of this book.

area that may affect the overall business in the power sector and, in particular, the operation of power plants and the supply of electricity services into the host state's market which is also related to investment (supply mode 3 of WTO). Therefore, the provisions included in the Trade in Services chapter of the respective EPAs are treated as complementary to what is provided under the Investment chapters. For example, in article 86 of the Japan-Thailand EPA (Chapter 7: Trade in Services), an exception from the right of free transfer of funds is introduced: "In the event of serious balance-of-payments and external difficulties or threat thereof, a Party may adopt or maintain restrictions on trade in services, including on payments or transfers for transactions."

However, the above restrictions are not unconditional. Their application shall always comply with some necessary principles. They shall be applied on a NT and MFN treatment basis, in consistency with IMF agreements, and shall avoid any unnecessary damage to the other Party and be temporary. The inclusion of all the above principles is important for the better protection of foreign investments and, as will be analysed in the findings section below, there are differences in the treaties' wording.

Finally, there are also some other legitimate restrictions to the right of free repatriation according to which a host country may "delay or prevent such transfers" in case of bankruptcy, issues related to the securities regulations, criminal offences and ensuring compliance with orders in adjudicatory proceedings. Such restrictions must be compelled in an "equitable, non-discriminatory, and good-faith application of its laws".[386] Thus investors should be mindful of any other limitations on the repatriation right, such as the prevention of the transfer of equity capital unless one year has passed since the time it entered the host country, or any prior approval that is required by the host state concerning transfers of currency.

5.3. The standard of protection from strife

5.3.1. In general

With regards to the international treaty framework of investment protection against the risk of damages in investment-property due to civil disturbance, disorder or violence, the general standard of full protection and security is not the only treatment that is provided to foreign investors. Especially in the most recent treaties, a specific guarantee is often found that provides remedy, both monetary (compensation) and restitution, in case of damages or losses that investors sustain due to war, civil disturbance, revolution.

The protection from strife standard consists of two important functions. It guarantees foreign investments with, first, a remedy against losses and, second, a provision of national treatment and most favoured nation treatment. It works as a guarantee by providing to foreign investors a compensation or restitution treatment. Foreign investors are more likely to assume political risk due to the explicit inclusion of indemnification obligation by host state. It is generally agreed that the standard of compensation is not a privilege granted only for expropriatory reasons. Even when it is not expressed exclusively by the treaty's

---

[386] For example, Article 67 of Japan-Indonesia EPA (Chapter 5 on Investment).

language, compensation is a recognised remedy that can be applied to any breach of a host state's treaty-based obligation. Thus, in the case of an emergency or crisis, foreign investors are particularly aware of host states' discriminatory tendencies against foreign investment's property and with respect to the protection that host states afford to theirs own investors.[387] Therefore, in most cases, the protection from strife standard emphasises the obligation of a host state to accord to foreign investments treatment no less favourable than that which it accords to its own investors (NT) or to any third-country's investors (MFN).

However, there is much confusion about the connection between the specific standard of protection from strife and the general standard of full protection and security when both of them are included in the provisions of an international investment treaty.

5.3.2. Application

As was noted in Chapter 4 on "General Standards of Treatment", the provision of the FPS standard does not cover all possible injuries that a foreign investor might suffer. First of all, the FPS standard requires from the states a general duty of police power to accord foreign investors protection against damages suffered in case of strife or violence by exercising due diligence. It is obvious that when there is no negligence of the government's FPS duty, then foreign investors cannot claim the host state's liability for any loss suffered due to strife. Moreover, when the FPS standard is limited (by the treaty's language or by the tribunal's interpretation) to the international minimum standard, the scope of protection owed is further diminished. Therefore, with the inclusion of a specific guarantee such as the protection from strife standard, the host state reaffirms its obligation to protect foreign investments in case of damage suffered due to wars or civil disturbance.

However, the standard of compensation that is accorded by the treaty's clause of protection from strife does not establish a right to full compensation.[388] On the contrary to what was analysed in the compensation for expropriation section, there is no requirement to treat investors with the Hull formula under the provisions of the protection against strife standard. Even if some BITs recognise the prompt, adequate and effective requirements of compensation only in case of requisition of or damage to investments suffered by the host state's authorities due to war or civil disturbance, most of the treaties do not contain any specific requirement except that the compensation be effectively realisable and freely convertible. Similarly, Japan's EPAs (investment chapters) recognise the effectiveness of the compensation and they do not grant a right to full compensation (no requirement for adequate compensation). For example, article 103.2 of the Japan-Thailand EPA states the following: "Any payments made pursuant to paragraph 1 shall be effectively realisable, freely convertible and freely transferable in a freely usable currency". The Japan-Vietnam BIT does include the requirement for freely transferable and convertible payment of compensation under the clause of protection against strife (article 10), but it provides it under

---

[387] Salacuse, *Law of Investment Treaties*, p. 336.

[388] *Ibid.*, p. 337.

the general clause for free transfer of funds (article 12.1.e).

Moreover, a right to full compensation cannot be established as most treaties require compensation to be treated in accordance with the NT and MFN treatment. For example, as a result of the NT, "foreign investors will be treated in the same way as are nationals of the host country",[389] which means that in case the host government provides inadequate indemnification to its nationals, it is likely that foreign investors will receive similar or no better treatment than that. Thus, it could be argued that with the MFN treatment, foreign investors could get better treatment than locals. Thus, the purpose of NT or MFN is not to define the amount of compensation but to reaffirm the host state's duty to compensate foreign investors for physical damage caused by armed conflict or civil strife and not any other damage related to regulatory measures.[390] Finally, all of Japan's reviewed EPAs and BIT follow a uniform language in the provision of the protection against strife standard.

5.4. The umbrella-clause standard

5.4.1. In general

As was explained in the beginning of this volume, the reality that investors are not able to "move out" after they have invested in a host country's sectors such as the power industry weakens their bargaining position towards the host government in the event of a later disagreement, conflict or unwarranted interference. Keeping alive governments' commitments in long term power-project investments is not an easy task. This problem of asset specificity or, as Raymond Vernon referred to it, "obsolescing bargains"[391] is related to the decline of the investors' bargaining power after making an investment. Given this situation, the most serious threat that investors need to face is the uncertainty about whether the host state will keep the promises that it made at the time of investment. This threat of uncertainty constitutes the essence of political risk and it is mainly associated with the possibility that the state will annul the contractual agreement that it had entered into with the foreign investor or compel a change in its terms. Therefore, the question is not only about how to strengthen the investor's bargaining position towards host state but also about how to protect the foreign investment's property from particular political risks such as the breach of contracts by the host state.

However, the state contract repudiation does not necessarily mean a breach of international law.[392] Especially when the government interferes in a contract not in its sovereign capacity as regulator but merely as a party to the contract, any breach of the contract does not constitute breach of state obligations under international law. The ICSID Tribunal in the *Noble Ventures* case has indicated as a well-established rule of general international law that "in normal circum-

---

[389] *Ibid.*

[390] Regulatory measures of the host government that cause loss or damage to foreign investment could be covered by the treaty provisions of compensation for regulatory expropriation or breach of FET standard depending on the specific circumstances in each case.

[391] Vernon, *Sovereignty at Bay, passim.*

[392] Salacuse, *Law of Investment Treaties*, p. 273.

stances per se a breach of a contract by the State does not give rise to direct international responsibility on the part of the State"[393] – or, as stated in another case, "a State may breach a treaty without breaching a contract and vice versa".[394]

In general, contractual rights are recognised by the majority of international investment treaties as subject to investment protection, being covered by the extensive definition of investment. Governmental interference with contractual rights could amount to expropriation or breach of the FET standard when the economic value is substantially damaged or when the legitimate expectations are hampered.[395] However, as analysed herein, in order for the investor to protect their rights under the international treaty's provisions, the behaviour of the host state needs to be at least unwarranted regarding specific obligations resulting in certain violations of the general and specific standards of treatment, e.g. FET, FPS, FTFs and others.

Therefore, the most important role of the umbrella clause included in the body of an investment treaty is the acceptance by the host state that, on the one hand, state contracts as well as any other obligation or commitment towards the foreign investors are governed by international law and, on the other hand, a breach of those obligation will result in state responsibility under international law. Foreign investors do not need to prove a breach of any other standard of treatment in order to claim repudiation of the contract, but only to justify the reasons of the state's violation of its contractual (or any other) commitments. This function of the umbrella clause is based on the international law principle *pacta sunt sevanda* and it establishes the so-called internationalisation of contracts.[396] In other words, breach of contract in its internationalised meaning is being assimilated into the breach of treaty.[397]

5.4.2. Application

The provision of an umbrella clause is not a common practice. It would be argued that it is more the exception than the rule in the international investment treaty practice. One reason for the rare provision of the umbrella clause could be the significant exposure of states to several contractual or other commitments with an increased level of obligation under international law. Another reason is the breadth of coverage of such clauses which are not always clear about what type of state-obligations should be covered. There is a divergence in the interpretation of umbrella clauses in both theory and jurisprudence, with the dominant view taking a broader approach towards the host state's liability for a violation of a large category of undertakings from contractual guarantees to some non-legal government representation and promises towards investors.[398]

---

[393] *Noble Ventures Inc. v. Romania*, ICSID Case No ARB/01/11, Award of 12 October 2005.

[394] *Compagnie Générale des Eaux v. Argentine Republic*, ICSID Case No ARB/97/3, Decision on Annulment of 3 July 2002, para. 95.

[395] Walde and Sabahi, 'Compensation', p. 1090 n. 172.

[396] McLachlan, Shore and Weiniger, *International Investment Arbitration*, pp. 109-117.

[397] See *Noble Ventures Inc. v. Romania*, ICSID Case No ARB/01/11, Award of 12 October 2005, para. 54, cited in Salacuse, *Law of Investment Treaties*, p. 274 n. 8.

[398] Rubins and Kinsella, *International Investment*, pp. 237-240.

In addition, the wordings of umbrella clauses that are found in investment treaties are not uniform. There is a variety in the formulation of umbrella clauses that creates problems in the interpretation of their meaning as well as in their effect on the protection of foreign investments. One of the wordings used by investment treaties in their umbrella clause that is believed to offer the maximum protection for the foreign investor's interests is the following: "Each Contracting Party shall observe any obligations it has entered into with an Investor or an Investment of an Investor of a Contracting Party".[399]

In spite of the divergence in the language used by international treaties, the existence of an umbrella clause increases significantly the degree of a foreign investment's protection against political risk. The intention of the umbrella clause is to create an international obligation on host governments to respect obligations they have undertaken towards investors of the home country.[400] Despite the fact that contractual or any other obligations that host state has made remain subject to the law they were made under (usually most state contracts are governed by the host state's law), the failure to respect such commitments will not only result in state liability under international law but will also give to investors the opportunity to select their preferred dispute resolution forum, between the one provided under the contract with the state and the dispute mechanisms provided by the respective international treaty.[401]

Finally, besides the problem in the different formulations of the umbrella clause, there is also a theoretical debate about whether government must be directly involved in the contracts or other agreements with the specific investment or whether quasi-governmental authorities such as SOEs can also create obligations covered under the treaty's umbrella clause by referring to international law. This issue is significant in relation to the power sector as, on many occasions, the foreign investor enters into an agreement not with the central government but with a state enterprise that operates and sometimes regulates the electricity industry. However, no matter how direct the connection between government and its enterprises (electrical and power utilities) is, when these utilities act in the state's sovereign capacity (i.e. regulate and operate the industry), then contractual obligations undertaken towards a specific foreign investment within formal agreements such as concessions or licences are also binding on the host government and any breach by the SOE constitutes state liability under international law.

5.5. The investor-state arbitration and the subrogation clause

5.5.1. In general

The final indicator concerns the applicability of an impartial dispute resolution comparable to an international adjudication. The general and specific standards of treatment that are guaranteed by the host state to foreign investors or to their investments would be pointless if there were not any appropriate

---

[399] Article 10.1 of the Energy Charter Treaty.

[400] R. Dolzer and M. Stevens, *Bilateral Investment Treaties*, International Centre for Settlement of Investment Disputes (Martinus Nijhoff Publishers, The Hague, 1995) p. 81.

[401] Salacuse, *Law of Investment Treaties*, p. 275.

dispute resolution systems to secure their application and implementation. In particular, the resolution of disputes occurring between states and foreign investors and the protection of investors' interests in case a violation of the treaty standards is established are the most important functions of international investment arbitration that results in the deterrence of host governments' unwarranted interference.[402] If a host state neglects or violates its international obligations derived from the standards of treatment clauses, its state responsibility can be established according to international law before the agreed arbitration forum. As was explained previously, the combined effect of various standards of treatment and dispute resolution mechanisms establishes the "rescue" or deterrence function of international treaties.

Thus, international arbitration is not the only method of dealing with disputes. Foreign investors can seek resolution of their disputes with host states through the domestic courts of the host country, diplomatic protection by their home countries as well as through direct negotiations with the host government.[403] The international arbitration method is certainly not the most preferred way for investors to achieve a settlement agreement with the host government.[404] More, looking into the Japanese or the Asian context in general, aggressive legalism could be seen as inappropriate and opposite to the amicable solutions and mediation-style approach. However, it is stated that the treaty-based mechanisms for resolving investment disputes are "the ultimate guarantee of protection for foreign investors"[405] which could be seen as a possible solution even in the context of the Japanese approach changing towards a more legally based framework of investment-protection.[406]

Within the international treaties' system, there are four independent methods for resolving disputes: consultation or negotiation between the states party to the treaty, interstate arbitration, consultation or negotiation between the host state and the covered investors and finally, investor-state arbitration.[407] This study adopts several criteria that are important elements for the effectiveness of the dispute resolution forum. However, it focuses on treaty-based dispute resolution, and in particular, on the most important method, investor-state

---

[402] Salacuse argues that dispute resolution mechanisms play a double role: "First, they are means for resolving disputes and securing the payment of compensation to injured investors. Second, such enforcement mechanisms deter states from disregarding their treaty commitments to other investors". *Ibid.*, p. 354.

[403] *Ibid.*, p. 357.

[404] In infrastructure projects it has been observed that most of the disputes between investors and host states usually result in renegotiations: J.L. Guasch, *Granting and Renegotiating Infrastructure Concessions: Doing it Right,* World Bank Institute Development Studies (World Bank, Washington, DC, 2004). Moreover, Salacuse states that 30% of ICSID cases as well as two thirds of ICC cases have been settled through negotiations rather than binding awards by arbitral tribunals; Salacuse, *Law of Investment Treaties*, p. 364.

[405] UNCTAD, *Bilateral Investment Treaties in the Mid-1990s*, p. 87.

[406] J. Nakagawa, 'No More Negotiated Deals? Settlement of Trade and Investment Disputes in East Asia', *Journal of International Economic Law* 10:4 (2007) pp. 840-841 and p. 863; see also: S.M. Pekkanen, *Japan's Aggressive Legalism: Law and Foreign Trade Politics Beyond the WTO* (Stanford University Press, Stanford, 2008) pp. 269 and 296.

[407] Salacuse, *Law of Investment Treaties*, p. 359.

international arbitration. Firstly, international investment treaties in most cases include a neutral dispute resolution forum that home states and their investors can utilise.[408] International investment arbitration offers states and investors an effective and impartial way to protect their interests and satisfy their claims by providing remedies such as adequate compensation or, in rare cases, restitution.

It is obvious that foreign investors would not feel secure about the ability of local courts to be completely neutral in resolving disputes between foreign investments and the host government. This is especially evident in developing countries where the rule of law and the independence of judiciary is at question. Moreover, with regards to infrastructure projects where social and economic interests are involved, and where host government is itself a party to the dispute with the foreign investor, it is stated that "the local judiciary may not always be relied upon as being independent from the political power".[409]

This study treats the investor-state arbitration mechanism as the most fundamental provision of international treaties with respect to the effective mitigation of political risk. Such a mechanism of dispute resolution provides to foreign investors "the right to pursue claims against foreign state in direct arbitration"[410] as they do not need to rely on their home countries through the state-to-state arbitration system. This capacity of foreign investors to initiate proceedings by themselves constitutes the "highest level" of foreign investment protection entitled by international investment treaties.[411] Moreover, by avoiding the home country's involvement in the private investor's dispute with the host government, it "depoliticises" the process as the dispute does not affect the countries' international relations.[412] Interstate arbitration has a number of implications that foreign investors would prefer to avoid. Some of the most crucial implications consist of the priority that home countries give to their national interests compared to private business interests, especially when they have established close political, diplomatic and economic relations with the offending host state. Such an implication could even result in the refusal of the home country to take any international action when "such an action would damage valuable relations with the host country".[413] In addition, in an interstate method of international investment arbitration, the investor is considered to be an outside-the-legal-process party, "with no control over the case, no formal role in the interstate proceeding, and no voice in decisions with respect to litigation strategy, settle-

---

[408] This depends on the provision of the arbitration clause: State-to-State or State-to-Investor arbitration forum.

[409] Sacerdoti, 'Source and Evolution', Section B, p. 12.

[410] *Ibid.*, Section B, p. 14.

[411] Sornarajah, *International Law*, p. 250.

[412] Ibrahim Shihata, former Vice-President and General Counsel of the World Bank and former Secretary-General of ICSID, drew attention to the depoliticisation of foreign investment disputes; I. Shihata, 'Towards a Depoliticisation of Foreign Investment Disputes: The Roles of ICSID and MIGA', *ICSID Review–Foreign Investment Law Journal* 1 (1986) p. 1, cited in Sornarajah, *International Law*, p. 250.

[413] Salacuse, *Law of Investment Treaties*, p. 373.

ment or abandonment of the claim".[414] These constraints faced in the state-to-state arbitration mechanisms can be efficiently avoided through the direct involvement of private parties in dispute resolution with the offending host state that is provided by investor-state international arbitration.

5.5.2. Application

An investor-state arbitration mechanism is provided by nearly all modern international investment treaties.[415] However, there are still treaties that are exceptions to this trend. Moreover, even when treaties include investor-state arbitration there are other exceptions that can significantly restrict the scope of foreign investment protection. Such strict provisions consist of the requirement that the foreign investor pursue his claim before an international tribunal only after he exhaust local remedies before the domestic courts. Other restrictions consist of treaties allowing investor-state arbitration only for disputes related to specific international standards' violations, excluding other types of complaints.[416]

In particular, with regards to the local remedies exhaustion requirement, Sornarajah argues that this duty exists even if there is a "provision for the overseas arbitration of the dispute" and even if "most of the treaties are silent on this issue"[417]. However, regarding the exhaustion of local remedies requirement, he distinguishes between disputes that are based on a treaty violation and those that have arisen from a violation of the contact between the foreign investor and the host state. In the prior situation, the foreign investor can directly address his claim before the agreed international tribunal without being required to resort to local remedies. However, the same does not occur if the dispute is concerning a violation of a contract. This, according to Sornarajah, is because "the contract and the treaty operate in two distinct realms, the first in national law and the second in treaty law".[418]

Moreover, the wording in each clause may differ from treaty to treaty and special attention must be taken with regards to the extent of the commitment created for the host state. Broches examined several treaties' international arbitration clauses with reference to ICSID jurisdiction and he was among the first scholars who identified the existence of four different types of arbitration provisions that constitute a different degree of foreign investment protection.[419] The difference among these types is based on the degree of consent given by the host state with regards to the jurisdiction created for an international arbitration

---

[414] *Ibid.*, p. 374.

[415] *Ibid.*, p. 362.

[416] Such exceptions are examined by the empirical analysis of Japan's investment treaties in the Findings section of this chapter.

[417] Sornarajah, *International Law*, p. 254.

[418] Sornarajah states that if the automatic right to arbitration is included in an international treaty then "the state should subject the dispute to arbitration"; *ibid.*, p. 255.

[419] A. Broches, 'Bilateral Investment Treaties and Arbitration of Investment Disputes', in J. Schulsz and J.A. van den Berg (eds.), *The Art of Arbitration: Liber Amicorum Pieter Sanders* (Kluwer, Deventer, 1982), cited in Sornarajah, *International Law*, p. 251.

as a dispute resolution mechanism. The first three types of clauses do not amount to consent to arbitrate. Foreign investors do not obtain a directly enforceable right to arbitrate before an international arbitration forum except under Broches' fourth type of arbitration clause. Thus, each type of arbitration clause constitutes different implications related to the international jurisdiction created, and therefore, it is necessary to examine the precise wording of each type of arbitration-clause. These types of arbitration clauses, along with other criteria, are incorporated into the assessment methodology of this volume as explained in the methodology section of this chapter.

Apart from Broches' categorisation of restrictions related to the consent to arbitration right, there are also some other implications which need to be examined. These implications are also related to the right to arbitration, thus they are procedural in nature. It is about the "conditions precedent to invoking investor-state arbitration", requiring the investors to first try resolving their disputes "amicably" through direct negotiation and conciliation with the host state.[420] Such a requirement should be treated as a non-actual restriction on the investor's right to arbitration and with no relevance to the issue of the host state's consent as examined above. However, when the respective treaty's clause does not specify a time limit for such negotiations it can then be argued that "delaying tactics" by the host government's agencies would impose serious constraints on an appropriate utilisation of an investor-state arbitration right.[421] Therefore, this work argues that for clauses that do not contain a specified period of negotiation or conciliation between the parties, the restriction imposed on the foreign investor's right to arbitration can be considered equal to those treaty clauses that do not include any investor-state arbitration at all. Nevertheless, most of the treaties specify a period of six months which is a necessary precondition to arbitration. Whether the negotiation results in a dispute settlement or not is not a requirement set by treaties, and therefore, investors are free to proceed after the expiration of the negotiation period to the arbitration.

Finally, apart from the provision of a direct right to an investor-state arbitration mechanism, modern investment treaties also include an additional provision that safeguards the interests of home states: the subrogation clause. This clause either comes under the arbitration clause or, most often, as a stand-alone article, and it is related to political risk insurance coverage that is provided by the home country's agencies to foreign investment implemented in the territory of the host countries.[422] According to the subrogation clause, when the home country satisfies the claims of the investor for insurance payment due to a damage suffered by the host state's behaviour, it can then substitute for the investor in its claims against the host country. This function of substitution of the subrogation clause is significant in mitigating political risk. It is stated that "this substitution has a deterrent effect on the host state as it would be loath to tangle

---

[420] Salacuse, *Law of Investment Treaties*, p. 386.

[421] *Ibid.*

[422] McLachlan, Shore and Weiniger, *International Investment Arbitration*, pp. 32-33.

directly with a powerful home state".[423] In particular, as Japanese overseas investments in the power sector of host countries are in their majority covered by PRI policies (usually offered by NEXI),[424] the inclusion of a subrogation clause in Japan's investment treaties can enhance substantially the degree of Japanese investments' protection through the clause's deterrence function.

However, even if most treaties contain a subrogation clause, the wording of such clauses may create uncertainty when their provision is vague or excludes certain investor's rights from subrogation. For example, it may be possible that subrogation to compensation rights may be limited to compensation from expropriation, excluding other risks such as civil strife or non-transferability of funds. Moreover, another implication of such a clause is that its function implies that it is more a political tool for use between sovereign states than a legal tool. As referred to in state-to-state arbitration, it is doubtful whether a home country would utilise such a clause when the betterment of the international relations with the particular host country is a national priority.[425] It is therefore argued that "subrogation acts as subtle threat, but it will not be put to extreme use".[426]

5.6. Assessment of specific standards of treatment-scoring

In order to assess the effectiveness of specific standards of treatment in managing political risk, this study analyses the provisions related to the standard of free transfer of funds, protection from strife, umbrella clause, investor-state arbitration, subrogation and it attempts to measure them adopting the following methodology.

The results of the assessment are shown in Table 14.

Table 14 Results of Assessment: Specific Standards of Treatment[427]

ASEAN-5	Indonesia	Malaysia	Philippines	Thailand	Vietnam
Free Transfer Fund (FTFs)	0.80	0.90	0.70	0.90	0.80
Protection from Strife & compensation	1.00	1.00	0.50	1.00	1.00
Umbrella Clause	0.00	0.00	0.00	0.75	0.00
Investor-state Arbitration	1.00	0.60	0.25	0.60	0.75
Subrogation	1.00	1.00	1.00	1.00	0.75

---

[423] Sornarajah, *International Law*, p. 257.

[424] PRI policy is analysed in Chapter 6, to follow.

[425] Sornarajah, *International Law*, p. 257. This scholar also questions the use of subrogation by stating that "the prejudice it would cause to the diplomatic relations between the two states deters resort to such extreme measures".

[426] *Ibid.*

[427] Table compiled by the author.

5.6.1. Methodology: The standard of free transfer of funds

The maximum score for the FTFs standard is a unit -1- which indicates the highest level of protection against political risk of restrictions on capital repatriation. This study analyses the relevant provision of free transfer of funds from the respective treaties' Trade in Services and Investment chapters. Both of these chapters are important for the overall assessment of investors' rights to capital repatriation. In particular, as mentioned above, there is no absolute right of free transfer of funds. It is acceptable practice that some restrictions are legitimate. However, when the restrictions are imposed based on balance of payments problem and external financial difficulties or any other threat, there are certain principles that shall be compelled. If these principles are recognised by the treaties' clauses, then they are treated with the maximum score: 1.00. If the wording of a treaty's clause excludes or does not invoke one of the principles, especially those relating to NT or MFN treatment, then a 0.90 score is given. If there is an exclusion of more than one principle (usually both NT and MFN) that should apply in the above restriction then a score of 0.80 is given. Additionally, the restriction of free transfer of rights, as previously analysed, can be justified on the basis of some other general cases. However, when a treaty includes some further reservations or excess restrictions such as prevention of equity capital's transfer and prior approval for the transfer of currency, then these restrictions are scored with a lower score: 0.70. Finally, when a treaty selects the exhaustive approach, listing the category of payments that should be protected with the FTF right, or when there is no clear provision of a freely convertible currency at the market rate of exchange prevailing on the date of transfer, then the respective clause is scored with 0.50. It should be mentioned that it is quite unusual in the conventional international law to find a treaty with no FTF-provision at all, according to which a zero-score (0.00) would be given. A detail of the FTFs standard's scoring-methodology is provided in the table below.

Table 15   Standard of Free Transfer of Funds/Scoring Methodology[428]

No FTFs provision	0.00
Exhaustive approach on FTF-payments & non-freely-convertible currency	0.50
Excess restrictions on FTFs right	0.70
Restriction on FTFs without application of NT & MFN standards	0.80
Restriction on FTFs by ensuring only one of NT/MFN standards	0.90
No restriction on FTFs unless complying with legitimate requirements	1.00

---

[428] Table compiled by the author.

5.6.2. The findings: The standard of free transfer of funds[429]

Analysing the six (including the Japan-Vietnam BIT) treaties between Japan and Indonesia, Malaysia, Philippines, Thailand and Vietnam, the study has found some differences in the wording of the "Payments and Transfer" (Trade in Services chapter) and "Transfers" (Investment chapter) clauses.

More specifically, all of them include (as was expected) transfer of funds provisions in both trade in services and investment chapters (in the Japan-Vietnam case a BIT), and they adopt the less strict, illustrative approach. However, in the case of restrictions based on the balance of payments problem, none of them is scored with maximum score (1.00). Japan's EPAs with Malaysia and Thailand receive higher score compared to the rest (0.90).

In the case of the Japan-Thailand EPA, article 85.1 recognises the general principle of unlimited right of free transfer of funds in trade in services unless there are restrictions to safeguard balance of payments problem (article 86). Thus, the Japan-Thailand EPA is the only Treaty that fulfils all the necessary requirements in order for restrictions to be applied. In particular, article 86.2 recognises that the restrictions shall be applied (a) on a NT basis, (b) MFN basis, (c) it shall be consistent with IMF articles, (d) shall avoid any unnecessary damage to the other Party, (e) shall not exceed the circumstance of the balance of payment problem and, finally, (f) shall be temporary measures and be phased out progressively when the situation improves. Moreover, article 86.5 provides that when a Party applies any restriction on the FTFs, it should start consultations with the other promptly in order to review the restrictions adopted. None of Japan's other treaties contains such a requirement that restrictions need to apply on a NT basis, and this omission affects their scoring as is explained below. Furthermore, none of the treaties repeats anything similar to the Japan-Thailand EPA's provision of article 86.5 about consultation. They merely mention that after a restriction imposed, the other Party should be notified promptly. However, the later provision of special consultations, even if it improves the position of the other Party in relation to getting some preparation for the FTF restrictions, is not measured in the study's overall political risk assessment.

When it comes to the protection of transfers under the Investment chapter, article 104.1 of the Japan-Thailand EPA assures that transfers relating to investments should be "made freely and in a freely usable currency and without delay", adopting the illustrative approach. Article 104.2 adds that the currency should be freely convertible "at the market rate of exchange prevailing on the date of the transfer". This wording is adopted by all the EPAs' investment chapters. In case of delay or prevention of transfers, article 104.3 refers to the classic circumstances in which such restrictions should be allowed, such as bankruptcy, securities trading, criminal matters and ensuring compliance with judicial orders "through the equitable, non-discriminatory and good-faith application of its laws relating to" the above circumstances. These circumstances are accepted in theory as being legitimate reasons for imposing restrictions to the free transfer of funds. However, when more cases are added by treaties, they are treated as one more restriction (see the case of the Japan-Philippines below).

---

[429] For detailed review of the findings, see appendix: "Scoring-Card of Japan's EPAs".

There is one requirement that only the Japan-Malaysia EPA contains. Each country shall accord to the transfers relating to investment "treatment no less favourable than that accorded to the transfer originating from investments made by investors of any third State".[430] This is an extra requirement that is not found in any other treaty, asking that MFN treatment should be provided to foreign investors in issues related to the transfer of funds. Even if we can argue that MFN treatment can be provided to investments by using the general clause for transfer of payments included in the "trade in services" chapter, the study takes into consideration what is explicitly included in the wording of each clause. Therefore, omission of such MFN provision is considered as a restriction of the particular EPA. In conclusion, even though Japan-Thailand EPA includes all the necessary conditions in the case of transfer relating to trade in services, the non-inclusion of MFN treatment for transfers relating to investment results in a restricted provision, and a score of 0.90.

In the case of the Japan-Malaysia EPA, article 107 provides the same provision as the Japan-Thailand EPA in relation to transfers connected to trade in services. However, as mentioned above, there is no reference to the requirement of NT that should be applied in case of restrictions to safeguard the balance of payments (art. 108.2). Despite that difference, the study assesses the Japan-Malaysia EPA with the same score 0.90 as Japan-Thailand because in the protection of transfers under its Investment chapter, article 83.3 is the only one among the reviewed treaties that provides that the MFN treatment shall be accorded as the FTFs right.

On the contrary, in Japan's EPAs with Indonesia and Vietnam (including the Japan-Vietnam BIT), there are omissions regarding the right of FTFs in both trade in services and investment chapters. In relation to trade in services, in article 88.2 of the Japan-Indonesia EPA and article 69.2 of the Japan-Vietnam EPA there is no provision of NT when restrictions to safeguard the balance of payments occur. In addition, article 69.1 of Japan-Vietnam EPA recognises the fact that Vietnam being in the process of economic development as one more reason to impose restrictions on the transfer of funds. Thus, this study treats this additional restriction as a legitimate reason being already included in the general wording of this clause: "in the event of serious balance-of-payments and external financial difficulties or threat". With regards to the protection of investments, article 67.2 of Japan-Indonesia EPA and article 12 of Japan-Vietnam BIT do not contain MFN treatment in relation to the right to the FTFs. Because of these omissions in the protection of transfers relating to trade in services and investment, both of Japan's treaties with Indonesia and Vietnam are scored more strictly: 0.80.

Finally, the Japan-Philippines EPA receives the lowest score among the reviewed treaties: 0.70. Besides the fact that this Treaty does not refer to the NT requirement relating to restrictions that safeguard the balance of payments (trade in services-art. 69.1) and to the MFN treatment relating to FTFs right (investment-art. 97) as in the above cases of Indonesia and Vietnam, the Japan-Philippines EPA adds one more restriction. Article 97.3, apart from the legitimate,

---

[430] Article 83.3 of Japan-Malaysia EPA (Chapter 7: Investment).

classic cases that justify delay or prevention of FTFs, adds one more case: "The registration, reportorial and prior approval requirement concerning transfers of currency or other monetary instruments". In a specific note, the Treaty explains that such a requirement of prior approval applies only to short-term foreign currency loans with maturity of up to one year. This study treats this additional case as an extra-restriction on the right to FTFs as it extends the capacity of the host state to delay or prevent a transfer related to investment.

5.6.3. Methodology: The standard of protection from strife

The maximum score for the protection from strife standard is a unit -1- which indicates the highest level of protection against political risk of a host state's interference with an investor's property in case of damage suffered due to armed conflict or civil strife. When the treaty does not make clear provision of non-freely-convertible non-transferable payments of compensation it is considered to be a limitation on the effectiveness requirement of the compensation and therefore it is scored with 0.75. In addition, when a treaty omits the requirement for either NT or MFN treatment in relation to the standard of compensation accorded to foreign investments, it is considered to be a stricter limitation and therefore scored with 0.50. It should be mentioned here that there is a divergence in theory about the importance of NT and MFN inclusion under the clause of protection against strife. It is argued that whether there is NT/MFN or not has no importance because foreign investors are covered in any case by the general standards of treatment requiring NT and MFN. However, this study asserts that NT and MFN provisions under this article are additional to the general standards requirement because they apply in times of war and civil disturbance. In other words, it is believed that during an emergency, without the NT or MFN provision, host states could exempt themselves from these requirements by referring to the exceptional circumstances or specific national interests. Finally, in the very rare case of no any provision of protection against strife, the treaty is scored with -0-. Further detail on the protection against strife standard's scoring methodology is provided in Table 16.

Table 16   Standard of Protection from Strife/Scoring Methodology[431]

No protection from strife (no any remedy)	0.00
No provision of NT or MFN with regards to compensation-payments	0.50
Non-freely-convertible & transferable payment of compensation	0.75
No any restriction	1.00

---

[431] Table compiled by the author.

5.6.4. The findings: The standard of protection from strife[432]

After the analysis of Japan's EPAs and BIT agreements, this study has found that all except one grants to their foreign investments protection against strife without any restriction in connection with the NT, MFN treatment or with regards to the free transferability and convertibility requirement of the compensation payments. Therefore, Japan's EPAs with Indonesia, Malaysia, Thailand and the BIT with Vietnam are given the maximum score of 1.00.

On the contrary, the Japan-Philippines EPA contains a restriction about the requirement of NT that should be accorded to Japanese investors with regards to the treatment of restitution, indemnification, compensation or any other settlement (article 96 of Japan-Philippines EPA). Therefore, the Japan-Philippines EPA receives the score 0.50.

5.6.5. Methodology: The umbrella-clause standard

The maximum score for the umbrella clause is a unit -1- which indicates the highest level of protection against political risk of a host state's interference with an investor's economic interests in case of damage suffered due to breach of contracts or any other type of agreement (broad definition of covered obligations). In case the language of the investment treaty is vague or includes restrictions by limiting the scope of the state-to-investors obligations that could be covered by the umbrella clause, the relevant treaty is scored with 0.75. In the most frequent situation, according to which there is not any umbrella clause provision, the treaty is scored with -0- . A detail of the protection against breach of contracts scoring methodology is provided in Table 17.

Table 17   Standard of Umbrella Clause/Scoring Methodology[433]

No provision of umbrella clause	0.00
Limitations on umbrella clause	0.75
Broad approach covering multiple cases	1.00

5.6.6. The findings: The umbrella-clause standard[434]

After analysis of Japan's EPAs and the BIT agreements, this study has found that only one includes an umbrella clause provision, that being the Japan-Thailand EPA. However, it is assessed that the relevant provision imposes some restrictions. In particular, article 100 of the Japan-Thailand EPA under the title "Acquired Treatment" states:

> "Each Party shall maintain, in accordance with its laws and regulations, the level of treatment which has been accorded to investors

---

[432] For further review of the findings, see appendix: "Scoring-Card of Japan's EPAs".

[433] Table compiled by the author.

[434] For further review of the findings, see appendix: "Scoring-Card of Japan's EPAs".

of the other Party and their investments with respect to investment activities."

The specification in article 100 that the contracting states are to respect their obligations connected to the level of treatment subject to "its laws and regulations" is considered to be a restriction on the umbrella clause meaning that the state's obligations are dependent on host country law (in this case on Thai law if Thailand is the host state of the Japanese investments). For this reason, the Japan-Thailand EPA is scored with 0.75. On the contrary, Japan's EPAs with Indonesia, Malaysia, Philippines and the BIT with Vietnam do not contain any relevant umbrella clause provision and therefore they are assessed with the minimum score -0-.

5.6.7. Methodology: Investor-state arbitration and subrogation clause

As discussed above, this work focuses on the provision of investor-state arbitration, considering such mechanism as the most influential with regards to the mitigation of political risk. Therefore, the present assessment exercise gives the lowest score, zero -0-, when the respective treaty does not include a state-investor arbitration process. Even if the majority of treaties include a dispute resolution article, it is possible that some of them may not provide for the particular resolution mechanism of investor-state arbitration. In addition, a low score (0.10) is given when treaty clauses require foreign investors to exhaust local remedies before activating the international arbitration procedure or to first resolve their disputes through negotiations and conciliations with no time limits. As analysed before, both requirements may result in long periods of dispute resolution as well as a large degree of uncertainty related to the host country's interference with the judicial procedures.

This volume also examines the various types of investor-arbitration clauses in relation to the degree of consent given by host states according to Broches' study, but also in relation to other exceptions which are found in treaty clauses. In particular, the first type of arbitration clause identified by Broches' study consists of the strictest requirement, scored with 0.25. It construes that the dispute "shall, upon, agreement by both parties, be submitted for arbitration by the Centre".[435] In such a wording, it is clear than no consent to arbitration is given by the host state. The second type requires that "sympathetic consideration to a request [for] conciliation or arbitration by the Centre" shall be given by the host state. This wording, according to Broches, may establish an "obligation not to withhold consent unreasonably", though it still does not constitute consent to arbitration, and therefore it is scored with 0.50.[436]

Between the second and third type of Broches category, there is one exception in the wording of several dispute resolution clauses which this study considers to be a stricter requirement: the exclusion of NT disputes or investments that do not comply with national laws from international arbitration. Such exclusions significantly limit the scope of arbitration, and therefore it is scored with 0.60.

---

[435] Broches, 'Bilateral Investment Treaties', cited in Sornarajah, *International Law*, p. 251.

[436] *Ibid.*

Following this category, the third type of Broche clause requires from the host state a higher degree of obligation "to assent to any demand on the part of the national to submit for conciliation or arbitration any dispute arising from the investment",[437] though a direct right to arbitration is still not established, so this clause is scored with 0.75. Only the fourth type of clause amounts to a full right to arbitration according to which it is explicitly stated that each party consents to submit to the ICSID tribunal for the settlement of disputes by means of arbitration or conciliation; it receives the maximum score -1-.

Finally, as far as the subrogation clause is concerned, if there is no subrogation provision, a case which is rather rare in modern investment treaties, a score of zero (0.00) would be given. In case a specific compensation right for damage due to risks such as expropriation, civil strife or non-transferability of funds is excluded from the subrogation clause, then a score 0.75 would be given, and eventually, if none of the above restrictions exist, a maximum score -1- would be given to the treaty-clause.

Table 18   Investor-State Arbitration/Scoring Methodology[438]

No provision of investor-state arbitration	0.00
Need to exhaust local remedies or negotiation/conciliation is required prior to arbitration without time limits	0.10
Dispute shall "upon agreement by both parties be submitted for arbitration" (Broches-1)	0.25
"Sympathetic consideration to a request for conciliation/arbitration" is required (Broches-2)	0.50
Exclusion of NT disputes or investments that not comply with national laws from the arbitration right	0.60
Host state required to "assent to any demand on the part of the national to submit for conciliation/arbitration any dispute arising from the investment" (Broches-3)	0.75
Directly jurisdiction to an international arbitration (binding clause, Broches-4)	1.00

Table 19   Subrogation Clause/Scoring Methodology[439]

No subrogation clause	0.00
Compensation-right for damage due to specific risk is excluded	0.75
Not any restriction	1.00

---

[437] *Ibid.*

[438] Table compiled by the author.

[439] Table compiled by the author.

5.6.8. The findings: Investor-state arbitration and subrogation clause

Examining the bilateral investment agreements between Japan and the five Asian countries, several differences are found with regards to the content of treaty clauses as well as in relation to each article's wording (dispute resolution clauses included in investment chapters of the respective treaties). All of the reviewed treaties include an investor-arbitration mechanism. However, the most significant finding is that several of them impose restrictions with regards to the consent of host states to direct arbitration as well as two of the treaties add certain exclusions from the right to investor-state arbitration.

Starting from the last observation (exclusions from arbitration right), there are two treaties that include several exclusions. The Japan-Malaysia EPA, in article 85.17, excludes from the investor-state arbitration provision disputes that arise on issues based on national treatment and on prohibition to performance requirements. Moreover, in the following paragraph, article 85.18 (b) also excludes investments that have not been made in compliance of laws, regulations and national policies of Malaysia. In a specific additional note, it defines investments that are not made in compliance with Malaysian laws by specifying those that have not been "endorsed by the Cabinet and announced and made publicly available in a written form by the Government of Malaysia". An additional restriction to the arbitration right is considered to be article 85.12 which requires that the parties hold their arbitration "in the disputing Country" (unless agreed otherwise). Such kinds of requirements are not included in any of the other examined treaties (except the Japan-Thailand EPA) and for this reason this study scores the Japan-Malaysia EPA with 0.60. Finally, the Japan-Malaysia EPA provides to the investor the right to choose an international arbitration forum from three alternatives: Kuala Lumpur Regional Centre for Arbitration, ICSID, and UNCITRAL or any other agreed centre. It also sets a time limitation to the consultation period (5 months–article 85.4). Similar to the Japan-Malaysia EPA, the Japan-Thailand EPA in article 106.15 (a), (b), (c), excludes from the investor-arbitration provision disputes that arose prior to the entry into force of this Agreement or disputes related to issues based on performance requirements or "with respect to measures other than those relating to the management, conduct, operation, maintenance, use, enjoyment, and sale or other disposition of investments". This study assesses such exceptions as strict requirements that do not exist in other treaties and therefore, as with the Japan-Malaysia EPA, gives it a score of 0.60. Other than these restrictions, the Japan-Thailand EPA provides the right to investor to choose an international arbitration forum from either ICSID or UNCITRAL rules. The Japan-Thailand EPA does not require the parties to settle an arbitration procedure within either country, thus the country of the arbitration "shall be held in a country that is a party" to the New York Convention on the Recognition and Enforcement of Foreign Arbitral Awards". It also sets a time limitation on the consultation period (6 months–article 85.4).

As for the three remaining treaties, the restrictions that are found by this study are related to the issue of the degree of consent given by the host state to the investor-state arbitration right. The Japan-Philippines EPA is considered to be the strictest among all treaties due to the low consent of the Philippines to Japanese investors' right to investor-state arbitration. In particular, article 107.2

states that: "In the absence of the mechanism for the settlement of an investment dispute between a Party and an investor of the other Party, the resort to international conciliation or arbitration tribunal is subject to mutual consent of the parties to the dispute. This means that the disputing Party may, at its option or discretion, grant or deny its consent in respect of each particular investment dispute and that, in the absence of the express written consent of the disputing Party, an international conciliation or arbitration tribunal shall have no jurisdiction over the investment dispute involved". Therefore, according to the Broches' study, such a wording is the strictest requirement that can be found. It means that the dispute "shall, upon, agreement by both parties, be submitted for arbitration".[440] The Japan-Philippines article, by requiring "mutual consent", is clear that no consent to arbitration has been given by the host state (the Philippines) and therefore, this study scores it with the score 0.25.

In the case of the Japan-Vietnam treaties, their EPA recognises only a state-to-state arbitration forum (articles 116-124), however, the Japan-Vietnam BIT, in article 14.1, it recognises the right to an investor-state international arbitration, stating that: "For the purpose of this Article, an investment dispute is a dispute between a Contracting Party and an investor of the other Contracting Party that has incurred loss or damage by reason of, or arising out of, an alleged breach of any right conferred by this Agreement with respect to investments of investors of that other Contracting Party". Article 14.3 provides the Japanese investors with the ability to choose an international arbitration forum from two alternatives, if the investment dispute cannot be settled through consultations within three months "from the date on which the investor requested the consultation in writing": arbitration in accordance with ICSID (and its additional facility rules) or in accordance with UNCITRAL rules. However, before the submission of an investment dispute to one of the international arbitration fora stated above, the host state (Vietnam) shall give its consent. According to article 14.4 "a contracting party which is a party to an investment dispute shall give its consent to the submission of the investment dispute to international conciliation or arbitration referred to in paragraph 3 above in accordance with the provisions of this Article". Such wording is similar to the third type of Broche clause requiring from the host state a higher degree of obligation "to assent to any demand on the part of the national to submit for conciliation or arbitration any dispute arising from the investment", though a direct right to arbitration is still not established, and therefore the Japan-Vietnam EPA is scored with 0.75.

Finally, the Japan-Indonesia EPA is considered to be the best treaty (among the five reviewed EPAs) in relation to the right to international investor-state arbitration. Article 69.1 recognises the settlement of investment disputes between a country and an investor of the other country and article 69.4 gives absolute right to foreign investors to choose an international arbitration forum from three alternatives: ICSID (including its additional facilities), UNCITRAL and, if agreed with the disputing party, any other arbitration forum. The right to arbitration to one of the fora mentioned above can be activated only if investor has first made an effort to negotiate with the host state for a period of five months (article 69.4).

---

[440] Broches, 'Bilateral Investment Treaties', cited in Sornarajah, *International Law,* p. 251.

Additionally, the arbitration can be held in any country that is a party to the New York Convention. In conclusion, such a dispute resolution clause under Japan-Indonesia EPA is not included in any other reviewed EPA, and therefore it is scored with one unit (1.00).

As for the subrogation clause, all the reviewed Japanese treaties include a subrogation article separate from the dispute resolution clause. Firstly, they all recognise the right of the home country's agency (e.g. Japan's NEXI or JBIC) to substitute the rights or claims of its investors.[441] Most importantly, they recognise the right of the home country (Japan) or its designated agency (NEXI or JBIC) to "exercise by virtue of subrogation such right or claim to the same extent as the original right or claim of the investor".[442] Moreover, they acknowledge that the right to compensation due to expropriation and protection from strife or the free transfer of such payment shall apply to the home country or its designated agencies with no any exception.[443] The Japan-Vietnam BIT is the only treaty that does not make any reference to the right of compensation due to damages caused from strife (article 11). For this reason, all Japan's treaties receive the best possible score 1.00, except the Japan-Vietnam BIT which is scored less (0.75).

5.7.   Chapter's conclusion

As has been analysed, the standard of FTFs functions in a similar way to a guarantee against the political risk of governmental interference with the investment's economic interests. This study argues that when the host state prevents investors from transferring their funds or converting them into hard currencies, substantial economic loss can occur, in a similar manner to the results of creeping expropriation. This economic loss is even more evident when the repatriation problem is connected to the devaluation of domestic currency. The currency convertibility and devaluation risk is particularly high in the case of power projects, such as IPPs, which involve intensive hard-currency denominated financing but where income is generated in local currency (project financing techniques). Thus, the risk of devaluation or the rate of currency exchange is usually considered to be a commercial risk and international law cannot mitigate it unless there is a particular state-to-investor contractual agreement. Moreover, the study asserts that even if the right to FTFs is a common practice for all investment treaties, investors need to be aware that, in times of financial crisis, restrictions on FTFs are allowed. Finally, the study has found several differences in the wording of the FTF-clauses related to trade in services and investments. In particular, it has been argued that omissions of NT and MFN treatment from the conditions that are required when the right to FTF is restricted affect the degree of investment-protection against political risk.

---

[441] Article 68.1 of the Japan-Indonesia EPA, article 84.1 of the Japan-Malaysia EPA, article 98.1 of the Japan-Philippines EPA, article 105.1 of the Japan-Thailand EPA, and article 11 of the Japan-Vietnam BIT.

[442] *Ibid.*

[443] Article 68.2 of the Japan-Indonesia EPA, article 84.2 of the Japan-Malaysia EPA, article 98.2 of the Japan-Philippines EPA, article 105.2 of the Japan-Thailand EPA.

Similarly, the standard for protection against strife works as a guarantee to foreign investors securing for them cases of protection and compensation which the general standard of full protection and security cannot cover. This international treaty-based standard provides to foreign investors a treatment for damage suffered as a result of armed conflict or similar circumstances for which they cannot be granted remedies under any other provision of the treaty or customary international law. However, it should be noted that the established right to compensation cannot be absolute as it is contingent, on the one hand, on NT and MFN treatment and, on the other hand, to the treaties' purpose in compensating only physical damage caused by armed conflict or internal disturbance.

The provision of the umbrella clause does not only stop the obsolescence of host state bargains but also tackles the political risk of contract repudiation which is one of the most important threats for private investors in the area of public infrastructure and, in particular, power projects. The umbrella clause mitigates political risk by increasing the cost to states of violating their obligations towards investors. The host states are imposed on with a treaty-based international duty not to breach their state-agencies' contractual obligations towards foreign investments. They are liable through the umbrella clause not only towards investors under the law of the contract but also towards the home country under international law. However, the lack of umbrella clause provisions in almost all of Japan's EPAs creates a serious consideration of the degree of effectiveness of the protection of the Japanese investments' interests in the power sector of the reviewed Asian economies. An alternative solution through political risk insurance or contractual practice is needed, which will be analysed in Part II of this volume.

Investor-state arbitration, being the most crucial method of dispute resolution, is also considered to be the ultimate mechanism of mitigating political risk due to its deterrent function against host governments' unwarranted behaviour. Similarly, the inclusion of a subrogation clause furthermore enhances the deterrence function of investment treaties. Moreover, the constraints faced in the state-to-state arbitration mechanisms can be efficiently avoided through the direct involvement of private parties in the dispute resolution process with the offending host state that is provided by the investor-state international arbitration. The rapidly growing number of investor-state arbitration cases is undoubtedly one of the most important developments in international investment law. However, even when treaties include investor-state arbitration, there are several variations in their wordings or exceptions within their content that significantly limit the scope of foreign investment protection. According to Broches' study, the most crucial difference among various types of arbitration clauses is the degree of consent given by host states with regards to the jurisdiction created for an international arbitration as a dispute resolution mechanism. Each type of arbitration clause constitutes different implications related to the international jurisdiction created and foreign investors do not always obtain a directly enforceable right to arbitrate before an international arbitration forum.

This study has examined the precise wording of each type of arbitration clause and, along with other criteria, different categories of arbitration clauses are incorporated into the assessment methodology. It was found that, in the cases of the analysed Japanese investment treaties, even if all EPAs and BIT include an investor-state arbitration clause, there are limitations related to the degree of the host country's consent to the Japanese investors' right to arbitration. The strictest limitation is the one contained in the Japan-Philippines EPA, according to which the Philippines (host state) can grant or deny, at its option or discretion, its consent in respect to each particular investment dispute with Japanese investors. The best wording of investor-state arbitration is included in the Japan-Indonesia EPA, which gives an absolute and direct right to foreign investors to choose an international arbitration forum from three alternatives, without requiring the prior consent of the host country (Indonesia). Finally, even if all examined treaties incorporate a separate article on the right to subrogation, the Japan-Vietnam BIT excludes the right of compensation due to protection from strife from the subrogation's scope of application.

PART II

POLITICAL RISK INSURANCE AND
INVESTOR-STATE AGREEMENTS

With regards to political risk mitigation-instruments, the most *active* (or *affirmative*) measures of home countries, international organisations and private investors, bearing some of the excessive burden that host states usually face and mobilising private financing, has been, on the one hand, the *political risk insurance* (PRI) offered by state or multilateral banks' sponsored agencies and, on the other hand, the *investor-State* contractual inclusion of specific guarantees against political risk.

Part II of the present volume will analyse in Chapter 6 the various schemes of protection provided by the political risk insurance (PRI) offered by Japanese institutions, mainly the export credit agency NEXI, comparing it with the role and the function of the World Bank's agencies such as MIGA. Finally, the study will investigate in Chapter 7 the role of specific guarantees that are provided to investors by looking into five power sector cases between Japanese investors and several East Asian countries (project finance techniques).[444] The analysis focuses on specific contractual-clauses such as: international arbitration with a choice of law clause, waiver of sovereign immunity including enforcement clause, stabilisation clause, and *force majeure* clause.

---

[444] These cases were provided by NEXI in relation to insurance that had been provided to Japanese investors (clients). They consist of five contracts between insured clients and their respective host countries. All of the cases are related to investments in the power sectors of the five countries that are subject of the book: Indonesia, Malaysia, Philippines, Thailand and Vietnam. However, due to reasons of confidentiality, the author is not allowed to reveal any information about the projects' identity or the host countries' or investors' names. The analysis is strictly limited to the contractual guarantees related to political risks and no other information is allowed to be revealed.

6

POLITICAL RISK INSURANCE, THE ROLE OF NEXI, AND COMPARISON WITH MIGA

6.1.   Introduction

Political risks have been traditionally seen as an area for governments to exercise their influence and capacity. As is mentioned in the following chapter, it is not only the host states which, as the main absorber of political risks, can mitigate them by offering certain promises and specific guarantees to foreign investors known as sovereign guarantees, it is also the home countries and the international organisations which function not only as financiers but also as insurers of investments through their specialised administrative agencies by providing political risk insurance (PRI) to their nationals' investments and by supporting their projects overseas. In particular, capital-exporting countries and IFIs have developed a policy of assuming several kinds of political risks that investors face when they invest overseas in risky investment environments. This policy is referred to as the strategy of the "prominent victims", indicating the deterrence of harmful behaviour by host government through the crucial involvement of powerful actors such as financial and insurance institutions of Multilateral Development Banks (MDBs) and home countries which act on behalf of the foreign investors.[445]

In addition, aside from the state sponsored insurance agencies, known as export credit agencies (ECAs), there are also investment insurers sponsored by international financial institutions as well as private sector insurers which are specialised in providing guarantees to investors in relation to political risk coverage.[446] Thus, this chapter focuses on the role of Japan's sponsored PRI through its agencies and on the World Bank Group's guarantee facilities.

6.2.   Main types of risks and mitigation instruments

Given the special nature of infrastructure projects and particularly of the

---

[445] S. Markwick, 'Trends in Political Risks for Corporate Investors', in T.H. Moran (ed.), *Managing International Political Risk* (Blackwell Publishers Ltd., Oxford, 1998) p. 54; see also: R.B. Shanks, 'Lessons in the Management of Political Risk: Infrastructure Projects (A Legal Perspective)' in Moran, *Managing International Political Risk*, pp. 96-98.

[446] Some of the most well-known private insurers are members of the Berne Union, such as Lloyds of London (including 10 syndicates) and around 10 private companies. Among them, Chartis Insurance, previously known as AIG (USA), Zurich (USA) Sovereign Insurance Ltd. (Bermuda) and Chubb (USA) account for about 43 percent of the total market share; thus, after the 2008 financial crisis with the "Lehman shock" (Lehman Brothers Corporation's bankruptcy) and the current sovereign debt crisis that many developed and developing countries face, there has been a significant retreat in the private sector's PRI-business. WB, 'World Investment and Political Risk: 2009', *MIGA* (World Bank, Washington, DC, 2010), Box 3.3, p. 49.

power sector, state and multilateral investment-guarantee agencies have developed a mix of risk-mitigation instruments that cover three broad types of risk: political risk, credit risk and exchange-rate risk (currency-devaluation risk).[447] From the first point of view, only the first category is related to the focus of this study, the mitigation of political risk. However, what a political risk is, it is not always well defined. There are cases of non-commercial risks that, though they are not directly related to political risk, they can be also covered under political risk mitigation instruments.[448]

Multilateral and state agencies increasingly focus on the mitigation of political risk in relation to the facilitation of infrastructure project financing. The instruments that are used by foreign investments to mitigate political risk are typically termed partial risk guarantees (PRG), such as the World Bank Group's guarantees and PRI used mainly by ECAs such as NEXI. Traditionally, political risk instruments cover expropriation risk (creeping expropriation was not usually covered), currency inconvertibility and transfer restriction, war and civil disturbance.[449]

Recently, however, there has been an expansion in PRI coverage, having come to include breach of contract, arbitration award default and more project-specific undertakings. It is a significant shift from the traditional general coverage of political risk, moving towards the coverage of specific governmental obligations that are contractually undertaken between the host state and the foreign promoter of an infrastructure investment.

In particular, as is analysed below, there are guarantees provided by third parties (ECAs or MDBs) that are used to mitigate the risk of governments' (or their SOEs') failure to meet specific obligations to a private project. Thus, when a government contractually agrees to undertake obligations such as the performance of a public counterparty (e.g. minimum revenue guarantee by a public electric utility) there are risks that do not fall clearly into the definition of political risk, though they are covered by political risk instruments. In addition, when a government's action or inaction related to the operation of a state-owned electric utility causes the bankruptcy of the SOE which consequently results in a debt-service default towards a foreign investor or private lender (being a counterparty of the SOE), then the SOE's default can be mitigated by the political risk guarantee because the reason for the default is considered to be political (i.e., governmental interference).

Similarly, while the coverage of currency risk does not result in political risk mitigation (governments have no control over the fluctuations of foreign exchange movements), under certain conditions currency risk becomes a government's binding responsibility. It has been observed in the contractual practice of power project financing between foreign investors and the host government (or its agencies and SOEs) that the tariff of electricity to be purchased is often indexed to foreign exchange rates under the host state's guarantee. If the

---

[447] UNCTAD, *World Investment Report 2008*, p. 171.

[448] Matsukawa and Habeck, 'Review of Risk Mitigation', pp. 1-5.

[449] WB, 'World Investment and Political Risk: 2010', *MIGA* (World Bank, Washington, DC, 2011) p. 56.

infringement of this guarantee results in a breach of contract by the host state, then the currency risk has materialised due to a non-commercial cause: government interference.[450]

Depending on the contractual arrangements in power project financing, guarantees of political risk can be expanded to issues such as a government's contractual payment obligations included in a PPA-contract, change of laws or regulations that have a negative impact on the project, and even a change in the contractual performance of public counterparties such as an electric utility which has several obligations as an off-taker towards a specific power project's investor.[451] These are only a few examples which can show the wide area of political risk coverage under the evolved function of new risk mitigation instruments such as the PRGs. However, it is also true that the borders between political and commercial risks have become more blurred and, as has been said, "[o]ne may argue that some of these risks fall in between traditional commercial risks and traditional political risks".[452]

6.3. The PRI market

6.3.1. Historic background

One of the first PRI investment programs was initiated by the US Government with the Marshall Plan in 1948. Its purpose was to encourage US investments overseas under the reconstruction policy in post-war Europe. Thus, it was not until the 1990s that the demand for PRI business increased significantly. After the fall of the Soviet Union, and especially as a result of the open-market policy, globalisation and liberalisation movements launched by the capital-exporting countries, unforeseen business opportunities were opened up for foreign investments, especially in the areas of natural resources, energy and infrastructure in many developing countries. This increased the demand for PRI. The PRI business had changed by the 2000s, with coverage capacity for a single risk growing from USD 250 million in 1992 to more than USD 1 billion in 2000 and tenors lengthening from 3 to 15 years.[453] However, the 11 September 2001 terrorist attack in the US and the Argentine financial crisis has affected the PRI industry significantly, changing the way investors and insurers assume political risks. The possibility of suffering extreme losses due to terrorism but also the rising uncertainty of the global financial crisis, with its potential sovereign and corporate defaults, has reinforced the debate as to whether, with such unpredictable situations, the PRI market should be allowed to continue at the same scale

---

[450] However, foreign exchange-currency risk should be treated as a commercial risk and should be borne by the private sector, as they are in a better position than governments to control such risks. T. Matsukawa, R. Sheppard and J. Wright, 'Foreign Exchange Risk Mitigation for Power and Water Projects in Developing Countries', Discussion Paper no. 9, *Energy and Mining Board Discussion Paper Series* (World Bank, Washington, DC, 2003).

[451] Matsukawa and Habeck, 'Review of Risk Mitigation', p. 5; see also: P. Gupta, R. Lamech, F. Mashar and J. Wright, 'Mitigating Regulatory Risk for Distribution Privatization: The World Bank Partial Risk Guarantee', no. 5 *Energy and Mining Sector Board Discussion Paper Series* (World Bank, Washington, DC, 2002) p. 10.

[452] Matsukawa and Habeck, 'Review of Risk Mitigation', p. 5.

[453] World Bank, 'World Investment and Political Risk: 2009', pp. 54-55.

or whether it should alter its policy on political risk coverage. At the G-20 economic summit held in London in April 2009 and at the G-8 summit held in Italy in July of the same year, the role of ECAs was reconfirmed and it was declared an excess need of underwriting globally insurance amounting to USD 250 billion until 2011.[454]

6.3.2. General characteristics

In general, the PRI market or political risk guarantee market[455] consists of two broad categories: guarantees for export or trade credit and investment insurance. For the purposes of this study, referring to the coverage of political risk in relation to overseas investment in power projects, it focuses on the role of investment insurance only.[456]

However, a potential protection of a foreign investment could be also offered by combining guarantees for political risk provided by export credit or trade tools. There are certain instruments that cover losses to exporters or lenders financing projects tied to the export of goods and services (trade coverage). In relation to investments in the power sector, the export credit guarantees can cover losses due to political risk for services that are connected to engineering, procurement and construction (EPC) contracts. For example, as mentioned above, sovereign and corporate debt-risk can be covered regardless of whether the reason for the default is commercial or political.[457]

6.3.3. PRI providers

As is mentioned above, the PRI market consists of multilateral and state insurers and a significant number of private enterprises. The multilateral agencies that provide risk mitigation instruments are mainly MDBs such as the WB, the ADB, the Inter-American Development Bank and the EBRD. Additionally, there are some multilateral agencies that specialise in providing political risk guarantees such as the African Trade Insurance Agency, the Inter-Arab Investment Guarantee Corporation, the Islamic Corporation for the Insurance of Investment and Export Credit, and the most important, the Multilateral Investment Guarantee Agency (MIGA) belonging to the WB Group.[458]

As far as the state or national agencies are concerned, they are generally bilateral development agencies and ECAs. ECAs are the most important type of PRI insurer, existing in almost all of the big capital-exporting countries, as well as in the recently transitioning economies such as Brazil, Russia, India, China and South Africa (BRICs) and other less-developed economies. ECAs can be considered a large category of national agencies including export-import banks, export

---

[454] Message from the Chairman and CEO of NEXI, Takashi Suzuki, October 2009.

[455] As was mentioned previously, they are the same but their names change depending on the provider: 'PRI' is used by NEXI and 'political risk guarantees' is used by MIGA.

[456] However, the area between traditional investment and export credit insurance has become blurred. Stephens, 'A Perspective', pp. 148-168.

[457] Matsukawa and Habeck, 'Review of Risk Mitigation', p. 4.

[458] World Bank, 'World Investment and Political Risk: 2010', p. 55.

credit guarantee agencies and investment insurance agencies.[459] Their organisational structures vary depending on their particular country's policies. For example, in the UK it is part of the government, in Germany and France they are private entities and in Japan and the US, ECAs are considered to be autonomous public agencies and thus not absolutely independent from public administration. ECAs are subject to international regulation by OECD and the WTO rules. Most of the ECAs provide guarantees for both political and commercial risks, though it has been questioned whether their role allows them to provide long-term commercial risk insurance for infrastructure project-financing.[460]

Finally, even if the bilateral agencies' objectives differ from those of multinational organisations, obtaining nationalistic purposes[461] their activities are often complementary in providing guarantees for many transactions related to infrastructure project financing.[462]

6.4. Japan's PRI-agencies: NEXI[463] in cooperation with JBIC

6.4.1. NEXI: Background

One of the largest state-sponsored insurance agencies is Japan's Nippon Export and Investment Insurance (NEXI)[464] which, along with the lending and guarantee function of the Japanese Bank for International Cooperation (JBIC), is Japan's public insurer, furnishing a variety of investment-related services to Japanese investors.[465]

Japan's investment insurance system was established in 1950 to support Japanese exports by providing guarantees against political risks such as war, currency controls and expropriation. The system was managed by the predecessor of NEXI, the Export-Import Insurance Division (EID) that was incorporated into the Ministry of Economy, Trade and Industry (METI). In April 2001, NEXI was established as an incorporated administrative agency taking over the ministry-managed service, acquiring administrative and operational autonomy.

---

[459] Matsukawa and Habeck, 'Review of Risk Mitigation', p. 9. For a list of the major bilateral agencies and their risk mitigation instruments, see *ibid.*, appendix B2, pp. 50-84.

[460] R. Short, 'Export Credit Agencies, Project Finance, and Commercial Risk: Whose Risk Is It, Anyway?', *Fordham International Law Journal* 24:4 (2001) p. 1371.

[461] ECAs usually serve their countries' national interests whereas MDBs do not tie their programs to the nationality of exporters or investors. Hoffman, *Law and Business*, p. 295.

[462] *Ibid.*, p. 73; see also: Matsukawa and Habeck, 'Review of Risk Mitigation', p. 10; T.H. Moran, 'Political Risk Insurance as a Tool to Manage International Political Risk', in T.H. Moran (ed.), *Managing International Political Risk* (Blackwell Publishers Ltd., Oxford, 1998) p. 140.

[463] The information in this section was provided by NEXI after conducting interviews and meetings in the period between March and August of 2010 with Mr. Haruyoshi Ueda (Senior Advisor of Structured & Trade Finance Insurance Dep.), Mrs. Natsuko Harada (Vice President of Power & Mining Team), Mr. Giichiro Hattori (Chief Senior Manager of Claims Service & Recovery Group) and Mr. Iwao Ogawa (Senior Manager of Asset Planning Group). Any misleading information provided herein, or any omission about NEXI's PRI policy, is solely the author's responsibility.

[464] NEXI web-address: www.nexi.go.jp.

[465] The three largest ECAs that are members of the Berne Union are OPIC (US), NEXI (Japan) and PwC Deutsche Revision (Germany); Rubins and Kinsella, *International Investment*, p. 70.

Thus, NEXI continues functioning under the auspices of METI which provides NEXI with its capital and reinsures insurance agreements underwritten by NEXI. As of 31 March 2009, NEXI's capital budget is JPY 104.4 billion and 152 officers are employed there.[466]

Since May 1970, NEXI has been a member of the Berne Union (the International Union of Credit and Investment Insurers), which is a forum where ECAs from various countries exchange information on common issues of export credit and investment insurance. The BU announced in October 2008 a new set of Guiding Principles which tie member-agencies to adopting a uniform policy about how to conduct investment insurance in general.[467] NEXI is also a member of the Paris Club, an informal international group that provides solutions to sovereign debt problems between debtor and creditor countries. Finally, NEXI is a member of the OECD's working party on Export Credits and Credits Guarantees, signing the Agreement on Officially Supported Export Credits called the OECD Consensus.[468] The OECD's working party issues recommendations in an effort to shape ECAs' behaviour towards export credit and investment insurance as well as issues of fair competition,[469] bribery, corruption and environmental protection.[470]

NEXI's mission is to facilitate the promotion of Japanese trade and investment by mitigating political and commercial risks in export and overseas investments through PRI provision.[471] NEXI provides insurance for investments and exports in both developing and developed countries (see Figure 4 below).[472] NEXI's PRI often operates in conjunction with other programs, such as those of JBIC's[473] and with development programs of Japan Investment and Cooperation Agency (JICA). NEXI is especially active in providing insurance for infrastructure investments, such as power projects, sponsored by Japanese entities.

One of the most recent cases is the support provided for the implementation of the BLCP coal-fired power plant project in Thailand. In this IPP project on a Build-Own-Operate basis (BOO), NEXI provided Buyer's Credit Insurance covering the amount of USD 163 million financed by commercial banks (among them the Bank of Tokyo-Mitsubishi UFJ, Ltd) for the construction and the provision of

---

[466] NEXI, *NEXI Introduction Brochure*, Nippon Export Insurance Agency, FY 2009.

[467] *Ibid.*, p. 26.

[468] Hoffman, *Law and Business*, p. 296.

[469] Each of the member countries in the OECD Consensus needs to limit export credit to no more than 85% of the contract value in order to protect competition from distortion; *ibid.*

[470] However, with regards to project financing, the OECD Consensus was amended in 1998, allowing member-countries' ECAs to support projects financed on a limited-recourse basis without any limitation; ibid. This exception is very important for foreign investments in the power sector, as most of the project-financing mechanisms are related to infrastructure projects.

[471] Japan's Trade and Investment Insurance Act of March 1950 (art. 4, No. 67/1950) and the Amendment Act of December 1999.

[472] As of July 2008, insurance can be provided for projects and exports to 181 countries.

[473] JBIC provides also some political risk guarantees but it mainly functions as a creditor of Japanese investments with NEXI being the main insurer providing PRI for loans and equity for overseas investment.

equipment as EPC contractors by Mitsubishi Corporation and Mitsubishi Heavy Industries, Ltd.[474]

Over the agency's history, NEXI has insured a total of about JPY 452 trillion and the amount of claims has totalled JPY 2.4 trillion. The insured amount has covered about 20% of the total amount of exports. Especially in FY 2008, insurance services related to investment have shown a substantial increase, e.g. overseas untied loan insurance increased by 866% and overseas investment insurance from JPY 155,228 million to JPY 281,717 million compared with FY 2007 due to increased large-scale projects and new coverage support provided for working capital used by the insured's overseas subsidiaries.[475]

NEXI has played a crucial role in protecting overseas investments against political risk. Until today, the majority of Japanese investors have been unaware about other alternatives in mitigating political risks such as through international law (EPA Treaties).[476] With regards to protection of overseas investments against political risk, NEXI is conceived of as a "last resort" mechanism.[477]

6.4.2. JBIC: Background[478]

The Japan Bank of International Cooperation is Japan's bilateral agency that provides debt financing to Japanese investors. It was organised in 1999 as a Japanese Government financial institution, thus its establishment is dated much earlier, to 1950, through its predecessor, the Export-Import Bank of Japan.[479] On 1 October 2008, JBIC became the international wing of the Japan Finance Corporation (JFC), continuing to use its name for its international finance operations.[480] JBIC has a similar mission to NEXI, promoting Japanese investors' "overseas development and acquisition of strategically important natural resources to Japan", as well as maintaining and improving the international competitiveness of Japanese industries".[481]

JBIC is the main financing arm of Japan's public borrowing. Its principal operation is to provide financial assistance including loans, bonds, and concessionary long-term and low-interest funds. JBIC offers limited PRI through its extended political risk guarantee (EPRG) which covers loans and bonds but not equity as NEXI does. It mainly functions as a creditor of Japanese investments

---

[474] NEXI, *Introduction*, p. 13.

[475] NEXI, Annual Report FY 2008 (Nippon Export Insurance Agency, April 2008-March 2009) p. 22.

[476] Meeting with NEXI managers, 10 June 2010.

[477] *Ibid.*

[478] Discussion-meetings were conducted in November 2009 and April 2010 with JBIC managers Mr. Takaya Naito (Executive Officer), Mr. Kaoru Nagata (Division-3 Chief), Mr. Yasushi Sunouchi (Division-2 Chief), and Mr. Taishi Sato (Division-3 Deputy Chief).

[479] Japan's Export Import Bank Law of 1950.

[480] Thus, due to the organisational realignment in 2008, the overseas economic cooperation operations (OECOs) of JBIC were taken by the expanded scope of the new Japan International Cooperation Agency (JICA); JFC, JBIC Annual Report-2009 (Japan Finance Corporation, 2009) p. 3.

[481] *Ibid.*, p. 6.

and not as an insurer in order to avoid "operation-overlapping" with NEXI.[482] Another reason for that is that JBIC can provide up to 60% of the total lending that is needed in each case. Therefore, the remaining 40% is covered by commercial banks (co-financiers) whose political risk is insured by NEXI. Thus, the practical contribution of agencies such as JBIC and NEXI is that private investors can achieve much better terms borrowing funds from the commercial markets. Without the guarantees of JBIC and NEXI, the maturity of loans offered by the markets cannot exceed a period of five, or maximum seven, years, which is very short if we consider that most power-financing cases have a project-life of a period between ten to fifteen years. With JBIC-NEXI guarantees, the maturity of loans can be extended to at least ten years and, if required, to a longer period.[483] JBIC provides financing tools such as overseas investment loans (OIL), overseas untied loans (OUL) and buyer's credit (BC), whose political risks are covered by NEXI's overseas investment insurance (OII), overseas untied loan insurance (OULI) and buyer's credit insurance (BCI) accordingly. Therefore, this book examines NEXI's PRI tools as being the main insurer of Japanese investors. However, it briefly refers to JBIC's political risk guarantees.

Table 20 Background Information about NEXI and JBIC[484]

NEXI	JBIC
• 1950: trade & invest. Insurance by the Government • 2001: administrative agency under METI • Article 4 of the Trade and Investment Insurance Law (Law No. 67 of 1950) • **Insurance** to both emerging & developed countries (181 countries as of July 2008) • Mostly **political risks** (but also some commercial) for **loans** & **equity** • No coverage if liability & negligence of the insured or default of the counter-part	• 1950 JEXIM-Export Bank Law • 1999 JBIC 2 functions: International financing & econ. cooperation • 2008 new JBIC: international financial wing of JFC-Finance Corporation Law (Law No. 57 of 2007) • **Loans, equity** & **guarantees** only to emerging countries (excl. nuclear plants) • Guarantees only for **loans/bonds** • **EPRG**: among others "off-taker risk" (vague but similar function with NEXI) • No coverage of natural disaster risk

6.5.   NEXI's PRI instruments: Political risk coverage

6.5.1.   In general

NEXI offers insurance for loans, equity investments, assets and rights or any other investment structure that is subject to long-term exposure to political risk. As mentioned above, NEXI's coverage is related to trade and investment and is provided for protection against both political and commercial risks. However, with regards to investments in the power sector, which is the focus herein, this study only analyses insurance coverage that is related to power investments and

---

[482]   Meeting with JBIC managers on 6 April 2010.

[483]   Meeting with JBIC managers on 6 April 2010.

[484]   Table compiled by the author (information based on NEXI's and JBIC's Organisation Laws and Annual Reports).

is provided for protection against losses caused by political risk. Therefore, it is important to identify, among different insurance instruments provided by NEXI, those that are appropriate for the protection of power investments against political risk.[485]

Figure 3   NEXI's Instrument for Trade and Investment[486]

- Export credit insurance
- Buyer's credit insurance: suitable for power projects
- Trade insurance for standing orders for specific buyer
- Export credit insurance for SMEs
- Overseas untied loan insurance: suitable for power projects
- Overseas investment insurance: suitable for power projects
- Export bill insurance
- Export bond insurance
- Prepayment import insurance
- Investment & loan insurance for natural resources and energy (excl. power)
- Trade & investment insurance for preventing global warming

Among the various instruments of PRI that NEXI uses, two are related to insurance of overseas power investments and they are subject of this book's analysis: Overseas untied loan insurance and the overseas investment insurance. In addition, the research examines one more PRI instrument which, despite the fact that it is considered to be an insurance covering trade, can also be a potential tool for securing power investments against political risk. One of the buyer's credit insurance functions can be suitable for power-projects' insurance when it covers EPC services of Japanese contractors in power project financing (trade in services: mode 3 of the WTO requirements).[487]

6.5.2.   Overseas Investment Insurance (OII)

6.5.2.1.   Scope

The most important insurance type suitable for investment in power projects is overseas investment insurance (OII). This type of insurance is offered as a hedge against both political and commercial risks. It covers overseas investment for capital subscription or equity, for acquisition of business rights and titles (real property, equipment, mining rights, licences, concession etc.) and it protects even reinvestments in a third country. This last function of insurance for reinvestment via an investment recipient is a unique type of investment insurance provided by NEXI. It increases the protection provided to the Japanese subsidiary in a host country by expanding the insurance to investments made in a third country (the Japanese subsidiary performs direct business without establishing its own subsidiary in the third country), and guarantees against losses suffered due to political risk not only in the host country but also in the

---

[485] See Figure 3.

[486] Source: Information compiled by the author.

[487] See the case of BLCP coal-fired power plant project in Thailand explained above.

third country. NEXI provides supplementary contracts to address these risks, subject to special agreement with NEXI.[488]

Figure 4   Overseas Investment Insurance[489]

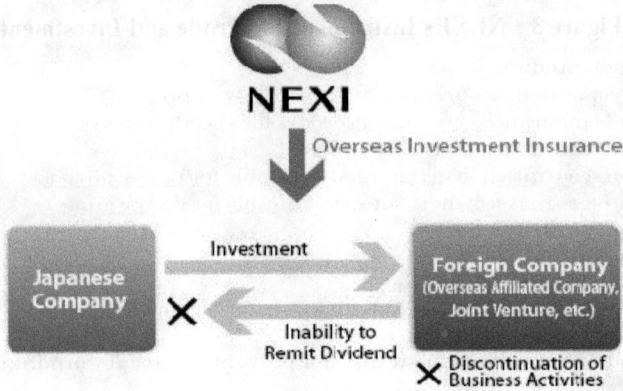

6.5.2.2. Covered political risks

Political risks covered by NEXI's OII include expropriation and infringement of rights, war, political violence or civil disturbance, currency inconvertibility and non-transfer of funds and natural disasters (*force majeure* risk).[490] In addition to these risks, OII covers some commercial risks such as insolvency of debtor and breach of contract by the other party which under certain conditions, could be considered to be political risks as well. For example, if the other party in the investment contract is the host government (central or local, public agencies or SOEs), which is the most usual case in power investments, any indemnity for losses suffered due to the government's breach of contract or due to insolvency caused by the government's political interference could be considered to be a PRI tool.

In particular, with regards to an expropriation case, OII makes NEXI liable to indemnify losses suffered by the insured investor that result from expropriation (direct and indirect) of stocks and equities caused by the host government's interference, actions or inactions of central or local public entities or any similar entity such as a SOE or public utilities e.g. an electric utility in the electricity industry.[491] Thus, in the case of a host government's claim that its actions are legitimate regulations, NEXI might not compensate for the damage that the insured suffered until an arbitration award has been issued.[492] In the case of an infringement of rights, investors are protected from deprivation of important rights and assets such as title of real estate, of licences or any other right that is

---

[488] NEXI, *Business Guide*, p.8.

[489] NEXI, *Introduction*, p. 18.

[490] Article 2 para. 16 item 1 of the Trade and Investment Insurance Act No. 67 of 1950.

[491] NEXI, *Policy Conditions for Overseas Investment Insurance*, Partial Amendment of 14 March 2007, Chapter 2, Art. 2, p. 1.

[492] Meeting with NEXI managers, 10 June 2010.

important in carrying out operations e.g. PPA in the supply of electricity (expropriation of rights) and equipment or raw materials etc. (expropriation of mobile assets).[493] Thus, NEXI will not insure losses due to an infringement of rights when a government's acts are in accordance with domestic or international law.[494]

Moreover, OII covers damages that result from war, revolutions, civil war, riots or disturbances and other acts of violence as long as they are politically motivated actions. A broader category of covering losses consists of the protection against *force majeure* risk, including natural disasters caused by extraordinary natural phenomena such as stormy winds, torrential rain, flooding, high tides, earthquake, tsunamis, nuclear contamination and even some general non-natural phenomena such terrorist attacks[495], breakdown of transportation facilities due to strikes and economic sanctions imposed by the UN or other international organisations and by any other country.[496] This insurance also covers losses incurred when a Japanese company is unable to remit dividends to Japan due to restrictions in foreign exchange transactions or imposition of controls on conversion of local currency into yen or US dollar or any other hard currency by the host government.

In addition, the breach of contract risk is also considered to be a political risk for which OII will cover the losses when the host government violates or unilaterally renounces a contract that was concluded between the Japanese company's subsidiary and the host government (a breach of contract). Thus, in order for this risk to be addressed by the OII, a supplementary contract between NEXI and the insured investor is required.[497] However, NEXI requires that investor shall exhaust all reasonable measures in order for the claim for insurance payment to be valid. By the term "reasonable", NEXI indicates that in case there is an arbitration clause in the investor's contract, investors should try to resolve the problem under the arbitration forum before seeking payment from NEXI. However, in general, NEXI shows flexibility in deciding about whether a measure is reasonable or not on a case-by-case basis.[498] Finally, the change of law or regulation risk is also mitigated by OII, which covers losses that result due to the imposition of new laws. In this case, the new law or regulation should be unfair and discriminatory or against an international treaty and cause losses.[499]

6.5.2.3. Insured events

According to NEXI's policy, in order for the abovementioned political risks to be considered materialised, there are certain events which need to have occurred.

---

[493] NEXI, *Policy Conditions*, p. 2.

[494] Meeting with NEXI managers, 10 June 2010.

[495] Investors are increasingly asking for insurance for losses due to terrorism especially after the "September 11" terrorist attack.

[496] NEXI, *Business Guide*, p. 12.

[497] *Ibid.*, p. 10.

[498] Meeting with NEXI managers, 10 June 2010.

[499] NEXI, *Business Guide*, p. 5.

Any of the following events that occur with respect to losses suffered by the investor due to the risks of expropriation or infringement of rights, war or political violence, the risk of breach of contract or the *force majeure* risk is insured by NEXI's OII mechanism:

- inability to continue business operations;
- bankruptcy of the investor's subsidiary;
- suspension of banking transactions; or
- suspension of business operations for three months (at least) or longer.

To invoke the remittance risk, the event that is required by NEXI is the inability of the investor to remit equity sales profits, dividends or any other funds to Japan for 2 months or longer.[500]

If at least one of the above events does not occur, then NEXI is not liable to insure the claim of the investor for losses suffered due to political risk. It is important to clarify that an event of suspension of business operations cannot be anything less than a total suspension. This is an important element, especially for complicated business operations such as a power-plant's. For example, when the host government or its public authorities decide to unilaterally alter their contractual obligation for provision of adequate fuel, supplying less than is needed for the operation of a power plant, it is questionable whether there is a right to insurance if the result of the government's action is only partial suspension of the plant's business operations. In this case, the insured investor will not be able to satisfy any claim for insurance of losses suffered due to the breach of contract, and NEXI will not indemnify the losses if the insured company continues the operation even partially. In relation to the above example, the covered event can only be "bankruptcy", complete "inability to operate" or complete suspension of operation for more than three months.

6.5.2.4. Claim ascertainment[501]

Even when the covered events occur, however, that does not mean NEXI will be automatically satisfied of the insured's claims and will pay out the insurance's agreed amount. NEXI has developed a list of check-points for claim ascertainment in order to examine whether the insured's claim in each case of the covered political risks analysed above is valid or not.

In relation to the expropriation risk and following the claim for insurance of the losses suffered due to the seizure of the investor's equity or rights, NEXI needs to investigate the following issues: the extent of the insured's right to the share and equity of the investment's company under the shareholders' agreement in accordance with the relevant laws and regulations in the host country. NEXI will indemnify the insured only up to the losses that are related to his equity share or to the seizure of his specific right when the investment company is a joint venture among many share-holders. With regards to investments in the

---

[500] NEXI, *Introduction*, p. 16.

[501] Information collected after conducting a meeting with Mr. Giichiro Hattori (NEXI) on 10 June 2010.

power sector, project-financing is the most standard form of investment. Power project finance is implemented through a special purpose vehicle (SPV), a joint-venture company consisting of a multi-level group of shareholders such as sponsors, lenders, operators, EPC contractors, suppliers and many others. In such a complicated mix of shareholders, NEXI needs to identify the extent of the insured's right to the equity or assets of the particular investment.

Similarly, in relation to the infringement on the right of business risk, NEXI needs to investigate: the importance of the asset for the operation of the invest-ment's company (e.g. if the asset is a right on a PPA regarding a power BOT project); if the particular asset is significant for the operation of the power company, the extent of the insured's right to the asset (e.g. in the previous example if the insured is the sponsor of the project or the EPC contractor, the extent of their rights to the asset varies); the commitment of the host government to permit the company's right (e.g. if the PPA agreement allows the government to unilaterally revoke the given right of the foreign investor); and the effect on the company's operation due to the infringement by the host government.

NEXI's check-point about "influence to the company's operation" is a crucial element for NEXI's insurance policy. It is also required for the cases of breach of contract risk, the change of law risk, the war risk and the force-majeure risk. With the term influence, NEXI indicates a concept different to the requirement of insured events explained above. "Influence" denotes the effect of causality. It deals with the method of causal analysis and calculation of the damages covered by the insurance policy. In particular, NEXI needs to examine how the cause of a particular political risk (e.g. breach of contract) affects the event (e.g. inability to operate) and its subsequent losses (e.g. claim of the insured). Since there are several causes that might co-exist at the same time e.g. slump of electricity sales (commercial market risk) and the host government's unilateral increase of the agreed fuel price supplied to the investor's power company (breach of contract risk or regulatory risk), both of these causes influence the company's operation, but only the second one can be an insured political risk covered by NEXI's insurance. Therefore, NEXI needs to assess and quantify only those effects on the company's operations that are invoked by political-risk causes. The covered losses will be calculated based on the decrease of the net worth of the company by comparing the worth of the company (a) before the event and (b) after the event and analysing how much related loss occurred due to that particular cause (the covered political risk).

In addition, with regards to the breach of contract risk, NEXI looks into the specific terms and conditions that are contained in the various clauses of the contract signed between the host government (or its agencies) and the insured investor. For this reason, the insured is obliged to submit the implementation contract or any other relevant contractual agreement that he has signed with the host government. There are certain clauses that are very important for the degree of protection that a foreign investor can obtain against political risk which are analysed in Chapter 7.

In the war and *force majeure* risk cases, in addition to the influence on the company's operation, NEXI needs to identify the occurrence of war, armed conflict or violence, or natural phenomena through various resources, mainly by utilising Japan's Ministry of Foreign Affairs' (MOFA) network and its embassy in the particular host state where the insured's investment is located. Moreover, when a remittance risk occurs, NEXI researches the situation of the foreign exchange market in the host country, any modifications undertaken in the laws and regulations of foreign exchange, the commitment of the foreign government to permit the remittance at a certain rate, and it also studies the local currency's necessary deposit for the remittance.

In conclusion, if one of the above-analysed check-points is not satisfied, NEXI ascertains that the insured's claim is invalid and it does not indemnify any damage suffered from the host government's interference with the investor's property. Additionally, NEXI does not indemnify the insured investor when the claimed losses or damages occurred due to the investor's own liability. Finally, it is important to state that it is not clear whether NEXI requires from the insured first to exhaust all local remedies, and only then, if no satisfaction can be obtained, to claim the insurance from NEXI. Under the policy conditions of NEXI, the insured is required to exhaust all *reasonable* measures for loss minimisation or damage prevention. It is clear that NEXI will not indemnify the investment if the insured investor neglects his obligations. Therefore the portion of damage which resulted due to the investor's fault will not be compensated. However, regardless the insured's liability, NEXI takes into consideration that when the counterpart of the insured is a foreign government or authority, the required level of such exhaustion of local remedies will depend on the condition of each case. That means that NEXI will treat each case with *ad hoc* flexibility in deciding to sometimes directly negotiate with the host state through public diplomacy with the co-operation of METI and local Japanese embassy.

Finally, after indemnifying the investor, NEXI will substitute the investor in all his legal rights and claims against the host government through derogation. For this reason, before compensation is paid, NEXI requires an assignment to itself of all the investor's rights, titles and interests that occur in his investment. Thus, if the host state has not obtained a bilateral investment treaty with Japan, there is a (very rare) possibility that the host state will not recognise NEXI's derogation right. For this reason, some bilateral ECAs and multilateral agencies offer insurance only to those investments that are sited in countries that have obtained investment agreements with the investors' home countries.

6.5.3. Overseas Untied Loan Insurance (OULI)

In addition to the OII, NEXI offers insurance covering long-term loans (and bonds) provided by Japanese companies. These funds or loans are provided to foreign companies or directly to a host government's agency or authority and they are not tied to exports from Japan. The purpose of the insurance's provision to loans can be either to finance a foreign partner in a joint venture for the acquisition of equity (e.g. a SPV in power project-financing), to provide funds to a foreign company for the operation of its business (e.g. operation of a power plant) or to finance a foreign company in order to develop natural resources that the Japanese investor will import to Japan.

Figure 5   Overseas United Loan Insurance[502]

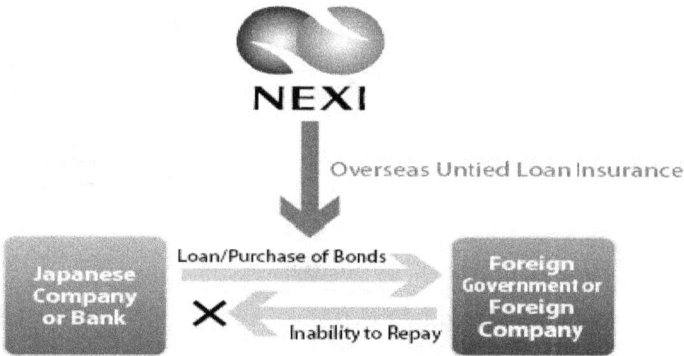

With the provision of OULI, the intention of NEXI is to support Japanese companies in cooperating with foreign companies in developing business in the complicated area of infrastructure projects with a particular focus on the energy industry. To develop business related to power projects is not only a capital-intensive but also a capacity-intensive effort which requires cooperation with other partners in technical, legal, and management practices. For successful participation in the bidding process of power mega-projects, strategic partner-ship with foreign companies is a *sine qua non*.

In particular, the OULI indemnifies the losses suffered by Japanese compa-nies or banks from being unable to collect the principal or the interest on a loan due to a reason which falls under one of the following political-risk reasons: war, revolution, or other civil disturbances (war risk), natural phenomena such as windstorms, floods, earthquakes, tsunamis or other natural calamities or even general strikes, terrorism, or nuclear disaster (force-majeure risk), prohibition on foreign exchange transactions (convertibility risk) or on remittance, suspension of remittance due to a debt-rescheduling agreement of the host government (remittance risk) and expropriation of the borrower/debtor's assets (expropria-tion risk). There are even some commercial risks that are covered by OULI such as the bankruptcy or default of the borrower or bond issuer who is the counter-party to the OULI-insured, and prohibition of exports or imports in the host country, being the country in which the project that is the subject of the OULI policy is implemented. Thus, if the counterparty is the host-government itself or any of its authorities, then based on the condition of the contractual obligations of host country these risks could be also considered to be non-commercial risks.[503]

To ascertain the occurrence of the above-mentioned risks, the event that is required by NEXI is the inability of the insured (lender) to remit to Japan the

---

[502] NEXI, *Introduction*, p. 16.

[503] NEXI, *Business Guide*, pp. 1-3.

principal or the interest on the loan for three months or longer in the performance of payment obligations by the counterparty.[504]

Similarly to the OII, NEXI adopts the same list of check-points for claim-ascertainment in order to examine whether the insured's claim in each case of the covered political risks under OULI is valid or not.[505] In the case of bankruptcy, NEXI requires checking whether the proceedings are verified by the host country's public institutions.[506] And finally, NEXI will not indemnify the insured if a delay in the payment obligations of the counterparty/borrower is attributable to the insured.[507]

6.5.4. Buyer's Credit (B/C) Insurance

The Buyer's Credit Insurance (B/C Insurance) is the last instrument that this study includes in the protection against political risk offered by NEXI. As mentioned before, B/C insurance is considered to be a mechanism covering trade transactions and not foreign investments. However, this study takes into consideration that this instrument has been applied on several occasions for securing power EPC services against political risk. In particular, one specific function of the B/C insurance can be suitable for power projects' insurance when it covers the EPC services of Japanese contractors in power project financing. EPC service is an area which overlaps with what is traditionally conceived of as investment. In cases such as EPC contracts (trade in services), the establishment of a subsidiary in the host country, which will undertake these services, is necessary. Therefore, this study asserts that any protection of EPC services against political risk is a contribution to the scheme of Japanese power investments overseas.

Figure 6   Buyer's Credit Insurance[508]

NEXI

Buyer's Credit Insurance

[figure continues to next page]

---

[504] *Ibid.*

[505] See accordingly to the OII-policy *mutatis mutandis.*

[506] However, according to this study, the bankruptcy of the counterparty is not considered to be political risk.

[507] NEXI, *Business Guide*, pp. 1-3.

[508] NEXI, *Introduction*, p. 13.

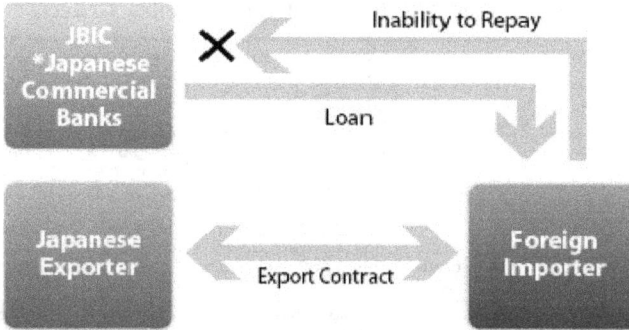

In particular, B/C insurance covers "losses suffered by a Japanese commercial bank or other financial institution as a result of providing loans to foreign importer who purchases goods and services from a Japanese exporter".[509] With regards to investments in the power sector, the Japanese bank lends an electric public utility, or any other authority of the host state, to purchase EPC services from a Japanese manufacturing company or trading-house. For example, in the BLCP coal-fired power plant project mentioned above, NEXI provided B/C insurance covering to a loan given by the Bank of Tokyo-Mitsubishi UFJ, Ltd for the construction and the provision of equipment as EPC contractors by Mitsubishi Corporation and Mitsubishi Heavy Industries, Ltd.

The risks covered by the B/C insurance as well as the insured events and the checkpoints that are required by NEXI for claim ascertainment are the same as in the case of the OULI instrument.[510]

As per JBIC, the types of political risks that are covered by EPRG tool are the same as for NEXI's insurance policy (currency convertibility and transfer risk, expropriation, political violence, and breach of contract by a sovereign obligor) excepting natural disasters and *force majeure* risk.

6.5.5. NEXI Eligibility Criteria[511]

NEXI's political risk insurance is issued under certain eligibility criteria with regards to the direct and indirect beneficiaries. First of all, NEXI provides insurance for projects that are sited in both emerging and developed countries. As of July 2008, 181 countries are eligible according to NEXI's insurance policy. JBIC's guarantees are allowed only for projects sited in developing countries. Moreover, as for the eligible forms of investment, NEXI provides insurance instruments for debt, bonds (domestic or foreign currency) and equity against political and commercial risks. JBIC, however, cannot offer guarantees for equity.[512]

---

[509] *Ibid.*

[510] See NEXI, *Business Guide*, pp. 1-7.

[511] Information collected by the author mainly through NEXI/JBIC Organisation Laws.

[512] For a better picture of NEXI/JBIC structure, see the information summarised in Table 20.

Table 21   NEXI/JBIC Tool and Eligibility Criteria[513]

Tools/ Criteria	Buyer's Credit Insurance	Overseas Untied Loan Insurance	Overseas Investment Insurance	JBIC- EPRG
Insured product	Loan for EPC services (principal+interest)	Long term business financing: loans or bonds (principal+interest)	Equity, assets (tangible & intangible), various rights	Loans/Bonds (no equity)
Eligibility of direct beneficiary	Japanese commercial bank or foreign affiliate based in Japan	Japanese commercial bank or foreign affiliate based in Japan	Japanese company	lenders/investors/ government (foreign also)
Eligibility of indirect beneficiary	Japanese EPC contractor	Foreign government/ company (untied)	Foreign JV with Japanese participation	Jap. participation in projects
Max. repayment Term	OECD standards (but for PF can be flexible)	No limit (equal to the duration of the underlying contract)	2-15 years (but can be extended for 1 more year)	Flexible-depends on contracts
Max. amount coverage	Political risk 97.5%, Commercial risk 95%	Political risk 97.5%, Commercial risk 95%	95% Political risk only	100%
Application of countries	Developed & emerging	Developed & emerging	Developed & emerging	Developing (exc. nuclear plants)

Of those investors who are eligible for NEXI's insurance, this book separates them in two categories: direct and indirect beneficiaries. Direct beneficiaries are considered to be those who sign the investment insurance agreement with NEXI and therefore directly benefit from NEXI's insurance policy. Indirect beneficiaries are those who, according to NEXI, are directly connected with the covered event of political risk, and they will benefit if the specific insurance tool is provided, thus they are considered to be third parties in relation to the signed insurance agreement.

As per NEXI's OULI and B/C insurance criteria, eligible direct beneficiaries can either be Japanese commercial banks or foreign bank's affiliates which need to be based and do business in Japan. Thus, for OII, eligible direct beneficiaries can only be Japanese companies. Indirect beneficiaries in the case of OULI are the host governments or foreign companies (untied policy), and in the case of B/C insurance are the Japanese EPC contractors.

In the case of JBIC's EPRG, there is no nationality requirement for direct beneficiaries. However, the project for which the guarantee is given needs to show that it has Japanese participation (indirect beneficiary). Moreover, JBIC's guarantees can only be offered for investment projects that are located in developing countries, except when the investment's purpose is to develop nuclear plants overseas by Japanese industry.

6.5.6.   NEXI: Repayment term, amount covered and cost

The term of NEXI's insurance depends on the specific instrument. The term of OII is set at a minimum of two years and at a maximum of fifteen years, but it can be extended for one further year unless the insured terminates the contract

---

[513] Table compiled by the author.

or does not apply for the extension on time.[514] In the case of OULI and JBIC's EPRG, the term is equal to the duration of the underlying contract, which is the maturity period of the debt (loan or bond). As per the B/C insurance, it is regulated by the exporters program in accordance with the general criteria of the OECD.[515]

As for the amount covered by the insurance tools, NEXI provides the highest insurance coverage compared with the coverage offered by other ECAs and multilateral agencies. OULI[516] and B/C insurance[517] insure and pay claims covering 97.5% of losses due to political risks and 95% due to commercial risks. As for OII, it covers 95% of losses due to political risk.[518] As for JBIC's EPRG, the amount covered depends on the contract between the insured and the counter-party, but under certain conditions it can reach up to 100% of losses due to political risk. Thus, the above numbers constitute the maximum coverage that NEXI and JBIC can offer. The insured investor is able to decide the appropriate percentage of coverage for his investment according to the specific requirements that exist in each case and he is free to request a lower percentage in order to reduce the cost of the premium.[519]

NEXI's cost for their insurance service is called premium amount and its calculation is based on the following formula (Figure 7):

Figure 7   Calculation Formula for NEXI Investment Insurance[520]

Total Value ✖ 95% ✖ Premium Rate = Premium Amount

For example, in relation to the purchase of investment insurance against political risk through the OII tool, the insured client needs to pay the covered amount that is insured by NEXI (95% of his equity's total value) multiplied by a premium rate that is set according to the specific host country's ability to service its external debt. The calculation of the premium rate is designed by OECD guidelines for pricing the default risk on export credit. The OECD-participating ECAs (among them NEXI) have all agreed to use these guidelines as minimum

---

[514] NEXI, *Business Guide*, p. 9.

[515] However, as mentioned before, project finance is not regulated by OECD guidelines and therefore each ECA is flexible as the conditions can be set according to each case.

[516] NEXI, *Business Guide*, pp.10-13.

[517] *Ibid.*, pp. 8-12.

[518] *Ibid.*, p.10.

[519] *Ibid.*, p.12.

[520] Figure compiled by the author.

premium rates that should be charged to their clients.[521] The country ratings are used not only for export credit insurance but also for the underwriting of investment insurance (as in the above example). The ratings are designed by classifying countries into eight groups, ranging from zero (least risky) to seven (riskiest), by assessing the ability of countries to service their external debt based on a quantitative method (model of a country credit risk, economic and financial factors) and on a qualitative exercise (analysis of a country's political factors).[522]

As the table below shows, each of the five Asian countries rank differently, with Malaysia obtaining a relatively good score (grade 4), and Indonesia and Vietnam a worse grade (grade 6).[523] In addition to the country ranking, NEXI provides different premium rates according to the "product" that is provided in each case. As can be seen in the table below, for the provision of OII, NEXI's charges depend on the type of investment (equity, dividend) and on the kind of political risks that are covered by the insurance policy.[524]

Table 22 Premium Rates According to Country-Risk and Type of "Product"[525]

Country/ Product	Indonesia grade-6	Malaysia grade-3	Philippines grade-5	Thailand grade-4	Vietnam grade-6
Equity	0.421%	0.259%	0.364%	0.301%	0.421%
Equity+ Dividend	0.580%	0.288%	0.412%	0.343%	0.580%
Dividend	0.580%	0.349%	0.504%	0.420%	0.580%
Equity without Transfer of fund risk	0.301%	0.185%	0.260%	0.215%	0.301%

6.6.   The World Bank's political risk guarantees: the role of MIGA

6.6.1. Background

Aside from Japan's state-sponsored agencies, Japanese investors participating in international infrastructure projects (especially in the energy and power sector) have utilised PRI coverage offered by multilateral development banks such as the World Bank Group's specific institutions. The World Bank Group comprises the WB (IBRD and IDA) and two more agencies that focus on private-

---

[521] The ratings came into effect in 1999 as part of an agreement known as "the Knaepen Package", seeking to create a unilateral approach for all participating ECAs by establishing common premium rates; WB, 'World Investment: 2010', Box 3.4, p. 63.

[522] However, the final assessment is made after confirmation with experts about country risk from each member ECA; *ibid.*

[523] Ranking provided by NEXI as of 02/11/2009.

[524] Premium rates provided NEXI as of 02/11/2009.

[525] Information compiled by the author.

sector projects, the IFC and the Multilateral Investment Guarantee Agency (MIGA).[526] These institutions, apart from MIGA, are typically more focused on lending operations than on providing guarantees (similar to the other MDBs). MIGA, however, is the exception among the various multilateral agencies in being a pure investment-insurance agency. Therefore, this section will look primary into MIGA's PRI instruments and secondarily into the other institutions' guarantee functions.

The World Bank was established in 1944 at the end of the World War II; the purpose of its first institution (the IBRD) was to provide financing for Western European countries' reconstruction, after their infrastructure had been left destroyed because of the disastrous war. However, in the 1960s, the Bank's purpose had changed to granting loans for the economic development of developing countries around the world, and most recently, its focus has (partially) shifted to the development of free-market economies by providing financing and guarantees for the encouragement and implementation of private projects, mainly project financing in infrastructure sectors.[527]

The WB's newest institution, MIGA was established in 1988 and it is owned by 170 member countries (Japan among them).[528] MIGA's purpose is to encourage the flow of investments to developing countries by supplementing the activities of IBRD, IFC and of other MDBs.[529] MIGA's objective is to provide insurance or "guarantees" (the term selected by MIGA)[530] to mitigate political risk in relation to investments carried out by the private sector (especially small- and medium-sized enterprises).[531] MIGA has, in coordination with bilateral ECAs (such as NEXI), played a significant role in facilitating investments made by investors from developing countries that do not have their own state-sponsored ECA in large infrastructure projects, using its experience in markets that are considered to be higher risk. It has also increased its activities in covering political risks in complicated investment projects such as PPPs.[532]

---

[526] The WB Group consists of one more institution, the International Centre for Dispute Resolution (ICSID) which is the arbitration forum of the WB; it is not involved in any of the Bank's lending or guarantees operations.

[527] Hoffman, *Law and Business*, p. 283.

[528] Ibrahim Shihata was the originator of the MIGA concept; in 1985, as the General Director of the WB, he repeated his previously successful experiment of creating in the 1970s the Inter-Arab Investment Guarantee Corporation. See: I. Shihata, *MIGA and Foreign Investment: Origins, Operations, Policies and Basic Documents of the Multilateral Investment Guarantee Agency* (World Bank, Washington, DC, 1988).

[529] Convention Establishing the Multilateral Investment Guarantee Agency (MIGA Convention), article 2 (11 October 1985).

[530] After a legal debate about whether to use the term insurance or guarantees for MIGA operations, the legal concept of guarantees prevailed as being more adoptable to diverse legal systems. Arghyris Fatouros was the first among legal scholars to use the term *guarantees*; see: Fatouros, *Government Guarantees*. However, in this book the meaning of insurance and guarantees is used interchangeably.

[531] Multilateral Investment Guarantee Agency, MIGA-Annual Report, FY 2009.

[532] UNCTAD, *World Investment Report*, Box V.13, p. 173.

6.6.2. Type of political risk guarantees

MIGA protects foreign investments against four types of political risks: expropriation, currency inconvertibility and transfer risk, breach of contract (including arbitration award default) and war and civil disturbance (including terrorism). Investors are free to choose from among these four types of coverage.[533]

MIGA insures against total or partial losses caused by a host government's nationalisation or expropriatory acts, whether they are direct or creeping. It covers expropriation of equity, debt, assets, funds and rights. The function of MIGA guarantees covering partial expropriation for funds and assets is compensable at the net book value for non-fund assets.[534] This function of covering partial losses does not exist in NEXI's insurance policy. However, MIGA also differs from NEXI in that it excludes from its expropriation coverage government actions that are non-discriminatory (bona fide) and are taken in the exercise of legitimate regulatory authority.[535] In relation to foreign investments in power sector, this exception may add additional uncertainty as a host government's interference with private projects is always high due to its regulatory authority over public infrastructure sector. This exclusion to MIGA's expropriation coverage may deteriorate the level of the investor's protection as it "may allow countries to enact legislation that has *de facto* the effect of expropriating an investment".[536]

MIGA covers also losses due to local currency inconvertibility into foreign exchange and inability to transfer funds (in foreign currency) outside the host state. Similar to NEXI's policy, this instrument protects against any potential reason, such as delays in acquiring foreign exchange caused by the host government, adverse changes in exchange laws or regulations and even lack of foreign exchange.[537] However, currency depreciation risk is not covered.

As for the war and civil disturbance risk, MIGA guarantees foreign investments against losses that result from physical damage or substantial interruption of business for at least one year due to war, revolution, insurrection, *coups d'ètat* or terrorism in the host country. However, the actions need to be politically motivated (as with NEXI). As for actions that cause interruptions to business, an event of this kind is insurable only when the interruption is related to operation that is essential for the business and when a total loss is experienced.[538]

Finally, in the case of contract breach or repudiation risk, MIGA covers the losses that an investor suffers due to a government's breach of its contractual obligations. MIGA guarantees investors in case they are denied access to an appropriate forum or they are denied the right to enforce an arbitration award or any other judgement. However, MIGA will not indemnify the insured unless the

---

[533] Matsukawa and Habeck, 'Review of Risk Mitigation', Table B1.3, p. 39.

[534] MIGA Convention, article 11, a [ii] (11 October 1985).

[535] *Ibid.*

[536] Ziegler and Gratton, 'Investment Insurance', p. 542.

[537] MIGA Convention, article 11, a [i].

[538] *Ibid.*, article 11, a, [iv].

investor has exhausted all remedies or until an award for damages has been made but after a period of non-payment by the host government.[539] These requirements for the coverage of breach of contract risk set by MIGA are considered to be strict as it is uncertain whether they can be effective in protecting investors or satisfying them in a reasonable amount of time.[540] As has been said, exhausting all local remedies can take a long period of time "during which time a project meltdown very likely will have occurred".[541]

As mentioned above, the WB (IBRD and IDA) provides a partial risk guarantee (PRG) complementary to the MIGA's PRI services. The WB guarantees loans made by commercial lenders to private projects (especially infrastructure investments) provided that the host country where these projects are located will issue a counter-guarantee to the WB.[542] The covered political risks are: currency inconvertibility and transfer risk, and breach of contract by the host state or its agencies, except for expropriation risk and war risk.[543] Additionally, the WB offers partial credit risk (PCR) which covers a borrower's credit risk (commercial risk). Regarding the guarantee against breach of contract risk, it is considered to be a useful tool for power project financing. With this guarantee, MIGA protects investors from various types of project risks that are associated with the host government's contractual undertaking in an agreement with the project company, such as termination payments or subsidy payments, government action or inaction having an adverse impact on the project (e.g. changes in law, non-allowance of agreed tariff rates) and any contractual performance of public agencies involved in the project's operation (e.g. under an off-take agreement or under a PPA).[544]

IFC does not include any genuine type of guarantees against political risks. However, under the IFC co-financing structure ("A" and "B" loans), it offers some protection against currency inconvertibility and transfer risk for the issuers of the "B" loans in order to attract commercial lenders to financing private investment projects.[545]

6.6.3. WB: Eligibility Criteria

MIGA requires that the insured investor be a national of a member country other than the host country.[546] The beneficiary-investor should be an entity operating on a commercial basis. This means that SOEs can also be eligible for MIGA's guarantees as long as they operate on a commercial basis.[547]

---

[539] *Ibid.*, article 11, a [iii].

[540] The adjudication process can sometimes last for a long period with unclear results.

[541] Shanks, 'Lessons', p. 98.

[542] Hoffman, *Law and Business*, p. 259.

[543] *Ibid.*

[544] Matsukawa and Habeck, 'Review of Risk Mitigation', p. 38 note e.

[545] Hoffman, *Law and Business*, p. 259.

[546] MIGA Convention, article 13 (October 11, 1985).

[547] *Ibid.*

Eligible countries for MIGA's policy (where an investment is made) are, as noted above, developing countries that are members listed on schedule A to the MIGA Convention.[548] In addition, the host country must approve the investment before MIGA issues the insurance coverage.[549] This approval reduces the risk of claims exposure for MIGA.

Finally, the forms of investment projects eligible to be covered under MIGA's guarantee policy are new projects (Greenfield Projects), projects for expansion, modernisation or financial restructuring of existing projects, privatisation and, in general, projects that satisfy specific requirements of MIGA (economic viability, promotion of economic development, compliant with local laws, protection of the host country's environment).

As per the WB and IFC guarantees, the eligible beneficiaries are private lenders, and eligible projects are new projects (in MIGA's case, including concession transactions) in a developing member country. According to IFC's criteria, eligible projects are private sector projects located in a developing member country.[550]

Table 23 MIGA/WB/IFC: Tools and Eligibility Criteria[551]

Agency/ Criteria	MIGA	WB-PRG	IFC-B Loan Guarantees
Insured product	Equity & Debt	Debt *loans only	B-loans (bank syndication)
Eligibility of direct beneficiary	Commercial lender, Host-governments & private sector. Only for: new project, or for expansion/modernization, restructuring, or privatization	Commercial lenders	Commercial lenders
Indirect eligibility/ criteria	Host government & project sponsor Need: econ. viability, development, local laws compliance, host country invest. environment +Specific approval by host country	Project sponsor Need: counter-guarantee by host government	Project sponsor Need: private sector develop. No need of host country counter-guarantee
Max. repayment Term	15 years (but if justified up to 20)	No limitation	N/A
Max. amount coverage	Equity 90%- Debt 95% (up to 200$ mil. /project)	No limitation (but according to IMF restrictions)	100% of B-loan
Application of countries	Developing	Developing	Developing

6.6.4. WB: Repayment term and amount covered

MIGA coverage is for up to fifteen years but it can be extended to twenty years on a case-by-case basis. MIGA may not terminate the insurance contract unless the insured investor infringes his contractual obligations towards MIGA.

---

[548] *Ibid.*, article 14.

[549] *Ibid.*, article 15.

[550] Matsukawa and Habeck, 'Review of Risk Mitigation', pp. 37-38.

[551] Table compiled by the author.

The insured, however, is able to terminate the contract after three years have passed.[552] There are no limitations for the WB and IFC. MIGA's political risk insurance covers equity and debt. Equity investment can be covered up to 90% and debt up to 95%. For technical assistance MIGA can cover up to 90% of total value of payments under the agreement. The remaining percentage of the risk is required to be covered by the investor.[553] There is no limitation on WB guarantees but there are some general guidelines set by IMF rules and for IFC "B-loan" guarantees, the total value (100%) can be covered.

Finally, according to the MIGA Convention, after the satisfaction of the insured's claims, all of the rights that the insured investor has acquired against the host state are transferred to MIGA as a result of subrogation. In addition, if negotiations between MIGA and the host country fail, disputes shall be submitted to ICSID arbitration.[554]

6.7. Chapter's conclusion

In conclusion, capital-exporting states (home countries) and multilateral organisations play an important role in the financing of foreign investments. However, regarding the high risks that occur in the infrastructure industries (power sector), the protection of foreign investments against political risk through the provision of various PRI tools is the most crucial task that bilateral and multilateral agencies undertake.

In general, purchasing PRI by the investor-insured, successfully enhances foreign investment by allocating the burden of political risk to third parties (ECAs) which play the role of prominent victims, which as a result provides further security in the financing needed by commercial lenders or for the participation of equity shareholders. Moreover, the application of various insurance instruments can directly mitigate specific political risks that investments face when implemented in the power sector of foreign countries. The political risk that can be covered by PRI are the expropriation risk, the currency inconvertibility and the transfer inability risk, the war or civil disturbance risk, the breach of contract and change in law risk and the *force majeure* risk. In addition, there are also types of risks that do not clearly fall under one of the above political risk categories and are difficult to define. Thus, PRI instruments can cover some of these risks, if not in full, in part and indirectly.

In the case of Japanese foreign investments, NEXI – as Japan's officially sponsored ECA – plays a dominant role in providing PRI to Japanese investors, while JBIC is the main public financier of Japanese investments but with a much smaller scope of political risk guarantees. Similarly, MIGA of the World Bank Group has played the most important role among multilateral agencies in guaranteeing foreign investments made in developing countries against political risks.

However, in relation to the benefits received by investments made by Japanese investors, NEXI is in a better position to support Japanese investments for

---

[552] Rubins and Kinsella, *International Investment*, p. 108.

[553] *Ibid.*, p. 107.

[554] MIGA Convention, articles 18 and 57 (11 October 1985).

various reasons: Firstly, because NEXI, including the JBIC, has in principle a "nation-based"[555] purpose of supporting the economic and industrial policy of the Japanese Government by promoting and securing Japanese investment projects overseas, while multilateral agencies such as MIGA apply more general criteria – economic development of the host countries, privatisation, open-markets and non-distortion of competition. However, with regards to power investments, both NEXI and MIGA have deployed a comprehensive set of instruments covering several contingencies of government's defaulting on its obligations towards its counterparty.

After examining the function of PRI, this study has noted the existence of a general problem – that the distinction between political and commercial risks is not always clear. For example, it is not easy to distinguish whether the default in the payment by the counterparty (e.g. an electric utility) is a political or commercial risk unless all necessary conditions and contractual obligations are clarified (e.g. default can result due to both political and commercial reasons). Moreover, the events that are required by the agencies' criteria to trigger political risk insurance are in some cases ambiguous. For example, NEXI requires, among others, the investor's inability to operate as a result of the political risk materiali-sation (e.g. breach of contract, infringement of rights, war risk, etc.). Thus, the suspension of operation requirement cannot be partial but it needs to be a full halt in the operation. This may cause uncertainty in the case of complicated power investments which consist of various kinds of operations (e.g. power plant operation, fuel supply operation, transmission through the grid etc.) and it raises questions about whether a claim for insurance is valid when a partial halt of one kind of operation causes substantial damage. MIGA's approach is different by accepting suspension of the essential operations, yet more clarity is needed.

Some of the other procedural implications (such as MIGA's requirement for not compensating the insured until all local remedies are exhausted and until an award for damages has been made) raise questions about the effectiveness of such a measure and about the prompt treatment of the investor's damage. NEXI differs on this requirement by requiring reasonable measures to be taken. NEXI is more flexible than MIGA as it can decide on a case-by-case basis. However, another implication is made with regards to "check points for claim ascertain-ment". ECAs need evidence of the influence on the investment's economic interests caused by the insured event, requiring a causal analysis between the event and the damage suffered. However, the investor is not always in a position to prove the causality of damages when the events (e.g. government actions or inactions) are indirectly connected with his damage, such as in the case of creeping expropriation or when the total result of the government's actions only becomes apparent much later.

The way ECAs assess the validity of the insured's claims in cases such as change in law risk is uncertain. In this case, MIGA accepts the claim as valid only if the new law is unfair or discriminatory or against International law and it causes losses to the investor. Thus, it is uncertain whether MIGA can intervene in

---

[555] A term borrowed from the non-political concept of "economic nationalism" which is based on the idea of countries supporting their national industries and products at any cost and protecting them against "open competition".

the host country's sovereignty and cast doubt on the fairness or the discriminatory nature of a domestic law. Similarly, in the case of the infringement of rights risk, MIGA accepts a claim for insurance as valid only if the host government's acts are discriminatory or against an international agreement or a domestic law. NEXI also does not insure losses due to an infringement of rights when government's acts are in accordance with domestic or international law.

Finally, the case of expropriation is also a complicated issue when the host government asserts that its actions are legitimate regulatory measures. MIGA does not compensate the insured if governmental actions are non-discriminatory (bona fide) and if taken in the exercise of legitimate regulatory authority. Thus, the protection against expropriation becomes an even more ambiguous issue as it is not clear how MIGA can investigate the legitimacy of the host government's measures. With regards to expropriation, another implication found is that NEXI can only insure investors against total losses suffered due to expropriation. Partial losses caused by a host government's nationalisation and expropriatory acts cannot be covered.

Due to the implications of the PRI mechanisms, investors need to take into consideration that signing an insurance contract does not mean elimination of all cases of political risks that they may face during a long-term investment project in the power sector of a foreign country. Especially in relation to power project financing, a more surgical and commercialised approach by insurance agencies is required. However, the effectiveness of PRI protection against political risk depends not only on the insurance policy but also, to a large extent, on the specific contractual arrangement between the investor and the host country or its agencies.

The occurrence of certain contractual clauses with the inclusion of specific guarantees toward investments provides a different level of protection against political risk, according to the content of each clause. National and multilateral PRI agencies pay attention to investor's contracts, looking into the content of specific guarantees. The next chapter analyses the role of specific contractual clauses in the protection against political risk, and it offers some empirical evidence by comparing five contracts signed between Japanese investors and Asian countries in relation to investment projects in the power sector.

7

GUARANTEES AGAINST POLITICAL RISK: CASE STUDY OF POWER-INVESTMENT CONTRACTS

7.1.   Introduction

Once an investor has decided to implement a power-project investment in a foreign country, due to what has been described as the "obsolescing bargain"[556] (investor's bargaining power diminishes as the investment project progresses), the investor should begin looking at methods to minimise certain political risks that they may face due to the host government's interference with the investment. In particular, as mentioned before, infrastructure is a special category of industry with services that have strategic importance, being essential for the economic development of the host state, and that have a public character sensitive to domestic politics. Given these factors, foreign investors need to take all available measures to mitigate political risk. Apart from the "passive" (or non-controllable) methods of minimising risks provided through the investor's "awareness" of the assurances available under international investment law and treaties, this chapter also focuses on the "affirmative" (or controllable) methods of reducing political risk exposure.[557] Along with the PRI measures explained before, it analyses the role of sovereign guarantees in general and the importance of specific contract clauses that are available for the protection of foreign investments against political risk under the investor-state international investment agreements. For the purpose of analysis, this study investigates the wording of five power-project contracts between Japanese investors and Asian countries.

7.2.   Sovereign guarantees

7.2.1.   General characteristics

Sovereign guarantees consist of a formal undertaking by a host government that various project risks will be placed within the government's agencies' control. These risks can be political, legal, regulatory or financial.[558] The sovereign guarantees are typically executed at the financial closing of an investment contract and are included in the implementation agreement. Thus, their provision is promised by the host government at an earlier time in order to achieve better conditions for the financing of the specific project. Sovereign guarantees indicate the strongest legal commitment of host governments to protect the foreign investment against any default of the public enterprises' obligations. It

---

[556] Vernon, *Sovereignty at Bay, passim.*

[557] Comeaux and Kinsella, *Protecting Foreign Investment*, p. 127.

[558] Hoffman, *Law and Business*, p. 147.

usually takes the form of a direct undertaking to the investors' company such as a guarantee of the off-taker's (SOE) performance obligations (under an off-take agreement, political risk buy-outs, the host state's engagement to support the power project, and other assurances about setting tariffs or rate of return for revenues).[559] Moreover, it is often the practice of host states to offer counter-indemnities to IFIs that have provided guarantees to project investors and lenders (as in the case of MIGA's guarantees).

Sovereign guarantees, as in the case of any other guarantees, are a mechanism for the transference of risks. For BOT-type infrastructure investments, sovereign guarantees are used to protect operators, sponsors and lenders against the risk of the public sector parties' default. Their function is crucial, especially when the creditworthiness of the foreign investor's counterparty (the public electric utility) is poor, when the political conditions in a host country is problematic or when the regulatory or business environment of the power sector is controversial due to lack of reforms. Under the above conditions, the foreign investor would desire or demand the government to directly counter-guarantee the obligations of its agencies and SOEs.[560]

7.2.2. Application: The case of NEXI

The existence of sovereign guarantees by a host government to a power project's investors is considered to be one of the most important determinants for ECAs and multilateral development banks in order to provide to the insured their various PRI mechanisms. NEXI has successfully provided PRI programs to a large number of Japanese investments in the power sector of Asian countries mainly because of the occurrence of sovereign guarantees from the host countries. Some of the successful cases of power projects insured by NEXI are shown in Table 24 (on the following page).

All of NEXI's insured transactions are provided to power projects that Japanese companies have obtained a substantial share or interest in, whether these companies are main sponsors of the project (debt or equity share), contractor (EPC services) or simply the financier. Most of the cases consist of a B/C type of insurance which is offered mostly for EPC services implemented by Japanese electric utilities (TEPCO, KEPCO, Kyushu Electric), and Japanese construction companies (Sumitomo, Mitsubishi Heavy Industry, Kawasaki Heavy Industry). In addition, important overseas investment activity in the power has been driven by Japanese trading houses such as Mitsui, Mitsubishi, Sojitsu and others by trading (EPCs services) and acquiring shares (equity), as well as lending to project sponsors. One characteristic of insurance provision found in almost all these cases is that NEXI complements the credit enhancement offered by JBIC (as shown in the table) by providing PRI to Japanese commercial lenders (OULI),

---

[559] *Ibid.*, p. 268.

[560] Sader, 'Attracting Foreign Direct Investment', p. 56.

Table 24   Examples of NEXI-Insured Transactions for Power Project[561]

Project Name sponsor/contractor)	Country	Year (period)	Insured Amount	Type of Insurance	Coverage (other ECAs)
Paiton 1 Coal-Fired Power Project (Mitsui,Tepco, International Power)	Indonesia	1995 (12)	USD Million	B/C	97.5% Political 75% Commercial JBIC,US EXIM, OPIC
Mindanao Coal-Fired Power Project (Sojitsu/Kawasaki Heavy)	Philippines	2004 (13)	USD 40 Million	B/C	97.5% Political+EPR (JBIC, KFW, GKA)
Tanjun Jati B Coal-Fired Power Project (Sumitomo)	Indonesia	2003 (9)	Yen 57.8 Billion	B/C	97.5% Political+EPR (JBIC)
PHU MY 3 BOT Power Project (Sojitsu / Kyushu Electric)	Vietnam	2003 (13)	USD 95 Million	OULI	97.5% Political+EPR (JBIC, ADB, MIGA)
TJB Expansion Power Project (Sumitomo)	Indonesia	2009 (7)	Yen 45 Billion	OII & OULI	97.5% Political+EPR (JBIC)
BLCP Power Project (Mitsubishi/MHI)	Thailand	2004 (15)	USD 163 Million	B/C	97.5% Political+EPR (JBIC, ADB)
Illiyan Gas Power Project (Mitsubishi/ Kepco)	Philippines	2000 (14)	USD104 Million	B/C	97.5% Political EPR (JBIC, US EXIM)

sponsors (OII) and contractors (B/C). Another important characteristic is that investments in the power sector are mega-projects, with long-term project operation and complicated structures that usually require the collaboration of multiple ECAs and multilateral agencies in the coverage of the political and commercial risks over many years (e.g. 15 years for the BLCP power project).

7.2.3.   Forms of sovereign guarantees

With regards to the above examples of insurance covering power investments against political risks, it is likely that NEXI (including the other ECAs) could not guarantee these projects (or could not guarantee them under the same conditions) if there were not any specific sovereign guarantees provided by the host governments. Host countries issued various forms of sovereign guarantees as shown in Table 25 (on the following page).

---

[561] Information provided by NEXI.

Table 25   Forms of Sovereign Guarantees and NEXI PRI[562]

Name of Project	Form of Guarantee	Issuer	Content of Guarantee	Direct Beneficiary	Indirect Beneficiary
Paiton-1 Project	Support Letter	MoF	Performance under PPA	PJ Company	PLN
Mindanao & Illiyan Projects	Performance Undertaking (PU)	GoP	Performance under PPA	PJ Company	NPC
TJB Project	Liquidity Facility Letter (LFL)	MoF	Performance under PPA	PJ Company	PLN
Phu My 3 Project	Government Guarantee Undertaking (GGU)	M. Pl. Inv.	Performance under PPA	PJ Company	PV
BLCP Project	National Budget	EGAT-Act (Law)	Financial Payment Duty	Any counterparty of EGAT	EGAT
TJB-Expansion Project	Umbrella Note of Mutual Understanding	GoI	Performance under PPA	NEXI	PLN

The form of these sovereign guarantees usually comes under different names as shown in the table above. The most used names are the government guarantee undertaking (GGU) as issued in the case of *Phu My 3 Project* by the Vietnamese Ministry of Planning and Investment or the performance undertaking (PU) as issued in the *Mindanao & Illiyan Projects* by the Government of the Philippines. In most of the cases, ECAs (as in the case of NEXI) perceive that all sovereign guarantees, even with different names, offer the same legal power in securing the project's investors against the default of their counterparty. However, there are different opinions expressed about whether general guarantees that come under a comfort letter, such as in the case of *Paiton Project*, are binding guarantees that can be legally enforceable.[563]

One of the most significant types of sovereign guarantees consists of the issuance by the host government or any of its ministries of a legally binding letter that discharges the performance obligations of the public electric utility under the power purchase agreement (PPA) towards the project company. The PPA is an off-take contract between the investment-consortium (power producer) and the public electric utility (SOE) which is the off-taker of the electricity produced. The PPA contract is considered to be the most important among all the contractual agreements because it contains the necessary arrangements about how much of the electricity produced, and at what price, the electric state utility should buy

---

[562] Information collected from NEXI's Annual Reports and meetings with managers.

[563] Sacerdoti argues that a comfort letter represents a statement of intent rather than a legal obligation: Sacerdoti, 'Source and Evolution', section A, p. 3. See also: Babbar and Schuster, 'Power Project Finance', p. 28.

from the project company.564 Based on the quantity and tariff of the output that is determined by the PPA, private investors and lenders can calculate the revenue of the particular power investment, which is important for project financing.565 Moreover, given the public character of the power sector in most countries and the sensitivity that arises from issues such as the price of electrical services, the government's interference with the utility's performance is a political rather than commercial issue that results in uncertainty. For this reason, foreign investors would like to see, along with the utility's contractual guarantee, a sovereign counter-guarantee in case the utility does not perform in accordance with the agreed PPA.

However, there are cases where power project financing could be implemented without a direct sovereign counter-guarantee of the utility's performance under a PPA. In the *BLCP Project*, the implementation contract between Thailand's public electric utility (EGAT) and the foreign investors (Mitsubishi Trading House and Mitsubishi Heavy Industry) was concluded without a specific inclusion of a counter-guarantee issued by the government or any of its ministries. Instead, investors conceived the provision of the EGAT's Act (Electricity Law) which in article 45 states that any EGAT's financial payment duty is guaranteed by national budget as a sufficient assurance. Moreover, NEXI also understood that the legal provision of EGAT's Act would be a sufficient guarantee without any additional commitment by the Government of Thailand to cover EGAT's payment obligations under the BLCP-Project's PPA.

Even if a domestic law can be a compelling mechanism for assuring investors, there are some implications that can create uncertainty over the extent of protection against certain political risks. A significant degree of uncertainty results due to the most common fear that investors face when investing in a foreign country: the change of law risk. The political risk that a future public administration will change the law becomes more uncertain if parties have not made concrete reference to the content of the law inside the body of their contract which could give some extent of protection under the breach of contract clause. Another implication, raised by NEXI during negotiations with the insured investors,566 is whether the law's provision about the commitment of the Thai Government will continue to prevail in the case of EGAT being privatised and the share of the government becoming less than 50%. If the possibility of privatisation is not clearly stated in the contract, it is likely that such legal provision as in article 45 will not be valid.

Moreover, there is a legal implication that the legal provision lacks specificity as it is addressed generally to any counterparty of EGAT. Even if the indirect beneficiary (EGAT) is clearly defined, the direct beneficiary, which is EGAT's

---

564 An early study by the World Bank had indicated that "the off-taker's ability to perform as contractually obligated may be the single most important risk facing private power projects"; Babbar and Schuster, 'Power Project Finance', p. 27.

565 In project financing (non-recourse financing) the only security for commercial lenders is the cash-flow of the particular project (or some limited mortgage used for limited-recourse financing).

566 Interview conducted with NEXI managers.

counterparty, is not specified by the law.[567] On the contrary, in the case of a sovereign guarantee, a specific support letter is issued by the government referring to a specific project and addressing concrete issues of a contract (PPA performance) and benefiting the specific sponsors of a project. Thus, it is asserted as a counter-argument for the above implications that, in reality, what always matters is the level of creditworthiness of the off-taker. In the case of *BLCP Project*, the risk is lower because of EGAT's strong balance sheet and historic record of good performance. Yet, even if the creditworthiness argument has practical value, it is an issue related to business and not political risk.

7.2.4. Present status

Today, however, sovereign guarantees such as those analysed above are very rare.[568] Sovereign guarantees do not come free for host governments. Depending on the extent of each type of guarantee, they represent a contingent liability and when the guarantee is called such liability can impose a budgetary burden on the central government.[569] Before, sovereign guarantees used to be considered as "off-budget" liabilities. However, macro-economic shocks such as the Argentinean crisis and the Asian financial crisis have shown that the previous perception by host governments and investors about the non-liability of sovereign guarantees over infrastructure BOT-type projects was an illusion.[570] Since then, and especially recently during another financial crisis with global effects influencing both developed and developing countries, the practice of sovereign guarantees for power-project investments has, for most host countries, diminished.

Accordingly, Japan's Ministry of Economy, Trade and Industry (METI) has recently started supporting the trend of PPP infrastructure projects for overseas investments without the inclusion of sovereign guarantees. NEXI, however, frequently finds this trend to be risky. On many project-occasions, NEXI has assessed that the overall exposure of its insurance business is very high unless there is a counter-guarantee from the host government. Even if NEXI, as most of ECAs, has changed its policy in accepting insurance coverage of projects without sovereign guarantees, it prefers markets that still provide sovereign guarantees or,

---

[567] As shown in Table 25, the direct beneficiary of the law provision is only generally specified as it can be anyone who becomes a counterparty of EGAT.

[568] However, it has recently been observed that, because of the financial and the sovereign debt crises, several countries are trying to attract foreign investments into their infrastructure sectors by offering comprehensive sovereign guarantees. For example, on 9 June 2011 the Cabinet Ministers of Ukraine (the "CMU") adopted Resolution No. 611 on the "Approval of the Procedure and Terms for Granting State Guarantees" for securing the debt obligations of businesses under borrowings attracted for the implementation of investment in infrastructure and other development projects. See: A. Mycyk and V. Kaplan, 'Ukraine: Procedure for State Guarantees for Certain Development Projects Approved', *Mondaq Legal News*, <www.mondaq.com>, retrieved 8 July 2011.

[569] "The US Government requires contingent liabilities to be reported if they are quantifiable, and to be calculated as full liabilities in case their probability of being called is above 50 percent". Sader, 'Attracting Foreign Direct Investment', p. 60.

[570] E. Woodhouse, 'Managing International Political Risk: Lessons from the Power Sector', in T.H. Moran, G.T. West and K. Martin (eds.), *Managing International Political Risk: Needs of the Present Challenges for the Future* (World Bank, Washington, DC, 2006) pp. 61-62; see also: Sader, 'Attracting Foreign Direct Investment', pp. 59-60.

at least, it provides insurance to investment projects that obtain other contractual guarantees that are essential for political risk mitigation.

7.3. Specific contract guarantees against political risks: power case studies

7.3.1. In general

Not all guarantees impose as heavy a contingent liability as the general government's counter-guarantee assuming all public-sector contractual obligations does. There are some specific guarantees that do not impose significant budgetary burdens on governments or that are not directly connected with the host government. As some political risks can be unbundled, specific risk-oriented guarantees can effectively achieve political risk mitigation.

This study analyses some of the most essential contractual clauses in mitigating political risks and contemplates their function by looking into the wording of five contracts that are related to power-project financing in Asian countries. These contracts are real cases that NEXI needed to assess in order to decide whether or not to provide PRI to Japanese investors. These contracts were concluded between state agencies or public electric utilities and investment consortia (with Japanese companies' participation) and they were not granted any sovereign guarantees similar to those of the cases explained in Table 25. Due to reasons of confidentiality, no information about the projects' names, the host countries or the projects' companies is allowed to be revealed. For analytical purposes, the five projects are named as follows: Alpha, Beta, Gamma, Delta, and Epsilon.

This section examines four contractual guarantees which are found in either separate or integrated clauses:

- provision of international arbitration forum (including choice of law ability)
- waiver of sovereign immunity (including enforcement capacity)
- stabilisation clause or legislative protection (including specific remedies), and
- protection against *force majeure*.

7.3.2. International arbitration clause

7.3.2.1. Scope

International arbitration is without any doubt one of the most essential elements in every investor-state contractual agreement mainly because of its importance as means of settling disputes arising between the parties of those contracts. With regards to international power-project investments in a host country, the significance of international arbitration is justified not only because of its advantages over litigation, but mainly because of the possibility of having an adjudication of disputes before an international tribunal that sits outside the host country. Moreover, an arbitration clause becomes indispensable for the effective protection of the foreign investor's rights against political risks when it includes provisions such as a "choice of law" applied in case of a dispute resolution, a "non-exhaustion of local remedies" requirement in order for an adjudication before a neutral forum to commence immediately after a dispute occurs, or the ability of an award to be enforcement by a jurisdiction different than the host state's legal system (related to the sovereign immunity issue). All of these requirements are necessary for the effective satisfaction of investors' interests.

Especially when the investment is related to public infrastructure such as the power sector, the disputes that may arise between foreign investors and public agencies can become politically and socially sensitive for the host country, touching upon "the core of State sovereignty".[571] If the investor-state contract does not provide the capacity to solve the dispute before a neutral forum, outside the host country, then the foreign investor faces the high possibility of the host government's interference in the country's judicial system, increasing the risk of a judgement being biased against the investor's interests,[572] something that, as explained before, may adversely affect the protection offered by ECAs through PRI mechanisms.[573] The parties in an international power contract have the freedom to select an arbitration forum between an ad hoc arbitration, which is conducted pursuant to their agreement and is usually self-executing, and an institutional arbitration, which consists of a permanent institution that administers an arbitration procedure with an exclusive list of arbitrators. The most well-known and established international arbitration institutions are the International Chamber of Commerce (ICC), the International Centre for the Settlement of Investment Disputes (ICSID) and the London Court of International Arbitration (LCIA).[574] There are also a number of nationally-based institutions that in addition to their domestic arbitration also offer services for international arbitrations. In East Asia, three such well-established national institutions are the Singapore International Arbitration Center (SIAC) in Singapore, the Hong Kong International Arbitration Center (HKIAC) in Hong Kong and the Kuala Lumpur Regional Centre for Arbitration (KLRCA) in Malaysia.

Additionally, an arbitration clause may provide a choice of law governing the parties' agreement which is different than the host state's law. Choosing a law other than the domestic law for the adjudication procedure of contracting parties plays an important role in reducing the political risk of changing laws and regulations by the host government. Especially in relation to power investments, state contracts can be manipulated by the host government by merely altering regulations according to its policies, which, as a result, affects the implementation of the contract. Therefore, by choosing another jurisdiction's law, especially from a legal system that is protective of creditor rights, such as English or New

---

[571] Rubins and Kinsella, *International Investment*, p. 44.

[572] Sornarajah, *International Law*, p. 413.

[573] If there is a judicial award by a local court that is against the investor's rights, ECAs usually reject the insurer's claim for insurance as non-valid.

[574] J. Paulsson, 'Dispute Resolution', in R. Pritchard (ed.), *Economic Development, Foreign Investment and the Law: Issues of Private Sector Development, Foreign Investment and the Role of Law in a New Era* (International Bar Association and Kluwer Law International, London, 1996) pp. 215-222.

York law,[575] adds some more stability and predictability for the foreign investors, and eventually lowers the change of law political risk.[576] Moreover, it is asserted that by including a clause that invokes the principles of international law or when it establishes a law other than the domestic law of the host state, the contract can be "internationalised".[577] Finally, in relation to the arbitration procedures that should be applied, more transparency and predictability is achieved by invoking a settlement under internationally-accepted arbitration rules, such as the United Nations Commission on International Trade Law's (UNCITRAL) arbitration rules.[578]

Thus, as explained in Part II, foreign investors can automatically benefit from an international forum of dispute resolution through the mere existence of an international investment treaty. Though, in the case of Japan, there was not, until recently, such a treaty with any Asian countries, and there are still many countries which are popular destinations for Japanese overseas investment but with whom there is still not any investment treaty yet signed. Moreover, even if there is an international treaty protecting foreign investments between the investor's home country and the host country where investment is located, it should not be taken for granted that an international arbitration system is provided or that a requirement of exhaustion of local remedies does not exist. Therefore, the inclusion of an international arbitration clause in the investor-State contracts should be a priority for foreign investors when negotiating and structuring their agreement with the host government.

7.3.2.2. The findings

All the contracts analysed herein included an arbitration clause, though their content varied significantly. There were differences in when parties could resolve their disputes in a neutral forum outside the host state by using the law of a third jurisdiction and when there was an inclusion of a clause that requires the host country's laws to be used as the governing law of the specific agreement.

Starting with the Alpha project's contract, under the "Dispute Resolution" clause, the agreement requires that the parties meet regularly "at not less than yearly intervals" in order to discuss the overall progress of the project and specifically about the operation of the power plant. It is acknowledged by the same clause that this requirement was set in order to "ensure that the arrangements between the Parties hereto proceed on a mutually satisfactory basis".

---

[575] Hoffman, *Law and Business*, p. 150.

[576] Moreover, "local law may be subject to alteration or manipulation to advance the economic interests of the State contracting party in the investment transaction"; Rubins and Kinsella, *International Investment*, p. 45.

[577] Cameron asserts that by exercising the right to choose public international law or any other jurisdiction's law except host state's law as the applicable law of the contract, it serves to internationalise the contract. See: Cameron, *International Energy Investment Law*, pp. 67-68.

[578] Lawyers and legal advisors are well-positioned to understand such legal procedures and to predict the results with regard to their application.

Table 26   Summary of Findings/International Arbitration[579]

Projects	Alpha (Satisfactory)	Beta (Best)	Gamma (Satisfactory)	Delta (Satisfactory)	Epsilon (Satisfactory)
Arbitration clause	-2 stages of consultation (+), 2nd formal but period not defied (-) -Gov. Law: N/A (-) -Place: Singapore (ad hoc) (+) -Arbitration: UNCITRAL Rules (+) -Language: ? (-) -Award final & binding (+)	-30 days friendly consultations (+) -Expert forum optional (+) -Gov. law: (+) Singapore Law -Place: (+) Kuala Lumpur (KLRCA) -Arbitration: (+) KLRCA Rules -Language: (+) English -Award final & binding (+)	-30 days consultation (+) -Expert forum mandatory (for technical matters) (-) -Gov. law: Host country's laws (-) -Place: Singapore (ICSID) (+) -Arbitration: (+) UNCITRAL Rules -Language: (+) English -Award apportion the costs of arbitration and is final & binding (+)	-45 days consultation (+) -Permanent Wise Counsellor ((for technical & commercial matters) (+) -Expert forum mandatory (hearing in Singapore) (-) -Gov. law: Host country's laws (-) -Place: Singapore (ICC) (+) -Arbitration: ICC Rules (+) -Language : English (+) -Award apportion the costs of arbitration and is final & binding (+)	-30 days consultation (+) -Expert forum mandatory (for technical matters) & if no decision new expert appointment (1 year limitation) (-) -Gov. Law: N/A, (-) -tribunal no bound by strict rules(-) -Place: Stockholm (ad hoc) (+) -Arbitration: UNCITRAL Rules(+) -Language: English (+) -Award apportion the costs of arbitration and is final & binding (+)

Moreover, in another paragraph of the same clause, under the title "Amicable Settlement", the Alpha project Agreement requires the parties to meet soon after there is a dispute, controversy or difference between them relating to the Agreement and resolve their dispute by discussion. In case such discussion does not help the resolution of the dispute, then the Agreement requires the chief executives of the project company and the public utility to meet and try again to resolve their dispute. The Agreement gives special importance to this second meeting not only because of the requirement for high level participation by the parties but because it states that in case the meeting comes to a joint decision by the chief executives of the parties, such decision "shall be binding upon the Parties". If these two attempts for amicable resolution fail, then the Agreement gives the right for any of the parties to settle the dispute by international arbitration.

The Agreement in Alpha project determines not only the neutral forum of the arbitration – "arbitration shall be conducted in Singapore" – but also the rules of the dispute-settlement arbitration procedure – "UNCITRAL Rules" – and the composition of the arbitration forum – "three arbitrators appointed in accord-ance to UNCITRAL Rules". Moreover, under the same clause, the parties agree to exclude any right of "application or appeal to any courts in connection with any question of law arising in the course of arbitration or with respect to any award made".

The structure of this clause is considered to be a sufficient method of mitigat-ing political risk resulting from dispute resolution procedural uncertainty. Thus, the Alpha contract does not specify the governing law of the agreement in case of a dispute. In the absence of a choice of law clause, it is most likely that the

---

[579] Table compiled by the author.

arbitration tribunal will apply the law of the host state, being the most appropriate because it is the place of contractual performance of the project investment (*lex loci*). For example, article 42.1 of the ICSID Convention clarifies that in the absence of any concrete choice of law by the parties, the particular tribunal of their dispute should apply the law of the contracting state (host state) and any rule of the international law as may be applicable.[580] This absence of a choice of law clause may be a reason for uncertainty for the investor's rights as mentioned above. Another element that might give some uncertainty to the procedure is that the Agreement does not mention the duration of the two meetings that parties should conclude in a decision during the attempt at an amicable settlement. That may create some anxiety on the private investor's side about the risk of dilatory procedural tactics by the state agency or the host government's intervention.

The Beta project also requires the parties in the contract to "attempt in the first instance to resolve such Dispute through friendly consultations". This contract does not specify whether the consultations shall be conducted by high level delegates from each side or whether there is a need for more than one attempt. Thus, the Beta contract comprises a more flexible requirement of amicable settlement than Alpha project by referring to "friendly" consultations and not any formal procedure. Moreover, it limits the period of such consultations to 30 days. If the dispute between the parties is not resolved within 30 days "after the commencement of discussions by notice from one Party to the other or such longer period as the Parties agree in writing at that time", then either party can submit a claim for settlement of the dispute to either an "Expert" or to an arbitration forum.

The Beta contract provides to either party an alternative ability to resolve their dispute before an expert that is an experienced and qualified independent engineering firm. This provision is available to the parties under two requirements: firstly, that they mutually agree to have an expert resolve their dispute, and secondly, that their dispute should involve a technical engineering issue of less than USD 2 million. Under these conditions, and given their good faith attempt to appoint "a reasonable satisfactory (firm) to both of them to act as an Expert", the parties can freely choose to bring their dispute before such a neutral forum which will render a final and binding decision.

In the event that the parties cannot choose such a forum or they are not willing to do so, they are able to resolve their dispute by an international arbitration process. Beta contract determines that the place of the arbitration shall be Kuala Lumpur, Malaysia (outside the host country), and the arbitration procedure be "in accordance with the Rules for Arbitration of Kuala Lumpur Regional Centre for Arbitration". The tribunal of arbitration should be composed of three members: one arbitrator appointed by each of the parties, and the two appointed arbitrators choosing the third who shall act as the presiding arbitrator of the tribunal. Nevertheless, the most important element of this contract is the choice of law clause providing that the day-to-day BOT Company operations "shall be carried out in compliance with the relevant laws of the host state", but in the

---

[580] Washington Convention on the Settlement of Investment Disputes between States and Nationals of Other States (ICSID Convention).

event of any dispute arising from this agreement the arbitration forum should apply the law of Singapore as well as the applicable rules of public international law. In addition, the language of arbitration shall be English and the decision of the tribunal be "final and binding". Finally, the parties agree to comply with any arbitral award and that they "shall not appeal to any court from the decision of the arbitral tribunal".

In the case of Gamma project, the contract requires the parties, as in the case of Beta project, to attempt settle any dispute "in the first instance by mutual discussions". These discussions should not last more than 30 days after the receipt of a notice by one party about the existence of a dispute. The Gamma contract does not set any requirement for a formal discussion as in the case of Alpha project. Thus, in case the nature of the dispute is technical, the parties are obliged (not as an alternative option as in Beta project) to resolve their dispute before an independent expert. The expert is appointed after the parties agree on his "identity and on the terms upon to which the Technical Dispute is to be referred". However, in case the parties are unable within a 14 day period to appoint an expert, the International Chamber of Commerce's (ICC) International Center for Expertise will appoint an expert for them. The decision of the expert, who acts as an expert and not as an arbitrator, shall remain confidential and is final and binding upon the parties.

In the event that the expert of the technical dispute cannot render a decision within 30 days or his appointment is terminated, and for any other dispute that is not of a technical nature, the parties are to resolve their dispute by international arbitration. Gamma contract's arbitration clause provides that dispute shall be settled under UNCITRAL's arbitration rules. The arbitral tribunal should be composed of three arbitrators, appointed in a similar way to the Beta contract.[581] However, in case a third arbitrator cannot be appointed according to the time limits set by this agreement, the Secretary General of the International Centre for the Settlement of Investment Disputes (ICSID) shall appoint the third arbitra-tor.[582] According to this agreement, the site of the international arbitration shall be the ICSID in Singapore, the language of arbitration English, the award rendered "shall apportion the costs of arbitration" and the decision of the tribunal will be "final and binding".

Finally as for the choice of law clause, the contract of the Gamma project explicitly determines that the governing law of any dispute between the parties shall be "governed and construed in accordance with the Laws of the host state". This is a direct reference to municipal law different from the Alpha project's clause, which is silent about the governing law. In the Gamma project, the tribunal will have no option other than to apply the domestic law of the host country wherein the Alpha project's case, there is at least a theoretical possibility

---

[581] One arbitrator is appointed by each party and then the two appointed arbitrators choose the third who shall act as the presiding arbitrator of the tribunal.

[582] Choosing an arbitrator is of great importance for the parties, who usually attempt to intervene in the process of selecting the third (neutral) arbitrator who acts as the Chairman of the particular tribunal. There are often objections about a proposed arbitrator when the parties believe that a particular arbitrator will be inappropriate with regards to the nature of the dispute. See also: Paulsson, 'Dispute Resolution', pp. 213-214.

that the tribunal would apply a different legal system outside the jurisdiction of the host country. Nevertheless, the application of the host country's laws is more likely to occur in either case.

In the case of the Delta project, the dispute resolution clause is very similar to that contained in the Gamma project's contract. Some differences are that initial discussions can last up to 45 days, and that the agreement requires the parties, regardless of the occurrence of a dispute, to mutually agree on the permanent appointment (for as long as the contractual agreement is in effect) of a "Wise Counsellor". The Wise Counsellor's appointment shall be made within three months after the date of the agreement and he should be knowledgeable about "technical and commercial aspects of the construction and operation of a coal-fired power plant". Similarly to the Gamma project, any dispute of a technical nature shall be resolved by the Wise Counsellor. Also, any hearing held by the Wise Counsellor shall be held in Singapore. In case discussions cannot resolve the dispute within a 45 day period or the Wise Counsellor cannot render a decision about a technical dispute or his appointment is terminated, and in case of any other dispute that is not of a technical nature, parties are able to resolve their disputes by international arbitration.

Moreover, any dispute shall be settled under the International Chamber of Commerce (ICC) arbitration rules. The arbitral tribunal is to be composed of three arbitrators in a similar way to the Beta and Gamma contracts. In case a third arbitrator cannot be appointed, then such an arbitrator shall be appointed by the International Court of Arbitration of the ICC within 30 days. The place of arbitration shall be Singapore and the language English, however, the Delta agreement allows the parties to submit testimony or documentary evidence in any other language provided that it "furnishes to the other Disputing Parties a translation into English". The award rendered shall be final and binding upon the parties. Finally, as for the choice of law clause, the contract of Delta project explicitly determines, as does the Gamma project, that the governing law of any dispute of the parties shall be "governed and construed in accordance with the Laws of the host state".

Finally, in the Epsilon project's case, any dispute or difference between the parties shall be settled by "mutual discussions" which can last no more than 30 days. If the dispute cannot be settled then the parties should resolve their dispute before an independent expert when that is specifically required by this agreement. Thus, when one of the parties (the Applicant) applies for a referral to an expert, it should give a "Notice of Intention" to the other party (the Respondent). This contract specifies the requirements that the notice of intention should meet, such as the inclusion of a description of dispute, the reasons for the applicant's claim, and the written materials that the applicant intends to submit to the expert. The respondent has 21 days after the receipt of the notice of intention to give to the applicant a notice of intention to defend, including the reasons for its claims and all the written materials that the respondent intends to submit. After this specific procedural requirement which is not found in the other reviewed contracts, the parties are required agree on an expert and on the terms under which their dispute should be referred. If the parties are unable within a 14-day period to appoint an expert then the ICC International Center for Expertise can appoint an expert for them, provided that he is "not a national of the Jurisdiction of either Party". Even if this contract includes specific provisions about the procedure of the referral of a dispute to an expert, it acknowledges that any proceeding "shall not be required to follow the procedural laws related to arbitrations". Moreover, the expert is flexible to resolve the dispute even without being "bound by strict rules of law" when he considers that some particular matters are "inconsistent with the spirit of this Agreement". The contract for Epsilon project seems to place more importance on the expert's dispute resolution that the other contracts do. For example, it provides more time to the expert in order to render his decision (90 days) compared with the available period of time in the other contracts (most of which use 30 days). In addition, in case the expert cannot render his decision within the above time, this agreement requires the parties to appoint a new expert who should be given the same period of time in order to solve the dispute. If the dispute is not resolved within the long period of one year (12 months), then the parties are allowed to refer their dispute for arbitration. This requirement of Epsilon contract for a second referral of a dispute to an expert and for a long period to resolve the dispute (one year) is not found in any of the other contracts.

As for the arbitration process itself, the dispute can be settled in accordance with the arbitration procedure of the UNCITRAL Arbitration Rules. Each party shall appoint one arbitrator within 30 days and then the two appointed arbitrators shall select a third one who will be the chairman of the arbitration tribunal. This agreement indicates that in case parties are not able to appoint their arbitrators within the above time, the arbitrators shall be appointed by the Secretary General of ICSID. As for the site of the arbitration forum, it shall be Stockholm, Sweden and the language shall be English. Also, this contract indicates that the arbitration forum "need not to be bound by strict rules of law" in case some particular matters are considered to be inconsistent with the spirit of the parties' agreement (the Epsilon project's contract). This provision is not included in any of the other contracts' arbitration clauses and therefore, it is considered that this contract offers to arbitrators a further degree of freedom in resolving the particular dispute, although it also creates more uncertainty about the following of some rules with regards to previous arbitration cases on similar matters. The parties also agree to waive their rights to appeal the award of the arbitral panel and they shall recognise that the decisions of such an award are final and binding. The award rendered shall apportion the costs of the arbitration. Finally, this contract does not specify any governing law and as referred to above, such an absence increases the possibility of the arbitration tribunal applying the host country's laws.

7.3.3. Waiver of Sovereign Immunity

7.3.3.1. Scope

Even if the foreign investor succeeds in negotiating a comprehensive international arbitration clause with the inclusion of a neutral forum outside the host state's jurisdiction, the question that still remains is whether the public counterparty in the contractual agreement will recognise such a forum and will not prevent it from assuming jurisdiction over the host state or allow the enforcement of an award and an attachment over the host state's or its agencies' assets.

There is a well-established rule in customary international law, known as the doctrine of sovereign immunity which gives to states and their instrumentalities (agencies and SOEs) a "favoured status" making them immune to a degree from the processes of domestic courts or any other forum.[583]

However, it is widely accepted today that when an SOE is engaged in commercial activity, as in the case of power project investments, the rule of sovereign immunity cannot be claimed by the SOE.[584] In other words, there is a distinction between sovereign acts or acts of public authority and commercial acts which are activities in which any private person could engage. State immunity can be recognised for the sovereign acts but not for those activities that look like any private sector entity's business undertakings. This discretion in the recognition of a state's immunity is known as "restrictive immunity", meaning the immunity that is limited to public acts only.[585]

Nevertheless, in relation to complicated foreign investments in the power sector of host states, it is not always easy to determine whether the interaction between private parties, state agencies and the host government itself results in actions that have a purely commercial or sovereign nature. In most of the cases, the host state acts through many instrumentalities and performs public and private activities simultaneously. Moreover, the immunity from suits in other jurisdictions and the immunity from the execution and enforcement of a judgement in local or foreign courts are quite different issues. The latter is related to the enforcement problem of state assets which are significant for the final satisfaction of investors' interests after an arbitral tribunal has awarded its decision. According to the ICSID Convention, all member states are obliged to recognise ICSID's arbitral awards as local judgements but in relation to the attachment of their assets their laws are preserved on sovereign immunity.[586] If these issues are not clarified in the investor-state implementation agreement, there is an increased degree of political risk that foreign investors will not effectively secure the protection of their investment from the host state's non-compliance with international law.

In order to mitigate the risk resulting from the sovereign immunity of states and their agencies, the inclusion of a waiver of sovereign immunity clause is very important. There is, however, no uniform type of clause that addresses the issue of sovereign immunity. Their variation depends on whether the public party in a power contract between a public utility and a foreign investor explicitly waives its sovereign immunity over the jurisdiction of an award or not, its enforcement in any competent jurisdiction, and attachment over state's assets or limits to the waiver. The waiver can be limited to a particular jurisdiction or assets and areas of activity, or it may omit important words such as "irrevocably" waiving sovereign immunity, thus increasing the possibility of alienating the waiver of

---

[583] Sornarajah, *International Law*, pp. 70-71.

[584] *Ibid.*, p. 70.

[585] State immunity is recognized with regards to *jure imperii* (public acts) but not to *jure gestionis* (private acts), as is discussed in Rubins and Kinsella, *International Investment*, p. 141.

[586] Washington Convention on the Settlement of Investment Disputes between States and Nationals of Other States (ICSID Convention), art. 55.

immunity by a later sovereign act or law. This section analyses the relative waiver of sovereign immunity clauses through the five power project contracts. Such clauses are linked to the arbitration clause, as in all of the cases they are provided under the "Dispute Resolution" section of the contracts.

7.3.3.2. The findings

Not all the contracts analysed herein included a waiver of sovereign immunity clause. Moreover, their wording varied according to whether they used an irrevocable and unconditional waiver or not, and in relation to their content whether a waiver from attachment is included or not.

Table 27   Summary of Findings/Waiver of Sovereign Immunity[587]

Projects	Alpha (Good)	Beta (Unsatisfactory)	Gamma (Best)	Delta (Best)	Epsilon (Poor)
Waiver of Sovereign Immunity clause	-Irrevocably (+) -In any jurisdiction -From suit, execution, attachment over assets & revenues (+) -No spec. Provision on attachment process (-) -Enforcement (irrevocably) (+) -Quezon City's courts (not exclusively) (+)	-Irrevocably not included (-) (only about the commercial nature of acts) -In any jurisdiction (+) -Attachment over assets & revenues not included (-) -Enforcement (+) -but (not irrevocably) (-) -Courts of England courts (not exclusively) (+)	-Recognition of commercial nature of acts (+) -Irrevocably & unconditionally (+) -From any legal proceedings (to the max. extent permitted by law) (+) -Spec.: (+) attachment prior to judgment or in aid of execution -Enforcement (irrevocably & unconditionally) (+) -Courts of: Singapore, Japan, England or USA (not exclusively) (+)	-Recognition of commercial nature of acts (+) -Irrevocably & unconditionally (+) -From any legal proceedings (to the max. extent permitted by law) (+) -Spec.: (+) attachment prior to judgment or in aid of execution -Enforcement (irrevocably & unconditionally) (+) -Courts of: Singapore, Japan, England or USA (not exclusively) (+)	-enforcement or execution of any award (general statement) BUT -No waiver of sovereign immunity clause (-)

Starting with the contract in the Alpha project, at the end of the "Dispute Resolution" section there is a clause under the title "Waiver of Immunity". This clause contains a comprehensive waiver of the public utility's immunity. In particular, the public utility agrees in the contract with the project company of the power investment that it will not claim and it will irrevocably waive from "suit, execution, attachment (before judgement or otherwise) or other legal process and to the extent that in any such jurisdiction there may be attributed to itself or its assets or revenues such immunity". Such a wording explicitly waives immunity from assuming jurisdiction by any court over the host state, from execution of any award and from an attachment over the agencies' assets or itself.

In addition, following the "Waiver of Immunity" clause, there is an "Enforcement of Award" clause. With the enforcement clause, the parties in the contract agree that an action of enforcement of the arbitration award can be

---

[587] Table compiled by the author.

submitted "in any competent court of Quezon City, Metro Manila". Thus, they irrevocably waive any objection they may have about any claim that "such a suit, action or proceeding has been brought in an inconvenient forum", recognising that the abovementioned courts are not an exclusive jurisdiction for any enforcement related to their contractual agreement. Therefore, this clause waives the state's immunity from the enforcement of an award not only before Quezon City's courts, but also in any other forum where there may be a related suit or proceeding.

Similarly, in the Beta project there is a clause under the "Choice of Law and Resolution of Disputes" section with the name "Sovereign Immunity". Firstly, in this clause it is stated explicitly that the state agency agrees irrevocably that actions such as "execution, delivery and performance" by the public utility "constitutes private and commercial acts" in order to make clear that there is no any public character to the utility's actions under this agreement with the project company. Furthermore, the public utility agrees to waive any right of immunity in any court assuming jurisdiction over it, to waive any right of immunity that now or in the future it may have in relation to its property, assets or revenues and finally agrees that it "consents to the enforcement of any judgement against it (public utility) in any such proceedings in any jurisdiction and to the giving of any relief ... in connection with such proceedings".

However, the wording of this clause does not contain two important elements: Firstly, the waiver of immunity from attachment and, secondly, it does not repeat the word irrevocably but only refers to it in relation to the character of the state agency's acts. These omissions create some uncertainty about the effectiveness of such a waiver. When any tribunal is asked to order an attachment against the state's assets it will need to see that there is an explicit intention of the state counterparty regarding the waiver of sovereign immunity related to attachment of its assets. Thus, in relation to the Beta contract, the clause refers to the immunity of the public utility's assets "in any such proceedings" without specifying whether the attachment legal process is included or not. Furthermore, if the state agency does not agree that the waiver is irrevocable, it may result in a later alteration of the state's willing with regards to this clause.

This clause also incorporates a waiver of immunity from enforcement of any judgement against the state party in any jurisdiction by using the word "consent" of the public utility to the enforcement of any judgement against it. A following clause, "Consent to Jurisdiction", addresses the enforcement issue by stating that the parties in the Agreement "consent to the non-exclusive jurisdiction of the courts of England for any action filed by each Party to enforce any award". However, the word irrevocably is again omitted in relation to the consent of the parties regarding waiving immunity from any enforcement.

As for the Gamma and Delta projects, they are identical with regards to the structure of their immunity clause. They are considered by this study to have the best structure among the reviewed contracts in relation to the waiver of sovereign immunity clause. Under the section concerning dispute resolution, the relevant clauses contain each party's unconditional and irrevocable agreement that their acts under this contract constitute "private and commercial acts rather than public and governmental acts" and that no immunity "from any legal proceedings" shall be claimed now or in the future with respect to assets "to the maximum extent permitted by law".

Referring to "any legal proceedings" is considered to be an inclusive wording implying all possible procedures including attachment. In a later paragraph, the clauses of both contracts explicitly state that each party irrevocably waives sovereign immunity from "suit, from the jurisdiction of any court...from attachment prior to judgement, from attachment in aid of execution of a judgement or from execution of a judgement, to the maximum extent permitted by law". This wording is clear enough to protect the project companies from any uncertainty about the enforceability of an award against the state counterparty and its assets. Finally, both clauses of the Gamma and Delta projects state that the parties in the Agreement agree not to claim immunity (irrevocably) from the jurisdiction of any court "including but not limited" to any court of Singapore, Japan, England or the United States of America.

Finally, the contractual agreement of the Epsilon project is considered by this study to be the worst in relation to the waiver of sovereign immunity clause compared to the other reviewed contracts. This contractual agreement contains no clause that addresses the issue of the waiving of sovereign immunity. The only exception is the acceptance of the enforcement or the facilitation of the execution of any award rendered by the arbitration forum; however this is still a general provision which does not explicitly include any condition of waiving sovereign immunity. Given the absence of a particular sovereign immunity clause, the contract of the Epsilon project increases the uncertainty about the political risk of state agency preventing any court from assuming jurisdiction over the host state or allowing the enforcement of an award and an attachment over the host state's or its agencies' assets. This risk of uncertainty also decreases the degree of protection that foreign investors can obtain before any tribunal as it is less likely that any court will order legal proceedings over the state agency or, even more difficultly, over the host state and its assets.

7.3.4. Stabilisation clause

7.3.4.1. Scope

One of the political risks that worry foreign investors, when assuming an investment project overseas, is the threat of being damaged during the operating life of the investment by the host state's change of the regulatory terms, laws or project conditions that existed on the date of signature of the project's contractual agreement. The inclusion of a so-called stabilisation clause or stabilisation guarantee is intended to strengthen the contract between the investor and the state counterparty by "freezing" the laws and regulations that are related to the particular investment agreement from the date that the contract takes effect until the expiration or termination of the contract.[588]

The inclusion of such clause concerning stability was started, and is usually adopted, by contracts between investors and host states in the international energy industry, such as concessions for oil exploration, gas and the mining

---

[588] Hoffman, *Law and Business*, p. 151.

sector.[589] In addition, the stabilisation clause has proven to be useful in capital-intensive infrastructure industry projects, especially in the power sector, such as for the project development of Independent Power Producers (IPPs) projects.[590] In relation to project financing, according to which the operating life is two or more decades, the stabilisation clause has the function of mitigating the political risk of governmental interference with significant investment assumptions over which the investor has no control.[591]

Such investment assumptions are related to the applicable host state's regulations, local laws and contractual engagements that deal with the fiscal regime of the particular project, especially taxation on the power investment, or with more specific assurances given by the government such as the agreed rate of return and the tariff-calculation method under the PPA contract, fuel price availability and price under the supply contract, guarantees for currency convertibility and transferability, environmental controls, as well as with any other commitment given to the project company when its alteration may result in serious damages or cancellation of the investment project itself. The primary purpose of the stabilisation clause is therefore to protect the investor from the possibility of the host government or its state enterprises changing the conditions of the agreement by ensuring that the contract's regime is "frozen from the time of signature over the life of the contract".[592]

However, it is not clear whether stabilisation clauses in investor-state contracts are always valid and whether they have an effect on the contractual relations between the parties when there is a breach of such clauses. The view has been expressed that stabilisation clauses are invalid when they are related to the natural resources of countries because of the concept of "permanent sovereignty" on them.[593] It is also asserted "as a matter of constitutional theory", that a contract with a private party and especially a foreign investor cannot restrict the legislative authority of a state, and that the obligation of the host state not to use its "legislative powers" cannot be committed to by officials of a state entity or even a minister.[594] Thus, under the internationalisation of contract theory, international tribunals generally confirm the states' practice of binding themselves by structuring stabilisation clauses in infrastructure investment contracts.[595] Moreover, it has been argued that a stabilisation clause does not restrict the state's legislative authority but that it only limits the enforcement of

---

[589] Cameron, *International Energy Investment Law*, p. 68.

[590] H. Inadomi, *Independent Power Producers*, p. 114.

[591] Sacerdoti, 'Source and Evolution', section A, p. 4. See also: Hoffman, *Law and Business*, p. 151.

[592] Cameron, *International Energy Investment Law*, p. 89.

[593] Brownlie, *Principles*, pp. 526-527.

[594] Such commitments on sovereignty matters shall be given by the state's parliament and not the executive branch. Sornarajah, *International Law*, pp. 407-408; see also Cameron, *International Energy Investment Law*, p. 91.

[595] A.D. Nwokolo, 'Is there a Legal and Functional Value for the Stabilisation Clause in International Petroleum Agreements?', *The Centre for Energy, Petroleum and Mineral Law and Policy (CEPMLP) Annual Review*, vol. 8 (2004) Section 4.2.

new rules against the specific investment in an investor-state contract.[596] Nevertheless, this study agrees with the view that the states' legislative power cannot by fettered in an unlimited fashion and for a non-reasonable period of time. Even if a host state takes regulatory measures that "diminishes the value of the contractual agreement", unless the measures are discriminatory or arbitrary, it is believed that "most stabilisation clauses would be unable to freeze the contract terms in practice".[597]

In investor-State contractual practice, there is not any uniform form of stabilisation clause. There are many types of stabilisation clause depending on each particular structure that the contractual parties agree to adopt in each case. In general, there are comprehensive clauses that freeze the law of the state as it was on the date it entered into force ("freezing" clauses) and there are clauses that offer stability to a lesser extent. For example, there is a "consistency" or "intangibility" clause which prohibits unilateral changes, requiring the mutual consent of both parties for the state to alter the conditions of a contract; and there are "balancing" clauses which do not prevent a change in the law by the host state as in the case of freezing and consistency clauses but they envisage "automatic adjustments or renegotiation of contract terms in the event of specified circumstances occurring".[598] The format of balancing clauses implies that in case a stabilisation clause is breached, there are generally two available remedies. One is that the foreign investor can be compensated by the state or its agencies for the disruption of the project's conditions through adjustments such as cost-recovery measures and, secondly, that the investor can renegotiate with the state party regarding the alleged change of regulations and be compensated for any damage. These damages are in generally available to investors but in most of the cases, contracts do not contain any reference to them. Finally, there is another type of remedy which is included in a form of stabilisation clause that "allocates the burden" in a loss created by a unilateral change of law. According to this form, the clause does not restrict the host state from changing the laws but in case a change of law occurs and as a result the project company suffers damages and losses, the clause "shifts the burden of change in the fiscal regime" to the state enterprise or the host government itself by requiring a specific remedial action.[599]

7.3.4.2. The findings

Not all of the contracts analysed herein include a type of stabilisation clause. Only one of the contracts provided a comprehensive and separate clause on the stability of laws while two others implicitly address the issue through the *force majeure* risk. There are two projects that do not contain any stabilisation clause.

The stabilisation clause that is provided for the Alpha project comes under a section entitled "Change in Circumstances". The first clause of this section states:

---

[596] Rubins and Kinsella, *International Investment*, p. 54.

[597] Cameron, *International Energy Investment Law*, p. 90.

[598] For more details see *ibid.*, pp. 70-81.

[599] *Ibid.*, p. 80.

Table 28   Summary of Finding/Stabilisation[600]

Projects	Alpha (Best)	Beta (Satisfactory)	Gamma (Poor)	Delta (Poor)	Epsilon (Satisfactory)
Stabilisation Clause	-No "freezing" clause (-) -Rebalancing requirement with 2 remedies (+): renegotiation (14 days limit) & automatic adjustments (restore financial return) -Burden allocation (+) requirement: if no agreement in 90 days indemnification of the investor by host state -Burden allocation (-) against investor in case of benefits decrease the fees payable -Transfer of currency risk (+) covered -State's liability (+) even after SOE's privatisation	-Stability of laws under force majeure section though "Government events or change-in law" -No "freezing" clause (-) -No rebalancing clause (-) -Alternative burden allocation: 1) During change-in-law or government event investor does not pay (+) 2) During change-in-law or government event host state or SOE need to make payments to investor (+)	No inclusion of any form of stabilisation clauses (-)	No inclusion of any form of stabilisation clauses (-)	-Change in laws as force majeure risk -No "freezing" clause (-) -No rebalancing clause (-) -Alternative burden allocation: 1) During change-in-law or government event investor does not pay (+) 2) During change-in-law or government event host state or SOE need to make payments to investor (+)

"In the event that as a result of any laws or regulations of the [electric public utility],[601] or any agency or other body under the control of the Government of [host state], or any regional, provincial or municipal authority or any political subdivision thereof, coming into effect after the bidding date, or as result of any such laws or regulations in force at the bidding date being amended, modified or repealed, and the Operator is able to establish that its interest in the Project or the Power Station and/or the Operator's financial return on its investment is materially reduced, prejudiced or otherwise adversely affected (including without limitation, any restriction on the ability to remit funds in Dollars outside of the [host country]) then, upon either Party giving notice to the other, the Parties hereto shall meet as soon as possible and in any event within 14 days from the date of such notice and endeavour to agree on amendments to this Agreement that will restore and preserve the Operator's financial return on its investment. [If] after ninety (90) days from the date of such notice, no such agreement has been reached the provisions of Article [x] shall apply".[602]

As an initial matter, it is clear under the above definition that this is a stabili-

---

[600] Table compiled by the author.

[601] Names of the host state and the state enterprise are omitted for confidentiality reasons.

[602] This Article states among others that if the rights of the Operator have been adversely affected by unilateral action by the host state resulting in losses or damages to the Operator's interests, then the host government shall indemnify the Operator for any deterioration of its economic situation.

sation clause. As per the form of this clause, it is not clear that it belongs to one of the categories of stabilisation clauses mentioned previously. Thus, this study argues that a combination of different forms of stabilisation clauses can exist. Actually, the clause of this contract (for the Alpha project) does not include any "freezing" requirement as it does not explicitly ban the possibility of the host state or its agencies from altering a regulation or law with regards to the Alpha project. Nevertheless, it requires that in case any change of law results in material damage or economic loss to the operator's interests on the project, then there will be an explicit rebalancing clause requiring that the parties agree in a limited time-frame (14 days) from the notice for meeting about amendments to their Agreement that "will restore and preserve the Operator's financial return on its investment". This wording includes both remedies of renegotiation and "automatic adjustments" about the fiscal position of the operator (Project Company), although it does not specify any measures to restore the economic condition of the investor. Following the last part of this clause, there is also a burden allocation form of stabilisation clause which requires in case of non-agreement in a period of 90 days that the host government will indemnify the project company for any deterioration of its economic situation. This last requirement increases the foreign investor's protection level by providing an additional remedial measure in case the rebalancing attempt is not successful.

However, this clause of the Alpha project includes one more paragraph stating the following:

> "Nothing in this provision shall be construed to prevent [the state agency] from initiating discussions with the Operator for possible amendments to this Agreement, including the possibility of decreasing the fees payable to the Operator under this Agreement, if the above circumstances material and favourably affect the Operator's financial return".

The above paragraph includes a stabilisation clause of "asymmetrical" character.[603] The project company is not only protected against adverse changes but in case there is a change in laws or conditions of the project that may result in benefits for the project company then it is the investor's side who is obliged to take the burden of this changes. As this paragraph states, the public utility has the right to decrease "the fees payable to the Operator" in order to rebalance the conditions of the project but this time in favour of the state agency and against the investor because of his unjust enrichment at the expense of the public counterparty. Even if the right of state to rebalance the conditions of a project against the private sector when the changes made in law have beneficial effects on the investor is widely recognised, it is unclear whether host governments will use this right properly or as an excuse to interfere in the project company's business by using unilateral modifications to the contract. Nevertheless, in the case of mismanagement of such a stabilisation clause by the host state, the in-

---

[603] Cameron, *International Energy Investment Law*, pp. 82-83.

vestor's interests may be protected if a claim for creeping or regulatory expropriation is successfully established.[604]

In addition, under a stabilisation clause, an explicit protection of the currency transferability is often included. The Alpha project's stabilisation clause, as referred to above, protects the project company against any change in laws that might result in "any restriction on the ability to remit funds in Dollars outside of the [host country]". This provision on the right to remit funds is not always included in the content of stabilisation forms, as it can be covered by the general content of protection against any law's change. However, most investors prefer the explicit wording because governments have many levers "within as well as outside the contract" to influence the private counterparty by undertaking changes in fiscal terms that must be accepted.[605]

Finally, the contract of Alpha project includes one more assurance for the project company under the stabilisation clause. In the case of the privatisation of the public utility which is the counterparty of the investor in the power project, this clause provides that the state enterprise or its successor (after the privatisation) "shall comply with its obligations under this Agreement" including the requirements under the Performance Undertaking contract and in particular, it "shall assure that the Operator's rights and net financial return ... are preserved". This is a form of stabilisation clause that restricts the legislative authority of the host state to a greater extent than is usual for stabilisation clauses as it limits its rights to liberalise the electricity sector given the constraints of the obligations that have been undertaken within Alpha project towards the private investor. Moreover, it is not clear whether the possibility of state enterprise's privatisation can be considered to be a political risk. It is not doubted that private investors should bear the business risk of open market competition. However, when the host government gives a specific guarantee to the foreign investor through a stabilisation clause that it will continue to be liable for the SOE's performance even after a privatisation event, then this study asserts that the "risk of privatisation" loses its business character and becomes at least "non-commercial" in nature due to the "political" engagement of the host state. According to this study, this risk is categorised as a non-traditional political risk.

As for the Beta project, its implementation agreement takes an alternative approach to the stabilisation clause. It does not contain any separate clause or a clear provision on the stability of laws and project's conditions, thus it refers to stabilisation issues within the *force majeure* clause. Even if this contact does not explicitly construe the stability of laws, it does offer guarantees for the protection of the project company against the political risk of damages suffered due to changes in laws and conditions related to the power project. In particular, under the "Force Majeure Event" section, this contract affirms that "Government Events" and "Change-in-Law" are not considered to be natural *force majeure* events and therefore, if the BOT company fails to perform due to such events it

---

[604] However, as Cameron implies, the distinction between unilateral modifications to the contract by the host state and illegal taking of the investor's rights is difficult to determine; *ibid.,* p. 69.

[605] *Ibid.,* p. 68.

shall be released from any of its obligations. This is considered to be a first kind of remedy in the case of a change in law risk. In addition, this clause determines that government event means, among others, the following:

> "Failure to obtain or renew any Government Authorisation (on terms and conditions at least as favourable as those contained in the original Government Authorisation) relating to the financing, construction, ownership, operation or maintenance of the Power Project"

Thus, it is not considered to be a government event if the failure occurred due to the project company's breach of the host state's laws or a breach of the agreement with the state enterprise. Another government event is the "issuance of an order, judgement or Laws of [the host state] denying the validity or enforceability of any Project Contract". Finally, and most importantly:

> "The making of, or any change in, any Laws of [the host state] after the date hereof and any Change-in-Law which adversely affects the BOT Company or any of its rights under this Agreement or any other Project Contract".

This clause can include any other law or regulation which is not covered by the previous clause's wording, such as environmental laws or regulations related to the transfer of funds. Under the above wording, this study considers that the main intention of these clauses is to mitigate the political risk of change in laws and conditions of the project-contract that were in effect when the Beta contract was signed. These clauses constitute neither any "freezing of laws" stabilisation clause, nor a rebalancing clause (it does not restore the financial return of investor). However, it could be argued that they consist of an alternative form of burden allocation. That is more obvious according to another provision in the same section referring to the period when the obligations of the project company or the state enterprise are affected by a government event or change in law. According to this provision, the parties shall meet to discuss about the problem before an "Authorised State Body" which will consider the situation and issue to the Parties

> "a decision as to whether the Capacity Charge payments and other payments due under this Agreement each month to the BOT Company shall be paid to the BOT Company (A) directly by [the host state], (B) by [the state enterprise] with funds specially provided by [the host state] or (C) by [the state enterprise] from its own resources".

Given the previously mentioned remedy – the project company being relieved from any of its obligations due to a government event or change in law – and combined with this last provision, it is obvious that the burden of change is allocated to the fiscal regime of the public counterparty or the host state itself as it needs to continue make payments in relation to the PPA agreement or any other payment to the project company. Even if this clause does not construe that these payments have a compensatory character (as in the case of Alpha project) towards the investor, it releases the project company from any of its obligations and, until the problem is solved, the burden of the changes is put on the host country's side.

Similarly to that of the Beta project, the contract of Epsilon project does not include a separate stabilisation clause, but provides guarantees on stability of laws within the "Force Majeure" section. One difference of the Epsilon project compared to the Beta project is that it treats changes in law as a *force majeure* risk. However, this has little practical importance as this contract includes similarly to Beta project a burden allocation provision by stating that in case of the occurrence of such *force majeure* events (including change in law), the project company "shall be deemed dispatched" from its performance obligations while "[the public utility] shall continue to be obligated to make payments for Net Dependable Capacity ... to the extent of such deemed dispatch".

In particular, this contract construes as events of *force majeure* eligible for the remedial treatment mentioned above, among others, the:

> "Adoption, enactment or application to Seller ... of laws by [the host state] (i) relating to the environment other than those set forth or referred to in [this Agreement] ... or (ii) not existing or not applicable to Seller, such Contractor or the Project on the date of this Agreement or any change in any such Legal Requirement or the application or interpretation thereof by a Governmental Instrumentality of [the host state] after the date of this Agreement".

Finally, as for the Gamma and Delta projects, their contracts are considered by this study to be the worst in relation to the stabilisation clause compared with the other reviewed contracts. These contractual agreements contain no clauses that address the issue of stabilisation and, therefore, the political risk of change in laws by the host state is considered to be high.

In general, this section of the book asserts that through the above-analysed *force majeure* clauses the Beta and Epsilon projects attempt to mitigate the political risk of investor's damage due to change in laws through an alternative method of stabilisation clause by transferring the burden of the changes onto the host country or its state-enterprise's side. However, this book acknowledges that this is not a comprehensive way to mitigate the change-in-laws risk and it would be preferable that contracts include explicit stabilisation clauses as in the case of the Alpha project by referring to remedies such as indemnification of foreign investments for damages suffered by the change in laws.

7.3.5. *Force majeure* clause

7.3.5.1. Scope

When a *force majeure* clause is included in the implementation agreement, it usually protects each party of the contract from carrying out its performance if events that are outside the control of the party make their obligation impossible.[606] The *force majeure* clause usually protects parties from natural disasters but also some other unforeseeable events such as war, insurrection and social

---

[606] Rubins and Kinsella, *International Investment*, p. 57.

strife. However, in power-contract practice, parties are flexibly able to include several events under the *force majeure* clause according to the particular circumstances in each case. One of the most significant forms of *force majeure* clause is when it allocates the risk of governmental interference to the state-utility. Under this design, *force majeure* protects only the private party (foreign investor) against certain political risks such as denial of licences and permits or cancellation of contracts. When such a provision is included, then the private party can be excused from its contractual obligations while the counterparty (SOE) is still responsible to perform its obligations toward the project company. This design of *force majeure* was used in power-project contracts between American investors and the Indonesian energy utilities (PLN and Pertamina) and, in some cases it effectively protected the interests of private parties. For example, during the Asian financial crisis, the American controlled enterprise *Karaha Bodas Company* could successfully protect its power-plant investment against the cancellation of contract ordered by the Indonesian Government because it had included in the implementation agreement with the state utility (PLN) a comprehensive design of *force majeure* specifying that the risk of "government related events" should be transferred to the state utility.[607] Finally, sometimes the contracts include a "buy-out" provision by the public utility or the host government at an agreed price, an obligation to pay debt and operating expenses to the project company during the *force majeure* event or specific "affirmative measures" that host state should take in order to protect the property of investors.[608]

7.3.5.2. The findings

Analysing the wording of the five power case studies provided by NEXI, all of the contracts have included a *force majeure* clause, although their wording varies. Firstly, one interesting finding is that most of the contracts provide for the mitigation of several types of risks under the *force majeure* clause, including an extensive list of natural and political events that constitute a *force majeure* risk. Although there is a variation among contracts about how the liability of the parties should be established according to different types of *force majeure* risk and about what the consequences are for the private party in case of a *force majeure* event. The reviewed contracts have a different structure in the allocation of *force majeure* risk between public and private parties, resulting in a different degree of exposure for foreign investors.

In the Alpha project, first of all, the *force majeure* clause protects both the public utility and the project company. There is an inclusion of an extensive list of traditional natural events such as natural disasters caused by earthquakes, fires, floods, volcanic activities, typhoons, or epidemics, and accidents resulting from navigation problems, perils of the sea, breakdowns of or injuries to vessels,

---

[607] *Karaha Bodas Company LLC v. Rerusahaan Pertabmangan Minyak Dan Gas Bumi Negara* (Pertamina), UNCITRAL Final Award of September 30 1999, cited in Rubins and Kinsella, *International Investment*, p. 58.

[608] Hoffman, *Law and Business*, p. 149.

Table 29   Summary of Finding/*Force Majeure*[609]

Projects	Alpha (Satisfactory)	Beta (Best)	Gamma (Unsatisfactory)	Delta (Unsatisfactory)	Epsilon (Satisfactory)
Force Majeure Clause	-Neither party liable for its failure to perform due to a FM event, not excused of their obligations(-) -extensive list of natural & political events(+) -any other event if not under the parties' control (+) -expropriation, imports/exports control -If events within or involving the host state & under its reasonable control, no release of State's obligations (-) -if natural events, the host state is not obliged to pay (-) -If events outside the host state, the host state is not obliged to pay (-) -Requirement to notify: extend & nature of problem, resume performance after force majeure condition (+)	-Neither party liable for its failure to perform due to a FM event, not excused of their obligations(-) -extensive list of natural & political events(+) -government and change in law events no FM: (+) nationalisation, political events within or involving the host state, stabilisation, breach of contract, government Guarantees (private party excused from its obligation but public party not excused) (+) -Any other event affecting private party; is only entitled to receive and public party only entitled to pay (+) -If event affecting the public party: parties not excused of their obligations(-)	-Neither party liable for its failure to perform due to a FM event, not excused of their obligations(-) -No list of natural & political events(-)	-Neither party liable for its failure to perform due to a FM event, not excused of their obligations (-) -No list of natural & political events(-)	-Both parties excused from their performance due to force majeure (-) -list of natural & political events (+) -SOE pay if unable to accept power due to political & natural FM events(+) -SOE no obligation to pay if PJCompany unable to deliver (-) -Inclusion of stabilisation clauses(+)

accidents to harbours, docks, canals or adjuncts of shipping. The list related to political events of *force majeure* is also extensive. It includes any wars (declared or not), or hostilities, belligerence, blockades, revolutions, insurrections, riots, public disorder, quarantines, strikes, lockouts or other labour disturbances. In general, the *force majeure* clause includes "any other event, matter or thing, wherever occurring, which shall not be within the reasonable control of the party affected thereby". In addition to these events, the Alpha project includes some political risks that do not generally fall under the definition of *force majeure* events such as: expropriation, requisition, confiscation or nationalisation, export or import restrictions by any governmental authorities, closing of ports, rationing, "whether imposed by law, decree or regulation ... of any governmental authority". This means that, if any of the above-described events occur neither of the contracting parties will be liable for the performance of their obligations, unless the event is within the reasonable control of the party.

However, there is an additional article indicating that when the above events (except the natural *force majeure* events) occur "within or involving the host state", then the state utility is not allowed to claim for itself the *force majeure* clause and is still obligated to make capacity payments to the project company, under the general requirement that the event is be "within the reasonable control

---

[609] Table compiled by the author.

of the public utility or the government or any agency, regional or municipal authority". This article secures the project company against the political *force majeure* and expropriation risk by mandating the public company's payment obligation towards the foreign investors. In addition, another article construes that this payment will also include an amount to repair any damage to the power plant, "ensuring the maintenance of the Operator's financial return on its investment in the Project". Nevertheless, under the Alpha project, the public utility is liable to make its payments only if political *force majeure* events occur inside the host state or if the host state or any public enterprise has been directly involved with it and it is within its reasonable control; it is excused from fulfilling its obligations due to any natural *force majeure* event or any political event occurring outside the host country. Finally, the relevant clause of this contract requires that the party invoking *force majeure* notify the other party, explain the nature and extent of the suspended obligation and resume its performance as soon as the *force majeure* condition no longer exists.

The Beta project excuses both parties from their performance obligations if natural *force majeure* events occur (including cases of fuel and water unavailability)[610] or when a political event of *force majeure* (war, insurrection, etc.) occurs outside the host country, "but only if and to the extent that such events (i) are not within the reasonable control of the affected Party, (ii) are without the fault or negligence of the affected Party and (iii) could not have avoided by the affected Party using reasonable care". The public utility cannot be excused from its obligations towards the project company for other *force majeure* events. Thus, this contract makes a separate category of events naming them as "Government Events" or "Change-in-Law Events" including political events inside the host state, nationalisation, breach of contract by the state enterprise, stabilisation clauses and others, which are not covered by the above rule and therefore from which the public party is not excused from its performance obligation.[611]

Moreover, the Beta project includes one additional obligation over the public agency and the host state that is not included in the Alpha project. In particular, with regards to *force majeure* events it states that "during the force majeure event affecting the project company, the project company shall only be entitled to receive and the state agency shall only be obliged to pay the capacity charges during such force majeure event pro-rated to reflect the portion of the power facility not affected thereby". This additional article of the Beta contract reduces the uncertainty about the necessary payments to the project company and for this reason, it is considered to be a more comprehensive guarantee against *force majeure* risks. However, this wording reduces the uncertainty of state enterprises' obligation only when the *force majeure* events affect the private party. Moreover, the Beta project provides within the *force majeure* clause requirements that are related to stabilisation clauses as analysed in the "stabilisation clauses" section.

---

[610] This might be an additional burden for the project company as fuel and water supply is the SOE's obligation and under the control of the host government.

[611] More details about the government events or change in law events are provided in the "Stabilisation Clause" section of this chapter (7.3.4).

The Gamma and Delta projects are similar. Their relative *force majeure* clauses are construed to be strict towards foreign investors because they treat public utilities and the project companies without any distinction. In particular, in reference to both of them, it states that "no extension or release of any obligation on the state agency or project company for the payment of money shall be permitted or granted by reason of a Force Majeure event". Moreover, these contracts do not make any extensive description or clarification about what kind of events constitutes a *force majeure* risk.

Finally, the Epsilon project obtains some strict conditions for the project company's protection with regards to *force majeure* clause compared to the other projects' provisions. Even if the Epsilon project acknowledges for both parties the general right to invoke a traditional political or natural *force majeure* event (as explained in the other projects) and the right thereby to be excused from their performance obligations, it establishes specific conditions of capacity payments that creates uncertainty for the project company. In the Epsilon project, the public utility is required to make capacity payments to the project company if political *force majeure* events prevent the public utility from accepting the delivery of the electric output. Thus, this means that in case these events prevent the project's company from generating power but do not affect the ability of the public utility to accept the delivery of power, then public utility is not obligated to make capacity payments. The public utility is also excused from its obligations to pay in case of natural *force majeure* events that do not affect its ability to accept power. These conditions make the protection of the project company unclear. Thus, the *force majeure* clause in the Epsilon contract acknowledges some other responsibilities of the state agency to pay in case of a change in an environmental law, a government denial of consent or in case of failure of the State's agency to supply coal to the project company.[612]

7.3.6. Contractual protections against other political risks

Aside from the four clauses analysed in the given power contracts, host governments or their state enterprises assume the risk of political events such as expropriation or nationalisation of the project company's assets, and they generally do not impede the ability of the project company to purchase foreign currency on the open market, to make foreign currency available and to allow the transfer of foreign currency abroad. With regards to the expropriation clause, the contracts usually grant to private parties the right to terminate their contract and receive a termination payment or the obligation of governmental entities to buy out the project.[613] Thus, sometimes, as in the case of the Alpha and Beta projects, there is a provision of protection against expropriation within the *force majeure* clause. For example, the Agreement in Beta project indicates that in case a state body nationalises all or any part of the investment facility or frustrates any of the Government's obligations, this is considered to be a "Government Event" according to which the public party cannot be relieved of any responsibility. A similar clause is included in the contract of the Alpha project. However, the

---

[612] Further detail about the government events or change in law events is given in section 7.3.4.

[613] Babbar and Schuster, 'Power Project Finance', p. 31.

public utility is relieved from its obligations in the Alpha contract if the expropriation event is not "within the reasonable control of the party affected", something that creates uncertainty about the purpose of such a clause. The currency convertibility clause is usually not included in the contracts as far as there is a stabilisation clause.[614] In addition, sometimes the host government assumes an alternative form of risks such as the risk of foreign exchange currency and interest rate, an off-taker's no-performance risk, or they undertake specific obligations such as the requirement to pay the project company directly to an international (offshore) account in order to reduce the risk of future expropriation.[615] Finally, there is sometimes a contractual inclusion of a co-operation or consultation clause which requires the host government or its state agencies and the project company to consult and co-operate before they proceed with actions that may cause losses or problems to the other party.[616] This kind of co-operation requirement is mostly found under either the *force majeure* clause or the resolution of dispute clause. A concrete provision of a consultation clause is found in the Alpha project contract under the title "Consultation" in which the parties are required to "consult with each other" in order to "take all reasonable steps to minimise the losses of either party resulting from Force Majeure".

7.4.   Chapter's conclusion

Investors need to take into consideration that PRI policies cannot result in the elimination of all possible cases of political risk. Moreover, the policy of insurance mechanisms is not always clear in determining the validity of an investor's claim regarding events related to political risk materialisation. Therefore this chapter has noted that sovereign and contractual guarantees constitute a practical method for power investments to mitigate certain political risks. Guarantees in general play the role of transferring risk from one party to another within a contractual agreement.

In particular, sovereign guarantees have been used extensively for BOT-type power investments to protect operators, sponsors and lenders against the risk of public sector parties' default. With regards to NEXI, it has successfully provided PRI programs to a large number of Japanese investments in the power sector of Asian countries mainly because of the occurrence of sovereign guarantees offered by host countries. However, sovereign guarantees do not come free for host governments. They impose a budgetary burden on the central government and for this reason the practice of including them has diminished in many host countries, especially in East Asia, where Japanese power investors are most active.

Investors, along with lenders and insurance agencies, need to protect overseas investments by looking at other ways of mitigating political risk. As some

---

[614] Rubins and Kinsella, *International Investment*, pp. 65-66. However, Cameron asserts that it is preferable that currency transferability be included in the stabilization clause; Cameron, *International Energy Investment Law*, p. 68.

[615] B. Sutherland, 'Financing Jamaica's Rockfort Independent Power Project: A Review of Experience for Future Projects', *RMC Discussion Paper Series* no. 121 (World Bank, Washington, DC, 1998) Annex 4, pp. 27-33.

[616] Hoffman, *Law and Business*, pp. 149-150.

political risks can be unbundled, specific risk-oriented guarantees can effectively achieve political risk mitigation without imposing the same degree of contingent liability on host governments as exist with sovereign guarantees. Thus, the parties in an investor-state contract need to take care with the structure and content of specific guarantees. This study selected four types of contractual clauses: international arbitration, waiver of sovereign immunity, stabilisation and *force majeure*. This study acknowledges that there are also other important clauses in contractual agreements, though it considers the four selected clauses to be the most essential in mitigating political risks after analysing their function and examining the wording of five contracts that are related to power-project financing in Asian countries with Japanese investors' participation.

This study asserts that the inclusion of an international arbitration clause in the investor-state contracts should be a priority for foreign investors and especially Japanese investors when negotiating and structuring their agreements with host governments. Overseas investments in the power sector are related to the economic development and growth of host countries, issues that are politically and socially sensitive for host governments and which touch upon the core of state sovereignty. It has been observed that host governments have a tendency to interfere with the country's judicial system, increasing the risk of a judgement being biased against the investor's interests. Therefore, having an adjudication of disputes before an international tribunal that sits outside the host country or includes a choice of law other than the domestic law is an important tool in mitigating the political risk of governmental interference within dispute resolution. This tool becomes indispensable for Japanese investors as there are many countries that have not signed yet an investment treaty with Japan. However, even though all the analysed project contracts included an outside the host country arbitration forum, only one provided for a choice of law clause (the Beta project). Four of the power projects require the parties of the contracts to either use domestic law as the governing law or they remain silent on this matter. In the absence of a choice of law clause, it is most likely that the arbitration tribunal will apply the law of the host state as being the most appropriate. Therefore, this study treats that both the inclusion of a domestic law clause and the omission of any choice of law clause increases the political risk of the host government changing local laws and regulations that are related to the particular power investment, especially when the parties in the contract have not included a stabilisation clause.

In addition, the arbitration clause does not have its desired effect if the host state refuses to recognise an outside arbitration forum, if it prevents the forum from assuming jurisdiction over itself or when it does not allow the enforcement of an award and an attachment over its, or its agencies', assets. States can enjoy a favoured status making them immune – to a degree – from the processes of domestic courts or any other fora. The waiver of sovereign immunity clause can mitigate the risk resulting from this sovereign immunity of states and their agencies. However, its degree of protection varies according to the wording of the clause, and depends on whether the public party explicitly agrees to irrevocably waive its sovereign immunity over the jurisdiction of an award, its enforcement in any competent jurisdiction and its attachment over state's assets. However, only two of the projects (Gamma and Delta) satisfy all of the above requirements, while one does not include any waiver of sovereign immunity clause (Epsilon) and the remaining projects provide a waiver clause but not a comprehensive one.

Moreover, the stabilisation clause or stabilisation guarantee strengthens the contract between the investor and the state counterparty by freezing the laws and regulations that are related to the particular investment agreement from the date that the contract takes effect until the expiration or termination of the contract. Especially in power project financing, according to which the operating life is two or more decades, the stabilisation clause has the function of mitigating the political risk of governmental interference with significant investment assumptions over which the investor has no control. However, unless the measures are discriminatory or arbitrary, this book asserts that stabilisation clauses are not always able to freeze the contract terms in practice because states' legislative authority cannot be fettered by an investor-state contract in an unlimited fashion. Moreover, the scope of the stabilisation clause depends on its form and content. The most representative forms of stabilisation clause are four: the freezing clause that provides a higher degree of protection against any change in laws, and other stabilisation clauses that offer stability to a lesser extent such as the consistency or intangibility clauses, the balancing clauses and those forms of stabilisation clause that allocate the burden of the changes between the parties. With regards to the analysed projects, there is only one contract that provides a comprehensive and separate clause on the stability of laws (the Alpha project), while two others implicitly address the issue through the *force majeure* risk (the Beta and Epsilon projects). Two of the remaining projects do not contain any form of stabilisation clause (the Gamma and Delta projects). The lack of stabilisation clauses in combination with the absence of a choice of law clause (arbitration clause) can significantly increase the political risk that Japanese investors may face in these projects.

Finally, a *force majeure* clause usually protects each party in the contract from carrying out its performance if events that are outside the control of the party make its obligation impossible. However, the most significant design of the force majeure clause is the allocation of risk. When it allocates the risk of damages due to certain events to only the state enterprise or the host government, then the private party can be excused from its contractual obligations while the public counterparty is still responsible to perform its obligations toward the project company. Under this design, *force majeure* increases the degree of protection against a variety of political risks such as denial of licences or permits, cancellation of contracts, or even non-controllable risks such as political and natural events. All the reviewed contracts included a *force majeure* clause providing mitigation of several types of risks through an extensive list of natural and political events, though there are variations in the liability of parties and in the effects on the Japanese investors. There is a different structure in the allocation of the *force majeure* risk in each project, resulting in a different degree of exposure for foreign investors. In particular, two of the projects (the Gamma and Delta projects) make no distinction between the private and public party in the contract. In these projects, if any of the *force majeure* events occur, the state party is not liable to perform its obligations under the contract unless the event is within the reasonable control of the party. This structure of *force majeure* clause increases the possibility that investors will not be paid for their services during the *force majeure* period. As for the remaining projects, there are some *force majeure* events during which state parties are not excused from their performance obligations to the project company but only limited cases (the Alpha project) or projects where the state party is obliged to pay only if it is unable to accept the output (power), but it is not responsible when the project company is unable to deliver power due to the *force majeure* event (the Epsilon project). Finally, as the best case of transfer of risk is considered to be a case according to which both parties are not liable for their performance due to *force majeure* risk, though when the event affects the private party's obligation, the state enterprise needs to continue make the payments even if the power is not supplied (as in the Beta project).

In conclusion, this chapter does not intend to assess the five projects' degree of protection against political risk. Each of the examined clauses has a different value according to the intentions of the contracting parties and the conditions that were set in each of the contracts. Furthermore, the needs of the parties vary in each phase of the implementation agreement. For example, a stabilisation clause may be more practicable than any other clause if there is a new government who attempts to change the conditions of a project, or a *force majeure* clause may protect the interests of a foreign investor better when a covered political event occurs.

Nevertheless, this study evaluates the significance of guarantees included in different clauses in protecting power investments through a mechanism of transferring political risk. When a specific guarantee comprehensively allocates more of a burden to the host state's side, then it is considered to be an effective tool in political risk mitigation (see the summary table below).

Table 30 Effectiveness of Transfer of Risk and Contractual Guarantee[617]

Guarantees/ Projects	Alpha	Beta	Gamma	Delta	Epsilon
International Arbitration	Satisfactory	Best	Satisfactory	Satisfactory	Satisfactory
Waiver of Sovereign Immunity	Good	Unsatisfactory	Best	Best	Poor
Stabilisation Clause	Best	Satisfactory	Poor	Poor	Satisfactory
Force Majeure	Satisfactory	Good	Unsatisfactory	Unsatisfactory	Satisfactory

---

[617] Table compiled by the author.

Finally, it is acknowledged that even the best contractual clauses will neither be able to eliminate the risk of host government repudiating its agreements nor be able to replace the need for PRI. However, it should be pointed out that a comprehensive structure of contractual guarantees can be a useful tool in providing the legal link between the investor's claim for protection and, on one side, the PRI coverage and, on the other, the international treaty law provisions.

8

NEXUS OF LEGAL REGIMES IN THE
PROTECTION AGAINST POLITICAL RISK

8.1.   Introduction

Having identified the legal elements in each tier of the legal framework dealing with managing political risk and assessing the level of each element's effectiveness with regards to risk mitigation, this chapter examines the interface (overlapping) among different tiers, and it tests whether there is any complementary result (nexus) in the protection of foreign investments against political risk. In order to identify the interrelationship between different tiers of legal protection, it is important to set the pairs of comparison and to realise what the strengths (advantages) and gaps (disadvantages) are in each tier with regards to the effective reduction of political risk. After doing that, it is then necessary to test what possible overlap can be experienced in order to construct the nexus-framework and especially, how the gaps that exist in one tier can be addressed by the mechanisms of another tier.

In this study the words *interface* and *nexus* are not used interchangeably. The notion of interface concerns the theoretical overlapping between pairs of legal tiers in connection to the coverage of political risk (i.e. the common boundary between two or more regimes). Nexus as a notion is preferred herein in order to explain not the theoretical overlapping between different tiers of legal regimes but to indicate the actual result of complementary functions, either between a pair of legal regimes or among all three tiers combined together. For instance, several types of political risks are mutually addressed by different legal regimes (interface), but many others are not. However, as analysed in this section, even when the tiers of legal protection do not have any interface between each other for a specific type of risk, an indirect nexus could be established according to which the risks that are not covered by one regime could be addressed by another legal framework (i.e., a complementary result).[618] Therefore, this study interprets nexus as a more sophisticated notion than interface. Interface is merely an overlapping of the coverage of political risk (direct interaction), but nexus is the indirect connection among different legal frameworks that could result to a more practical binding of legal measures.[619]

---

[618] Nevertheless, in reality, the different regimes' interaction depends on the extent of the protection offered related to the limitation or to the practical implications that exist within its regime's functionality.

[619] The etymology of nexus derives from the Latin *nectere*, which means "to bind".

8.2. Pairs of comparison

As is explained in this study, the mechanisms of managing political risk are derived from two main frameworks (PIL and contractual agreements) that consist of three legal regimes:

a) the standards of treatment that exist in public international law and in particular in treaty law consisting of five EPAs and one BIT between Japan and five Asian countries (*public international law-treaty standards*);

b) the political risk insurance provided by bilateral and multilateral agencies and in particular PRI instruments offered by NEXI and JBIC and guarantees provided by World Bank Group, mainly MIGA (*contractual agreements: investment insurance*); and

c) the specific guarantees against political risk negotiated in five power contracts between Japanese private companies and Asian governments or their state agencies (*contractual agreements: investor-state contracts*).

Therefore, the potential pairs of interactions of such legal regimes can be three: first, the interface between public international law and investment insurance (a+b), second, the interface between public international law and investor-state contracts (a+c), and third, the interface between investment insurance and investor-state contracts (b+c).

8.3. Nexus between public international law and investment insurance [(a)+(b)]

8.3.1. Interface (overlapping risks)

This study asserts that the legal frameworks of managing political risk through international treaty-based standards of treatment (a) and through PRI instruments (b) are considered to be equally important regimes in securing foreign investment's legal rights and economic interests against host governments' (or their state agencies) unwarranted interference, each of them for different reasons. Moreover, this section asserts that the interaction of these two legal regimes could further enhance the degree of protection against political risk through their direct (interface) and indirect (nexus) connection, resulting in complementary results.

In order to test these regimes in relation to this study's subject, Japanese overseas power-investments, it is first necessary to compare the types of political risk that are covered by these two regimes in general, provisions under international law and the PRI industry, and in particular, the effectiveness of each EPA treaty and each agency, mainly NEXI and MIGA.

There is an overlap of political risk coverage by these two regimes with regard to the following types of political risk: expropriation (both direct and indirect types), infringement of rights (or breach of contract), convertibility and transfer risk, political violence for events occurred within the host country, the non-honouring of sovereign financial obligations (including SOEs performance) and finally with regard to the subrogation right which could be established through a concrete clause under investment treaties as well as through a specific agreement between the home country's ECA and the host country. Finally, it should be added that the mechanism of diplomatic protection can be provided under both tiers. In the case of PIL, home countries are directly involved in the treaty as counterparties to the agreements with the host states and as per PRI-policy, the ECA is also a state agency of the home country which can intervene in the dispute between the investor and the host government through diplomatic contacts (formal or informal). However, there are also many differences between the two regimes resulting in the absence of interface in relation to the coverage of several types of political risk.

Figure 8   Nexus between Public International Law and Investment Insurance [(a)+(b)][620]

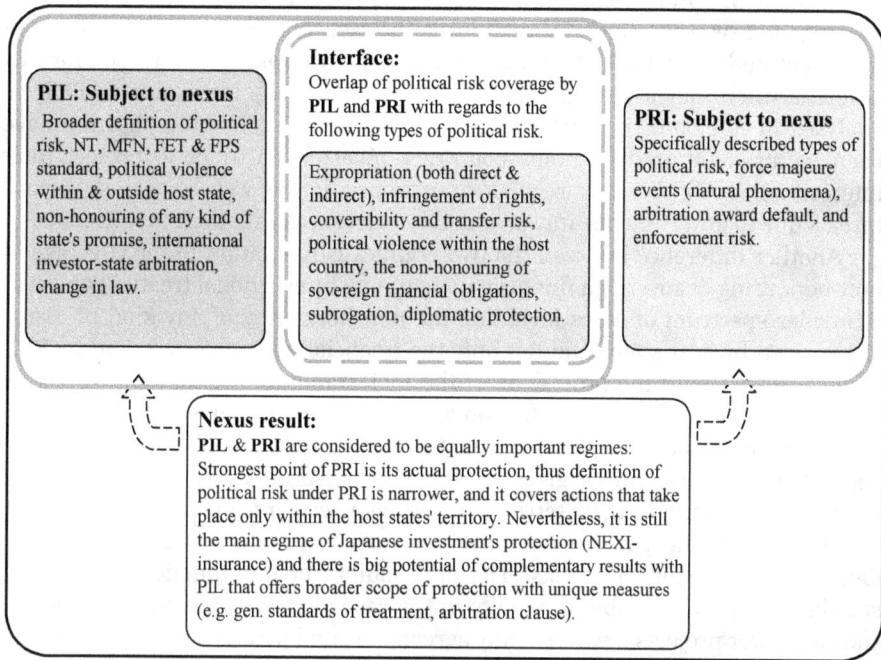

Interface:
Overlap of political risk coverage by PIL and PRI with regards to the following types of political risk.

PIL: Subject to nexus
Broader definition of political risk, NT, MFN, FET & FPS standard, political violence within & outside host state, non-honouring of any kind of state's promise, international investor-state arbitration, change in law.

Expropriation (both direct & indirect), infringement of rights, convertibility and transfer risk, political violence within the host country, the non-honouring of sovereign financial obligations, subrogation, diplomatic protection.

PRI: Subject to nexus
Specifically described types of political risk, force majeure events (natural phenomena), arbitration award default, and enforcement risk.

Nexus result:
PIL & PRI are considered to be equally important regimes: Strongest point of PRI is its actual protection, thus definition of political risk under PRI is narrower, and it covers actions that take place only within the host states' territory. Nevertheless, it is still the main regime of Japanese investment's protection (NEXI-insurance) and there is big potential of complementary results with PIL that offers broader scope of protection with unique measures (e.g. gen. standards of treatment, arbitration clause).

8.3.2.   Types of political risk with no interface that are subject to nexus

This study asserts that political risk could be determined in a broader way within PIL and according to international treaties and arbitration tribunals' jurisprudence than the approach of PRI market. The different approach between these legal regimes results in a broader coverage of political risk under PIL; however, the issue of coverage is not connected with the effectiveness in mitigating these types of risk. As analysed by the assessment-exercise in the previous chapters, the degree of protection varies according to the comprehensiveness of each element.

On the contrary, PRI follows a narrower definition of political risk.[621] In particular, PRI only covers actions that take place within the host states' territory

---

[620] Figure compiled by the author.

(*force majeure* events),[622] though there is no such distinction found in international treaty-based law. For example this distinction results in quality differences in the protection against the risk of political violence. In general, war, civil disturbance, terrorism (political violence), can be covered either by PRI instruments or through international treaty standards such as the specific standard of protection against strife and the general standard of FPS. However, in the case of international standards of treatment, the coverage is broader, also addressing events of political violence even when they occur outside the host country's territory.

Another important difference found by this study with regards to the risk-coverage between PIL and PRI regimes is the fact that the general standards of treatment under PIL (NT, MFN, FET and FPS) do not constitute a reason for PRI coverage when they are violated by host state. Especially in relation to FET, as analysed in this book, its evolved function and broad scope of application have been increasingly used by home countries' investors in order to protect their interests against indirect or regulatory expropriation as well as against various threats due to governments' unwarranted interferences with their investments.

Another difference between the two regimes is in relation to the coverage of non-honouring of sovereign financial obligations. International treaties can cover a broader spectrum of cases including the non-honouring of any kind of assurances given by host states and not only the financial guarantees covered by PRI. In particular, under the provisions of the FET standard of treatment, investors can establish their claim for protection against any action or inaction of host state based on the violation of their legitimate expectation. As analysed herein, even general or oral assurances given by the host government in order to attract foreign investments to their territory could be a reason for violation of the FET standard when the government later revokes its promises causing losses or damages to investors' interests. The applicability of this function of the FET standard could be valuable especially in the case of mega-project investments – such as power projects – where many agreements and parties are concerned.

In addition, the risk of adverse changes in law could also be covered by PIL through different standards of treatment according to each specific case. For example, when a new regulatory measure meets the criteria of indirect or regulatory expropriation, the expropriation and compensation clause could be applied. In case a new regulation is in favour of domestic or third countries' investors and discriminatory towards the home country's investors, then protection can be applied through the use of NT or MFN treatment accordingly, as well as through the FET standard in the case of the new regulation violating the legitimate expectations of the particular foreign investment. Finally, international investor-state arbitration provision is an important measure of deterrence which is preferred by the majority of foreign investors compared to domestic dispute-resolution methods that face the risk of unfairness and impartiality. Such an arbitration mechanism is not available under the PRI regime; thus, as is

---

[621] WB, 'World Investment and Political Risk: 2009', *MIGA* (World Bank, Washington, DC, 2010) p. 28.

[622] Actually, in the case of NEXI, actions that take place outside Japan are covered.

explained below, an instrument that obtains an indirect connection with the PRI legal regime is a unique case.

With regards to risks that are covered only by the PRI regime, there are some particular cases which the present study considers to be political risk according to the determination given by PRI instruments. Natural events of *force majeure* are covered by PRI instruments, thus they are not included in the provisions of treaty-based standards of treatment. Finally, in the case of claims based on the infringement of rights and breach of contracts under PRI policies, they require the insured investor to obtain an arbitral award for damages first or in case the host government has failed to honour the award and there is a denial of justice. Especially in relation to the frequent situation when host states do not comply with the decision of an international tribunal, most PRI policies provide a specific insurance instrument that covers the investor against the risk of arbitration award default. This is a crucial measure offering actual protection to foreign investments as in many cases developing countries do not abide by the legal requirements set by tribunals' decisions[623] or in case the foreign investors cannot find seizable assets to enforce the arbitral awards.[624]

8.4. Nexus between public international law and investor-state contracts [(a)+(c)]

8.4.1. Interface (overlapping risks)

Comparing the types of political risk that are covered by international investment treaties (a) and investor-state contracts (c) there are some interfaces. Nevertheless, the most important finding is that there are more indirect nexuses rather than direct interrelations. These indirect nexuses constitute *one way* to approach the coverage of certain types of political risk. The direct interface between these two legal regimes consists of the mutual coverage of the following types of political risk: expropriation (both direct and indirect), breach of contract, convertibility and free transfer of funds, war and political violence risk, as well as the provision of international arbitration which is considered to be an important mechanism of deterrence against host states' violations of treaty or contract provisions.

In the case of expropriation and transfer of funds risks, there is some variation in how contracts address these provisions. In the majority of the cases, they incorporate provisions for these risks in the stabilisation or *force majeure* clauses. In addition, as analysed previously, protection from strife and FPS standards of treatment address the mitigation of political violence and strife risk (in the case of contracts, these risks are often covered under the *force majeure* clauses). As for the international arbitration clause, this is considered to be the most important overlap between these two regimes. The investor is likely to be doubly benefited when an availability of state-investor international arbitration forum is

---

[623] WB, 'World Investment and Political Risk: 2009', *MIGA* (World Bank, Washington, DC, 2010) p. 50.

[624] T.H. Moran and G.T. West, 'Overview', in T.H. Moran, G.T. West and K. Martin (eds.), *International Political Risk Management: Needs of the Present, Challenges for the Future* (World Bank, Washington, DC, 2008) p. 3.

provided by both legal regimes, by an international treaty between his home government and the host state as well as by the specific implementation agreement between the investor and the host government or its state agency. In this case, the foreign investor can choose the arbitration forum whose provisions are more appropriate according to the needs of each case and the specific circumstances at each time.

However, the provision of an arbitration forum by each of these two regimes does not always result in the same protection against political risk. The most important difference is related to the determination of the actor of violation for which the investor seeks protection through a dispute resolution forum. In the case of an investor-state contract, the investor can claim his rights as recognised by the particular contract only in relation to actions or inactions that are provoked by the counterparty of the contract. In power investment contracts, the foreign investor's counterparty is usually the host government itself (though it may also be a ministry or local government) or the public utility responsible for the supply of power services in the country. These actors will be responsible for any violation that is caused directly or indirectly in relations to guarantees that were given. Nevertheless, in case a damage is caused to a foreign investment due to another public agency, whose performance is not guaranteed by the agency who signed the contract with the project company, then as Hansen argues, the foreign investor "could find itself with no arbitration rights against the offending agency and thus no basis for a claim under its political risk insurance policy".[625] This implication related to contract-based arbitration is particularly prominent in infrastructure sectors where investors usually conclude a concession or project finance contract with a central or local government and an off-take agreement (PPA) with a public utility company but face problems from outside the contract-parties' agencies, such as from customs officials who deny the importation of certain goods (e.g. fuel) or machinery that are necessary for the operation of the project company. In the above example, Hansen asserts[626] that if the state parties to this contract have not guaranteed the performance obligation of the customs office, then the foreign investment cannot invoke the protection of the arbitration clause specified in the contract. This problem does not exist with regards to the protection provided through the provisions of a treaty-based international arbitration forum, as the foreign investor can address his rights against any state agency that violated any treaty-based recognised standard, either specific (e.g. creeping expropriation) or general standard (e.g. legitimate expectations in FET standard). Therefore, in this case, public international law should be the preferred regime. However, another implication with regards to arbitration provision is related to the insurance of the awards. PRI policies insure for a default of award risk only if awards are based on contract-clauses and not on treaty arbitration clauses. This implication means that foreign investment is benefited only through the nexus of investment insurance with investor-state

---

[625] K.W. Hansen, 'A BIT of Insurance', in T.H. Moran, G.T. West and K. Martin (eds.), *International Political Risk Management: Needs of the Present, Challenges for the Future* (World Bank, Washington, DC, 2008) p. 10.

[626] *Ibid.*

contracts (b+c), which is explained in the following section and not through the nexus of PIL and investment insurance (a+c).

Figure 9   Nexus between Public International Law and Investor-State Contracts [(a)+(c)][627]

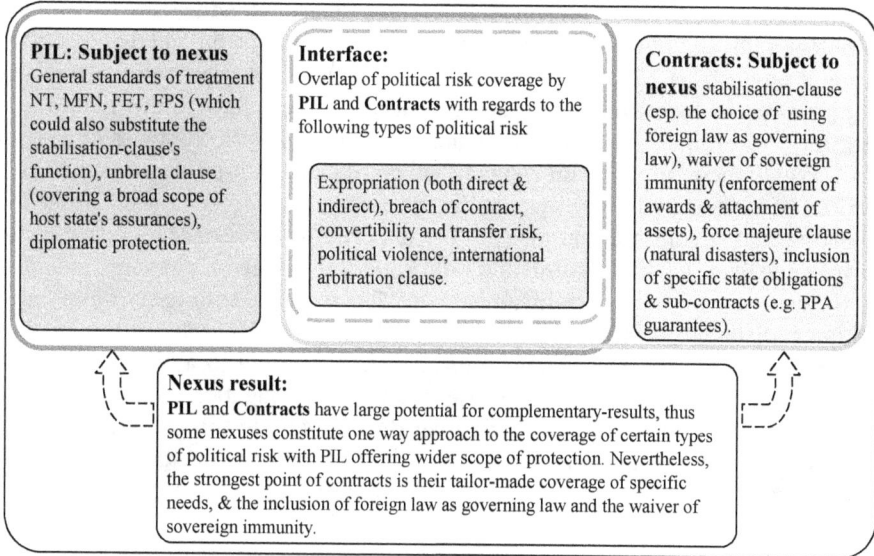

PIL: Subject to nexus	Interface:	Contracts: Subject to
General standards of treatment NT, MFN, FET, FPS (which could also substitute the stabilisation-clause's function), umbrella clause (covering a broad scope of host state's assurances), diplomatic protection.	Overlap of political risk coverage by **PIL** and **Contracts** with regards to the following types of political risk Expropriation (both direct & indirect), breach of contract, convertibility and transfer risk, political violence, international arbitration clause.	**nexus** stabilisation-clause (esp. the choice of using foreign law as governing law), waiver of sovereign immunity (enforcement of awards & attachment of assets), force majeure clause (natural disasters), inclusion of specific state obligations & sub-contracts (e.g. PPA guarantees).

Nexus result:
PIL and Contracts have large potential for complementary-results, thus some nexuses constitute one way approach to the coverage of certain types of political risk with PIL offering wider scope of protection. Nevertheless, the strongest point of contracts is their tailor-made coverage of specific needs, & the inclusion of foreign law as governing law and the waiver of sovereign immunity.

8.4.2. Types of political risk with no interface that are subject to nexus

There are types of political risk that cannot be mutually covered by these two legal regimes (a+c). With regards to risks that are covered only by the international treaty-law regime (a), these risks are the general standards of treatment (NT, MFN, FET and FPS), the umbrella clause and the diplomatic protection that is derived from the character of this regime as an international treaty between states. In particular, the umbrella clause is an important standard requiring the host state to respect not only the investor's rights under the treaty-law but also any right related to contractual agreements between the investor and any state agency or general assurances provided to the project company. On the contrary, the investor-state contract only requires the parties to respect their obligations recognised under the specific contractual agreement.

As for the investor-state contract (c), there are specific provisions that treat political risk without any direct connection with international law. These unique provisions are provided under the stabilisation clause, the waiver of sovereign immunity and the *force majeure* clause with respect to protection against losses due to natural disasters. The stabilisation clause is a unique provision, first because of the inclusion of a foreign law as governing law of the contract and second, because the host state directly undertakes the obligation to "freeze" its laws and to restrain its legislative power for the benefit of a particular project

---

[627] Figure compiled by the author.

company. However, as analysed herein, such an obligation cannot be absolute or unlimited be according to public international law and, moreover, there are various wordings in contract clauses that significantly alter the effectiveness of this provision.

The waiver of sovereign immunity clause is, in its full capacity (unconditional and irrevocable waiver), the most important clause. It addresses a common problem that all investors face when host governments do not comply with awards or obstruct the enforcement process. This clause becomes particularly valuable when investors locate seizable assets of the host state outside its territory, allowing courts of any jurisdiction to proceed with the investor's claim and execute their enforcement rights based on the *unconditional* and *irrevocable* waiver of sovereign immunity. Finally, as far as the *force majeure* clause is concerned, it is common practice for the majority of investor-state contracts to cover an extensive list of natural and political event-threats. However, in relation to the coverage of natural events, most contracts treat the counterparties equally without distinction in their rights and obligations. Therefore, the project company (private party) becomes unprotected when, due to a natural disaster, the state enterprise (public party) is excused from its obligation to pay in case the project company cannot perform its own duty to supply the power. Thus, the exposure of the private party differs according to the specific structure of each contract with regards to the allocation of the *force majeure* risk between the state and private parties.

Nevertheless, the advantage of investor-state contracts, especially in relation to power projects that are implemented through project financing, is the structuring of several sub-contracts which are all included in the main agreement between the project company and the host government (usually referred to as the implementation agreement or project agreement) and whose protections can be tailor-made according to the specific needs of each investor. Under this multiple set of legal documents, there is an explicit listing of parties' obligations and rights. Moreover, the host government usually gives specific assurances towards the project company which are provided either by sovereign guarantees or within sub-contracts such as the PPA agreement. These provisions guarantee risks of a commercial nature, such as the amount and the price of power purchased (demand risk), the supply of energy that is need for the operation of the power plants (supply risk e.g. oil, coal, gas etc. according to the technology used) and with a fixed price (price fluctuation risk) or they can even secure the foreign investors from currency risks pegging the local currency to a hard currency. As explained herein, when such commercial risks are allocated to the host government, then the private parties are excused from their mitigation and they have the right to claim for protection when state parties do not conform to their promises. In the case of disputes over one of the above non-commercial risks, international tribunals are more likely to accept violation based on contracts rather than on the more general and abstract framework of international treaty standards.

Notwithstanding the absence of a direct interface, this study asserts that an indirect connection between public international law and investor-state contracts can be established. Thus, such an indirect connection does not consist of a mutual coverage of political risk as in the case of the direct interface, but to some extent, it is *one way* nexus effect. One way means that what is covered by one regime can be covered by the other but not the reverse. The one way effect of such nexus could be experienced in the case of the stabilisation clause. The essence of the stabilisation clause is the prohibition of changes in law that adversely affect the interests of the project company. This function could be also exerted through the use of general standards of treatment. In particular, when the new law violates the investors' legitimate expectations, the evolved type of FET standard may be applied, or when a new law sets some discriminatory rules between the foreign investor and domestic or third-countries' investors, NT or MFN standards may be applied accordingly. Therefore, under specified conditions set by international law, general standards of treatment may substitute for stabilisation clauses. However, the reverse effect does not prevail. Stabilisation clauses do not extend their scope of protection to all cases of measures that are discriminatory or violate the legitimate expectations of the private party to a contract.

8.5. Nexus between investment insurance and investor-state contracts [(b)+(c)]

8.5.1. Interface (overlapping risks)

The possibility of the third potential pair of legal regimes in managing political risk is the most common case especially with regards to the protection of Japanese investments. The combination of PRI by NEXI (b) and a power contract between a consortium of companies and a host state (c) is prevalent with regards to the business practices of most Japanese investors in the power sector. Not only the fact that Japanese investors are more risk-averse than competitors from western countries (e.g. American) or markets in transition (Chinese companies), but also the nature of most power investments overseas require a higher degree of security than a mere contractual agreement between the private and the public parties. However, the interface of these two regimes is dependent on the content of the particular power contract which NEXI (as all ECAs) usually require before signing the insurance coverage contract. It is rather a rare case that an ECA will provide PRI to a power investor unless there is a legally binding contractual agreement between the project company and the host government or a state enterprise. Moreover, most insurance-agencies, besides the necessary examination of the legal conditions under a specific contract, also investigate the business settings of the project itself, such as the revenue flow, the profit forecast and other issues related to the business plan. Therefore, in terms of timing, an investor-state contractual agreement precedes the negotiation and signing of an investment insurance contract.

Notwithstanding the applicability of the two regimes mentioned above, in a theoretical approach, the types of political risk that are mutually addressed by both legal regimes are related to the: non-honouring of state-party's financial obligation, expropriation, convertibility and transfer of funds, infringement of rights or breach of contract, and *force majeure* events, though with many differences between political or natural events that occur inside and outside the host country. Nevertheless, the interface tested in this pair of legal regimes is more a result of the content of each particular power contract. For example, with regard to the infringement of rights risk, the PRI covers only those cases which are recognised as rights by the contract's provisions and not anything that exceeds these provisions.

Figure 10   Nexus between Investment Insurance and Investor-State Contracts [(b)+(c)][628]

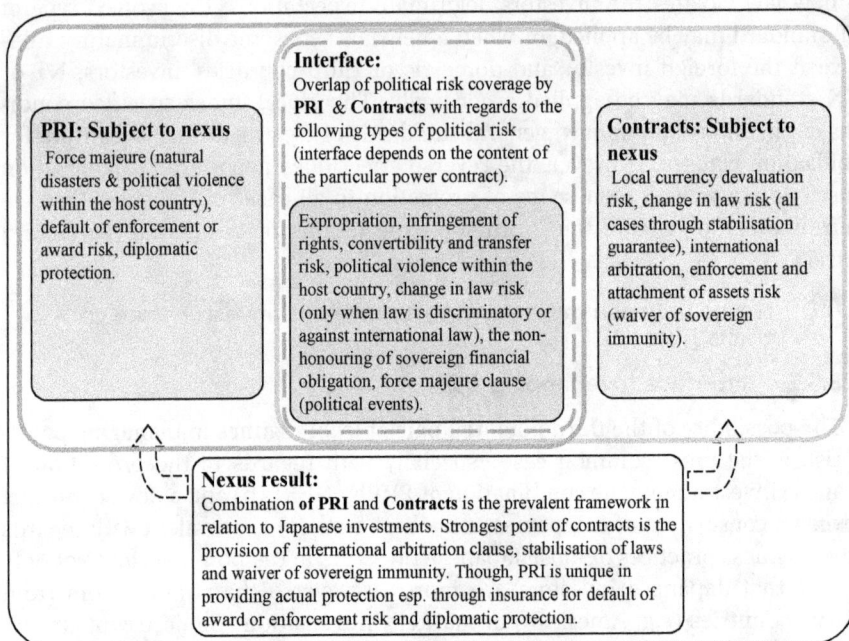

Interface:
Overlap of political risk coverage by **PRI** & **Contracts** with regards to the following types of political risk (interface depends on the content of the particular power contract).

Expropriation, infringement of rights, convertibility and transfer risk, political violence within the host country, change in law risk (only when law is discriminatory or against international law), the non-honouring of sovereign financial obligation, force majeure clause (political events).

PRI: Subject to nexus
Force majeure (natural disasters & political violence within the host country), default of enforcement or award risk, diplomatic protection.

Contracts: Subject to nexus
Local currency devaluation risk, change in law risk (all cases through stabilisation guarantee), international arbitration, enforcement and attachment of assets risk (waiver of sovereign immunity).

Nexus result:
Combination **of PRI** and **Contracts** is the prevalent framework in relation to Japanese investments. Strongest point of contracts is the provision of international arbitration clause, stabilisation of laws and waiver of sovereign immunity. Though, PRI is unique in providing actual protection esp. through insurance for default of award or enforcement risk and diplomatic protection.

8.5.2.   Types of political risk with no interface that are subject to nexus

This study asserts, however, that there is a difference between these two regimes in relation to their approach toward protection against political risk. First, with regard to the investor-state contract regime, as explained above, several investor-state contracts may include sovereign guarantees on foreign exchange protecting the project company against the risk of the local currency's devaluation. In addition, the change in law risk that is covered by most stabilisation clauses is only partly addressed by PRI tools. For example, NEXI covers the insured investors only when the new law is discriminatory or it is against the provisions of an international treaty. With regards to the arbitration clause, ECAs satisfy a claim against the infringement of rights only after an award is attributed in favour of the insured investor. Therefore, arbitration clause has complementary result to PRI. Moreover, as is explained in the section on the nexus between PIL and investment insurance (a+c), PRI policies insure the default of award risk

---

[628] Figure compiled by the author.

only if awards are based in contract clauses and not in treaty arbitration clause. In addition, the waiver of sovereign immunity clause is a unique provision to foreign investors which varies significantly according to the scope of each contract's clause.

In addition to the above difference, many others occur in relation to *force majeure* risk. For the investment insurance regime, PRI tools cover the risk of losses due to the occurrence of a large list of natural events. On the contrary, contract-based protection against the *force majeure* risk usually treats the public and private parties with no distinction in relation to rights and obligations due to losses or damages caused by natural disasters. The PRI market does not distinguish between natural and political events and covers a broad category of *force majeure* risks without any distinction; but it does not cover the insured's claim if he is found responsible for the losses and when the event was within his reasonable control or outside the jurisdiction of the host state.[629] However, in contrast with NEXI's coverage of the natural *force majeure* risk, MIGA does not cover any losses due to natural disasters. Finally, a crucial advantage of PRI policy compared with any other legal regime is that foreign investors can obtain actual protection against the insured risk with an immediate response to their claims by various state (e.g. NEXI) or multilateral agencies (e.g. MIGA). A representative example of this actual protection is the coverage of the arbitration default risk by PRI tools. Host states not honouring the decisions of international tribunals is one of the most severe cases of non-controllable risk which foreign investors need to tackle. This has become especially clear during the current global financial crisis, as had previously been shown in the Argentinean crisis.[630] PRI is the best choice available to foreign investors for the mitigation of arbitration-award default risk, thus the insurance policy does not cover the treaty-based arbitration default. Nevertheless, the legal regime of PRI policy is enhanced by another determinant which is not a legal factor, the diplomatic protection that ECAs as NEXI, usually provide in order to resolve disputes between the insured investor and the host government. The diplomatic way may constitute the most actual measure of protection of foreign investments against political risk and NEXI, through its parent ministry METI, has played a crucial role in promoting and defending Japanese companies' interests abroad.

8.6. Nexus of three tiers of protection: [(a)+(b)+(c)]

Notwithstanding the importance of comparing the three pairs of interactions of the legal regimes, it is also needed to assess the nexus among all three facets of legal means. In addition to the three sets of nexuses, in reality all legal regimes co-exist and function as a means of mitigating political risk.

First of all, it is not necessary to investigate the interface (overlapping) result of all three legal frameworks together, as every possible combination of risks being covered mutually by each framework has already been analysed above. Nevertheless, the following figure (Fig. 11) shows the nexus of all regimes bound together, namely PIL, PRI and Investor-State Contracts.

---

[629] If the event is attributable to parties then there is no coverage under the PRI.

[630] WB, 'World Investment Report: 2009', p. 50.

Figure 11 Nexus between Public International Law, Investment Insurance and Investor-State Contracts [(a)+(b)+(c)][631]

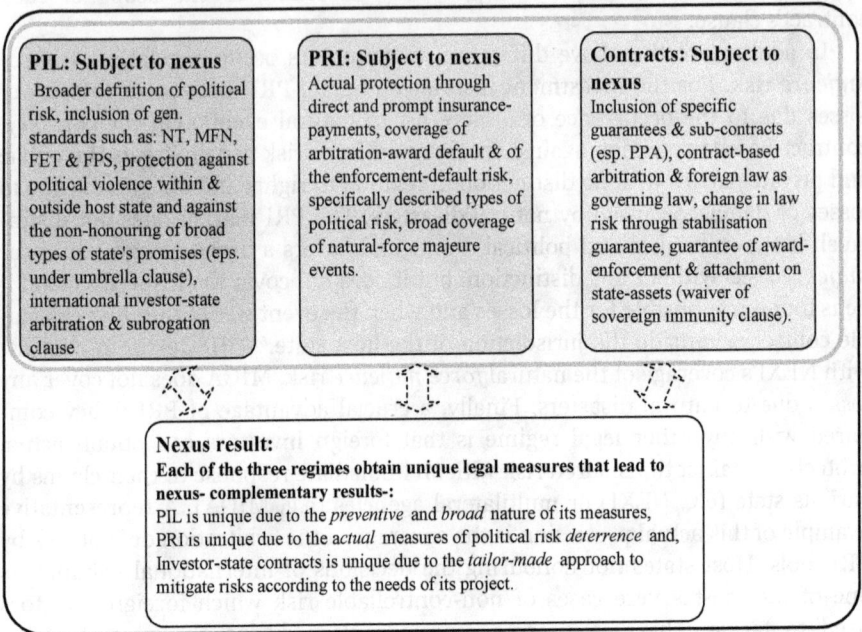

PIL: Subject to nexus	PRI: Subject to nexus	Contracts: Subject to nexus
Broader definition of political risk, inclusion of gen. standards such as: NT, MFN, FET & FPS, protection against political violence within & outside host state and against the non-honouring of broad types of state's promises (eps. under umbrella clause), international investor-state arbitration & subrogation clause	Actual protection through direct and prompt insurance-payments, coverage of arbitration-award default & of the enforcement-default risk, specifically described types of political risk, broad coverage of natural-force majeure events.	Inclusion of specific guarantees & sub-contracts (esp. PPA), contract-based arbitration & foreign law as governing law, change in law risk through stabilisation guarantee, guarantee of award-enforcement & attachment on state-assets (waiver of sovereign immunity clause).

Nexus result:
Each of the three regimes obtain unique legal measures that lead to nexus- complementary results-:
PIL is unique due to the *preventive* and *broad* nature of its measures,
PRI is unique due to the actual measures of political risk *deterrence* and,
Investor-state contracts is unique due to the *tailor-made* approach to mitigate risks according to the needs of its project.

This figure indicates what each legal regime is able to contribute in the complementary function of the combined legal framework. In other words, it shows what the uniqueness of each legal regime is in providing legal means of managing political risk.

Beginning with the PIL, there are several contributions to the nexus-assessment. This study selects as the most important elements the fact that political risk can be determined in the most flexible and broad manner, increasing the coverage of unpredicted cases of political risk materialisation. Such an effect occurs mainly because of the existence of the general standards of treatment, such as NT, MFN, FET and FPS. As analysed by this study, the nature of such standards is based on the general principles of rule of law, non-discrimination, transparency and respect by host state of its promises (especially through the evolved function of FET). It is this nature that can contribute to the combined framework flexibility and *lato-sensu* application of protection mechanisms against political risk. Apart from the general standards, a unique contribution is made through some specific standards, such as the protection from strife covering cases of political violence occurring not only within the borders of host states (mainly covered by PRI and contracts) but also outside them, as well as the special role of umbrella clauses which *internationalise* host states' contractual assurances without the need to specialise them (on the contrary, contracts need to be specific in what they cover and on parties' rights and obligations). Finally,

---

[631] Figure compiled by the author.

the investor-state international arbitration standard is considered to be one of the most significant developments of PIL. This measure of treaty-based arbitration is different from contract-based arbitration mainly because it provides to foreign investors the choice to pursue their claims on a different legal-basis, according to what best matches their specific needs.

In the case of PRI, the uniqueness of this regime consists of its direct and prompt (if all conditions are satisfied) coverage of the investor's loss through insurance payment. Such an insurance payment is characterised as an actual method of mitigating political risk which is absent from the legal measures of the other regimes. One representative example of actual coverage of political risk is the insurance against the risk of award-default by a host government or the risk of enforcement-default. When such risks are occurred, PRI is unique in addressing them in a direct and immediate way which is absent from any other legal regime. In addition, despite the fact of the broad and flexible definition of political risk under PIL, PRI can add specificity that sometimes is needed with regards to a specific listing of various types of political risk. It is also significant the way PRI policies, such as NEXI's tools, address the risk of natural events and disasters which, contrary to contractual agreements, compensate investments for damages without reference to whether host state performs its obligations or not.

Finally, as for investor-state contracts, their most important contribution to the three facets' nexus is the inclusion of specific guarantees and sub-contracts which specifically address the risks that are related to the implementation of power projects, such as PPA arrangements. Most importantly, apart from the contract-based arbitration – which is different than the treaty-based arbitration (explained above), – provisions of a foreign law as governing law, and guarantees against the change in law risk (the stabilisation clause) or against the risk of state's immunity over the enforcement process and over its assets (the waiver of sovereign immunity clause), are unique legal measures that significantly complement the process of effectively managing political risk.

8.7. Chapter's conclusion

This chapter has shown the nexus of three potential combinations among different legal regimes, as well as the nexus of all regimes combined together, by investigating on the complementary result and identifying the uniqueness that occurs within each legal regime.

The first pair of public international law and investment insurance (a+b) is considered to contain the most interactions but also many differences. The international treaty standards are *non-controllable* measures obtaining a preventive function. On the contrary, PRI instruments are active measures taken by the insured-investor and they provide an *actual* protection. These two different legal regimes overlap by covering similar political risks and complement each other by providing preventive and actual measures respectively against these risks. The interface of these regimes consists of overlapping related to most of the specific standards of treatment. However, there are also differences in political risk coverage which creates chances for a complementary result (nexus). The most important one is related to the general standards of treatment which are provided under PIL but not addressed under PRI. In addition, the notion of political risk covered under international law can be broader than the PRI-market's determination. In that sense, there is significant potential for nexus-effect between these two regimes.

In the second pair of public international law and investor-state contracts (a+c), as with the first pair, PIL offers non-controllable measures and power contracts include active measures consisting of *specific guarantees* taken by the state parties for the benefit of the private parties. This combination of measures results in a complementary function of both a preventive and deterrent nature. One of the most significant overlaps is the double provision of international arbitration clauses under both regimes. Under this combination of legal regimes, foreign investors can have more choices of international arbitration fora and can select the one that is more appropriate to the needs of each case. However, there are implications and differences about the degree and the scope of protection provided by each regime. Power investment contracts have the advantage of being specific, providing concrete guarantees of a government's obligations and addressing *ad hoc* risks that are not determined by the general and abstract structure of international treaties' standards (e.g. SOEs performance in PPA contract). Nevertheless, it is the general language of standards of treatment that may be preferable for protection against political risk, when several disputed circumstances of a government's interference are not determined by the particular investor-state contract. This function of international law has been especially observed in relation to the evolved coverage of the FET standard under the interpretation of the most recent international jurisprudential cases.

Finally, the third pair of investment insurance and investor-state contracts (b+c) is the most prevalent combination of legal regimes with regards to the business practice of most Japanese investors in the power sector. There is a mutual coverage of different types of political risk that result in a high degree of interface. Thus, such overlapping depends on the content of each particular power contract according to which PRI is applied. As per the nexus possibility, the investor-state contractual agreement is the primary source of protection, and in which investors should be careful to pay attention to the details when negotiating with the state counterparty and structuring the final agreement with a focus on the dispute resolution mechanisms through the arbitration clause. The protection of PRI comes at a later stage. Nevertheless, the investment insurance offers to foreign investors two indispensable tools. The first is the *actual* and *immediate* protection against the risk of the host government not honouring the decisions of arbitration tribunals. When the award default occurs, foreign investors can claim the payment of the award from their insurer-agency and then the agency substitutes for them in their rights against the host state. This capacity is available only under the investment insurance regime (most significant evidence of the actual protection). Furthermore, there is also the diplomatic protection that bilateral agencies like NEXI and multilateral organisations like the World Bank can provide to their insured-investors.

The nexus among all three legal regimes shows that there is a substantial opportunity to complement each other in the coverage of a broad spectrum of political risk categories. Each of the regimes has its own strong and unique aspects, and also its own weaknesses. Therefore, this chapter has explained that all three facets of legal means should be grasped and assessed as a whole, each facet playing complementary roles in political risk mitigation. Synthesising the core argument of such complementary roles, nexuses are the strongest in mitigating political risk when:

1) PIL provides comprehensive wording of general standards of treatments and the evolved nature of FET/FPS, includes specific standards such as the umbrella and protection against strife clauses, as well as the direct right to investor-state arbitration and subrogation clauses;

2) PRI offers clear criteria for the actual and direct payment of several types of political risk, including, among others, the deterrence of arbitration award and enforcement default, and the coverage of natural and political *force majeure* events; and finally,

3) Investor-state contracts provide tailor-made solutions by including specific sub-contracts and specific guarantees, such as the choice of a foreign law as governing law of the contracts (the arbitration clause), protection against changes of the domestic laws and regulations (the stabilisation clause) and security over the judicial enforcement and the attachment of host-state's assets.

On the contrary, legal means of mitigating political risk are the weakest when there are no nexuses, as in some of the following examples. The most notable case is when the *breach of contract risk*, the *infringement of rights risk*, the *change in law risk* and the *indirect expropriation risk* cannot be determined clearly by legal regimes and as a result cannot be covered by any risk-mitigation measure. Such a case is apparent especially due to innate implications that exist when:

1) PIL obtains only limited provisions with regards to general standards of treatment (especially when the limited form of the FET standard is established – as an *international minimum standard* – or when NT and MFN are excluded from applying to power investments), and using the expropriation clause cannot adequately distinguish between regulatory expropriation and non-compensable measures or there is not any umbrella clause provision to cover breach of contracts or other defaults of assurances by the host state;

2) PRI does not indemnify the insured investor unless an arbitration award is issued for expropriation or infringement of rights and in favour of the investor, or it does not ascertain the investor's claim for payment due to infringement of rights unless it is proved that host state's actions were discriminatory or against international law, and similarly no insurance payment is recognised for the change in law risk unless it is proved that the new law was unfair and discriminatory or against international law and it caused losses to the investor; and finally,

3) investor-state contracts are not likely to mitigate the risk of change in laws if there is not any stabilisation guarantee included, and similarly, they cannot protect against a breach of contract risk unless the specific type of breach is explicitly contained and referred to the contract-agreement.

Such a result of nexus-absence becomes even more evident for investors when their choices of the right to international arbitration diminish either because PIL does not recognise their direct right to investor-state arbitration without the prior consent of the host state, or because contract-based arbitration clauses do not cover disputes between investors and state agencies that are not recognised as party to the investor-state contractual agreement. Such a lack of complementary roles is even more apparent when PRI policies provide insurance only after the investor exhausts all available local measures.

However, the above assessment of nexuses among each legal regime's capacity has been applied through a nominal and theoretical approach to the legal protection against political risk, without taking into consideration the variations that occur within each regime. After conducting an empirical assessment, this book has concluded that, in the case of Japan as home country of overseas power-investments, within each legal regime there are several variations and exceptions. The degree of the legal framework's effectiveness varies significantly according to each international treaty's content, to the specific requirements set by state (NEXI, JBIC) or multilateral (MIGA and WB) insurance agencies, as well as in the divergence in the wording of several power contracts' clauses. The most crucial illustrations of the divergence found in each legal regime (tier of protections) are demonstrated in the following chapter, the conclusion of this study.

9

CONCLUSION

9.1.   Research

This study has analysed the multi-tier legal regime of foreign investment protection focusing on how to manage political risk in the power sector. In particular, political risk is broadly defined as a host government's unwarranted interference with a foreign investment, which should be political in nature (laws, actions or inactions should be based on political reasons) and should adversely affect the investment's operation or damage its economic interests. Nevertheless, the main focus of this study has been the assumptions that international treaty standards of treatment (Part I), PRI policies and several contractual guarantees (Part II) can be effectively applied to mitigate different types of political risk and furthermore, that there is an interface among these legal regimes which, under certain conditions, can result in complementary nexuses.

In relation to these assumptions, this study has attempted to respond to several questions, such as what the legal response of each regime's elements to the mitigation of political risk is, what the factors that increase or decrease the possibility of political risk occurrence are, and how the multiple tiers of legal framework interact with each other. Moreover, a question central to the methodology is how effective the legal response of each regime is in relation to political risk management and how the effectiveness of the multi-tier legal framework can be assessed.

9.2.   List of findings

9.2.1.   In general

In order to address these questions, this study was based on empirical legal research focused on the protection granted to Japanese overseas investments in a particular industry, the power sector. The analysis has demonstrated that there are several important legal factors in each regime that positively influence the management of political risk. These legal factors are related to three categories (legal measures) of analysis, namely expropriation and compensation standards, general standards and specific standards of treatment provided by international treaties (Part I), and two more legal measures of analysis, namely PRI tools and contractual guarantees provided by investment insurance agencies and investor-state contracts (Part II). The empirical analysis consists of examining the wording, the content and the application-mechanisms related to power investments in the following cases: five Japanese EPAs and one BIT entered into force with five Asian countries, PRI instruments provided by NEXI and JBIC in comparison with the World Bank's guarantees (mainly MIGA) and finally, specific clauses included in five real-world power cases between Japanese investors and Asian Governments. The results of the analyses have illustrated that the international treaty standards of treatment consist of non-controllable (*passive*) functions or self-help measures (meaning that investors do not control these measures) acting as preventive measures against political risk that are internationally binding. Moreover, PRI policies and contractual guarantees consist of *active* or *affirmative* functions (meaning that investors do control these measures) that result either in actual and immediate protection (PRI coverage) or deterrence against the host government's actions (specific obligations under contract combined with an international arbitration forum and a subrogation capacity).

However, building on the result of the qualitative and scoring assessment of the above mechanisms, this study has examined each case of the multi-legal framework and has identified, apart from strengths, some weaknesses in relation to political risk management as well.

9.2.2. Public international law

In relation to the assessment study of the Japanese bilateral treaties (public international law regime) with the five Asian countries (Indonesia, Malaysia, Philippines, Thailand and Vietnam), this study has found that all treaties clauses included either several reservations in the wording of their respective clauses, or restrictions and exceptions with regards to the protection of power investments that resulted in lower scoring. Some of the most important illustrations of the assessment exercise are enlisted in the following summary-table and further details of the findings are contained in the Appendix.

Table 31 International Treaties' Findings[632]

PIL: Standards	Strengths	Weaknesses
Expropriation	-All Japan's treaties require the 4 principles of lawful expropriation: public purpose, non-discrimination, due process and compensation; otherwise illegal expropriation -Protection against direct & indirect expropriation with a reference to taxation measures when used as creeping expropriation (**Japan-Malaysia EPA**)	-Difficulty in distinguishing regulatory expropriation from non-compensable measures (**no treaty** applies any specific expropriation test) -Tribunals' tendency to reject claims of indirect expropriation -No compliance with expropriation clause in case of necessity: health, environmental, security measures etc. (**Japan-Philippines EPA & Japan-Vietnam BIT**) -Taxation measures exempted from the 4 principles of lawful expropriation (**Japan-Philippines EPA**)

---

[632] Table compiled by the author.

Compensation standard	-Full standard: prompt, adequate, effective (Hull formula included in most Japan's treaties)	-No uniform practice about calculation of compensation-amount by international tribunals -Difficult to diagnose causality between government interference & investor's deprivation -Uncertainty about the conditions of compensation carrying appropriate interest from the time of expropriation (**Japan-Thailand EPA**)
NT	-Enhances the rule of law and predictability of host state's behaviour -Uncertainty is minimised as Japanese investors receive the same treatment with SOEs (important for subsidies and privileges)	-Local standards may not be adequate -All treaties have several limitations as below -General restrictions applied to all sectors: e.g. NT shall not be accorded in the provision of loans, grants, incentives and other subsidies (**Japan-Malaysia EPA**) -Specific restrictions applied to power sector: Exception of NT to power plants & electricity network services (**Japan-Indonesia EPA**)
MFN	-Reduce the risk of discretionary behaviour of host governments -Unfair competition is minimised as Japanese investors receive the same treatment as third-countries' investors -Important in the age of *FTAs trend*	-Most treaties have limitations as below -MFN only to services conducted after the agreement entered into force (**Japan-Thailand EPA**) -Exceptional measures are allowed in the future (**Japan-Vietnam BIT**) -Specific restrictions applied to power sector: Exception of MFN to power plants & electricity network services (**Japan-Indonesia EPA**)
FET	-Most influential standard under its evolved function (**Japan: Indonesia & Malaysia EPA**) -includes the risk of denial of justice, lack of transparency & proportionality, violation of good faith, and legitimate expectations -Recent jurisprudence accepting indirect expropriation based on FET	-Limited function if recognised as "minimum standard of treatment": no protection of legitimate expectations (**Japan: Thailand & Philippines EPA**) -not easy to clarify if loss is due to government's behaviour or investor's negligence -protection against physical damage only (not legal damage)
FPS	-protection against the risk of losses due to civil disturbance -More influential under its evolved function (**Japan: Indonesia & Malaysia EPA**)	-Limited function if recognised as "minimum standard of treatment" (**Japan: Thailand & Philippines EPA**) -not easy to clarify if loss is due to government's behaviour or investor's negligence -protection against physical damage only (not legal damage) -Duty of *police power* by host state is abstract

FTFs	-All Japan's treaties follow the illustrative approach (more inclusive) -transfer right in a freely convertible currency & at the market rate (all Japan treaties) -provision of FTFs in both chapters (trade in services & investment)	-FTFs right covers funds related only to an investment-activity -no absolute right of FTF (exception in case of balance of payments constraints, financial difficulties etc.) -More uncertainty when exceptions do not conform with NT & MFN standards (**Japan: Indonesia & Vietnam EPA**) -Restriction on FTFs right requiring prior approval (**Japan-Philippines EPA**)
Protection From Strife	-Protection against risk of loss due to armed conflict or war -Freely convertible & transferable payments of compensation & even restitution (all Japan's treaties)	-No NT to Japanese investors with regards to compensation right (**Japan-Philippines EPA**) -protection against physical damage only -no full compensation payment (as in *Hull formula*) under protection from strife standard
Umbrella clause	-**Japan-Thailand EPA** contain umbrella clause -Protection against the risk of breach of contract (broad approach covering any kind of host state's undertakings)	-Almost **none** of Japan's treaties have umbrella clause -Restriction when host state's obligation is subject to its laws & regulations (**Japan-Thailand EPA**)
Arbitration	-All treaties include an investor-arbitration mechanism which "depoliti-cises" the dispute resolution process - Disputes that are based on violation of treaties can be directly addressed before international tribunal without being required to resort to local remedies (deterrence) -The right to choose one among many neutral arbitration fora -Direct & absolute right to arbitration without the involvement of home country or the consent of host state (**Japan-Indonesia EPA**)	-The default of treaty-based award by host state is not an event covered by PRI -Exclusion of several disputes from being subject of investor-state arbitration: e.g. violation of NT & prohibition to performance requirements or for investments that are not endorsed by the Cabinet (**Japan-Malaysia EPA**) or disputes that arose prior to the entry into force of this Agreement (**Japan-Thailand EPA**) -Various restrictions with regards to the degree of consent of host states to direct investor-state arbitration right (Broches categories) -Majority of Japan's treaties do not contain a direct consent to arbitration right e.g. **Japan-Philippines EPA** imposes the strictest requirement: the arbitration right is subject to mutual consent of the parties to the dispute

Subrogation	- All reviewed Japanese treaties include a separate subrogation article - They all recognise the right of Japan's agency (e.g. NEXI or JBIC) to substitute the rights or claims of its investors & the right to exercise such rights or claims to the same extent as the original rights or claims of the investor -most treaties acknowledge that the right to compensa-tion due to expropriation and protection from strife or the free transfer of such payment shall apply to the home country or its designated agencies with no exceptions (deterrence)	- Subrogation clause's function implies it is more a of political tool than a legal measure used between sovereign states -**Japan-BIT** is the only treaty that does not make any reference to the right of compensation due to protection from strife which is excluded from the provision of the subrogation article

9.2.2.1. Strengths

The legal response of public international treaty law to the management of political risk is strong when an expropriation clause provides protection against all direct and indirect forms of foreign property taking (especially in relation to taxation and other regulatory measures when these result in creeping expropria-tion) and requires a full compensation payment (the Hull formula) as a remedy due to the damage suffered by the host government's actions (e.g. Japan-Malaysia EPA). Moreover, legal responses can effectively prevent political risk when general standards of treatment comprehensively address problems such as the uncertainty of the rule of law and the predictability of the host state's behaviour (NT), minimise the risk of unfair competition with investors from third countries (MFN treatment), and most importantly, reduce the risk of denial of justice, lack of transparency and proportionality, or the violation of good faith and legitimate expectations (evolved function of FET-standard), as well as protect against the risk of losses due to civil disturbance through the FPS standard (e.g. Japan-Indonesia and -Malaysia EPAs).

Finally, certain types of political risk can be effectively deterred when specific standards of treatment fully tackle issues related to: FTFs in a freely convertible currency, at the market rate and in respect to the NT and MFN standards; compensation payments (which should be freely transferable and convertible) for losses due to armed conflict or war (protection from strife standard); guarantees against the host state's breach of contractual undertakings (umbrella clause e.g. Japan-Thailand EPA); and finally, being the most crucial task for political risk deterrence, the direct and absolute right of the investor to arbitration without the involvement of the home country or the consent of host state (arbitration clause, e.g. Japan-Indonesia EPA), along with the recognition of the home country's (Japan) or its agencies (e.g. NEXI or JBIC) right to substitute the claims and interests of its investors and the ability to exercise such claims to the same extent as the original right or claim of the investors without exceptions (most of Japan's treaties include the subrogation clause).

9.2.2.2. Weaknesses

The assessment exercise of this study has found that the above comprehensive structure of international standards of treatment, however, does not occur in all Japanese international treaties. Several weaknesses exist due to the treaties' variations in relation to the wording and the limitations of their provisions. In particular, this book asserts that the legal response to the management of political risk is weak (or weaker) when investors' claims are only based on the protection provided by the expropriation clause. Evidence from international jurisprudence has shown that Tribunals tend to reject claims for indirect expropriation, especially due to the difficulty in distinguishing regulatory expropriation from non-compensable measures (e.g. expropriation clause: no Japanese treaty applies any specific expropriation test), and in some cases taxation measures do not need to comply with the requirements of a lawful expropriation (e.g. Japan-Philippines EPA). Furthermore, with regards to the compensation right, it is difficult to determine the causality between governmental interference and the damage which occurred to the investor's property, and some treaties are not clear about whether appropriate interest from the time of expropriation is recognised (e.g. Japan-Thailand EPA). As for the general standards of treatment, the assessment exercise has found several limitations or restrictions included in all of the analysed treaties. Such limitations are related to general exceptions from NT and MFN standards, applied to all sectors (e.g. Japan-Malaysia and -Thailand EPAs) or restrictions applied specifically to power sector (e.g. Japan-Indonesia EPA), as well as limitations with regards to the function of FET and FPS standards with some treaties recognising them as "minimum standards of treatment" and excluding crucial provisions such as investors' protection of the legitimate expectations and "legal damage" (e.g. Japan-Thailand and -Philippines EPAs).

Finally, certain types of political risk cannot be effectively managed when the FTFs standard covers funds related only to investment activities and not to trade in services or when exceptions from FTFs right do not comply with the NT and MFN standards (e.g. Japan-Indonesia and -Vietnam EPAs). In addition, protection against strife cannot be comprehensively addressed when the investor's compensation right does not comply with the NT standard (e.g. Japan-Philippines EPA). Moreover, the absence of an umbrella clause from the majority of Japan's treaties, which leads to uncertainty related to the host state's observance of its contractual obligations, is considered to be a crucial weakness. Most importantly, investment treaties lose a significant degree of their level of deterrence against political risk when several disputes are excluded from being subject of investor-state arbitration (e.g. Japan-Malaysia and -Thailand EPAs) or when the investor's right to arbitration is dependent on the host state's prior consent (e.g. Japan-Philippines EPA).

9.2.3. PRI policies

In relation to the comparison of Japanese agencies such as NEXI and JBIC with the World Bank agencies, especially MIGA, this study has found that there are several similarities in the provision of PRI policies towards foreign investments which have particularly benefited power projects in mitigating political risk. However, there are also differences which apply to either the specific criteria required by each agency or they are related to the eligibility requirements for the insured investors. Moreover, this study has examined the weaknesses of NEXI's and MIGA's PRI policies that are related not only to the scope of political risk coverage but also to the comprehensiveness of the criteria required for the validity of the investors' claims. A summary of the most important findings are detailed in Table 32.

Table 32 PRI Findings[633]

PRI: Policy	Strengths	Weaknesses
NEXI: OII, OULI, B/C.I, EPRG (JBIC)	-Risk-coverage: expropriation, infringement of rights, war & civil disturbance, convertibility & transfer risk, breach of contract, insolvency of debtor (when debtor is an SOE & bankrupted due to political reasons), *force-majeure* (natural & non-natural phenomena), change in law risk, arbitration award default.	-no indemnification until arbitration award is issued for expropriation & infringement of rights -no indemnification for claims of infringement of rights if host acts in accordance with domestic or international law -insurance paid only after investor exhausts all reasonable measures (uncertain what is reasonable) -change in law risk covered only if new law: unfair & discriminatory or against international law and causes losses -FM only if it is within host state's jurisdiction & only physical damage -breach of contract: covers what is contained explicitly in the contract-agreement -EPRG (JBIC) does not cover FM risk
MIGA guarantees & PRG **(WB)**	-Risk-coverage: expropriation, currency convertibility & transfer risk, breach of contract, arbitration award default, war & civil disturbance	-*force-majeure* risk is not covered -no indemnification until arbitration award is issued -compensation paid only after investor exhausts all local measures (time consuming process – stricter than NEXI) -WB does not cover expropriation & war risk

---

[633] Table compiled by the author.

NEXI: Insured events due to political risks	-inability to continue business operations, bankruptcy of the investor's subsidiary, suspension of banking transactions, suspension of business operations for at least 3 months, inability to remit funds to Japan for at least 2 months (transfer risk)	-partial inability or partial suspension of business is not covered for compensation -partial losses from expropriation are not covered -NEXI covers the extent of the insured's right to the expropriated asset or right (but sometimes difficult to define that); -need to check the importance of the expropriated asset or right and its influence to the project's operation (uncertainty) -in case of bankruptcy, it must be verified by host country's state-agencies (it may be time consuming)
MIGA: Insured events due to political risks	-covers both partial & total losses from expropriation -delays in acquiring foreign exchange, inability to remit funds and even lack of foreign exchange -substantial interruption of business for at least 1 year due to political violence	-expropriation not recognised if governmental actions are bona fide & exercised with legitimate regulatory authority (unclear to determine specific conditions) -interruption of operation shall be essential for the business (uncertainty)
NEXI: Eligibility & policy criteria	-focus on the promotion & protection of Japanese interests -developed & developing countries -NEXI provides PRI even for countries with no treaty with Japan -debt & equity are covered -diplomatic protection through Japanese embassies and METI	-Difficulty in covering power-projects with no sovereign guarantee -Policy influenced by METI
MIGA: Eligibility & policy criteria	-developing countries -focus on economic development -promote especially S&M enterprises -great influence on many countries as an agency of the World Bank Group -debt & equity are covered	-more difficult for Japanese investors (more criteria for guarantee application: e.g. environmental concerns, economic development, compliance with host country's laws) -focus on developing countries only -WB PRG covers loans only -developed countries not eligible

9.2.3.1. Strengths

NEXI, as Japan's public agency for overseas investment insurance, covers a broad range of political risk categories that occur in power investments through three insurance tools: OII, OULI, B/C.I (and EPRG in the case of JBIC). The covered types of political risk are: expropriation, infringement of rights, war and civil disturbance, convertibility and transfer risk, breach of contract, insolvency of debtor (when the debtor is an SOE and it is bankrupted due to political reasons), *force majeure* (covering both natural and non-natural phenomena), arbitration-award default and change in law risks. MIGA also covers several types of the above political risks through its guarantees (PRGs in the case of WB), though with some limitations as explained later.

It is also an important to note that both agencies introduce several criteria in order to justify in an objective manner the validity of insured investor's claim for compensation payment. As for NEXI, the mere occurrence of such criteria is based on the following events: inability to continue business operations, bankruptcy of the investor's subsidiary, suspension of banking transactions, suspension of business operations for at least three months, inability to remit funds to Japan for at least two months (transfer risk). In the case of MIGA there is a slight variation in the criteria required: partial or total losses due to expropriation, delays in acquiring foreign exchange, inability to remit funds or even incapacity due to lack of foreign exchange and substantial interruption of business for at least one year due to political violence.

Finally, there is a positive effect on the PRI coverage due to the eligibility-policy of insurance agencies especially with regards to NEXI. According to NEXI policy criteria, investment in both equity and debt forms that are implemented in any country (developed or developing) is eligible for insurance coverage. Moreover, NEXI's goal is to promote and protect the national interests, and therefore Japanese companies' competitiveness and expansion overseas, by using all kinds of direct or indirect diplomatic methods of intervention. In MIGA's case, the goal is the economic development of developing countries and on the promotion of S&M enterprises, rather than MNCs. However, being a member of the WB Group, it has great leverage on the politics of most aid-receiving countries.

9.2.3.2. Weaknesses

The assessment exercise of this study, nonetheless, has found that there are several weaknesses in the NEXI and MIGA PRI policies. Firstly, according to the analysis of NEXI's policies and insurance practice, the scope of the political risk coverage is considered to be problematic. For instance, when expropriation or an infringement of investor's rights materialises, NEXI does not compensate the insured investor unless an arbitral award has redressed his claims. This policy may result in an ineffective insurance measure because of the investor's dependency on the appropriateness of the selected adjudication procedure and due to time-consuming processes. Moreover, if the host state argues that, in spite of the infringement of investor's rights, its acts were in accordance with domestic or international laws, NEXI is not likely to indemnify the insured's claim for insurance. The NEXI policy may also result in ineffective coverage when it requires from the insured investor to exhaust all *reasonable* measures before indemnification (there is uncertainty about how to define "reasonable" in each case), or when insurance for the change in law risk is recognised only when the new law is *unfair* and *discriminatory* (or against international law) and causes losses (there is uncertainty about how to define "unfair" and "discriminatory" in each case). MIGA, among other criteria, in some of the cases explained above imposes stricter limitations on risk coverage by requiring the insured investor to exhaust *all local measures* (instead of the "reasonable measures" that NEXI requires), creating more uncertainty about the effectiveness of the coverage of several types of political risk by PRI.

In relation to the criteria about the insured events that are recognised, there is also a lack of comprehensiveness. For instance, NEXI does not ascertain claims for compensation when the insured investor suffers only a *partial* inability to operate its business (partial suspension of business or partial losses due to expropriation risk). As explained herein, the various types of political risk that can occur in complicated power project financing structures may result in several consequences; it is often not immediately clear and cannot easily be determined to what degree they are responsible for the losses suffered by the investor. In particular, NEXI requires for the ascertainment of expropriation claim validity that the expropriated asset shall be important or the expropriated right shall be influential to the project's operation and business. However, such a requirement may be not always be clearly able to be determined with regards to complicated power investments where many different private parties are involved and each investor's right (or asset) plays a significant role in the overall success of the project company. Similarly, MIGA does not recognise that expropriation has occurred if the host government claims that its actions were *bona fide* and exercised with *legitimate regulatory authority* (it is unclear how to determine the specific conditions of such vague criteria), or the requirement that the interruption of the project's operation that occurred due to the government's interference shall be *essential* for the overall business (as explained above, there is uncertainty about how "essential" can be defined in each case).

Finally, even if NEXI sets as its goal (eligibility) the support of Japanese investments overseas, it is still unclear, in relation to power projects, whether NEXI can provide insurance for projects that do not obtain sovereign guarantees by host governments, and how METI (the political supervisor of NEXI that sets its goal for broader insurance provision) will influence the insurance policy on this matter during the current global financial crisis. As for MIGA's eligibility criteria, it is rather more difficult for Japanese investors alone to comply with the more detailed and development-oriented policy, unless certain joint-ventures with corporations of other countries can be achieved.

9.2.4. Investor-State contracts (guarantees)

Finally, with regards to the non-numerical assessment exercise taken for the last legal regime of managing political risk, this study analysed five power projects implemented in Asian countries with the participation of Japanese investors. It has examined the wording and content of four clauses: arbitration, stabilisation, waiver of sovereign immunity and *force majeure* clauses, and has assessed their influence on the deterrence of political risk. However, it was found that there are several weaknesses that consist of either exceptions or reservations related to important elements in each clause, or merely of the non-inclusion of some clauses in some of the contracts. Some of the most crucial observations in the assessment exercise are indicated in the summary table (Table 33).

Table 33   Investor-State Contracts Findings[634]

Investor-State Contracts / Guarantee	Strengths	Weaknesses
Arbitration clause	-all projects include international tribunal outside the host country -choice of law other than the domestic law (**Beta project**)	-Most projects use either domestic law or omit any choice of law (**Alpha, Gamma, Delta, Epsilon projects**) -arbitration covers disputes addressed only against the state-agency that is counterparty in the contract (limitation)
Waiver of sovereign immunity clause	-host state permits outside arbitration forum to assume jurisdiction over itself, allows enforcement of its award & attachment over state's or SOE's of assets (**Gamma & Delta projects**)	-No inclusion of any related clause (**Epsilon** project) -no comprehensive clause (**Beta projects**)
Stabilisation clause	-freezes the laws & regulations related to an investment from date of contract until expiration or termination (**Alpha project**)	-restriction on legislative authority is not unlimited + several forms with variation -Limited form through force-majeure clause (**Beta & Epsilon projects**) -No any stabilisation-form included (**Gamma & Delta projects**)
Force majeure clause	-most significant design: the risk of damage allocated to the state-party while private-party excused from its performance (**Beta project**)	-structure in the allocation of risks varies significantly (different degree of investor's exposure) -Great uncertainty when both parties equally liable (**Gamma & Delta projects**) -when investor unable to deliver the output due to FM event, state-party is excused from paying (**Epsilon project**) -Natural events of FM: parties equally liable

9.2.4.1. Strengths

As to the arbitration clause, all of the analysed project contracts include arbitration clauses that recognise the investors' right to resolve their disputes with the host states before an international tribunal that sits outside the host country. In addition, one contract (Beta project) specifies that the governing law of the contract be other than the domestic law. Both provisions result in an important safeguard for the impartial and appropriate resolution of investment disputes, decreasing the risk of legal-process unpredictability. Regarding the waiver of sovereign immunity, two contracts fully include the necessary consent of host states that an outside arbitration forum can assume jurisdiction over them, and

---

[634] Table compiled by the author.

proceed with the enforcement of its award and attachment over host states or over their SOEs of assets and property (Gamma and Delta projects). In the case of the stabilisation clauses, Alpha project provides comprehensive guarantees about freezing the laws and regulations of the host country that are related to the project's investment from the date of the contract until its expiration or termination. This type of guarantee effectively mitigates the political risk of change in laws and reduces the uncertainty over the continuation of the promised legal framework. Finally, the most adequate design in managing *force-majeure* risk occurs when the risk of damage or losses is allocated to the state-party of the contract while the private-party (Japanese investor) is excused from its performance obligations (Beta project).

9.2.4.2. Weaknesses

However, according to this analysis, the majority of the reviewed project contracts contain exceptions or reservations related to important elements in each clause and some of them lack of any relevant provision at all. In particular, arbitration clauses in most of the projects restrict the use of foreign law as the governing law of the contract by either requiring the use of domestic laws only or by omitting any ability to choose the law, which according to this study is equal to a denial of using foreign law as the governing law (e.g. Alpha, Gamma, Delta and Epsilon projects). Moreover, a general limitation of the contact-based arbitration process is that the investor can claim his rights before the agreed tribunal only if the dispute (violation of the investor's rights) is related to the specific state-agency that is the counterparty in the investor-state contractual agreement. Such a procedural restriction limits the deterrent effect of the arbitration clause as it does not cover any potential violation of the investor's rights by any other agency or SOE of the host state. The weaknesses in relation to the waiver of sovereign immunity clause are even larger, as one project contract does not contain any relevant provision (e.g. Epsilon project) and others lack comprehensive provisions (e.g. Beta project does not allow for attachment over assets and revenues of state agencies). Similarly, with regards to the stabilisation guarantee, two of the project-contracts have no provision for any stabilisation form (e.g. Gamma and Delta projects) and some contain only limited provisions of stabilising laws included not in a separate article, but within the *force majeure* clause (e.g. Beta and Epsilon projects). Finally, according to the present findings, the structure of most *force majeure* clauses vary significantly, as they have different degrees of allocation of *force majeure* risks between the contract-parties, which results in a higher degree of Japanese investors' exposure. For instance, two of the projects treat both public and private parties in the contract as equally responsible for the risk of *force majeure*, considering private parties as being in the position to control such risks, and therefore requiring from them an equal degree of liability (e.g. Gamma and Delta projects).

9.3.   Contributions and concluding remarks

This study has made three contributions to the legal literature on investment protection: the determination of political risk under new areas of law (e.g. under PIL); the structure of a comprehensive framework composed of multi-legal regimes analysed separately and in a nexus manner; and the assessment of the framework's effectiveness by using qualitative and scoring methodology.

The management of various types of political risk has been analysed primarily from a legal-empirical perspective, examining the multi-tier legal framework that is available to Japanese investments in the power sector of Asian countries. Especially with regards to PIL, this study is unique in exploring the relation between certain international standards of treatment and political risks. Moreover, each of the legal regimes assessed herein plays a determinant and effective role in the management of political risk. In particular, the effectiveness of each regime's legal responses depends on the precise wording of its legal components and on their interaction, as the impact of these regimes becomes higher when their nexus is investigated. This study has found that several types of political risk can be covered simultaneously by different legal regimes, addressing mechanisms that either prevent or deter the occurrence of these risks. Moreover, risks that are not mutually covered can be mitigated by the nexus of potential combinations among different legal regimes. Such nexuses were tested by investigating the complementary results that occur among the three legal facets.

These legal facets can enhance the degree of legal protection against political risk when bound together. In particular, as Figure 12 illustrates, synthesising the core argument of such complementary roles:

Figure 12   Nexus of Legal Regimes[635]

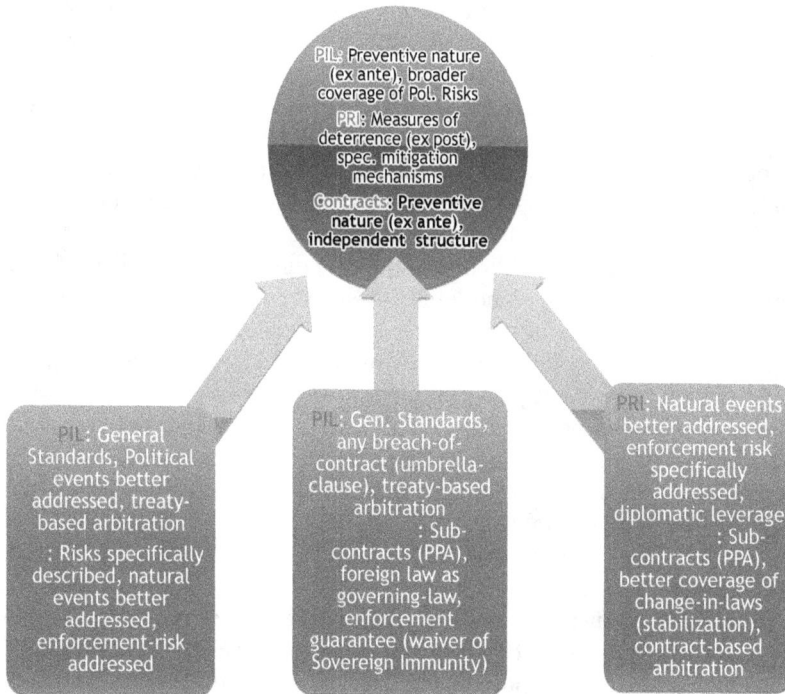

PIL: Preventive nature (ex ante), broader coverage of Pol. Risks

PRI: Measures of deterrence (ex post), spec. mitigation mechanisms

Contracts: Preventive nature (ex ante), independent structure

PIL: General Standards, Political events better addressed, treaty-based arbitration
: Risks specifically described, natural events better addressed, enforcement-risk addressed

PIL: Gen. Standards, any breach-of-contract (umbrella-clause), treaty-based arbitration
: Sub-contracts (PPA), foreign law as governing-law, enforcement guarantee (waiver of Sovereign Immunity)

PRI: Natural events better addressed, enforcement risk specifically addressed, diplomatic leverage
: Sub-contracts (PPA), better coverage of change-in-laws (stabilization), contract-based arbitration

---

[635] Figure compiled by the author.

The PIL regime is unique for its preventive nature of measures (*ex-ante protection*) and for its broader coverage of political risk due to the inclusion of general standards of treatment; PRI is unique for offering measures of deterrence (*ex-post protection*) that can address on-time specific types of political risk better than any other regime (e.g. natural events-*force majeure*); Finally, investor-state contracts are unique for their specific-preventive nature (*tailor-made protection*) offering an independent structure of risk-transfer design, according to the needs and priorities of the parties. However, such nexus constitutes an ideal situation occurring in nominal terms, and it does not take into consideration the variations that exist under each regime. In reality, as assessed by this study, due to several limitations or weaknesses in each legal regime, the actual nexus is more limited than the nominal case described above.

In relation to Japanese investors, political risk insurance, provided primarily by NEXI and secondarily by MIGA, is considered to be the most important tool for managing political risk when investing in the power sector overseas. PRI agencies are considered to be the *prominent victims* that assume the risks investors face as the last-resort protection. According to Japanese investors' perception, NEXI still plays a dominant role, being considered as not only the last resort but also as the only reliable resort of protection. There are two facts that have contributed to such a perception. The first consists of the unawareness among Japanese business about the existence and applicability of other more *institutionalised* mechanisms of protection. The second and more crucial reason is related to the *imbalance* between the number of international investment treaties that Japan has signed and number of countries that are eligible for investment insurance covered by NEXI. The countries which are signatories with a BIT or EPA with Japan are, at the time of writing, twenty-two (22). However, the applicable countries to receive investment covered by NEXI are one hundred eighty-one (181) as of July 2008. Both of these facts are responsible for the fact that investment insurance has monopolised, until the present moment, the legal framework of protection available to Japanese investors.

However, in times of global financial and economic crises as well as of intense economic competition between not only developed countries but also economies in transition, the necessity of a multi-tier legal framework is evident. No matter the significant role of PRI industry, public international law remains the primary source of foreign investment protection, addressing the management of political risk in a broader and more inclusive perspective. In particular, given the situation that Japan has recently entered into EPA treaties with several Asian countries, the awareness of the new framework's capacity and the choices available within it, it should be more than desirable.

Notwithstanding the primary role of PIL, the investor-state contract remains an equally important legal regime in addressing the mitigation of political risk, as in power project financing, formal contractual agreements are a *sine qua non* condition for the implementation of an investment. Nevertheless, given the fact that sovereign guarantees impose budgetary burdens on the central government and their provision is becoming rarer today, alternative solutions are required. Accordingly, NEXI finds it difficult to provide insurance to Japanese projects that do not obtain sovereign guarantees by the respective host states. Therefore, except from PIL, some specific contractual guarantees are also needed for the structuring of an effective framework of political risk management. This study has asserted that four particular contractual guarantees can establish an adequate legal framework with respect to the effective protection against political risk. In particular, the investor-state arbitration clause with a choice of governing and procedural law other than domestic law, legislative stability through the stabilisation guarantee, and the responsibility of host state to respect any foreign award and allow attachment over state-owned assets have proven to be unique mechanisms in deterring the risk of a host government's unwarranted interference with foreign investment. Nevertheless, this study has emphasised that the strength of legal responses to political risks by each legal regime depends, on the one hand, on the comprehensiveness of their provisions (clear wording and policy without limitations), and, on the other hand, on the awareness of their complementary results obtained by combining their preventive and deterrent functions.

9.4. Limitations

There are issues that this study has not investigated or that otherwise remain to be analysed by future research. One limitation of this research is the method used to assess the effectiveness of political risk management. The assessment exercise was based only on legal elements (extracted from treaties and contractual agreements) and not on other factors. For example, it could be argued that, besides laws and contracts, there are also other determinants of political risk management such as the quality of governance or the level of corruption in a particular host country, the ease of doing business, the reliability of the electricity companies (SOEs), the state's judicial system, and many others. However, such an assessment focusing only on legal factors was intentionally elected in an attempt to isolate the effect of specific legal elements to the mitigation of political risk from any other factor that plays a similar role in the political risk management. Thus, as was explained in the introduction chapter, this research is an empirical study of law focusing on the legal protection of Japanese-foreign investments within a specific sector (the power industry).

9.5. Policy implications

Even if the protection of foreign investments against political risk is a subject well acknowledged by both public and private parties in Japan, when it comes to the legal means of managing political risks, most of the effort is concentrated in two processes: firstly, in a non-institutional method, which avoids litigious processes, focusing on a strategy of negotiating with host governments through formal or informal diplomatic channels; and secondly, in a more traditional and quasi-institutional mechanism that combines, on the one side, the PRI legal regime of protection (provided by NEXI to the Japanese insured-investors) and, on the other side, the leverage of NEXI and JBIC (in influencing host country's state agencies and public actors) as well as the desire of host states to amicably resolve disputes with important economic partners such as Japan. Generally, in the case of Japan and Asia, such a model, consisting of informal, non-legal and definitely non-litigious processes, has been successfully applied to the whole area of international economic cooperation, both interstate and private-public or trade and investment relations. Nevertheless, in the last five years, there has been evidence of Japan displaying an increasing interest in more institutionalised means of shaping its international economic relations by focusing not only on the WTO and multilateral trade agreements (as was the case until today), but also signing bilateral EPA treaties with trade partners such as the ASEAN member-countries.

In an era of rapid economic, political and social developments around the globe, the public international law regime could add a new perspective to Japan's businesses and economic policies. As mentioned in the introduction of this study, comparing Japan with some of the main capital-exporting countries, Japan lags behind in terms of the number of IIAs signed. This is one reason that the trend of EPA treaty-signing by Japan should be continued in order to challenge its economic competitors in the new environment of preferential trade and investment, providing competitive advantages to its businesses and corporations.

However, focusing on Japanese overseas investment protection, this study indicates that the creation of an institutionalised legal regime, based on a multi-tier legal framework, should not be seen only as a means for market openness and the creation of new business opportunities (as examined by liberalisation theory studies), but rather it is a way to enhance *stability* and *security* which is threatened by the possibility of political risk occurrence. More specifically, this study has demonstrated that the awareness of international treaty standards of treatment would not necessarily lead to a more litigious approach or aggressive legalism (which is seen so-far as inappropriate in the Asian context of amicable solutions and mediation-style approaches). International law standards could provide to Japanese investments the necessary guarantees to pursue their business structuring with less reliance on the home country's diplomatic protection and less allocation of resources in the negotiation phase with local authorities. For instance, as analysed by this study, the existence of comprehensive general standards of treatment could decrease the uncertainty over the risk of discriminatory treatment by the host country's authorities favouring local businesses (NT standard), or tackle the risk of unfair competition with third-countries competitors (MFN standard) and, most importantly, prevent the risk of discretionary behaviour by host state towards the legitimate expectations of Japanese investments (FET standard). Such general standards of treatment can be utilised as a unique mechanism to improve the rule of law and the transparency of insufficient local legal regimes. Such general standards are not met by other legal regimes; they are uniquely addressed under the framework of modern investment treaties such as EPAs and therefore, public and private actors should utilise them in either formal mechanisms (dispute resolution) or informal processes (negotiation with the host state agencies and SOEs).

In addition, specific standards of treatment can also provide useful safeguards for the Japanese business sector. Thus, their application becomes much more effective if they are applied in combination with other legal regimes either in a set of nexuses or all together. For instance, contractual guarantees gain an *internationalised* protection level when umbrella clauses are included in investment treaties. This is something that future Japanese treaties should utilise more often than in current treaties, which have not included such a clause (except in one instance). Similarly, an arbitration clause may not succeed its deterrent function if there is not any comprehensive waiver of sovereign immunity included in investor-state contracts. Especially, the issue of enforcement and attachment of state assets are among the issues that have imposed constraints in the execution of international awards. Moreover, the risk of change in laws and change of regulations could be effectively mitigated by using a combination of the FET treatment (legitimate expectations), and the stabilisation clause (legislative stability) which could *freeze* legislation that is related to specific investment guarantees given by host states in the beginning of the project-implementation. The legal stability, being a main concern of most business actors when investing overseas, has been also connected with another crucial risk of most foreign investments: indirect or regulatory expropriation. PRI policies have offered useful safeguards against more obvious and direct cases of foreign property takings, but it is questionable how these insurance policies can be applied to the latest phenomenon of *creeping* expropriations. Modern investment treaties such as the Japan's EPAs could broaden the scope of investment protection against creeping expropriatory acts through a combination of expropriation and FET clauses that offer more flexible criteria of expropriation recognition than PRI policies do.

Finally, there are two important factors that should be reconsidered when private actors are in the process of making their investment protection strategy. The first is the current unpredictable environment which affects both private businesses and sovereigns. The financial crisis that started as mostly a private banking problem in 2008 has already metastasised into a sovereign debt crisis and resulted in world-wide economic stagnation. Thus, it is not only the financial problems but also several other implications that we are experiencing today such as inter-state maritime disputes and tensions (especially in Asia Pacific region), social unrest and revolutions (Middle East), up-rise of terrorism (especially after 11 September 2001), on-going protectionism and resource re-nationalisation (Latin America) that constitute an environment of multi-faceted political risk that one legal framework alone (e.g. PRI) is not likely to effectively challenge. In such an environment, businesses need to utilise all the potential tools of managing political risk and therefore, examination of all potential nexuses among different tiers of legal protection is necessary, especially by taking advantage of the international law standards of full protection and security (FPS), protection form strife and *force majeure* clauses that can provide solutions to unpredictable political and natural events, as well of free transfer of funds necessary to challenge the risk of currency convertibility and balance of payments constraint in a period of sovereign debt crises.

The second fact that should be reconsidered is more directly connected to the Japanese business sector. It is evident that a transformation is ongoing in Japan's approach to its international economic relations, with emphasis on a more litigious approach related to its trade disputes, namely under the WTO. Thus, such legalism is still untried in relation to the protection of Japanese investments before international arbitration tribunals such as the ICSID of the WB or other institutional or *ad hoc* arbitration fora. The new legal regime, created after the inclusion of the investor-state arbitration standard in the recently signed Japanese EPAs, could be the most challenging development in the management of political risk, especially in the field of mega-projects such as the power-investments. Japanese private actors could acquire a larger degree of autonomy and independence by not relying only on the State's political agenda with each host country which to some extent could be reluctant to make a direct confrontation with partner states for the sake of a private actor's economic interests. Moreover, evidence has shown that investor-state arbitration is a unique tool to *depoliticise* complicated sovereign relations by avoiding state-to-state litigation processes.

Under such circumstances, a new multi-tier based legal approach to managing political risk would provide benefits not only for private businesses, but also for both Japan and host states. For Japan, a new policy relying more on legal regimes could result in a more transparent and formal means of dealing with international economic disputes, which, in turn, could be a new opportunity for Japan to become a *rule-maker* in its bilateral or regional economic relations. As for the host states, a formalised legal approach based on *high-standards* of international treatment provisions could be the most preferable way to attract investment opportunities into industries crucial for their economic development, such as the power sector, without sacrificing too much on contingent liabilities (sovereign guarantees) that are often required for the implementation of mega-projects. Therefore, the goal of managing political risk through more transparent and legal approaches could be the means of achieving a *win-win* situation for both private and public actors with regards to the sensitive and complicated issue of overseas energy-investment protection.

APPENDIX

Scoring-Card of Japan's EPAs[*]

Countries: Indonesia
Type of IIAs: EPA
Dateof entry into force: 2008/7/1

A. Expropriation and Compensation Standards of Treatment		B. General Standards of Treatment
(1) Protection against expropriation	(2) Compensation treatment	(3) National treatment
0.75 In the article 65.1 (investment chapter) there is a provision of the general 4 principles that are required (alltogether) in order an expropriation to be lawful: public purpose, non-discriminatory, due process of law and compensation. Moreover, this EPA adds one more requirement that the other EPAs do not contain: Article 65.1 (c) of the treaty requires that the host state's measures shall be compatible not only with the classic concept of "due-process of law" but also with FET and FPS standards. The study argues that this is a positive requirement that can strengthen the protection against indirect expropriation. According to article 73.1, it is acknowledged that art. 65 of the Treaty (expropriation) shall also apply to taxation measures unless the above principles occur. However, article 73 of the Treaty establishes a "sub-committee on investment" which among others is responsible to discuss any related to taxation measures as expropriation (art. 73.4). That means the investors cannot directly claim before a court the expropriatory character of a taxation measure unless they consult the respective Committee first. Moreover, if the committee determine that the taxation measure is not expropriation, the investor cannot submit the investment dispute before the international tribunal. According to the study, this adds more uncertainty about the protection of investments against creeping expropriation (taxation). This is one more restriction that results to a lower score. The Japan-Malaysia EPA does not have such restriction.	**1.00** The Treaty refers to the Hull formula by stating that expropriation or its equivalent is not allowed except "upon payment of prompt, adequate and effective compensation" (art. 65.1 [d]), and that "such compensation shall be equivalent to the fair market value of the expropriated investments (a) at the time when the expropriation was publicly announced or (b) when the expropriation occurred, whichever is the earlier" (art. 65.2). Considering the effective compensation, article 65.3 states that "effective realisable, freely transferable and freely convertible at the market exchange rate prevailing on the date of the expropriation into the currency of the country of the investors concerned and freely usable currencies". This guarantee is repeated in the relevant article concerning "transfer of payments" (art. 67.1[f]). Finally, in according to the prompt-compensation requirement, art. 65.3 states that "compensation shall be paid without delay and shall carry an appropriate interest, taking into account the length of time from the time of expropriation until the time of payment".	**0.50** There is an inclusion of a general restriction (art. 59.2): "Notwithstanding paragraph 1, each Party may prescribe special formalities in connection with investment activities of investors of the other Party in its area, provided that such formalities do not materially impair the protection afforded by the former Party to investors of the other Party and to their investments pursuant to this Chapter". It is argued that these special formalities introduce some form of limitation to the standard of national treatment and they consist of an exemption that other treaties do not require (i.e. Japan EPAs with the Philippines, Thailand and Vietnam). According to art.76.2 (c) of the Japan-Indonesia EPA-Agreement (trade in services), subsidies provided by a Party or a state enterprise thereof, including grants, government supported loans, guarantees and insurance do not apply in the treaty. According to National Treatment art. 79 (services) and annex 8 provides an exemption from NT concerning income-tax of non-resident taxpayers if their income derives from Indonesian source (interest, royalties, dividend, fee from service performed in Indonesia). Investment Chapter: art. 59 but in case of inconsistency between chapter on services and ch. on investment, ch. on services prevails (art. 82). Article 62 also provides NT on the access to the courts of Justice. But, according to art. 64.1, it adds some reservation and exceptions on certain sectors that are included in Annex 4. among them, there are EPC-construction services, power plant, transmission & distribution of electric power, M&O of electric power instrument, nuclear power plant. Finally, in case of inconsistency between chapter on services and ch. on investment, ch. on services prevails.

[*] The originals of the Scoring-Cards reproduced in this Appendix may be obtained, in PDF format, by contacting the author at <t.papanastasiou@nup.ac.cy>.

| | | | C. Specific Standards of Treatment |
(4) Most Favoured Nation treatment	(5) Fair & equitable treatment	(6) Full protection & security	(7) Free transfer of funds
According to Annex 9 (services), MFN restriction may be posed in all sectors through all measures affecting tade in services in all modes of supply (same as No 4). Investment chapter: art. 60 but in case of inconsistency between chapter on services and ch. on investment, ch. on services prevails (art. 82). Article 62 also provides MFN on the access to the courts of Justice. But, according to art. 64.1, it adds some reservation and exceptions on certain sectors that are included in Annex 4. among them, there are EPC-construction services, power plant, transmission & distribution of electric power, M&O of electric power instrument, nuclear power plant (similarly to NT). **0.50**	Article 61 of the Treaty (Investment Chapter) provides the general treatment of fair & equitable treatment. (There is no any note that reduces the scope or exlude from the meaning any treatment like it happens in the case of Philippines or Thailand). Therefore, FET clause under this Treaty is considered as providing full protection levels. There is no any exemption for the power sector. **1.00**	Article 61 of the Treaty (Investment Chapter) provides the general treatment of full protection & security. (There is no any note that reduces the scope or exlude from the meaning any treatment like it happens in the case of Philippines or Thailand). Therefore, FPS clause under this Treaty is considered as providing full protection levels. There is no any exemption for the power sector. **1.00**	There are omissions regarding the right of FTFs in both trade in services and investment chapters. According to Art. 87, a country shall not apply restrictions on international transfers & payments for transactions related to trade in services, unless in case of art. 88 which describes such cases as serious balance of payments and external financial difficulties or threat. Any restriction taken should be under concrete conditions: MFN (but no referrence to NT) treatment, according to IMF rules, avoid unnecessary damage, shall not exceed those necessary to deal with above circumstances, be temporary and be phased out progressively (art. 88.2). Finally, art. 88 does not provide after request of the other party, consultations in order to review the restrictions adopted above. Moreover, with regards to the protection of investments, art. 67.2 does not contain MFN treatment in relation to FTFs right. **0.80**

		C. Specific Standards of Treatment					
(8) Protection from Strife & Compensation		(9) Umbrella clause		(10) Arbitration provision		(11) Subrogation clause	
Article 66 grants protection against strife without any restriction in conection with NT, MFN or with regards to the free transferability and convertibility requirement of the compensation payments.	1.00	No any relevant clause of protection of contractual commitments.	0.00	The article 69 recognizes settlement of investment disputes between a country and an investor of the other country. It gives absolut right to the investor to choose an international arbitration forum with 3 alternatives: ICSID, UNCITRAL or any other agreed center. Though, art 69.4 requires a negotiation period of 5-months before the investor submit an application for an international arbitration to one of the forum above. Additionally, the arbitration can be held in any country that is a party to NY Convention (similar provision in Japan-Thailand EPA). Such clause under Japan-Indonesia EPA is not included in any other reviewed EPA, and therefore it is scored with one unit (1.00	0.90	There is a separate subrogation-article from the dispute resolution clause. First, article 68.1 recognises the right of home country (or its agencies) to substitute rights or claims of its investors and the right to exercise such rights or claims to the same extent as the original right or claim of the investor. Moreover, art. 68.2 acknowledges that the right to compensation due to expropriation and protection from strife or the free transfer of such payment shall apply to the home country or its designated agencies with no any exception.	1.00

Countries:	Thailand
Type of IIAs:	EPA
Dateof entry into force:	2007/11/1

A. Expropriation and Compensation Standards of Treatment		B. General Standards of Treatment	
(1) Protection against expropriation	(2) Compensation treatment	(3) National treatment	
In the article 102.1 (investment chapter) there is a provision of the general 4 principles that are required (alltogether) in order an expropriation to be lawful: public purpose, non-discriminatory, due process of law and compensation. According to article 110.1, it is aknowledged that art. 102 of the Treaty (expropriation) shall also apply to taxation measures unless the above principles occur. However, article 110 of the Treaty establishes a "sub-committee on investment" which among others is responsible to discuss any related to taxation measures as expropriation (art. 110.3 [a], [b]). That means the investors cannot directly claim before a court the expropriatory character of a taxation measure unless they consult the respective Committee first. Moreover, if the committee dtermine that the taxation measure is not expropriation, the investor cannot submit the investment dispute before the international tribunal. According to the study, this adds more uncertainty about the protection of investments against creeping expropriation (taxation). This is one more restriction that results to a lower score. The Japan-Malaysia EPA does not have such restriction. **0.75**	The Treaty refers to the Hull formula by stating that expropriation or its equivalent is not allowed except "upon payment of prompt, adequate and effective compensation" (art. 102.1 [d]), and that "such compensation shall be equivalent to the fair market value of the expropriated investments (a) at the time when the expropriation was publicly announced or (b) when the expropriation occurred, whichever is the earlier" (art. 102.2). Considering the effective compensation, article 102.3 states that "effective realisable, freely transferable and freely convertible at the market exchange rate prevailing on the date of the expropriation into the currency of the country of the investors concerned and freely usable currencies". This guarantee is repeated in the relevant article concerning "transfer of payments" (art. 104.1[f]). Finally, in according to the prompt-compensation requirement, this treaty introduces one restriction compared to the other treaties by reffering in art. 102.3 that "compensation shall be paid without delay and shall carry an appropriate interest, in accordance with the laws and regulations of the Party making the expropriation". This difference is treated by the study as a main restriction increasing the uncertainty about the prompt compensation. **0.75**	According to art.72.2 (c) of the Japan-Thailand EPA- Agreement (trade in services), subsidies provided by a Party or a state enterprise thereof, including grants, government supported loans, guarantees and insurance do not apply in the treaty and are exempted from the NT. Finally, in case of inconsistency between chapter on services and chapter. on investment, chapter on services prevails. Aditionally, there are some minor limitations with regards to power sector included in Annexes.	**0.75**

(4) Most Favoured Nation treatment		(5) Fair & equitable treatment		(6) Full protection & security		**C. Specific Standards of Treatment** (7) Free transfer of funds	
Thailand does not retain any reservation for the power sector on the MFN treatment. But, art. 79 does not provide MFN treatment to Japanese investments in respect to agreements with third parties that were conducted before this Agreement entered into force. For this reason, a low score has been given; also similarly, art. 96.1 in regards to establishment & acquisition of investments (investment chapter) and 96.2 provides MFN treatment only in regards to management, O&M, use, sale or other disposition of investments. Finally, in case of inconsistency between chapter on services and chapter. on investment, chapter on services prevails.	0.50	Article 95 of the Treaty (Investment Chapter) provides the general treatment of fair & equitable treatment. There is also a note that specifies the meaning of this treatment like the case of Philippines as "minimum standard of treatment instead of "general standard of treatment". Under this wording, the Treaty provides only as much protection as foreign investors receive in their capacity as aliens under the customary international law minimum standard of protection of aliens and not any higher level than that. For this reason, it is considered as a restriction to the FET full-capacity standard of treatment excluding the concept of "legitimate expectations" as jurisprudence has interpreted.	0.75	Article 95 of the Treaty (Investment Chapter) provides the general treatment of full protection and security. There is also a note that specifies the meaning of this treatment like the case of Philippines as "minimum standard of treatment instead of "general standard of treatment". Under this wording, the Treaty provides only as much protection as foreign investors receive in their capacity as aliens under the customary international law minimum standard of protection of aliens and not any higher level than that. It is considered as a restriction excluding the protection against legal damage that jurisprudence could acknowledge.	0.75	According to article 85.1, a country shall not apply restrictions on international transfers & payments for transactions related to trade in services, unless in case of art. 86 which describes such cases as serious balance of payments and external financial difficulties or threat. Any restriction taken should be under concrete conditions: MFN & NT treatment, according to IMF rules, avoid unnecessary damage, shall not exceed those necessary to deal with above circumstances, be temporary and be phased out progressively (art. 86.2). Also, art. 86.5 provides after request of the other party, consultations in order to review the restrictions adopted above. Protection of transfer of funds is also guaranteed under the Investment Chapter (art. 104). However, MFN treatment is not accorded for the transfers originating from investments (restriction).	0.90

		C. Specific Standards of Treatment		
(8) Protection from Strife & Compensation	(9) Umbrella clause	(10) Arbitration provision	(11) Subrogation clause
Article 103 grants protection against strife without any restriction in conection with NT, MFN or with regards to the free transferability and convertibility requirement of the compensation payments. **1.00**	The Japan-Thailand EPA is the only Treaty that contains an umbrella-clause provision. In article 100 it is stated: "Each Party shall maintain, in accordance with its laws and regulations, the level of treatment which has been accorded to investors of the other Party and their investments with respect to investment activities." However, the expression "with its laws and regulations" is considered as a restriction on the effectiveness of umbrella clause limiting its scope of protection. **0.75**	Art. 80.2 (trade in services) requires parties to institute as soon as posible judicial ar arbitral procedures in order to provide prompt review or appropriate remedies in case a service supplier is affected. The article 106 (Invest, Chapter) recognizes settlement of investment disputes between a country and an investor of the other country. It gives absolut right to the investor to choose an international arbitration forum. Article 106.15 (a), (b), (c), it excludes from the investor-arbitration provision disputes that aroused prior to the entry into force of this Agreement or disputes related to issues based on performance requirements or "with respect to measures other than those relating to the management, conduct, operation, maintenance, use, enjoyment, and sale or other disposition of investments". For this reason, the score is discounted. Other than these restrictions, Japan-Thailand EPA provides the right to investor to choose an international arbitration forum from ICSID and UNCITRAL rules. The Japan-Thailand EPA does not require the parties to settle an arbitration procedure within either country, thus the country of the arbitration "shall be held in a country that is a party" to the New York Convention on the Recognition and Enforcement of Foreign Arbitral Awards". It also sets a time limitation to the consultation period (6 months-article 85.4). **0.60**	There is a separate subrogation-article from the dispute resolution clause. First, article 105.1 recognises the right of home country (or its agencies) to substitute rights or claims of its investors and the right to exercise such rights or claims to the same extent as the original right or claim of the investor. Moreover, art. 105.2 acknowledges that the right to compensation due to expropriation and protection from strife or the free transfer of such payment shall apply to the home country or its designated agencies with no any exception. **1.00**

Countries: **Malaysia**
Type of IIAs: **EPA**
Dateof entry into force: **2006/7/13**

A. Expropriation and Compensation Standards of Treatment					B. General Standards of Treatment	
(1) Protection against expropriation		(2) Compensation treatment			(3) National treatment	
In the article 81.1 (investment chapter) there is a provision of the general 4 principles that are required (alltogether) in order an expropriation to be lawful: public purpose, non-discriminatory, due process of law and compensation. According to article 81.5, it is aknowledged that art. 81.1 of the Treaty (expropriation) shall also apply to taxation measures unless the above principles occur. The Japan-Malaysia EPA has no restriction requiring the establishment of a sub-committee for taxation measures. In article 85.1 (Settlement of Investment Disputes), it is confirmed with a special note that any settlement related to investment disputes "shall apply in respect of taxation measures". Similar provision exists in the Japan-Thailand EPA. For this reason, perfect score (1.00) is given.	1.00	The Treaty refers to the Hull formula by stating that expropriation or its equivalent is not allowed except "upon payment of prompt, adequate and effective compensation" (art. 81.1 [d]), and that "such compensation shall be equivalent to the fair market value of the expropriated investments (a) at the time when or immediately before the expropriation was publicly announced or (b) when the expropriation occurred, whichever is the earlier" (art. 81.2). Considering the effective compensation, article 81.4[a,b,c] states that "effective realisable, freely transferable and freely convertible at the market exchange rate prevailing on the date of the expropriation into the currency of the country of the investors concerned and freely usable currencies". This guarantee is repeated in the relevant article concerning "transfer of payments" (art. 83.1[f]). Finally, in acording to the prompt-compensation requirement, art. 81.4 states that "compensation shall be paid without delay and shall carry an appropriate interest, taking into account the length of time from the time of expropriation until the time of payment".	1.00		There is an inclusion of a general restriction (art. 75.3): "Notwithstanding paragraph 1, each Party may prescribe special formalities in connection with investment activities of investors of the other Party in its area, provided that such formalities do not materially impair the protection afforded by the former Party to investors of the other Party and to their investments pursuant to this Chapter". It is argued that these special formalities introduce some form of limitation to the standard of national treatment and they consist of an exemption that other treaties do not require (i.e. Japan EPAs with the Philippines, Thailand and Vietnam). Art. 97 (market access) of Jp.-Mal. EPA agreement, it provides national treatment with the specific commitments & limitations of Annex 6, and the additional commitments of art. 98. According to art.94.2C of the Japan-Malaysia EPA-Agreement (trade in services), subsidies provided by a Party or a state enterprise thereof, including grants, government supported loans, guarantees and insurance do not apply in the treaty. Annex 6 (services): incentives are limited to eligible Malaysia-owed corportions engaged in service sectors promoted by the Government. Also annex 4-Investment- provides that national treatment may not be accorded in the provision of loans, grants, incentives and other subsidies. Other exceptions in providing NT: in land transactions, ownership and lease of land, restrictions on licensing by reg. authorities, acquisition of shares, mergers and takeovers of Malaysian companies by foreigners, privatization or divestment of assets owned by the gov.-annex 4-. Article 78 provides NT on the access to the courts of Justice. Art. 80.6 imposes a possibility of discriminatory restriction. Finally, in case of inconsistency between chapter on services and chapter. on investment, chapter on services prevails.	0.50

					C. Specific Standards of Treatment	
(4) Most Favoured Nation treatment		(5) Fair & equitable treatment		(6) Full protection & security	(7) Free transfer of funds	
Art. 101 provides MFN treatment unless there is an exemption in Anex 7. Malaysia does not retain any reservation for the power sector thus, there are major general restrictions that affect MFN in relation to power sector as indicated below. Art. 101.3 expands MFN treatment to also future preferential agreements of Malaysia and third countries. Article 78 also provides MFN treatment on the access to the courts of Justice. Art. 80.6 imposes a possibility of discriminatory restriction. Annex 4-Investment- provides that MFN treatment may not be accorded in the provision of loans, grants, incentives and other subsidies. MFN may not be accorded in privatization or divestment of assets owned by the gov.-annex 4-. It may also not be accorded to foreign investors with respect to preferential treatment granted under any ASEAN agreement. -annex 4-. According to Annex 7, Part II (services), MFN restriction may be posed in all sectors through all measures affecting tade in services in all modes of supply. Finally, in case of inconsistency between chapter on services and chapter. on investment, chapter on services prevails.	0.50	Article 77 of the Treaty provides the general treatment of fair & equitable treatment. (There is no any note that specifies the meaning of this treatment like the case of Philippines). The FET clause receives full-capacity standard of treatment.	1.00	Article 77 of the Treaty (Investment Chapter) provides the general treatment of full protection & security. (There is no any note that reduces the scope or exlude from the meaning any treatment like it happens in the case of Philippines or Thailand). Therefore, FPS clause under this Treaty is considered as providing full protection levels. There is no any exemption for the power sector. [1.00]	According to article 107.1, a country shall not apply restrictions on international transfers & payments for transactions related to trade in services, unless in case of art. 106 which describes such cases as serious balance of payments and external financial difficulties or threat. Any restriction taken should be under concrete conditions: MFN (but no refferrence to NT) treatment, according to IMF rules, avoid unnecessary damage, shall not exceed those necessary to deal with above circumstances, be temporary and be phased out progressively (art. 108.2). Thus, there is no any provision for consultations in order to review the restrictions adopted above. Art. 83 (investment chapter) defines the categories of transfers and confirms that those shall be done freely, in any currency and without delay. Art. 83.3 accords MFN treatment to the transfer of funds (the other Treaties do not accord MFN treatment). Thus, due to the non-reference of NT in case of restrictions to safeguard the balance of payments (trade in services), the score is discounted.	0.90

C. Specific Standards of Treatment							
(8) Protection from Strife & Compensation		(9) Umbrella clause		(10) Arbitration provision		(11) Subrogation clause	
Article 82 grants protection against strife without any restriction in conection with NT, MFN or with regards to the free transferability and convertibility requirement of the compensation payments.	1.00	No any relevant clause of protection of contractual commitments.	0.00	The article 85 recognizes settlement of investment disputes between a country and an investor of the other country. It gives absolut right to the investor to choose an international arbitration forum with 3 alternatives: Kuala Lumpur Regional Centre for Arbitration or ICSID or UNCITRAL or any other agreed center. Though, the art. 85.17 excludes from this provision disputes that arise on issues based on national treatment, prohibition to performance requirements. Article 85.18 also excludes investments that have not been made in compliance of laws. regulations and national policies of Malaysia.In a specific additional note, it determines investments that are not made in compliance with Malaysian laws by specifying those that have not been "endorsed by the Cabinet and announced and made publicly available in a written form by the Government of Malaysia". Such strict requirements are not included in any of the other examined treaties For this reason, the score is discounted. Japan-Malaysia EPA sets a time limitation to the consultation period (5 months-art. 85.4). An additional restriction to the arbitration right is considered to be the art. 85.12 which requires the parties to hold their arbitration "in the disputing Country" (unless agreed otherwise).	0.60	There is a separate subrogation-article from the dispute resolution clause. First, article 84.1 recognises the right of home country (or its agencies) to substitute rights or claims of its investors and the right to exercise such rights or claims to the same extent as the original right or claim of the investor. Moreover, art. 84.2 acknowledges that the right to compensation due to expropriation and protection from strife or the free transfer of such payment shall apply to the home country or its designated agencies with no any exception.	1.00

Countries:	Philippines
Type of IIAs:	EPA
Dateof entry into force:	2008/11/11

A. Expropriation and Compensation Standards of Treatment			B. General Standards of Treatment	
(1) Protection against expropriation		(2) Compensation treatment		(3) National treatment

(1) Protection against expropriation	0.50	(2) Compensation treatment	1.00	(3) National treatment	0.75
In the article 95.1 (investment chapter) there is a provision of the general 4 principles that are required (alltogether) in order an expropriation to be lawful: public purpose, non-discriminatory, due process of law and compensation. According to article 104.1, it is aknowledged that art. 95 of the Treaty (expropriation) shall also apply to taxation measures unless the above principles occur. However, the Japan-Philippines EPA provides an additional note under the article 104 (taxation measures as expropriation) that introduces an exemption from the general rule of the 4 principles that are needed in order an expropriation to be lawful. From the 4 principles, only "non-discriminatory" is required in order a taxation measure to be lawful. This exemption is fount only in case of Japan-Philippines EPA. For this reason, the study treats this exemption of the "expropriation clause" with a lower score than it treats the others, as the risk of indirect expropriation through taxation measures becomes higher. Furthermore, article 106 of the Treaty establishes a "sub-committee on investment" which among others is responsible to discuss any related to taxation measures as expropriation (art. 106.2 [c]). That means the investors cannot directly claim before a court the expropriatory character of a taxation measure unless they consult the respective Committee first. According to the study, this adds more uncertainty about the protection of investments against creeping expropriation (taxation). This is one more restriction that results to a lower score. The Japan-Malaysia EPA does not have such restriction. Finally, article 99 of the Treaty permits the Parties to take any measure without obligation to comply with the expropriation-clause (art. 95) if there is a necessity to adopt measures for the protection of health, life, environment, to maintain morals & public order, to protect essential security interests and finally to comly with their obligation under UN Charter for the maintenance of international peace and security (art. 99.1 [a], [b], [c], and [d]). Similar provision is fount only in the Japan-Vietnam BIT (art. 15). The study does not give any score for the above reservation of the Treaty.		The Treaty refers to the Hull formula by stating that expropriation or its equivalent is not allowed except "upon payment of prompt, adequate and effective compensation" (art. 95.1 [d]), and that "such compensation shall be equivalent to the fair market value of the expropriated investments (a) at the time when the expropriation was publicly announced or (b) when the expropriation occurred, whichever is the earlier" (art. 95.2). Considering the effective compensation, article 95.3 states that "effective realisable, freely transferable and freely convertible at the market exchange rate prevailing on the date of the expropriation into the currency of the country of the investors concerned and freely usable currencies". This guarantee is repeated in the relevant article concerning "transfer of payments" (art. 97.1[f]). Finally, in according to the prompt-compensation requirement, art. 95.3 states that "compensation shall be paid without delay and shall carry an appropriate interest, taking into account the length of time from the time of expropriation until the time of payment".		Art. 73 of Jp.-Phil. EPA agreement, provides national treatment but according to the specific commitments about access in Annex 6. According to art.70.2C of the Japan-Philippines EPA-Agreement, subsidies provided by a Party or a state enterprise thereof, including grants, government supported loans, guarantees and insurance do not apply in the treaty. Also, according to Annex 6, horizontal section, there is a limitation on national treatment: all foreign firms engaged in services other than manufacturing shall prescribe 50:50 debt-to-equity ratio when avail of peso borrowings. Finally, article 92 also provides NT on the access to the courts of Justice. Finally, in case of inconsistency between chapter on services and chapter. on investment, chapter on services prevails.	

				C. Specific Standards of Treatment	
(4) Most Favoured Nation treatment		(5) Fair & equitable treatment		(6) Full protection & security	(7) Free transfer of funds

(4) Most Favoured Nation treatment	1.00	(5) Fair & equitable treatment	0.75	(6) Full protection & security	0.75	(7) Free transfer of funds	0.70
Art. 76 provides MFN treatment unless there is an exemption in Annex 6, Part II. Philippines does not retain any reservation for the power sector. Article 92 also provides MFN on the access to the courts of Justice. Finally, in case of inconsistency between chapter on services and chapter. on investment, chapter on services prevails.		Article 91 of the Treaty provides the general treatment of fair & equitable treatment. There is a note that specifies the meaning of this treatment by referring to it as "minimum standard of treatment" instead of "general standard of treatment". Under this reference, the Treaty provides only as much protection as foreign investors receive in their capacity as aliens under the customary international law minimum standard of protection of aliens and not any higher level than that. For this reason, it is considered as a restriction to the FET full-capacity standard of treatment similarly to Thailand.		Article 91 of the Treaty (Investment Chapter) provides the general treatment of full protection and security. There is also a note that specifies the meaning of this treatment like the case of Philippines as "minimum standard of treatment instead of "general standard of treatment". Under this wording, the Treaty provides only as much protection as foreign investors receive in their capacity as aliens under the customary international law minimum standard of protection of aliens and not any higher level than that. It is considered as a restriction excluding the protection against legal damage that jurisprudence could aknowledge.	According to Art. 81, a Party shall not apply restrictions on international transfers & payments for transactions related to trade in services and if so, art. 82.1 and 97.3 describe the cases of such restrictions as serious balance of payments and external financial difficulties or threat. Any restriction taken should be under concrete conditions: MFN (but no reference to NT) treatment, according to IMF rules, avoid unnecessary damage, shall not exceed those necessary to deal with above circumstances, be temporary and be phased out progressively. Moreover, art. 82.2 ensures measures of treatment & protection in case of transfer restrictions. Art. 97 (investment chapter) defines the categories of transfers and confirms that those shall be done freely, in any currency and without delay and respecting MFN treatment.However, art. 97.3 adds one more element that can justify delay or prevention of FTts right: prior approval is required (though applying only to short term foreign currency loans). Because of this additional requirement, the score is discounted more than in the other Treaties.

C. Specific Standards of Treatment			
(8) Protection from Strife & Compensation	(9) Umbrella clause	(10) Arbitration provision	(11) Subrogation clause
0.50 Article 96 grants protection against strife only with regards to the free transferibility and convertibility requirement of the compensation payments.. Thus, it contains a restriction about the requirement of NT that should be accorded to Japanese investors with regards to the treatment of restitution, indemnification, compensation or any other settlement.	**0.00** No any relevant clause of protection of contractual commitments.	**0.25** According to art. 107.2 it is stated that "in the absence of the mechanism for the settlement of an investment dispute between a Party and an investor of the other Party, the resort to international conciliation or arbitration tribunal is subject to mutual consent of the parties to the dispute. This means that the disputing Party may, at its option or discretion, grant or deny its consent in respect of each particular investment dispute and that, in the absence of the express written consent of the disputing Party, an international conciliation or arbitration tribunal shall have no jurisdiction over the investment dispute involved". The Japan-Philippines article, by requiring "mutual consent", it is clear than no consent to arbitration is given by the host state (Philipines) and therefore, this thesis scores it with the score 0.25.	**1.00** There is a separate subrogation-article from the dispute resolution clause. First, article 98.1 recognises the right of home country (or its agencies) to substitute rights or claims of its investors and the right to exercise such rights or claims to the same extent as the original right or claim of the investor. Moreover, art. 98.2 acknowledges that the right to compensation due to expropriation and protection from strife or the free transfer of such payment shall apply to the home country or its designated agencies with no any exception.

Countries: Vietnam
Type of IIAs: EPA
Dateof entry into force: BIT: 2004/12/19   EPA: 2009/10/1

A. Expropriation and Compensation Standards of Treatment		B. General Standards of Treatment
(1) Protection against expropriation	(2) Compensation treatment	(3) National treatment
In the article 9.2 of the BIT, there is a provision of the general 4 principles that are required (alltogether) in order an expropriation to be lawful: public purpose, non-discriminatory, due process of law and compensation. According to article 19.2, it is acknowledged that art. 9.2 of the Treaty (expropriation) shall also apply to taxation measures unless the above principles occur. In article 4 of the Agreed Minutes of the BIT agreement, the Parties record their understanding in relation to the taxation measures stating that "the imposition of taxes does not generally constitute expropriation". This is only a recognition of a general principle of international law and it is not considered as restriction to what constitutes expropriation. However, article 20 of the Treaty establishes a "sub-committee on investment" which among others is responsible to discuss any related to taxation measures as expropriation. That means the investors cannot directly claim before a court the expropriatory character of a taxation measure unless they consult the respective Committee first. According to the study, this adds more uncertainty about the protection of investments against creeping expropriation (taxation). This is considered as a restriction that results to a lower score. The Japan-Malaysia EPA does not have such restriction. Finally, article 15 of the Treaty permits the Parties to take any measure without obligation to comply with the expropriation-clause (art. 9.2) if there is a necessity to adopt measures for the protection of health, life, environment, to maintain morals & public order, to protect essential security interests and finally to comly with their obligation under UN Charter for the maintenance of international peace and security (art. 15.1 [a], [b], [c], and [d]). Similar provision is fount only in the Japan-Philippines EPA (art. 99). The study does not give any score for the above reservation of the Treaty. **0.75**	The Treaty refers to the Hull formula by stating that expropriation or its equivalent is not allowed except "upon payment of prompt, adequate and effective compensation" (art. 9.2 [c]), and that "such compensation shall be equivalent to the fair market value of the expropriated investments (a) at the time when the expropriation was publicly announced or (b) when the expropriation occurred, whichever is the earlier" (art. 9.3). Considering the effective compensation, article 9.3 states that "effective realisable, freely transferable and freely convertible at the market exchange rate prevailing on the date of the expropriation into the currency of the country of the investors concerned and freely usable currencies". This guarantee is repeated in the relevant article concerning "transfer of payments" (art. 12.1[e]). Finally, in according to the prompt-compensation requirement, art. 9.3 states that "compensation shall be paid without delay and shall carry an appropriate interest, taking into account the length of time from the time of expropriation until the time of payment". **1.00**	Article 2.1 of BIT recognizes NT for all investments unless exceptional measures adopted in Annex I (there is no any such measure in relation to electricity sector). Also, in relation to exceptional measures existed before the BIT agreement (art. 6.1), parties may maintain them and specify in Annex II (electricity is included in the sectors of maintaining some exceptional measures) Even though there is this inclusion, relevantly to the other countries, Vietnam has less restrictions and for this reason, it still receives a 0.75 score. Also, in respect to Annex II, in exceptional financial, economic or industrial circumstances, new exceptional measures may be adopted (art. 6.7). In case of new exceptional measures adopted in Annex I, the Parties shall a) notify the other party and b)hold upon request, consultations in good faith with view to achieving mutual satisfaction (art. 5.3). In case of new exceptional measures adopted in Annex II, the Parties shall keep more requirements: a) notify the other party, b) provide upon request, particular explanations, c)allow reasonable time for the other Party to make comments in writting, d)hold upon request, consultations in good faith with view to achieving mutual satisfaction and e) take an appropriate action based on (c) or (d) (art. 6.7) According to the trade in services chapter of the Japan-Vietnam EPA, article 60.1 provides that "each Party shall accord to the services of the other Party, treatment no less favorable than that it accords to its own like services". One exception from the above treatment is included in Annex 5, under the horizontal section, limitations on National Treatment: "Eligibility for subsidies may be limited to Vietnamese service suppliers and the granting of one-time subsidization to promote & facilitate the process of equitization is not in breach of this commitment". In regards to electricity sector, there is no any specific restriction to NT. **0.75**

		C. Specific Standards of Treatment	
(4) Most Favoured Nation treatment	(5) Fair & equitable treatment	(6) Full protection & security	(7) Free transfer of funds
Article 2.2 of BIT recognizes MFN treatment for all investments unless exceptional measures adopted in Annex I (no any measure adopted in relation to electricity sector). Also, in relation to exceptional measures existed before the BIT agreement, parties may maintain them and specify in Annex II (electricity is included in the sectors of maintaining some exceptional measures but exceptionnaly MFN treatment shall be accorded for all sectors incl. electricity). In case of new exceptional measures adopted in Annex I, the Parties shall a) notify the other party and b)hold upon request, consultations in good faith with view to achieving mutual satisfaction (art. 5.3). In case of new exceptional measures adopted in Annex II, the Parties shall keep more requiremnts: a) notify the other party, b) provide upon request, particular explanations, c)allow reasonable time for the other Party to make comments in writting, d)hold upon request, consultations in good faith with view to achieving mutual satisfaction and e) take an appropriate action based on (c) or (d) (art. 6.7). According to article 63.1 of the EPA, "each Party shall accord to services of the other Party, treatment no less favorable than that it accords to like services of any non-Party", unless there is a limitation/restriction in Annex 6 of the EPA. But, according to article 63.2 & 63.3, and Annex 6, all sectors related to "commercial presence" (electricity sector is included), are exempted from the MFN treatment in regards to measures extending preferential treatment pursuant to bilateral investment treaties between Vietnam and other countries. The reason of this exemption is to foster investment in Vietnam. **0.50**	Each Party shall accord in its area of investments of the other Party fair & equitable treatment (art. 9.1, BIT). (There is no any note that specifies the meaning of this treatment like the case of Philippines). The FET clause receives full-capacity standard of treatment. **1.00**	Each Party shall accord in its area of investments of the other Party full and constant protection and security. (There is no any note that reduces the scope or exlude from the meaning any treatment like it happens in the case of Philippines or Thailand). Therefore, FPS clause under this Treaty is considered as providing full protection levels. There is no any exemption for the power sector. **1.00**	There are omissions regarding the right of FTFs in both trade in services and investment chapters. Article 12 of BIT requires free transfer of payments and defines the categories of payments (art. 12.1) and confirms that those shall be done freely, in any currency and without delay (art. 12.2). A Party may delay or prevent a transfer through the equitable, non discriminatory & good faith of its laws (but no any exact referrence to NT & MFN) relating to: bankruptcy/insolvency or protection of creditors, trading in securities, criminal or penal offenses or ensuring compliance with judgements. When a Party does not conform with the free transfer of funds, there shall be some concrete conditions such as: serious balance of payments and external financial difficulties or threat (art. 16.1); and shall be referred to IMF rules, avoid unnecessary damage, shall not exceed those necessary to deal with above circumstances, be temporary and be phased out progressively (art. 16.2). (But MFN treatment is not referred). The above conditions & requirements are also repeated by the article 68 and 69 of Japan-Vietnam EPA: "A Party shall not apply restrictions on international transfers and payments for current transactions relating to its specific commitments" (art. 68), except under the circumstances of art. 69.1 and the conditions in 69.2. An interesting addition in the Japan-Vietnam EPA, which is not found in any other EPA, is the article 69.3, which legitimizes such restrictions especially when occur to the supply of services that are essential for the economic development of the Party (electricity sector could be included in those services). However, the same article clarifies that "such restrictions shall not be adopted for the purpose of protecting a particular service sector". **0.80**

C. Specific Standards of Treatment							
(8) Protection from Strife & Compensation		(9) Umbrella clause		(10) Arbitration provision		(11) Subrogation clause	
Article 10 of the BIT provides specific treatment measures & compensation on the base of NT and MFN and also payments freely transferable (art. 12.1e) and convertible (art. 12.2).	1.00	No any relevant clause of protection of contractual commitments.	0.00	The Japan-Vietnam EPA provides only State-to-State dispute settlement (articles 116-124). However, article 14.1 of the BIT recognizes the right to investor-state dispute settlement/arbitration. Article 14.3 offers to the investor the chance to choose an international arbitration forum, if investment dispute cannot be settled through consultations within 3 months, with 2 alternatives: arbitration in accordance to ICSID or under the UNCITRAL rules. However, before the submission of an investment dispute to one of the international arbitration forums stated above, the host state shall give its consent Art. 14.4 states that: "A contracting party which is a party to an investment dispute shall give its consent to the submission of the investment dispute to international conciliation or arbitration referred to in paragraph 3 above in accordance with the provisions of this Article". Such wording is similar to the third type of Broche-clause, and therefore the Japan-Vietnam EPA is scored with 0.75.	0.75	There is a separate subrogation-article from the dispute resolution clause. First, article 11 recognises the right of home country (or its agencies) to substitute rights or claims of its investors and the right to exercise such rights or claims to the same extent as the original right or claim of the investor. However, art. 11 acknowledges that the right to compensation shall apply to the home country or its designated agencies only due to expropriation. Compensation right due to protection from strife is excluded and therefore this article's score is discounted.	0.75

BIBLIOGRAPHY

Adams, R., P. Dee, and G. McGuire, 'The Trade and Investment Effects of Preferential Trading Arrangements – Old and New Evidence', Australian Productivity Commission Staff Working Paper, Canberra, 2003.

ADB, *Developing Best Practices for Promoting Private Sector Investment in Infrastructure*, Asian Development Bank, Manila, 2000.

Ali, A.H. and K. Tallent, 'The Effect of BITs on the International Body of Investment Law: The Significance of Fair and Equitable Treatment Provisions', in C. Rogers and R. Alford, eds., *The Future of Investment Arbitration*, Institute for Transnational Arbitration-The Center for American and International Law, Oxford University Press, Oxford, 2009, p. 199-221.

Amerasinghe, C.F., 'Issues of Compensation for the Taking of Alien Property in the Light of Recent Cases and Practice', *International and Comparative Law Quarterly* 41:1, 1992, pp. 22-65.

Babbar, S. and J. Schuster, 'Power Project Finance: Experience in Developing Countries', *RMC Discussion Paper series*: no. 119, World Bank, Washington DC, 1998.

Bacon, R. and J. Besant-Jones, 'Global Electric Power Reform, Privatisation and Liberalisation of the Electric Power Industry in Developing Countries', *Energy and Mining Sector Board Discussion Paper*: no. 2, World Bank, Washington DC, June 2002.

Bernardini, P., 'Development Agreements with Host Governments' in R. Pritchard, ed., *Economic Development, Foreign Investment and the Law: Issues of Private Sector Development, Foreign Investment and the Role of Law in a New Era*, International Bar Association and the Kluwer Law International, London, 1996, pp. 161-174.

Bowett, D.W., 'State Contracts with Aliens: Contemporary Developments on Compensation for Termination or Breach', *British Year Book of International Law* 59:1, 1988, pp. 49-74.

Broches, A., 'Bilateral Investment Treaties and Arbitration of Investment Disputes' in J. Schulsz and J. A. van den Berg, eds., *The Art of Arbitration: Liber Amicorum Pieter Sanders*, Kluwer, Deventer, 1982.

Brownlie, I., *Principles of Public International Law*, 6th edn, Oxford University Press, New York, 2003.

Bubb, R.J. and S. Rose-Ackerman, 'BITs and Bargains: Strategic Aspects of Bilateral and Multilateral Regulation of Foreign Investment", *International Review of Law and Economics*, 27:3, 2007, p. 291-311.

Cameron, P.D., *International Energy Investment Law: The Pursuit of Stability*, Oxford University Press, Oxford, 2010.

Chen, A., 'A New Perspective on Infrastructure Financing in Asia', *Pacific-Basin Finance Journal* 10:3, 2002, pp. 227-242.

Comeaux, P. and S.N. Kinsella, 'Reducing Political Risk in Developing Countries: Bilateral Investment Treaties, Stabilization Clauses, and MIGA & OPIC Investment Insurance', *New York Law School Journal of International and Comparative Law* 15:1, 1994, pp. 1-48.

— — and S.N. Kinsella, *Protecting Foreign Investment under International Law: Legal Aspects of Political Risk*, Oceana Publications Inc., New York, 1997.

Covindassamy, M.A., D. Oda and Y. Zhang, 'Analysis of Power Projects with Private Participation under Stress' no. 311/05 Joint UNDP/WB (ESMAP) Report, World Bank, Washington DC, 2005.

Crawford, J., *The International Law Commission's Articles on State Responsibility: Introduction, Text and Commentaries*, Cambridge University Press, Cambridge, 2002.

Delmon, J., 'Mobilizing Private Finance with IBRD/IDA Guarantees to Bridge the Infrastructure Funding Gap', Finance, Economics and Urban Development Department/Sustainable Development Network, World Bank, Washington DC, 2007.

Doh, J.P. and R. Ramamutri, 'Reassessing Risk in Developing Country Infrastructure', *Long Range Planning* 36:4, 2003, pp. 337-353.

Dolzer, R., 'New Foundations of the Law of Expropriation of Alien Property', *American Journal of International Law* 75, 1981, pp. 553-589.

— — 'Indirect Expropriations: New Developments?', *New York University Environmental Law Journal* 11:1, 2002, pp. 64-93.

— — 'Fair and Equitable Treatment: A Key Standard in Investment Treaties', *International Lawyer* 39:1, 2005, pp. 87-106.

— — and M. Stevens, *Bilateral Investment Treaties*, International Centre for Settlement of Investment Disputes, Martinus Nijhoff Publishers, the Hague, 1995.

Dugan C.F., D. Wallace Jr. and R.D. Noah, *Investor-State Arbitration*, Oxford University Press, Oxford, 2008.

EIB, 'Evaluation of PPP Projects Financed by the EIB', Evaluation Report, Operations Evaluation Department, European Investment Bank, Luxembourg, 2005.

Estache, A., 'Argentina's 1990s Utilities Privatization: A Cure or a Disease', Mimeo, World Bank, Washington DC, 2002.

— — and A. Coicoechea, 'How Widespread Were Infrastructure Reforms During the 1990s?', *World Bank Research Working Paper*, no. 3595, World Bank, Washington DC, 2005.

— — and M. Fay, 'Current debates on Infrastructure Policy', *Policy Research Working Paper*, no. 4410, World Bank, Washington DC, 2007.

Fatouros, A.A., *Government Guarantees to Foreign Investors*, Columbia University Press, New York and London, 1962.

Freyer, D.H. and D. Herliby, 'Most Favored Nation Treatment and Dispute Settlement in Investment Arbitration: Just How Favored is Most-Favored?", *ICSID Review–Foreign Investment Law Journal*, 20, 2005, p. 58-83.

Gagné, G. and J.F. Morin, 'The Evolving American Policy on Investment Protection: Evidence from Recent FTAs and the 2004 Model BIT'. *Journal of International Economic Law* 9:2 2006, pp. 357-382.

Gaillard, E., 'Establishing Jurisdiction through a Most-Favored-Nation Clause', *New York Law Journal* 233:105, 2005.

Gazzini, T., 'The Role of Customary International Law in the Field of Foreign Investment', *Journal of World Investment & Trade*, 8:5, 2007, pp. 691-716.

Ginsburg T., 'International Substitutes for Domestic Institutions: Bilateral Investment Treaties and Governance', *International Review of Law and Economics* 25:1, 2005, pp. 107-119.

Glavinis, P., *Diethnes Oikonomiko Dikaio: Genikes Arhes, Diethnes Emporio, Xenes Ependiseis* [*International Economic Law: General Principles, International Trade, Foreign Investments*], Sakkoulas Publications, Athens, 2009.

Golub, S.S., 'Measures of Restrictions on Inward Foreign Direct Investment for OECD Countries', *OECD Economic Studies*, no. 36, OECD, Paris, 2003.

Gomez-Ibanez, J.A., 'Private Infrastructure in Developing Countries: Lessons from Recent Experience', paper presented to the Commission on Growth and Development at the workshop 'Global Trends and Challenges', New Haven, 28-29 September 2007.

Grierson T., J. Weiller and I.A. Laird, 'Standards of Treatment', in P. Muchlinski, F. Ortino and C. Schreuer, eds., *The Oxford Handbook of International Investment Law*, Oxford University Press, Oxford, 2008, pp. 259-304.

Guasch, J.L., *Granting and Renegotiating Infrastructure Concessions: Doing it Right*, World Bank Institute Development Studies, World Bank, Washington DC, 2004.

Gupta, P., R. Lamech, F. Mashar and J. Wright, 'Mitigating Regulatory Risk for Distribution Privatization: The World Bank Partial Risk Guarantee' no. 5 *Energy and Mining Sector Board Discussion Paper Series*, World Bank, Washington DC, 2002.

Hansen, K.W., 'A BIT of Insurance' in T. H. Moran, G. T. West and K. Martin eds., *International Political Risk Management: Needs of the Present, Challenges for the Future*, World Bank, Washington DC, 2008, pp. 7-12.

Harms, P., *International Investment, Political Risk, and Growth*, Kluwer Academic Publishers, Boston/Dordrecht/London, 2000.

Hill, C.A., 'How Investors React to Political Risk', *Duke Journal of Comparative and International Law* 8:2, 1998, pp. 283-313.

Hoffman, S.L., *The Law and Business of International Project Finance*, 3rd edn, Cambridge University Press, New York, 2008.

Houde, M.F. and F. Pagani, 'Most Favored Nation Treatment in International Investment Law', OECD Working Paper on International Investment no. 2004/2, OECD Financial and Enterprise Affairs Directorate, 2004.

— — and K. Yannaca-Small, 'Relationships between International Investment Agreements', OECD Working Paper on International Investment no. 2004/1, OECD Financial and Enterprise Affairs Directorate, 2004.

Inadomi, H.M., *Independent Power Producers in Developing Countries: Legal Investment Protection and Consequences for Development*, Wolters Kluwer Law and Business, Austin, 2010.

International Institute for Sustainable Development, 'The European Union's Future International Investment Policy: What to Expect in the Wake of the Lisbon Treaty', *Investment Treaty News* 1:1, Sept. 2010, <www.iisd.org/itn/wpcontent/uploads/2010/09/IISD_ITN_newsletter_SEPT_WEB.pdf>

Irwin, T., M. Klein, G.E. Perry and M. Thobani, eds., *Dealing with Public Risks in Private Infrastructure*, World Bank Latin American and Caribbean Studies, World Bank, Washington DC, 1997.

Islam M.R., 'The Most Favored Nation Clause', in K.C D.M. Wilde, M.R. Islam, eds. *International Transactions: Trade and Investment, Law and Finance*, The Law Book Company Limited, Sydney, 1993, pp. 215-224.

Jamasb T., 'Between the State and the Market. Electricity Sector Reform in Developing Countries', *Utilities Policy* 14:1, 2006, pp.14-30.

JBIC, 'JBIC Project Finance Initiatives: Japanese Enterprise and Global Prosperity', Japan Bank for International Cooperation, 2009.

JFC, JBIC Annual Report – 2009, Japan Finance Corporation, 2009.

Kalinova, B., A. Palerm, and S. Thomsen, 'OECD's FDI Restrictiveness Index: 2010 Update', OECD Working Paper on International Investment no. 2010/3, OECD Financial and Enterprise Affairs Directorate, 2010.

Kaushal, A., 'Revisiting History: How the Past Matters for the Present Backlash against the Foreign Investment Regime', *Harvard International Law Journal* 50:2, 2009, pp. 491-534.

Kessides, I.N., *Reforming Infrastructure: Privatization, Regulation, and Competition*, World Bank, Washington DC, and Oxford University Press, New York, 2004.

Kill, T., 'Don't Cross the Streams: Past and Present Overstatement of Customary International Law in Connection with Conventional Fair and Equitable Treatment Obligations', *Michigan Law Review* 106, 2008, p. 853-880.

Kishoiyian, B., 'The Utility of Bilateral Investment Treaties in the Formulation of Customary International Law', *Northwestern Journal of International Law & Business*, 14:2, 1994, pp. 327-375.

Kolo, A., 'Transfer of Funds: The Interaction between the IMF Articles of Agreement and Modern Investment Treaties: A Comparative Law Perspective' in S. Schill, ed., *International Investment Law and Comparative Public Law*, Oxford University Press Inc., Oxford, 2010, pp. 345-374.

Koyama, T. and S. Golub, 'FDI Regulatory Restrictiveness Index: Revision and Extension to More Economies', OECD Working Paper on International Investment no. 2006/4, OECD Financial and Enterprise Affairs Directorate 2010.

Lesher, M. and S. Miroudot, 'Analysis of the Economic Impact of Investment Provisions in Regional Trade Agreements,' *OECD Trade Policy Working Papers* no. 36, OECD, Trade Directorate, Paris, 2006.

Lessard, D.R., 'Country Risk and the Structure of International Financial Intermediation' in D.K. Das, ed., *International Finance–Contemporary Issues*, Routledge, London, 1993, pp. 451-470.

Lucas, R.E. Jr., 'Why doesn't Capital Flow from Rich to Poor Countries?', *American Economic Review* 80:2, 1990, pp. 93-96.

Mankiw, N.G., D. Romer and D.N. Weil, 'A Contribution to the Empirics of Economic Growth', *Quarterly Journal of Economics* 107:2, 1992, pp. 407-437.

Markwick, S., 'Trends in Political Risks for Corporate Investors', in T.H. Moran, ed., *Managing International Political Risk*, Blackwell Publishers Ltd., Oxford, 1998, pp. 44-56.

Matsukawa, T., R. Sheppard and J. Wright, 'Foreign Exchange Risk Mitigation for Power and Water Projects in Developing Countries', Discussion Paper no. 9, *Energy and Mining Board Discussion Paper Series*, World Bank, Washington DC, 2003.

— — and O. Habeck, 'Review of Risk Mitigation Instruments for Infrastructure Financing and Recent Trends and Developments', *Trends and Policy Options Paper*, no. 4, PPIAF, World Bank, Washington DC, 2007.

McLachlan C. QC., L. Shore and M. Weiniger, *International Investment Arbitration: Substantive Principles*, Oxford University Press Inc., New York, 2008.

Moran T.H., 'The Changing Nature of Political Risk' in T.H. Moran, ed., *Managing International Political Risk*, Blackwell Publishers Ltd., Oxford, 1998, pp. 7-14.

— — 'Political Risk Insurance as a Tool to Manage International Political Risk', in T. H. Moran, ed., *Managing International Political Risk*, Blackwell Publishers Ltd., Oxford, 1998, pp. 139-147.

— — 'Political and Regulatory Risk in Infrastructure Investment in Developing Countries: Introduction and Overview', *The Centre for Energy, Petroleum and Mineral Law and Policy Journal* (CEPMLP), vol. 5-6, 1999.

— — and G.T. West, 'Overview' in T.H. Moran, G.T. West and K. Martin eds., *International Political Risk Management: Needs of the Present, Challenges for the Future*, The World Bank, Washington DC, 2008, pp. 3-6.

— — G.T. West and K. Martin, eds., *Managing International Political Risk: Needs of the Present Challenges for the Future*, World Bank, Washington DC, 2006.

Muchlinski, P.T., 'The Rise and Fall of the Multilateral Agreement on Investment: Where Now?', *International Law*, 34, 1999, p. 1033-1053.

— — 'Caveat Investor? The Relevance of the Conduct of the Investor under the Fair and Equitable Treatment Standard', *International and Comparative Law Quarterly* 55:3, 2006, 527-558.

— — F. Ortino and C.H. Schreuer, eds., *The Oxford Handbook of International Investment Law*, Oxford University Press, Oxford, 2009.

Mycyk, A. and V. Kaplan, 'Ukraine: Procedure for State Guarantees for Certain Development Projects Approved', *Mondaq Legal News*, <www.mondaq.com>, retrieved on 20 July, 2011.

Nakagawa, J., 'No More Negotiated Deals? Settlement of Trade and Investment Disputes in East Asia', *Journal of International Economic Law*, 10:4, 2007, pp. 837-867.

NEXI, Policy Conditions for Overseas Investment Insurance, Partial Amendment of March 14, Nipon Export Insurance Agency, 2007.

— — Annual Report FY 2008, Nipon Export Insurance Agency, April 2008-March 2009.

— — *NEXI Business Guide*, Nipon Export Insurance Agency, 2009.

— — *NEXI Introduction Brochure*, Nipon Export Insurance Agency, FY 2009.

Nwokolo, A.D., 'Is there a Legal and Functional Value for the Stabilisation Clause in International Petroleum Agreements?', *The Centre for Energy, Petroleum and Mineral Law and Policy Journal* (CEPMLP) Annual Review, vol. 8, 2004.

Ochiai R., P. Dee and C. Findlay, 'Services in Free Trade Agreements' in C. Findlay and S. Urata, eds., *Free Trade Agreements in the Asia Pacific*, World Scientific Studies in International Economics vol. 11, World Scientific Publishing Co., Singapore, 2010, pp. 29-80.

Papanastasiou, T.N., 'Protecting Foreign Investments against Expropriation: A Comparative Study of Japan's EPAs', *International Journal of Public Law and Policy* 1:2, 2011, pp.171–201.

— — 'The Role of Economic Partnership Agreements in Protecting Foreign Investments against Political Risk: An Analysis of Japan's EPAs', *Journal of the Graduate School of Asia-Pacific Studies* 21:2, 2011, pp. 95-124.

Paterson, C., 'Investor-to-State Dispute Settlement in Infrastructure Projects', OECD Working Paper on International Investment no. 2006/2, OECD Financial and Enterprise Affairs Directorate, 2010.

Paulsson, J., 'Dispute Resolution' in R. Pritchard ed., *Economic Development, Foreign Investment and the Law: Issues of Private Sector Development, Foreign Investment and the Role of Law in a New Era*, International Bar Association and the Kluwer Law International, London, 1996, pp. 209-246.

PECC, 'An Assessment of Impediments to Foreign Direct Investment in APEC Member Economies', Pacific Economic Cooperation Council, Tokyo, 2002.

Pekkanen, S.M., *Japan's Aggressive Legalism: Law and Foreign Trade Politics Beyond the WTO*, Stanford University Press, Stanford, 2008.

Pritchard, R., 'The Contemporary Challenges of Economic Development', in R. Pritchard, ed., *Economic Development, Foreign Investment and the Law: Issues of Private Sector Involvement, Foreign Investment and the Rule of Law in a New Era*, the Kluwer Law International, International Bar Association, London, 1996, pp. 1-11.

Reinisch, A., 'Expropriation' in P. Muchlinski, F. Ortino and C. Schreuer, eds., *The Oxford Handbook of International Investment Law*, Oxford University Press, Oxford, 2008, pp. 407-458.

Rodriquez, A.F., 'The Most-Favored-Nation Clause in International Investment Agreements–A Tool for Treaty Shopping?' *Journal of International Arbitration* 25:1, 2008, pp. 89-102.

Rogers, C.A. and R.P. Alford, eds., *The Future of Investment Arbitration*, Institute for Transnational Arbitration–The Center for American and International Law, Oxford University Press Inc., New York, 2009.

Rowat, M.D., 'Multilateral Approaches to Improving the Investment Climate of Developing Countries: The Cases of ICSID and MIGA', *Harvard International Law Journal* 33:1, 1992, pp. 103-144.

Rubins, N. and S. Kinsella, *International Investment, Political Risk and Dispute Resolution: A Practitioner's Guide*, Oceana Publications, New York, 2005.

Sabahi, B. and N.J. Birch, 'Comparative Compensation for Expropriation' in S. Schill, ed., *International Investment Law and Comparative Public Law*, Oxford University Press Inc., Oxford, 2010, pp. 755-785.

Sacerdoti, G., 'Bilateral Treaties and Multilateral Instruments on Investment Protection', *Recueil de Cours* 269, 1997, pp. 251-460.

— — 'The Source and Evolution of International Legal Protection for Infrastructure Investments Confronting Political and Regulatory Risks', *The Centre for Energy, Petroleum and Mineral Law and Policy Journal* (CEPMLP) vol. 5-7, 1999.

Sader, F., 'Attracting Foreign Direct Investment into Infrastructure: Why Is It So Difficult?', *Foreign Investment Advisory Service–IFC*, occasional paper no. 12, World Bank, Washington DC, 2000.

Salacuse, J.W., 'BIT by BIT: The Growth of Bilateral Investment Treaties and their Impact on Foreign Investment in Developing Countries", *International Law*, 24:3, 1990, p. 655-675.

— — 'The Emerging Global Regime for Investment', *Harvard International Law Journal* 51:2, 2010, pp. 427-473.

— — *The Law of Investment Treaties*, Oxford University Press, Oxford, 2010.

Schill, S.W., ed., *International Investment Law and Comparative Public Law*, Oxford University Press Inc., New York, 2010.

Schreuer, C.H., 'Protection against Arbitrary or Discriminatory Measures', in C.A. Rogers and R.P. Alford, eds., *The Future of Investment Arbitration*, Institute for Transnational Arbitration-The Center for American and International Law, Oxford, Oxford University Press, 2009, pp. 183-198.

— — 'Full Protection and Security', *Journal of International Dispute Settlement*, 2010, pp. 1-17.

Shanks, R.B., 'Lessons in the Management of Political Risk: Infrastructure Projects (A Legal Perspective) in T.H. Moran, ed., *Managing International Political Risk*, Blackwell Publishers Ltd., Oxford, 1998, pp. 85-108.

Shihata, I., 'Towards a Depoliticisation of Foreign Investment Disputes: The Roles of ICSID and MIGA', *ICSID Review–Foreign Investment Law Journal* 1, 1986, pp. 2-35.

— — *MIGA and Foreign Investment: Origins, Operations, Policies and Basic Documents of the Multilateral Investment Guarantee Agency*, World Bank, Washington DC, 1988.

— — *Legal Treatment of Foreign Investment: The World Bank Guidelines*, World Bank, Washington DC, 1993.

Short, R., 'Export Credit Agencies, Project Finance, and Commercial Risk: Whose Risk Is It, Anyway?', *Fordham International Law Journal*, 24:4, 2001, pp. 1371-1381.

Sornarajah, M., *The International Law on Foreign Investment*, 2nd edition, Cambridge University Press, Cambridge, 2004.

Stephens, M., 'A Perspective on Political Risk Insurance' in T.H. Moran, ed., *Managing International Political Risk*, Blackwell Publishers Ltd., Oxford, 1998, pp. 148-168.

Sutherland, B., 'Financing Jamaica's Rockfort Independent Power Project: A Review of Experience for Future Projects', RMC Discussion Paper series no. 121, The World Bank, Washington DC, 1998.

Sykes, A., 'International Law', in M. Polinsky and S. Shavel, eds., *Handbook of Law & Economics*, vol. 1, Elsevier, Amsterdam, 2007, pp. 757-821.

Thomson, B., 'Laos and Thailand: Exploring Cross-Border Hydropower Projects', *Allen & Overy*, note written on 17 May, 2010 retrieved on June 20, 2011.

UNCTAD, *Bilateral Investment Treaties in the Mid-1990s*, United Nations, New York and Geneva, 1998.

— — *Bilateral Investment Treaties 1995-2006: Trends in Investment Rulemaking*, United Nations, New York and Geneva, 2007.

— — 'Foreign Direct Investment and Financing for Development: Trends and Selected Issues', Doc. TD/B/COM.2/80, United Nations, New York and Geneva, 2008.

— — *World Investment Report 2008: Transnational Corporations and the Infrastructure Challenge*, United Nations, New York and Geneva, 2008.

— — 'Latest Developments in Investor-State Dispute Settlement', *IIA Monitor no. 1* (UNCTAD/WEB/DIAE/IA/2009/6), United Nations, New York and Geneva, 2009.

— — *The Role of International Investment Agreements in Attracting Foreign Direct Investment to Developing Countries*, United Nations, New York and Geneva, 2009.

Urata, S. and M. Ando, 'Investment Climate Study on ASEAN Member Countries' in J. Corbett and S. Umezaki, eds., *ERIA Report no 1, 2008: Deepening East Asian Economic Integration*, ERIA Institute, Jakarta, 2009, pp. 125-195.

— — and J. Sasuya, 'Analysis of the Restrictions on Foreign Direct Investment in Free Trade Agreements' in C. Findlay and S. Urata, eds., *Free Trade Agreements in the Asia Pacific*, World Scientific Studies in International Economics vol. 11, World Scientific Publishing Co., Singapore, 2010, pp. 81-130.

Valenti, M. 'The Most Favored Nation Clause in BITs as a Basis for Jurisdiction in Foreign Investor-Host State Arbitration', *Arbitration International* 24:3, 2008, pp. 447-466.

Vanndevelde, K.J., 'The Political Economy of Bilateral Investment Treaty', *American Journal of International Law*, 92:4, p. 621-641.

Velde, D.W. te and D. Bezemer, 'Regional Integration and Foreign Direct Investment in Developing Countries', 2004, <www.odi.org.uk/iedg/Projects/ec_prep2.pdf>.

Vernon, R., *Sovereignty at Bay: The Multinational Spread of U.S. Enterprises*, Basic Books Inc., New York/London, 1971.

Walde, T.W. and K. Hober, 'The First energy Charter Treaty Arbitral Award', *Journal of International Arbitration* 22:2, 2005, pp. 83-104.

— — and B. Sabahi, 'Compensation, Damages, and Valuation' in P. Muchlinski, F. Ortino and C. Schreuer, eds., *The Oxford Handbook of International Investment Law*, Oxford University Press, Oxford, 2008, pp. 1052-1124.

Wells, L.T., 'God and Fair Competition: Does the Foreign Direct Investor Face Still Other Risks in Emerging Markets?' in T.H. Moran, ed., *Managing International Political Risk*, Blackwell Publishers Inc., Oxford, 1998, pp. 15-43.

— — and E.S. Gleason, 'Is foreign infrastructure investment still risky?', *Harvard Business Review* September/October 1995, pp. 44–53.

William, L., 'Political and Other Risk Insurance: OPIC, MIGA, EXIMBANK and Other Providers', *Pace International Law Review* 5:1, 1993, pp. 59-113.

Williamson, O.E., *The Economic Institutions of Capitalism*, Free Press New York, 1985.

Woodhouse, E., 'Managing International Political Risk: Lessons from the Power Sector', in T.H. Moran, G.T. West and K. Martin, eds., *Managing International Political Risk: Needs of the Present Challenges for the Future*, World Bank, Washington DC, 2006, pp. 59-86.

WB, 'World Development Report 1994: Infrastructure for Development', World Bank, Washington DC, 1994.

— — 'World Investment and Political Risk: 2009', *MIGA*, World Bank, Washington DC, 2010.

— — 'World Investment and Political Risk: 2010', *MIGA*, World Bank, Washington DC, 2011.

Yannaca-Small, C., 'Fair and Equitable Treatment Standard in International Investment Law', OECD Working Paper on International Investment no. 2004/3, OECD Financial and Enterprise Affairs Directorate, Paris, 2004.

— — '"Indirect Expropriation" and the "Right to Regulate" in International Investment Law', OECD Working Paper on International Investment no. 2004/4, OECD Financial and Enterprise Affairs Directorate, Paris, 2004.

— — 'Interpretation of the Umbrella Clause in Investment Agreements', OECD Working Paper on International Investment no. 2006/3, OECD Financial and Enterprise Affairs Directorate, 2006.

Zeitler, H.E., 'Full Protection and Security', in S. Schill, ed., *International Investment Law and Comparative Public Law*, Oxford University Press Inc., Oxford, 2010, pp. 183-212.

Ziegler, A.R. and L.P. Gratton, 'Investment Insurance' in P.T. Muchlinski, F. Ortino and C.H. Schreuer, eds., *The Oxford Handbook of International Investment Law*, Oxford University Press, Oxford, 2008, pp. 526-548.

¶P

Visit us at *www.quidprobooks.com*.